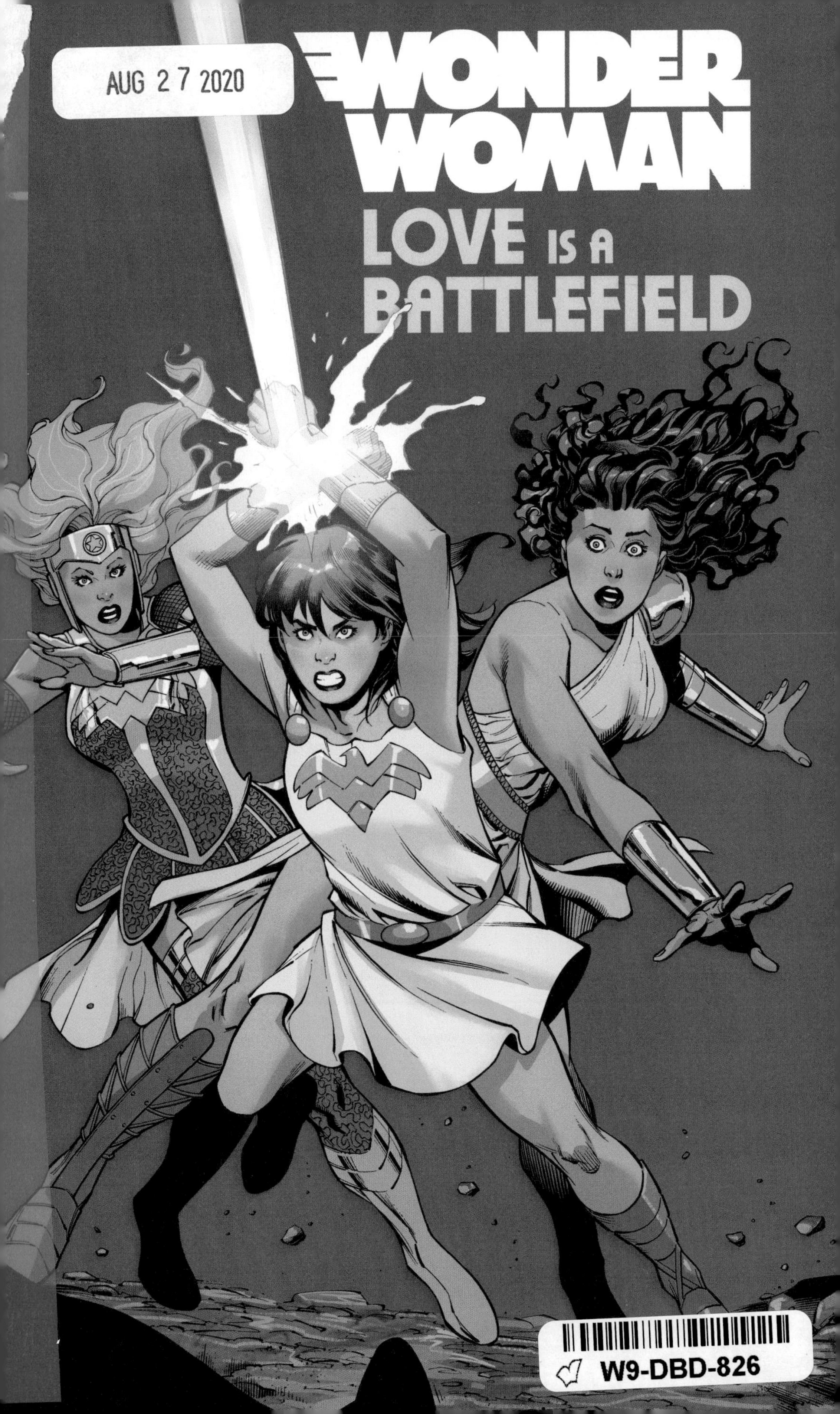
WONDER WOMAN
LOVE IS A BATTLEFIELD

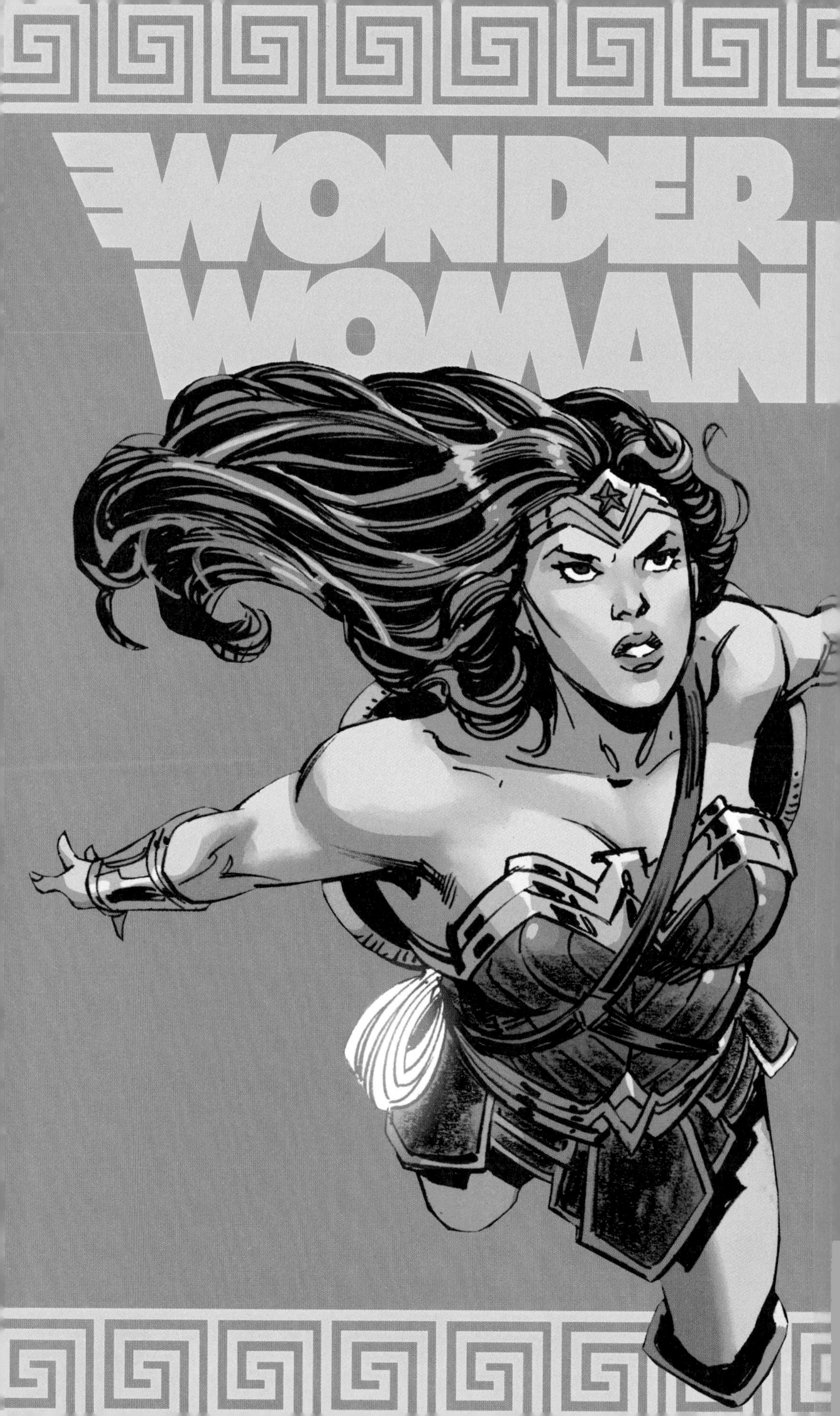
WONDER WOMAN

LOVE IS A BATTLEFIELD

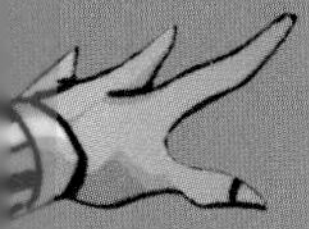

G. WILLOW WILSON
STEVE ORLANDO
WRITERS

CARY NORD
XERMANICO
RONAN CLIQUET
TOM DERENICK
AARON LOPRESTI
JESÚS MERINO
PENCILLERS

MICK GRAY
XERMANICO
RONAN CLIQUET
SCOTT HANNA
JESÚS MERINO
MATT RYAN
INKERS

ROMULO FAJARDO JR.
COLORIST

PAT BROSSEAU
LETTERER

TERRY DODSON & RACHEL DODSON
COLLECTION COVER ARTISTS

WONDER WOMAN **CREATED BY** WILLIAM MOULTON MARSTON

CHRIS CONROY
BRIAN CUNNINGHAM
Editors – Original Series

BRITTANY HOLZHERR
Associate Editor – Original Series

DAVE WIELGOSZ
Assistant Editor – Original Series

JEB WOODARD
Group Editor – Collected Editions

ERIKA ROTHBERG
Editor – Collected Edition

STEVE COOK
Design Director – Books

JOHN J. HILL
Publication Design

ERIN VANOVER
Publication Production

BOB HARRAS
Senior VP – Editor-in-Chief, DC Comics

DAN DiDIO
Publisher

JIM LEE
Publisher & Chief Creative Officer

BOBBIE CHASE
VP – New Publishing Initiatives

DON FALLETTI
VP – Manufacturing Operations & Workflow Management

LAWRENCE GANEM
VP – Talent Services

ALISON GILL
Senior VP – Manufacturing & Operations

HANK KANALZ
Senior VP – Publishing Strategy & Support Services

DAN MIRON
VP – Publishing Operations

NICK J. NAPOLITANO
VP – Manufacturing Administration & Design

NANCY SPEARS
VP – Sales

JONAH WEILAND
VP – Marketing & Creative Services

MICHELE R. WELLS
VP & Executive Editor, Young Reader

WONDER WOMAN VOL. 2: LOVE IS A BATTLEFIELD

DC Comics, 2900 West Alameda Ave., Burbank, CA 91505
Printed by Transcontinental Interglobe, Beauceville, QC, Canada. 7/10/20. First Printing.
ISBN: 978-1-77950-711-2

Library of Congress Cataloging-in-Publication Data is available.

PEFC Certified

This product is
from sustainably
managed forests and
controlled sources

PEFC
PEFC/01-31-106
www.pefc.org

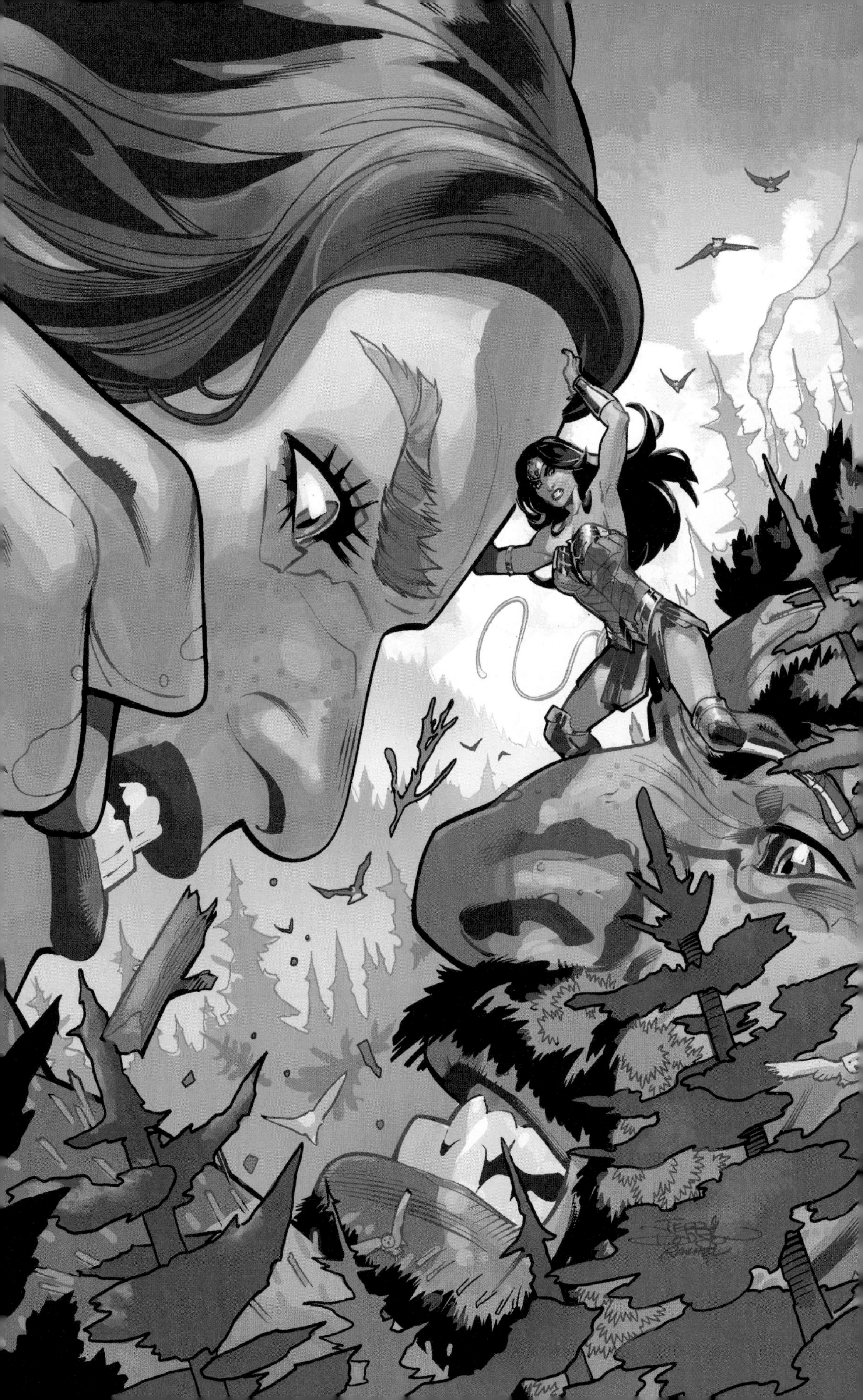

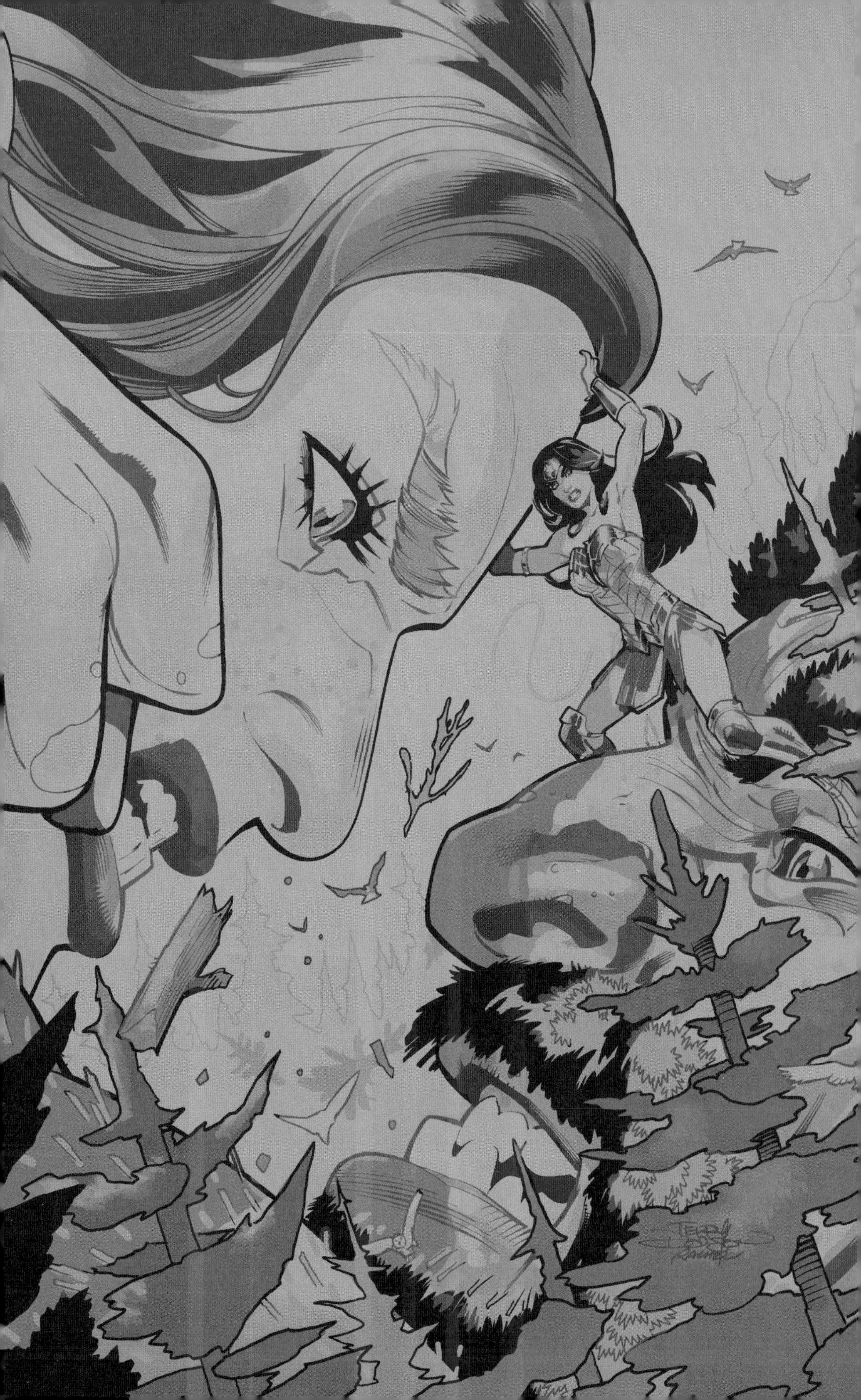

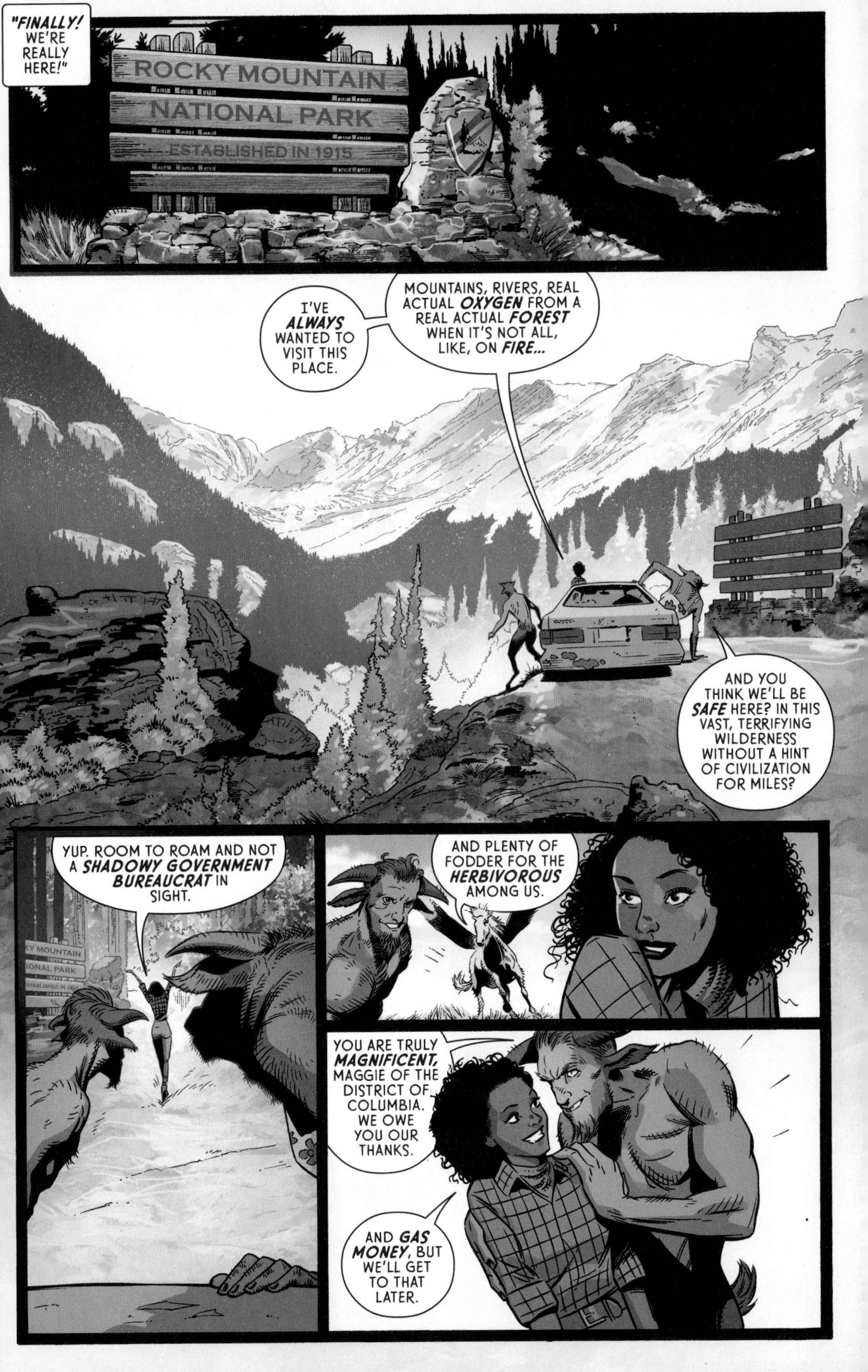
"FINALLY! WE'RE REALLY HERE!"
ROCKY MOUNTAIN
NATIONAL PARK
ESTABLISHED IN 1915
I'VE ALWAYS WANTED TO VISIT THIS PLACE.
MOUNTAINS, RIVERS, REAL ACTUAL OXYGEN FROM A REAL ACTUAL FOREST WHEN IT'S NOT ALL, LIKE, ON FIRE...
AND YOU THINK WE'LL BE SAFE HERE? IN THIS VAST, TERRIFYING WILDERNESS WITHOUT A HINT OF CIVILIZATION FOR MILES?
YUP. ROOM TO ROAM AND NOT A SHADOWY GOVERNMENT BUREAUCRAT IN SIGHT.
AND PLENTY OF FODDER FOR THE HERBIVOROUS AMONG US.
YOU ARE TRULY MAGNIFICENT, MAGGIE OF THE DISTRICT OF COLUMBIA. WE OWE YOU OUR THANKS.
AND GAS MONEY, BUT WE'LL GET TO THAT LATER.

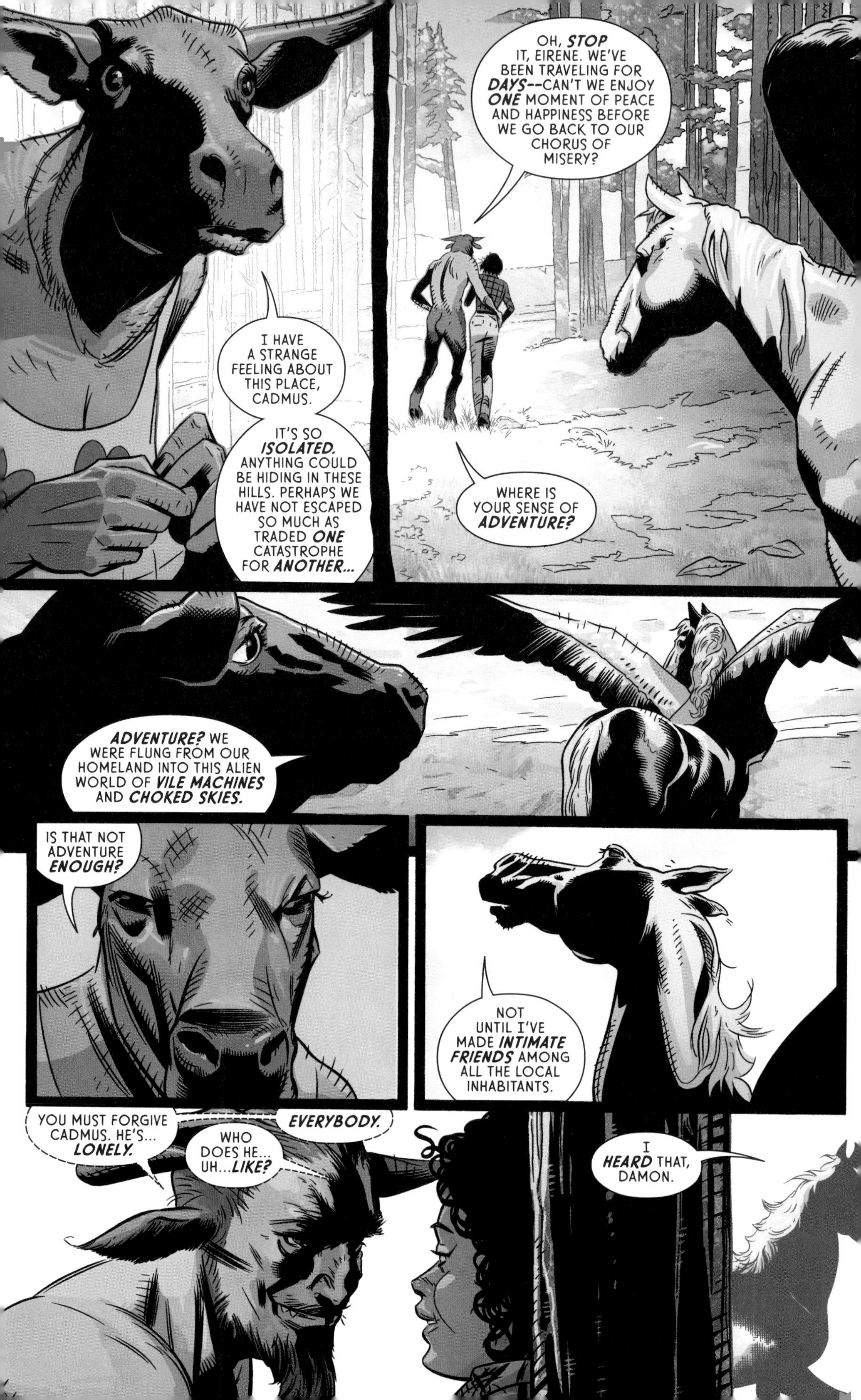
I HAVE A STRANGE FEELING ABOUT THIS PLACE, CADMUS.
IT'S SO *ISOLATED.* ANYTHING COULD BE HIDING IN THESE HILLS. PERHAPS WE HAVE NOT ESCAPED SO MUCH AS TRADED *ONE* CATASTROPHE FOR *ANOTHER...*
OH, *STOP* IT, EIRENE. WE'VE BEEN TRAVELING FOR *DAYS*--CAN'T WE ENJOY *ONE* MOMENT OF PEACE AND HAPPINESS BEFORE WE GO BACK TO OUR CHORUS OF MISERY?
WHERE IS YOUR SENSE OF *ADVENTURE?*
ADVENTURE? WE WERE FLUNG FROM OUR HOMELAND INTO THIS ALIEN WORLD OF *VILE MACHINES* AND *CHOKED SKIES.*
IS THAT NOT ADVENTURE *ENOUGH?*
NOT UNTIL I'VE MADE *INTIMATE FRIENDS* AMONG ALL THE LOCAL INHABITANTS.
YOU MUST FORGIVE CADMUS. HE'S... *LONELY.*
WHO DOES HE... UH...*LIKE?*
EVERYBODY.
I *HEARD* THAT, DAMON.

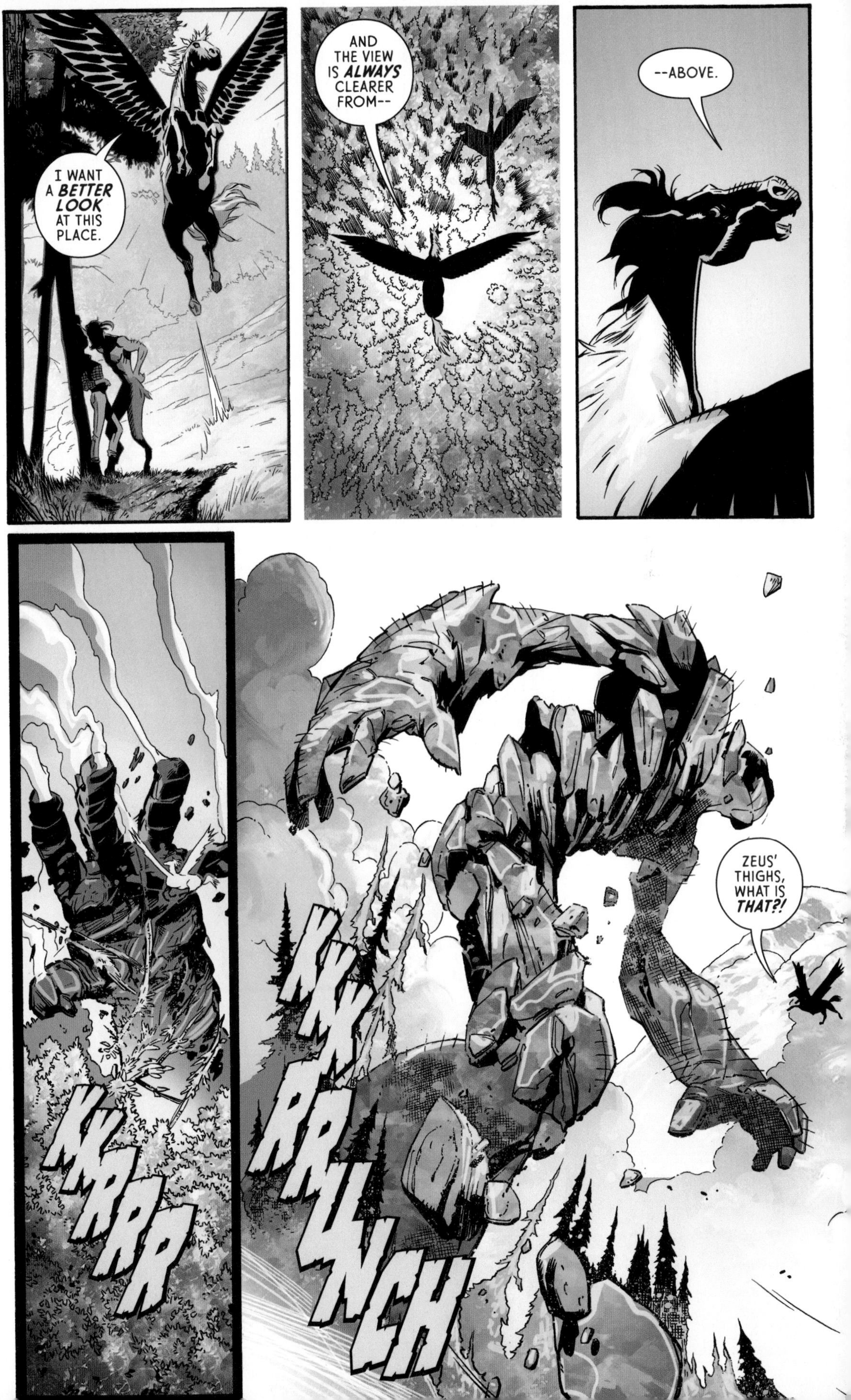
I WANT A BETTER LOOK AT THIS PLACE.
AND THE VIEW IS ALWAYS CLEARER FROM--
--ABOVE.
KRRRR
KKKRRUNCH
ZEUS' THIGHS, WHAT IS THAT?!

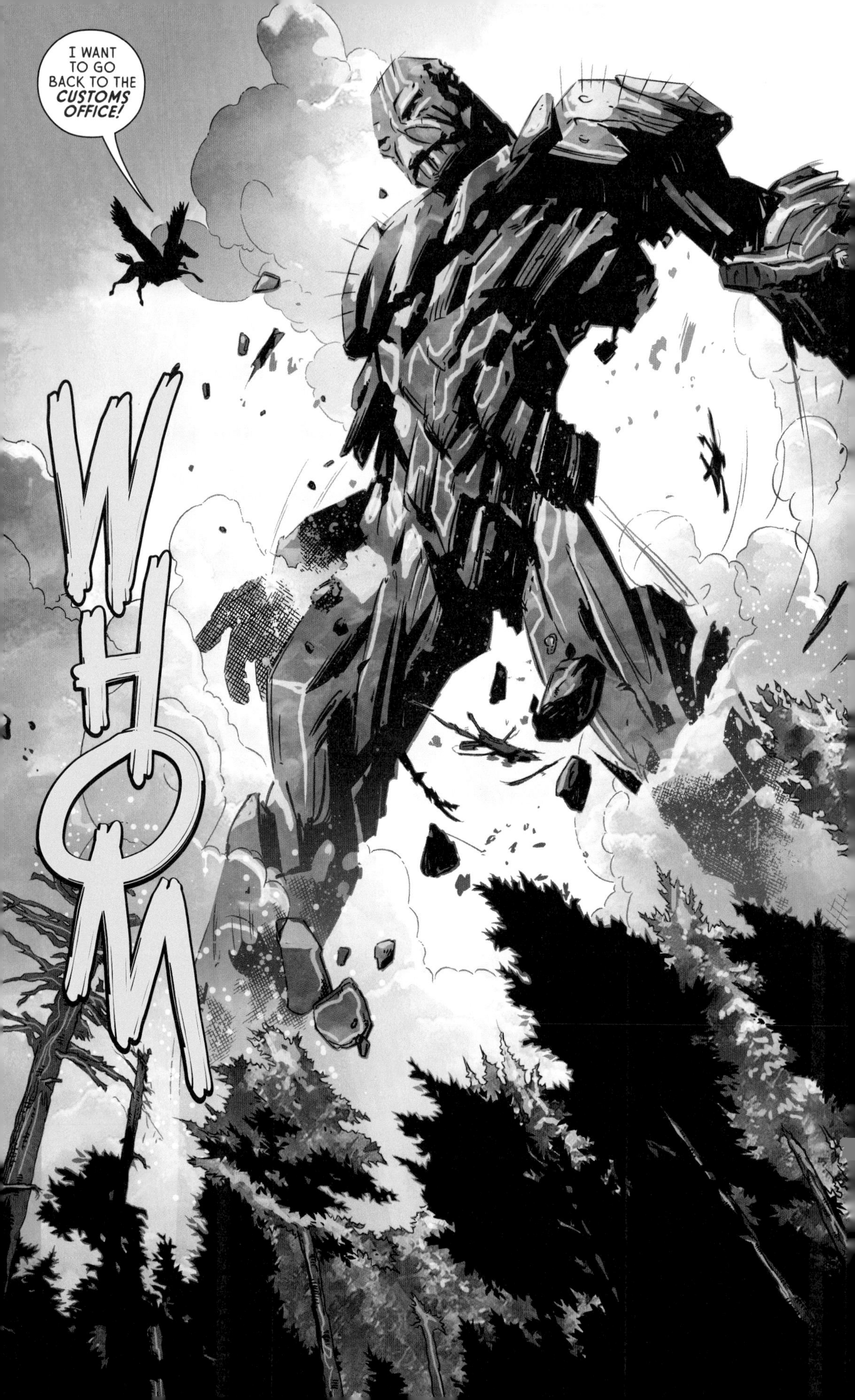
I WANT TO GO BACK TO THE *CUSTOMS OFFICE!*
WHOOM

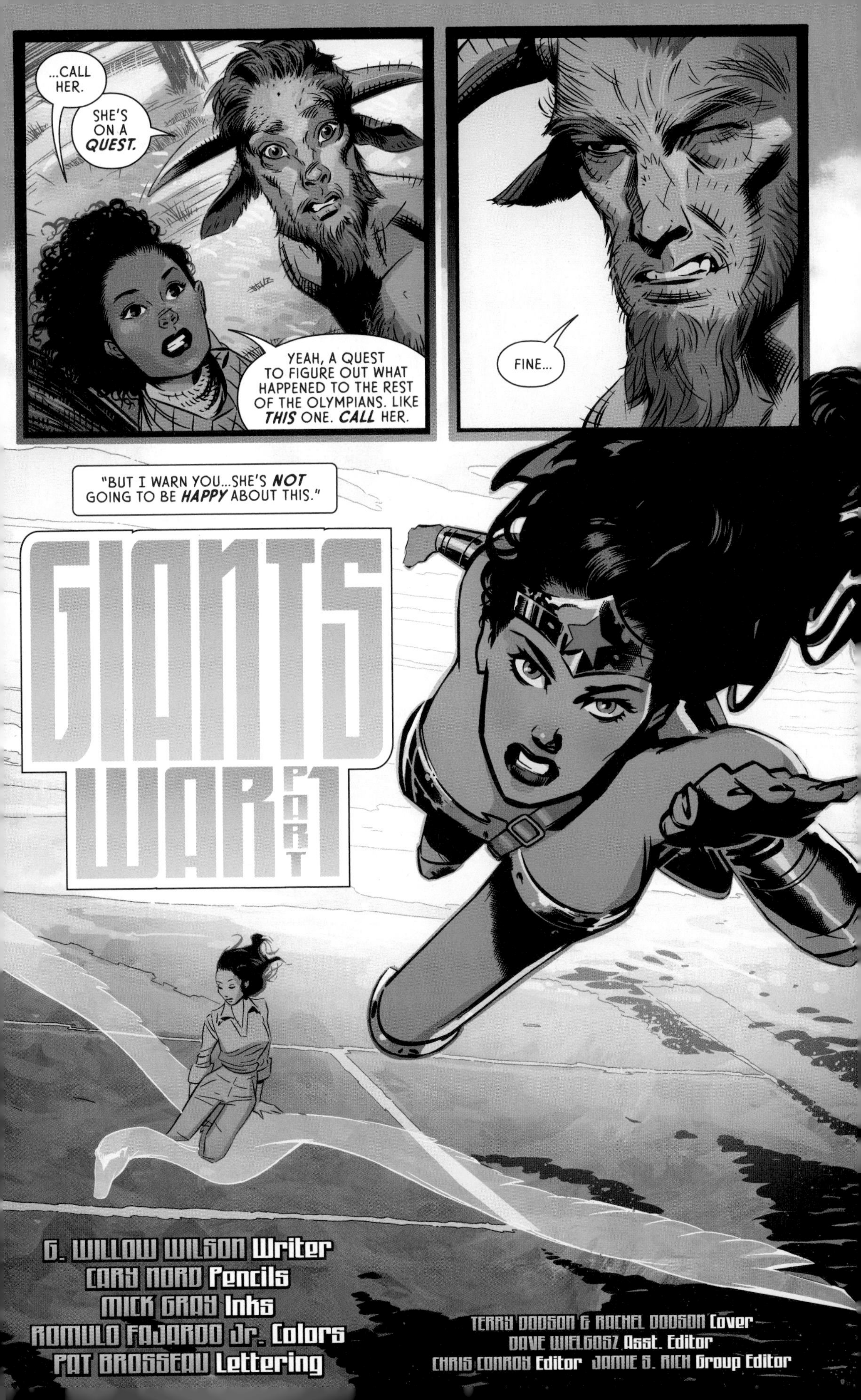

...CALL HER.
SHE'S ON A QUEST.
YEAH, A QUEST TO FIGURE OUT WHAT HAPPENED TO THE REST OF THE OLYMPIANS. LIKE THIS ONE. CALL HER.
FINE...
"BUT I WARN YOU...SHE'S NOT GOING TO BE HAPPY ABOUT THIS."
GIANTS WAR PART 1
G. WILLOW WILSON Writer
CARY NORD Pencils
MICK GRAY Inks
ROMULO FAJARDO Jr. Colors
PAT BROSSEAU Lettering
TERRY DODSON & RACHEL DODSON Cover
DAVE WIELGOSZ Asst. Editor
CHRIS CONROY Editor JAMIE S. RICH Group Editor

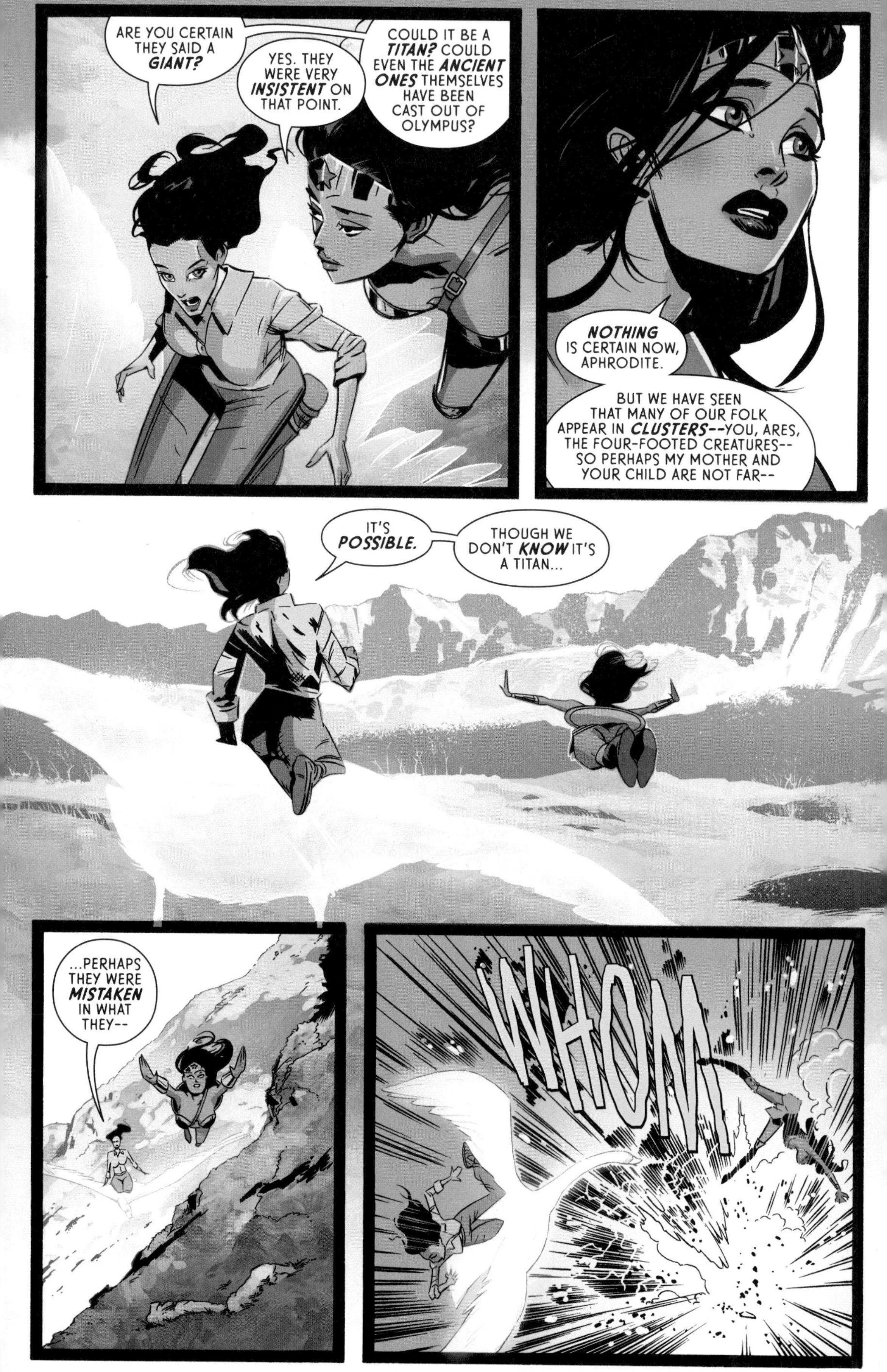

ARE YOU CERTAIN THEY SAID A *GIANT?*
YES. THEY WERE VERY *INSISTENT* ON THAT POINT.
COULD IT BE A *TITAN?* COULD EVEN THE *ANCIENT ONES* THEMSELVES HAVE BEEN CAST OUT OF OLYMPUS?
NOTHING IS CERTAIN NOW, APHRODITE.
BUT WE HAVE SEEN THAT MANY OF OUR FOLK APPEAR IN *CLUSTERS--*YOU, ARES, THE FOUR-FOOTED CREATURES-- SO PERHAPS MY MOTHER AND YOUR CHILD ARE NOT FAR--
IT'S *POSSIBLE.*
THOUGH WE DON'T *KNOW* IT'S A TITAN...
...PERHAPS THEY WERE *MISTAKEN* IN WHAT THEY--
WHOM

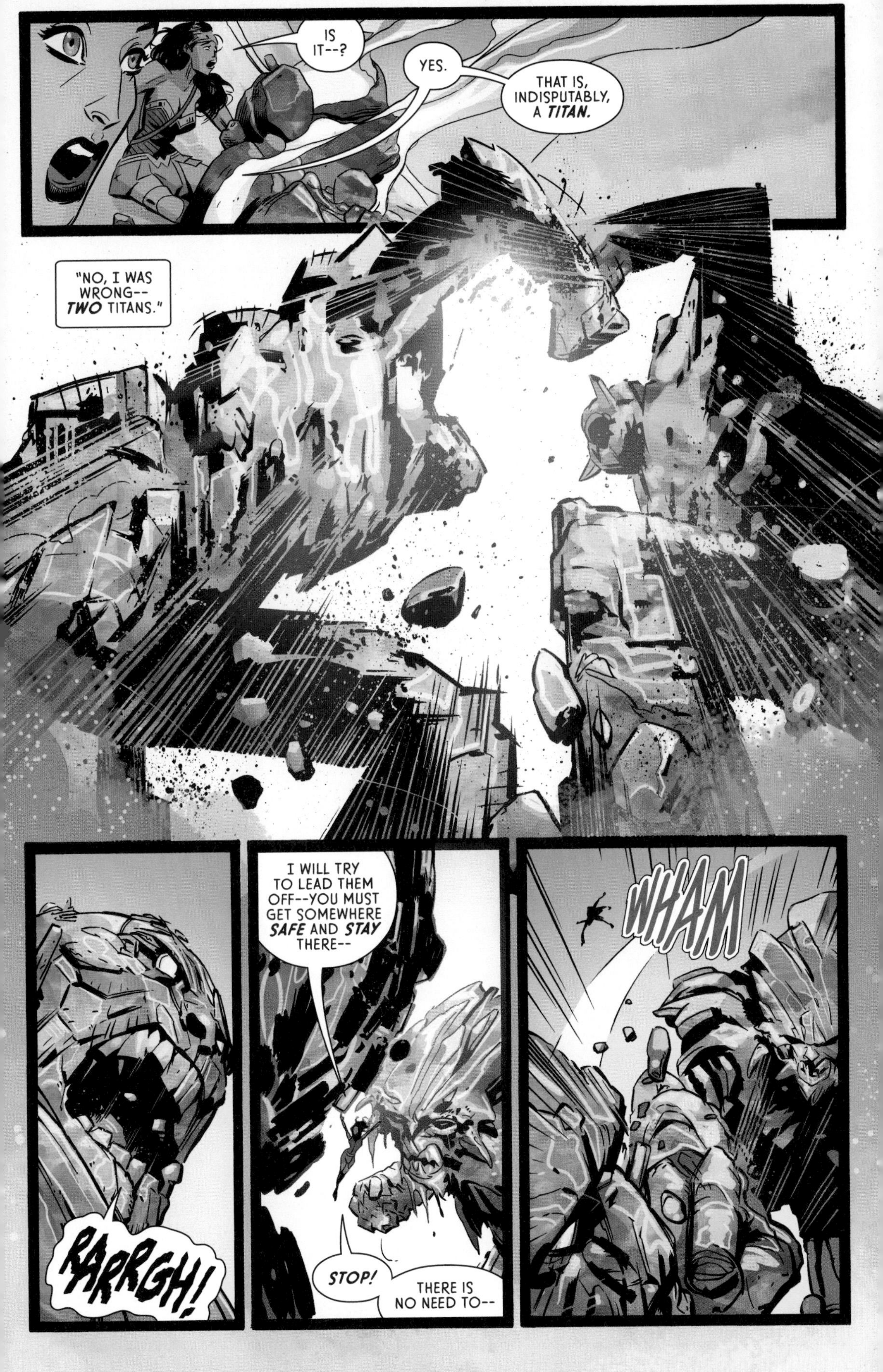
IS IT--?
YES.
THAT IS, INDISPUTABLY, A TITAN.
"NO, I WAS WRONG-- TWO TITANS."
RARRGH!
I WILL TRY TO LEAD THEM OFF--YOU MUST GET SOMEWHERE SAFE AND STAY THERE--
STOP!
THERE IS NO NEED TO--
WHAM

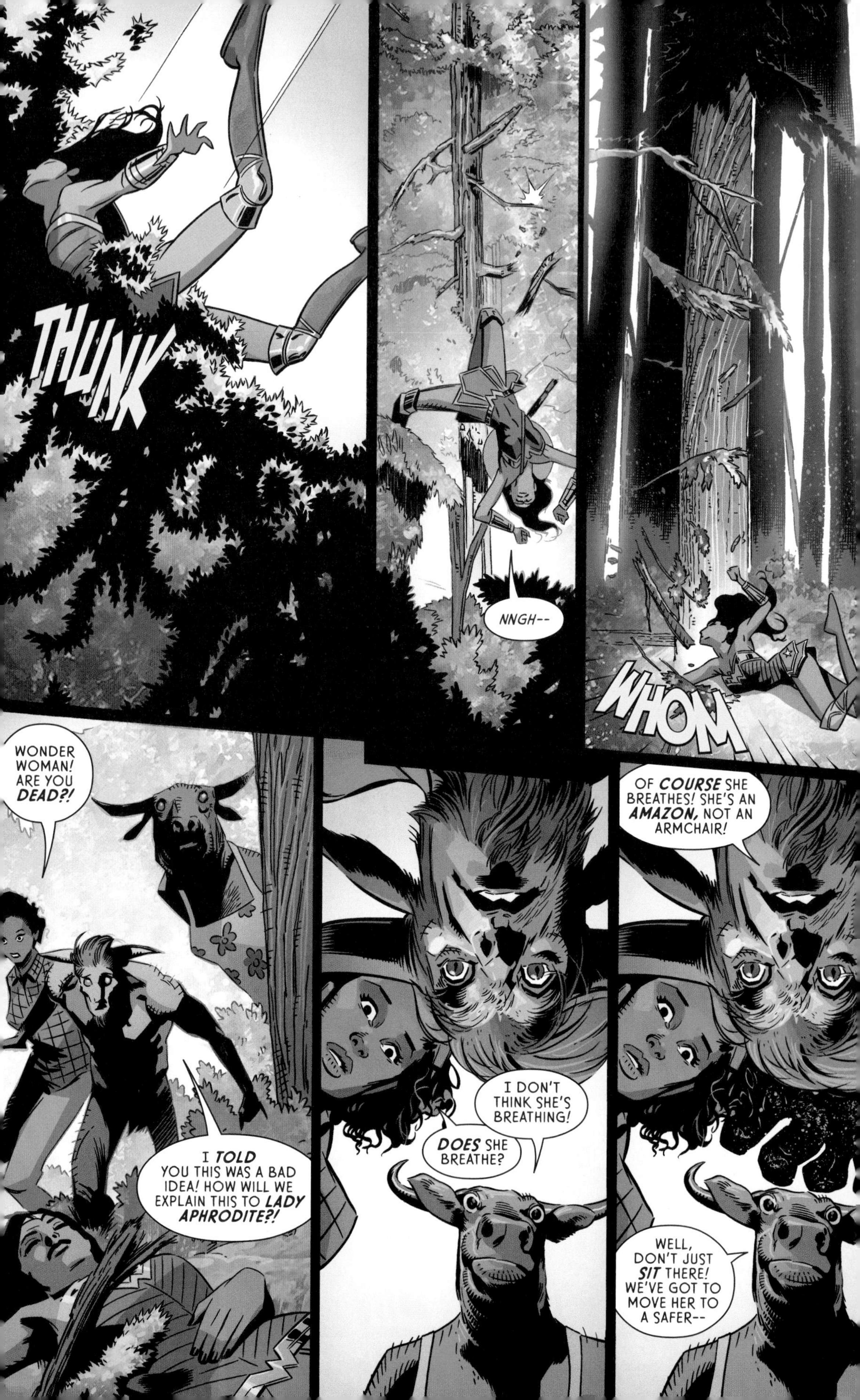
THUNK
NNGH--
WHOM
WONDER WOMAN! ARE YOU DEAD?!
I TOLD YOU THIS WAS A BAD IDEA! HOW WILL WE EXPLAIN THIS TO LADY APHRODITE?!
I DON'T THINK SHE'S BREATHING!
DOES SHE BREATHE?
OF COURSE SHE BREATHES! SHE'S AN AMAZON, NOT AN ARMCHAIR!
WELL, DON'T JUST SIT THERE! WE'VE GOT TO MOVE HER TO A SAFER--

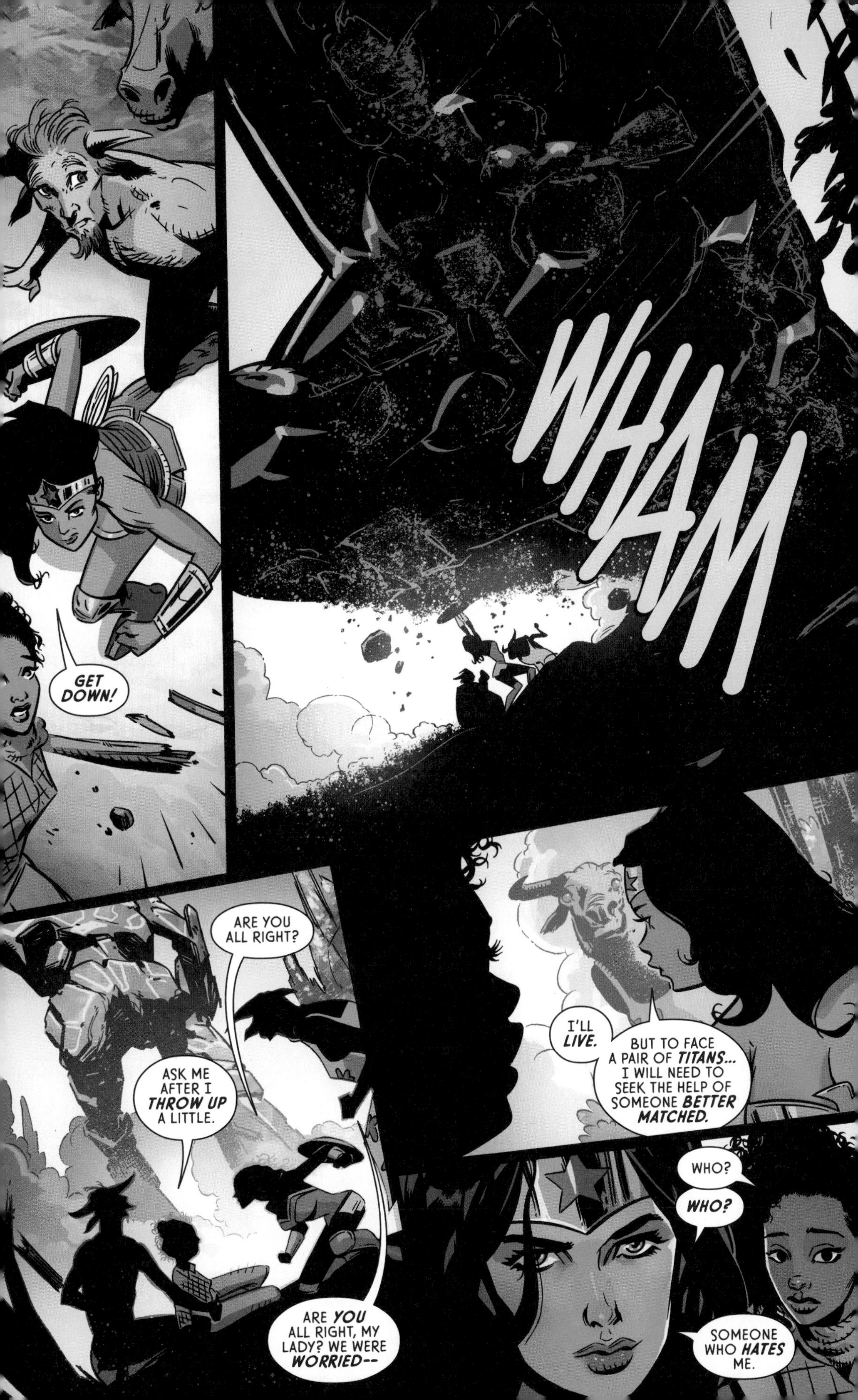
GET DOWN!
WHAM
ARE YOU ALL RIGHT?
ASK ME AFTER I THROW UP A LITTLE.
ARE YOU ALL RIGHT, MY LADY? WE WERE WORRIED--
I'LL LIVE.
BUT TO FACE A PAIR OF TITANS... I WILL NEED TO SEEK THE HELP OF SOMEONE BETTER MATCHED.
WHO?
WHO?
SOMEONE WHO HATES ME.

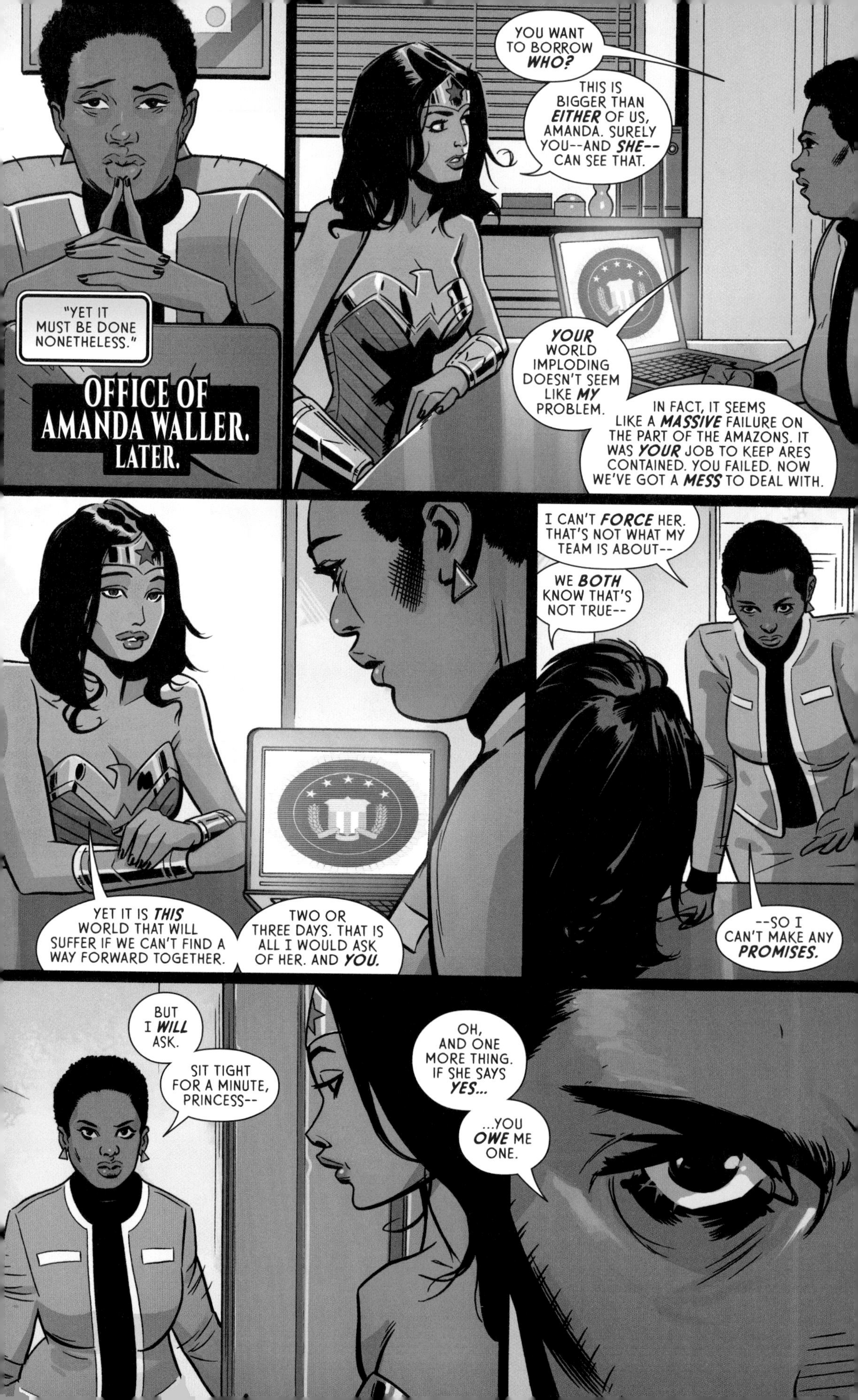
"YET IT MUST BE DONE NONETHELESS."
OFFICE OF AMANDA WALLER. LATER.
YOU WANT TO BORROW WHO?
THIS IS BIGGER THAN EITHER OF US, AMANDA. SURELY YOU--AND SHE--CAN SEE THAT.
YOUR WORLD IMPLODING DOESN'T SEEM LIKE MY PROBLEM.
IN FACT, IT SEEMS LIKE A MASSIVE FAILURE ON THE PART OF THE AMAZONS. IT WAS YOUR JOB TO KEEP ARES CONTAINED. YOU FAILED. NOW WE'VE GOT A MESS TO DEAL WITH.
YET IT IS THIS WORLD THAT WILL SUFFER IF WE CAN'T FIND A WAY FORWARD TOGETHER.
TWO OR THREE DAYS. THAT IS ALL I WOULD ASK OF HER. AND YOU.
I CAN'T FORCE HER. THAT'S NOT WHAT MY TEAM IS ABOUT--
WE BOTH KNOW THAT'S NOT TRUE--
--SO I CAN'T MAKE ANY PROMISES.
BUT I WILL ASK.
SIT TIGHT FOR A MINUTE, PRINCESS--
OH, AND ONE MORE THING. IF SHE SAYS YES...
...YOU OWE ME ONE.

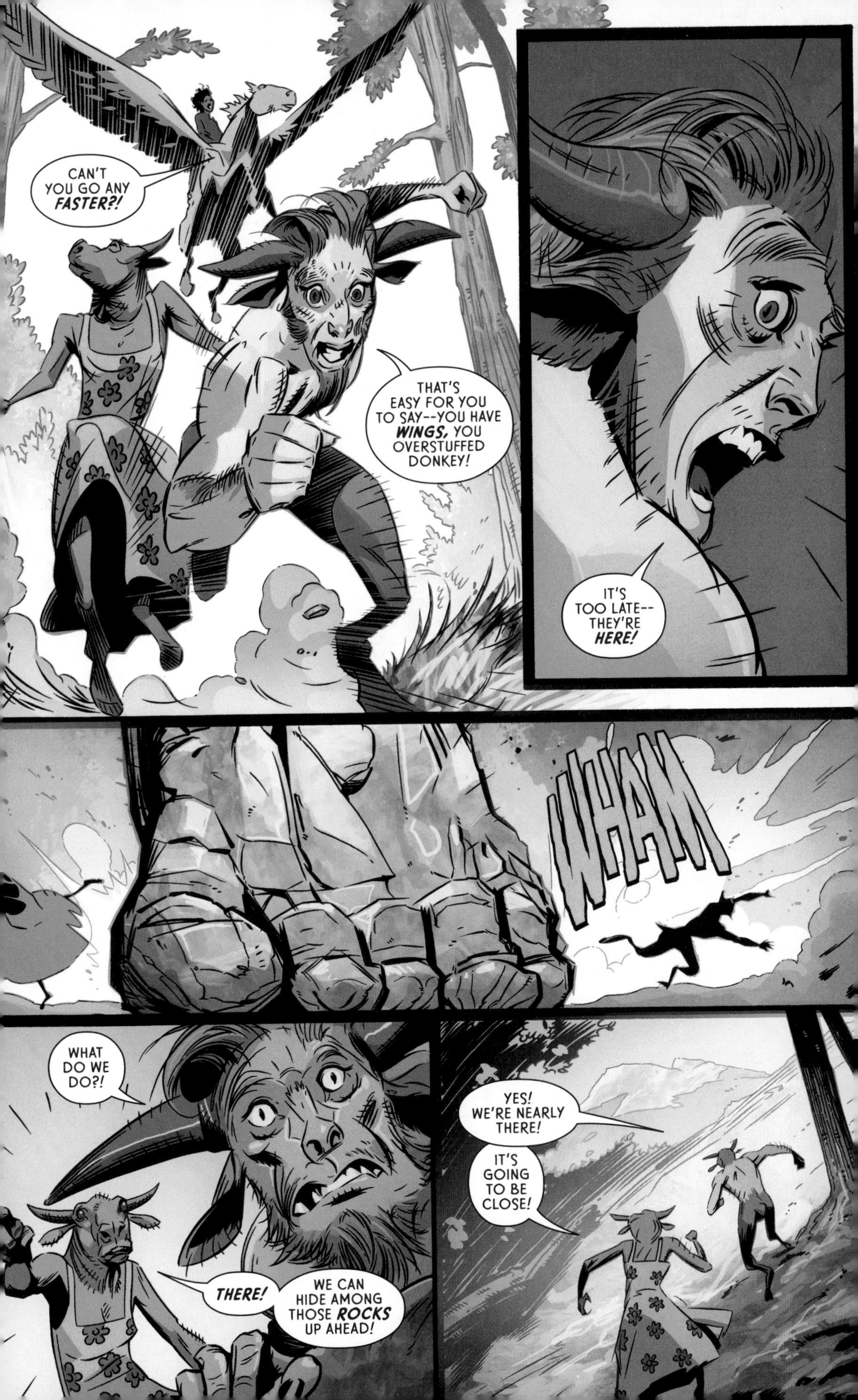
CAN'T YOU GO ANY *FASTER?!*
THAT'S EASY FOR YOU TO SAY--YOU HAVE *WINGS,* YOU OVERSTUFFED DONKEY!
IT'S TOO LATE--THEY'RE *HERE!*
WHAM
WHAT DO WE DO?!
THERE!
WE CAN HIDE AMONG THOSE *ROCKS* UP AHEAD!
YES! WE'RE NEARLY THERE!
IT'S GOING TO BE CLOSE!

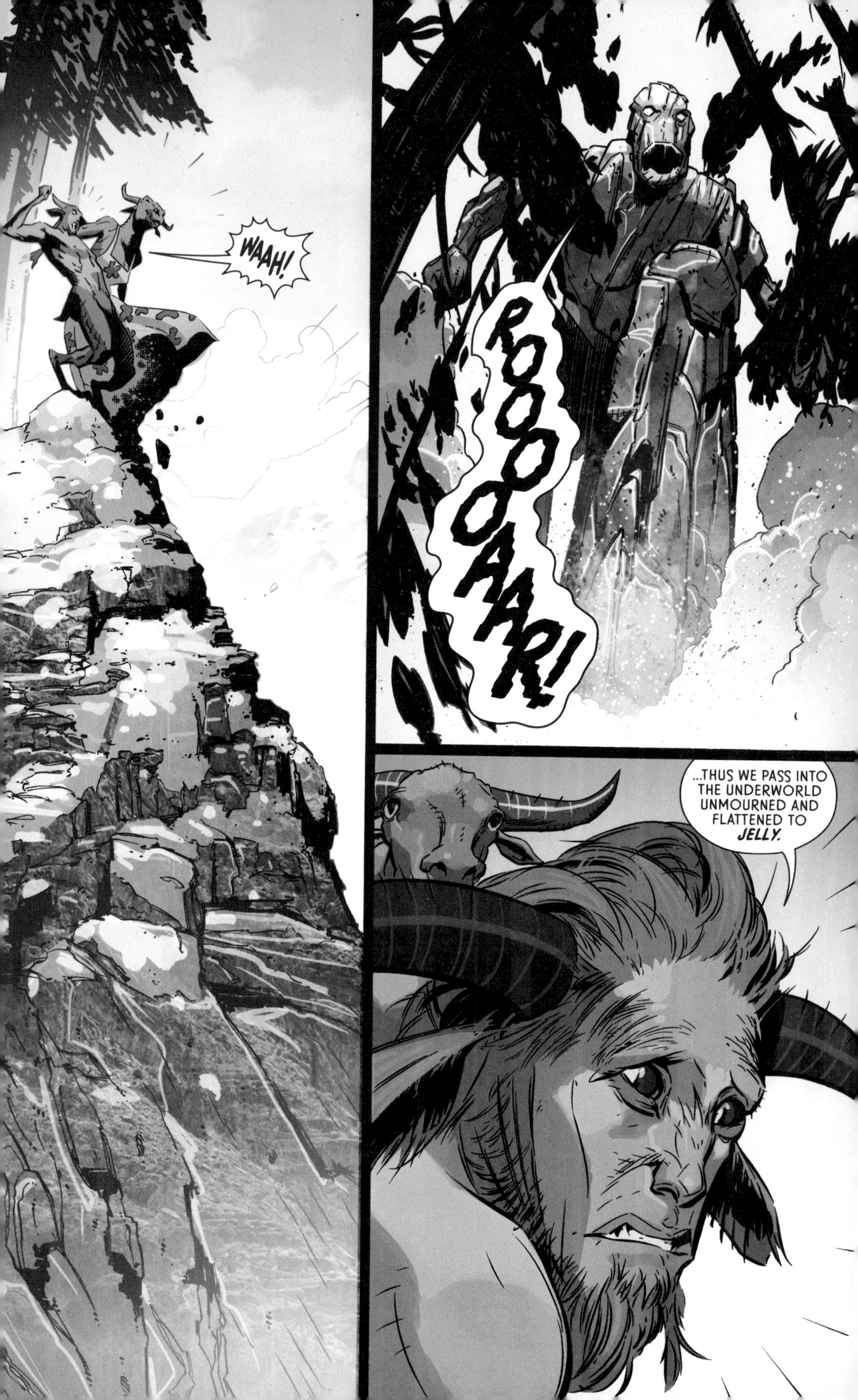
WAAH!
ROOOOAAAR!
...THUS WE PASS INTO THE UNDERWORLD UNMOURNED AND FLATTENED TO JELLY.

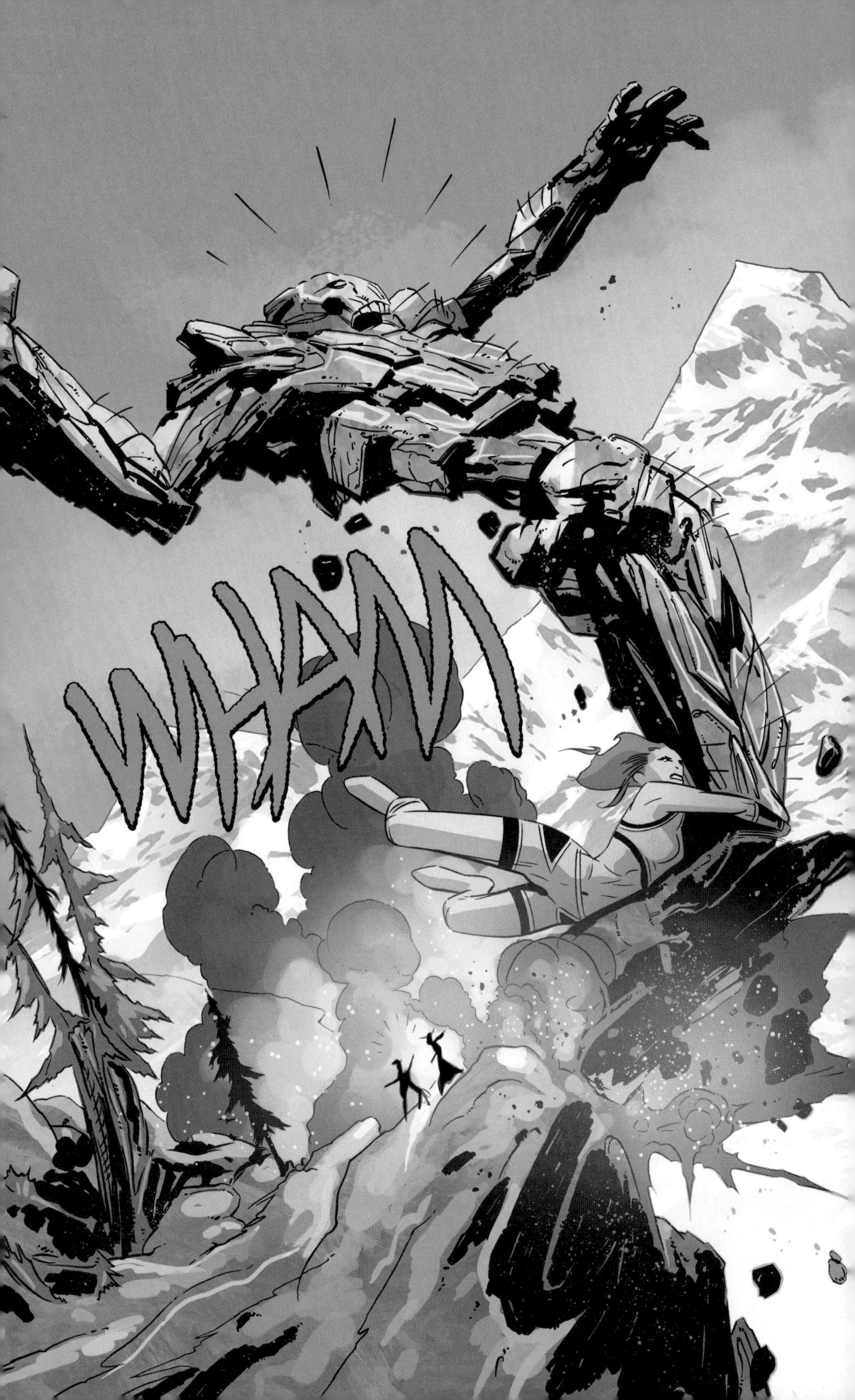
WHAM

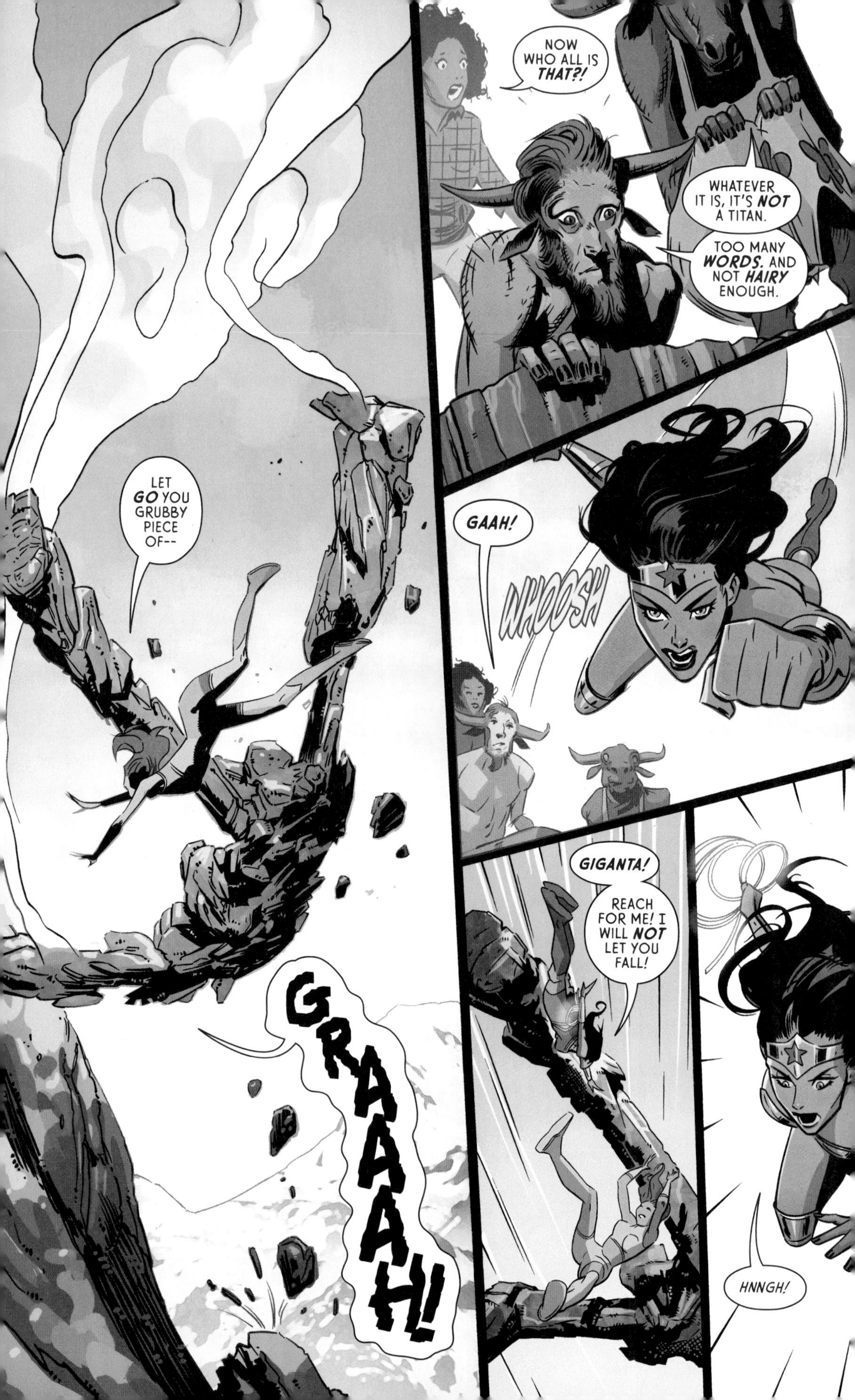
LET GO YOU GRUBBY PIECE OF--
GRAAAAH!
NOW WHO ALL IS THAT?!
WHATEVER IT IS, IT'S NOT A TITAN.
TOO MANY WORDS. AND NOT HAIRY ENOUGH.
GAAH!
WHOOSH
GIGANTA!
REACH FOR ME! I WILL NOT LET YOU FALL!
HNNGH!

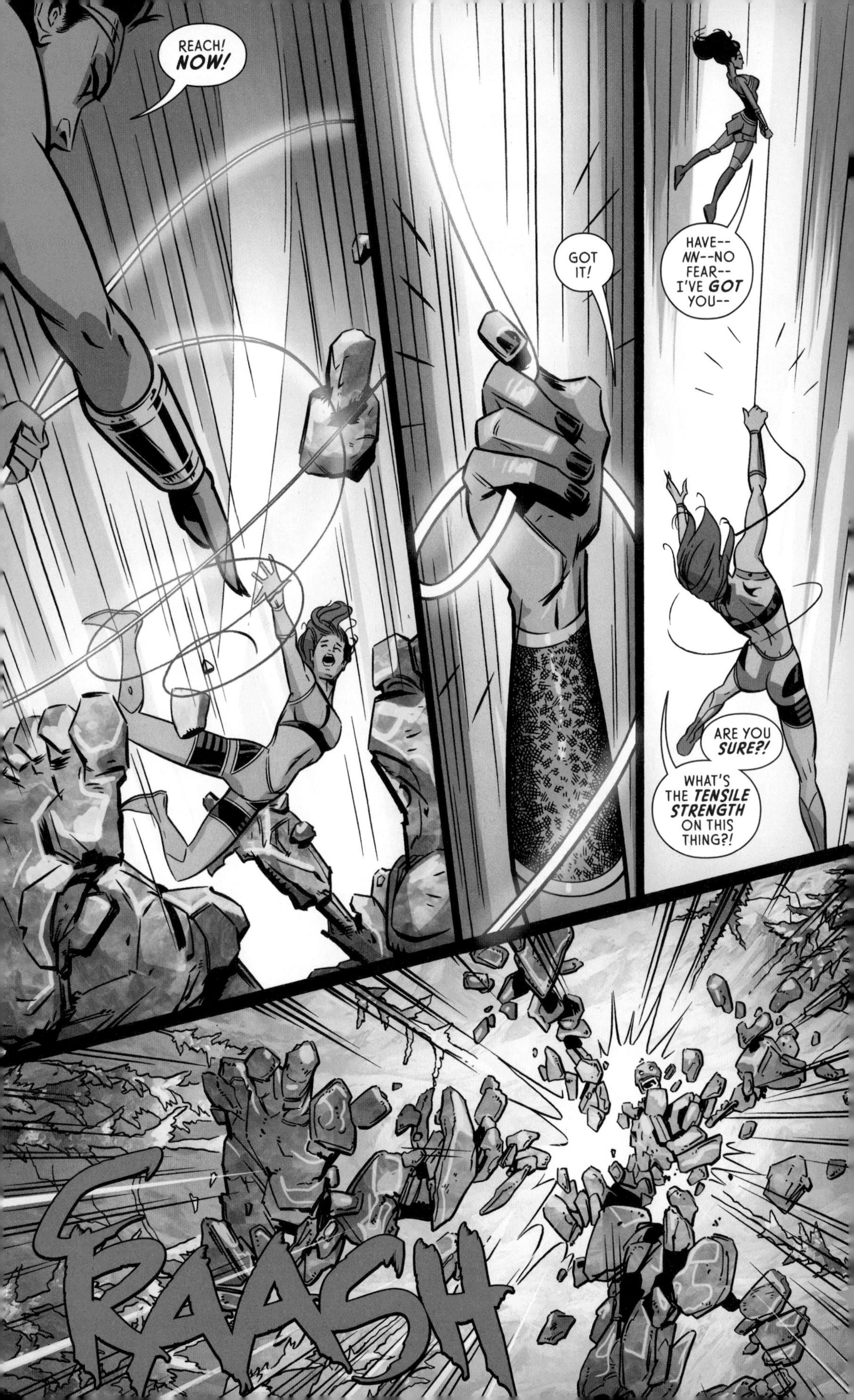
REACH! NOW!
GOT IT!
HAVE-- NN--NO FEAR-- I'VE GOT YOU--
ARE YOU SURE?!
WHAT'S THE TENSILE STRENGTH ON THIS THING?!
KRAASH

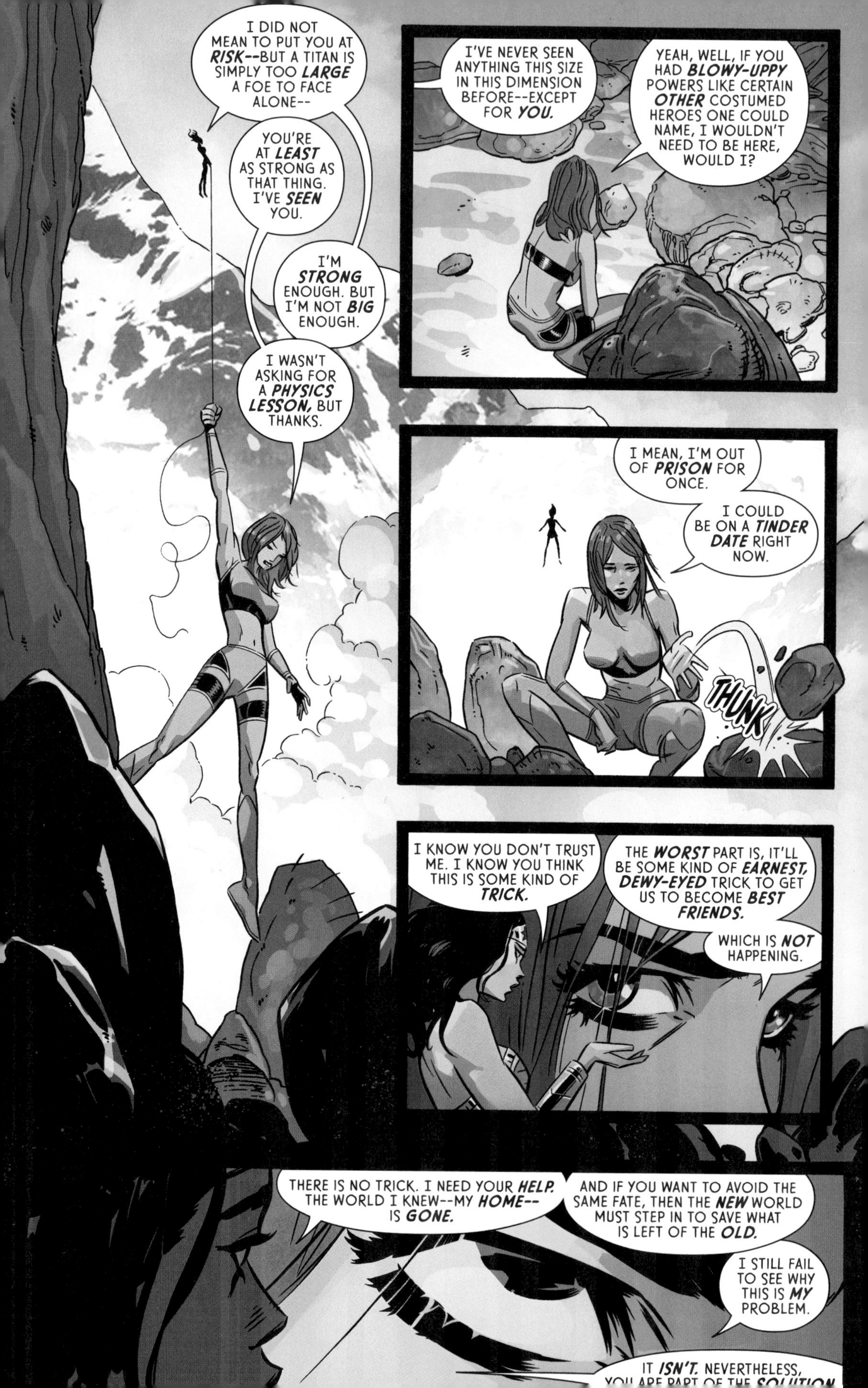
I DID NOT MEAN TO PUT YOU AT RISK--BUT A TITAN IS SIMPLY TOO LARGE A FOE TO FACE ALONE--
YOU'RE AT LEAST AS STRONG AS THAT THING. I'VE SEEN YOU.
I'M STRONG ENOUGH. BUT I'M NOT BIG ENOUGH.
I WASN'T ASKING FOR A PHYSICS LESSON, BUT THANKS.
I'VE NEVER SEEN ANYTHING THIS SIZE IN THIS DIMENSION BEFORE--EXCEPT FOR YOU.
YEAH, WELL, IF YOU HAD BLOWY-UPPY POWERS LIKE CERTAIN OTHER COSTUMED HEROES ONE COULD NAME, I WOULDN'T NEED TO BE HERE, WOULD I?
I MEAN, I'M OUT OF PRISON FOR ONCE.
I COULD BE ON A TINDER DATE RIGHT NOW.
THUNK
I KNOW YOU DON'T TRUST ME. I KNOW YOU THINK THIS IS SOME KIND OF TRICK.
THE WORST PART IS, IT'LL BE SOME KIND OF EARNEST, DEWY-EYED TRICK TO GET US TO BECOME BEST FRIENDS.
WHICH IS NOT HAPPENING.
THERE IS NO TRICK. I NEED YOUR HELP. THE WORLD I KNEW--MY HOME--IS GONE.
AND IF YOU WANT TO AVOID THE SAME FATE, THEN THE NEW WORLD MUST STEP IN TO SAVE WHAT IS LEFT OF THE OLD.
I STILL FAIL TO SEE WHY THIS IS MY PROBLEM.
IT ISN'T. NEVERTHELESS,

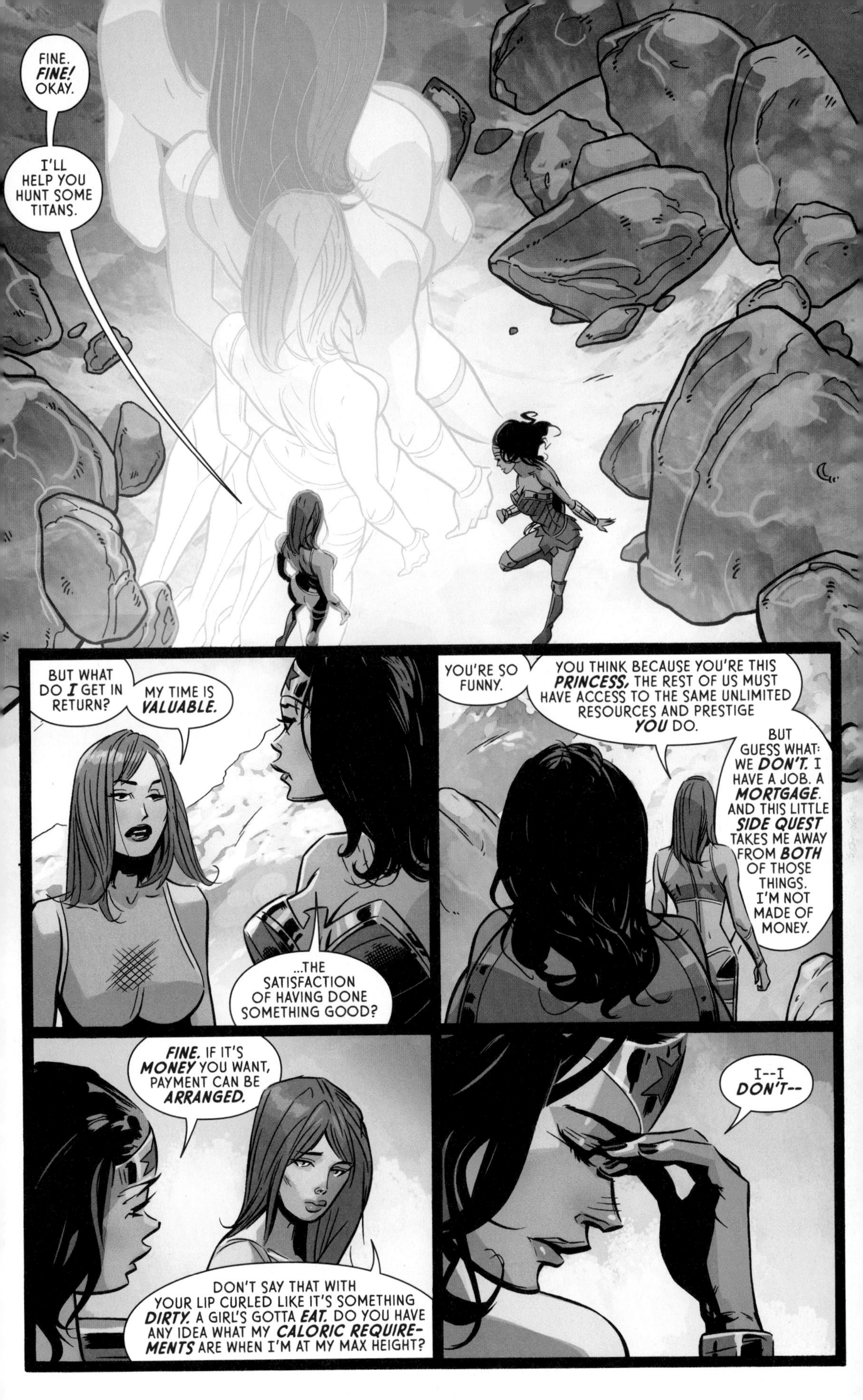
FINE. *FINE!* OKAY.
I'LL HELP YOU HUNT SOME TITANS.
BUT WHAT DO *I* GET IN RETURN?
MY TIME IS *VALUABLE.*
...THE SATISFACTION OF HAVING DONE SOMETHING GOOD?
YOU'RE SO FUNNY.
YOU THINK BECAUSE YOU'RE THIS *PRINCESS,* THE REST OF US MUST HAVE ACCESS TO THE SAME UNLIMITED RESOURCES AND PRESTIGE *YOU* DO.
BUT GUESS WHAT: WE *DON'T.* I HAVE A JOB. A *MORTGAGE.* AND THIS LITTLE *SIDE QUEST* TAKES ME AWAY FROM *BOTH* OF THOSE THINGS. I'M NOT MADE OF MONEY.
FINE. IF IT'S *MONEY* YOU WANT, PAYMENT CAN BE *ARRANGED.*
DON'T SAY THAT WITH YOUR LIP CURLED LIKE IT'S SOMETHING *DIRTY.* A GIRL'S GOTTA *EAT.* DO YOU HAVE ANY IDEA WHAT MY *CALORIC REQUIREMENTS* ARE WHEN I'M AT MY MAX HEIGHT?
I--I *DON'T--*

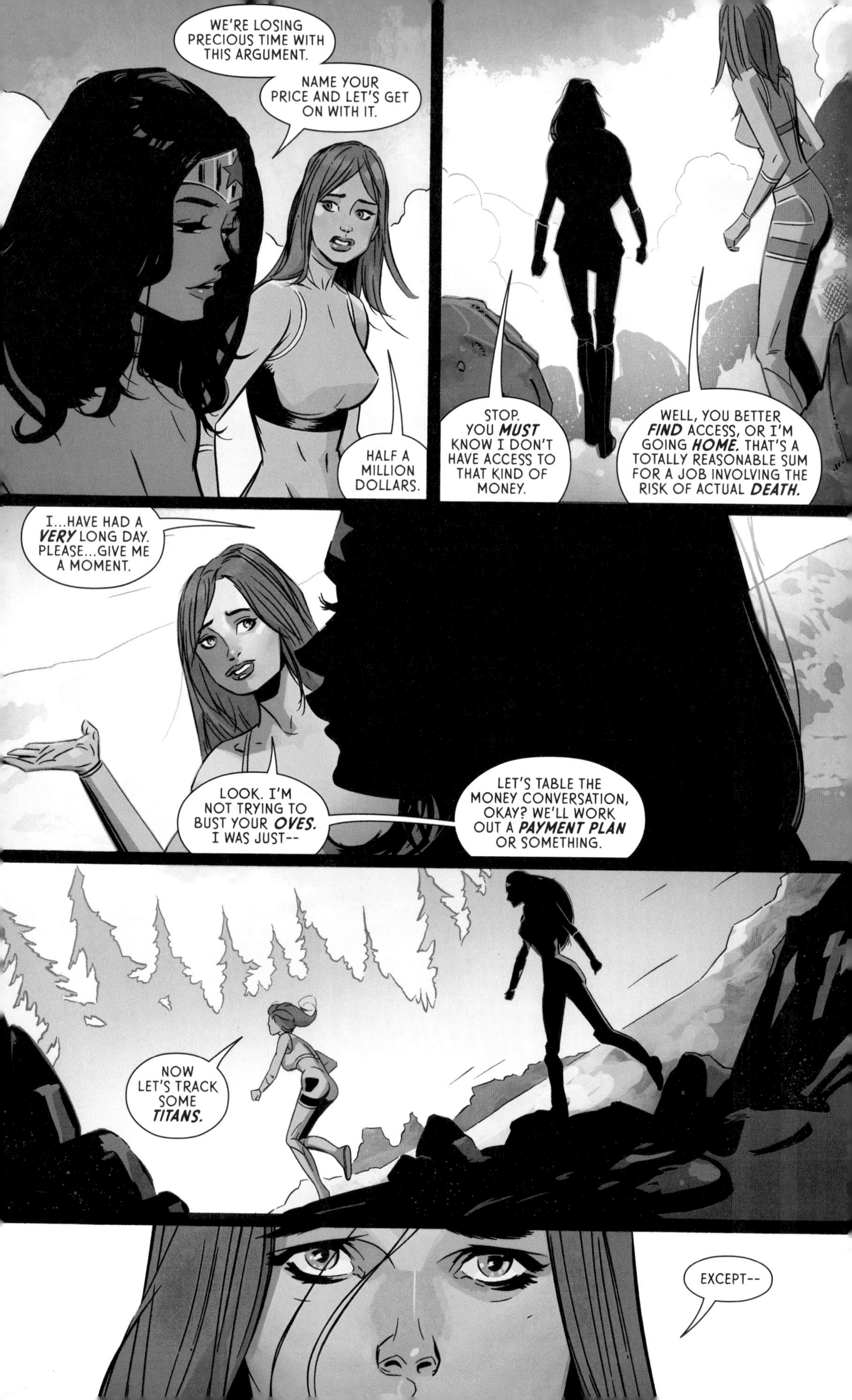
WE'RE LOSING PRECIOUS TIME WITH THIS ARGUMENT.
NAME YOUR PRICE AND LET'S GET ON WITH IT.
HALF A MILLION DOLLARS.
STOP. YOU MUST KNOW I DON'T HAVE ACCESS TO THAT KIND OF MONEY.
WELL, YOU BETTER FIND ACCESS, OR I'M GOING HOME. THAT'S A TOTALLY REASONABLE SUM FOR A JOB INVOLVING THE RISK OF ACTUAL DEATH.
I...HAVE HAD A VERY LONG DAY. PLEASE...GIVE ME A MOMENT.
LOOK. I'M NOT TRYING TO BUST YOUR OVES. I WAS JUST--
LET'S TABLE THE MONEY CONVERSATION, OKAY? WE'LL WORK OUT A PAYMENT PLAN OR SOMETHING.
NOW LET'S TRACK SOME TITANS.
EXCEPT--

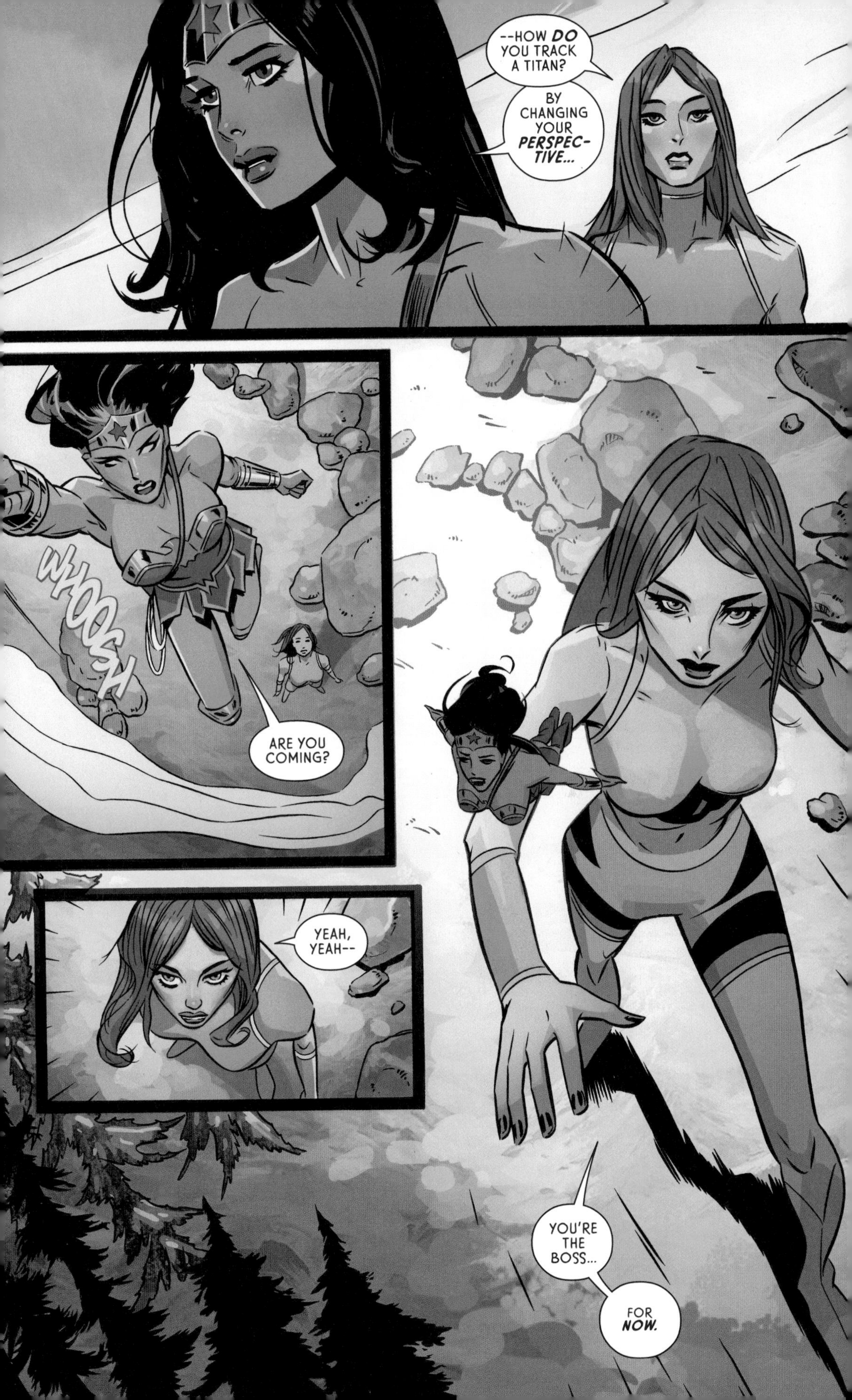
--HOW DO YOU TRACK A TITAN?
BY CHANGING YOUR PERSPECTIVE...
WHOOSH
ARE YOU COMING?
YEAH, YEAH--
YOU'RE THE BOSS...
FOR NOW.

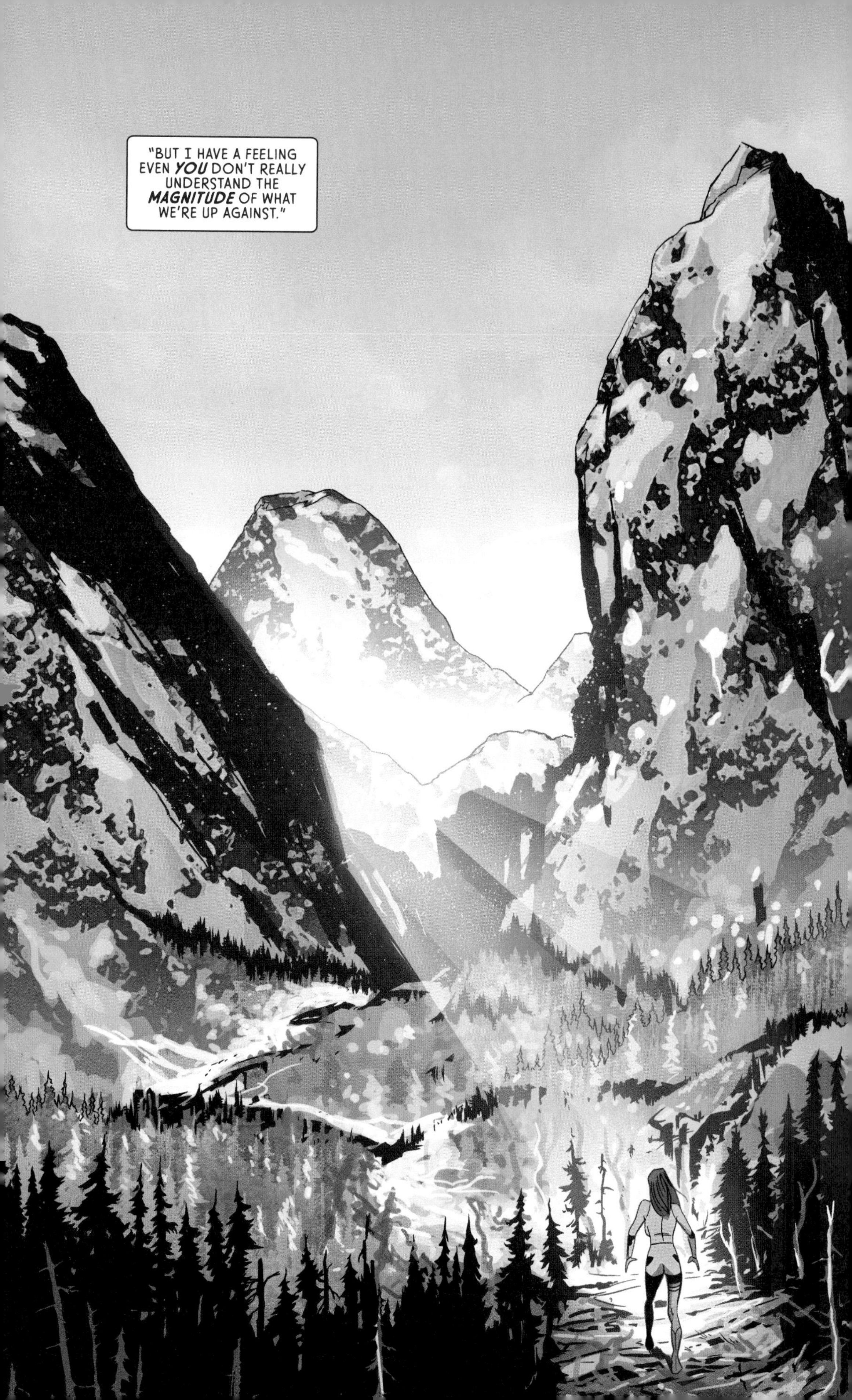
"BUT I HAVE A FEELING EVEN ***YOU*** DON'T REALLY UNDERSTAND THE ***MAGNITUDE*** OF WHAT WE'RE UP AGAINST."

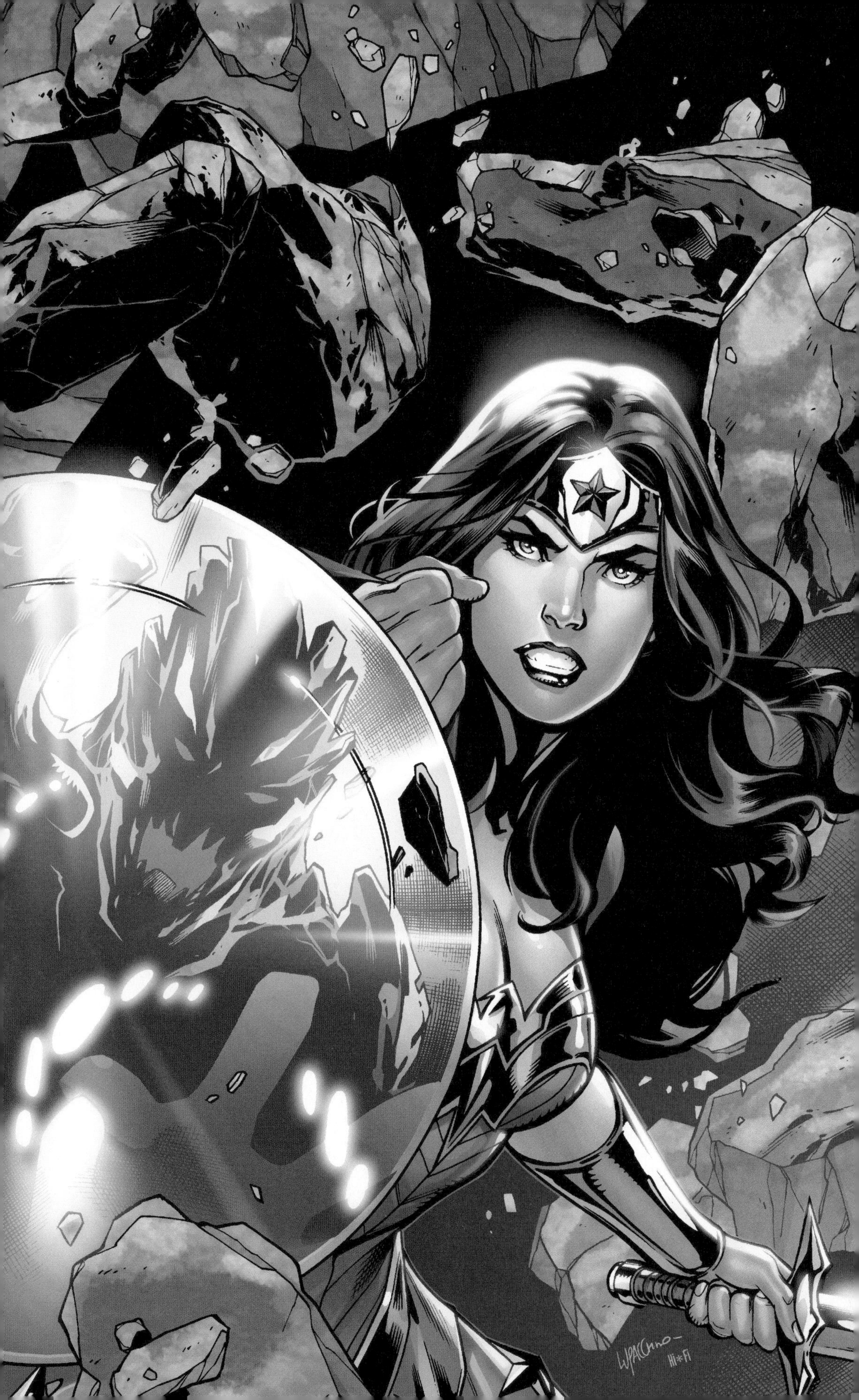

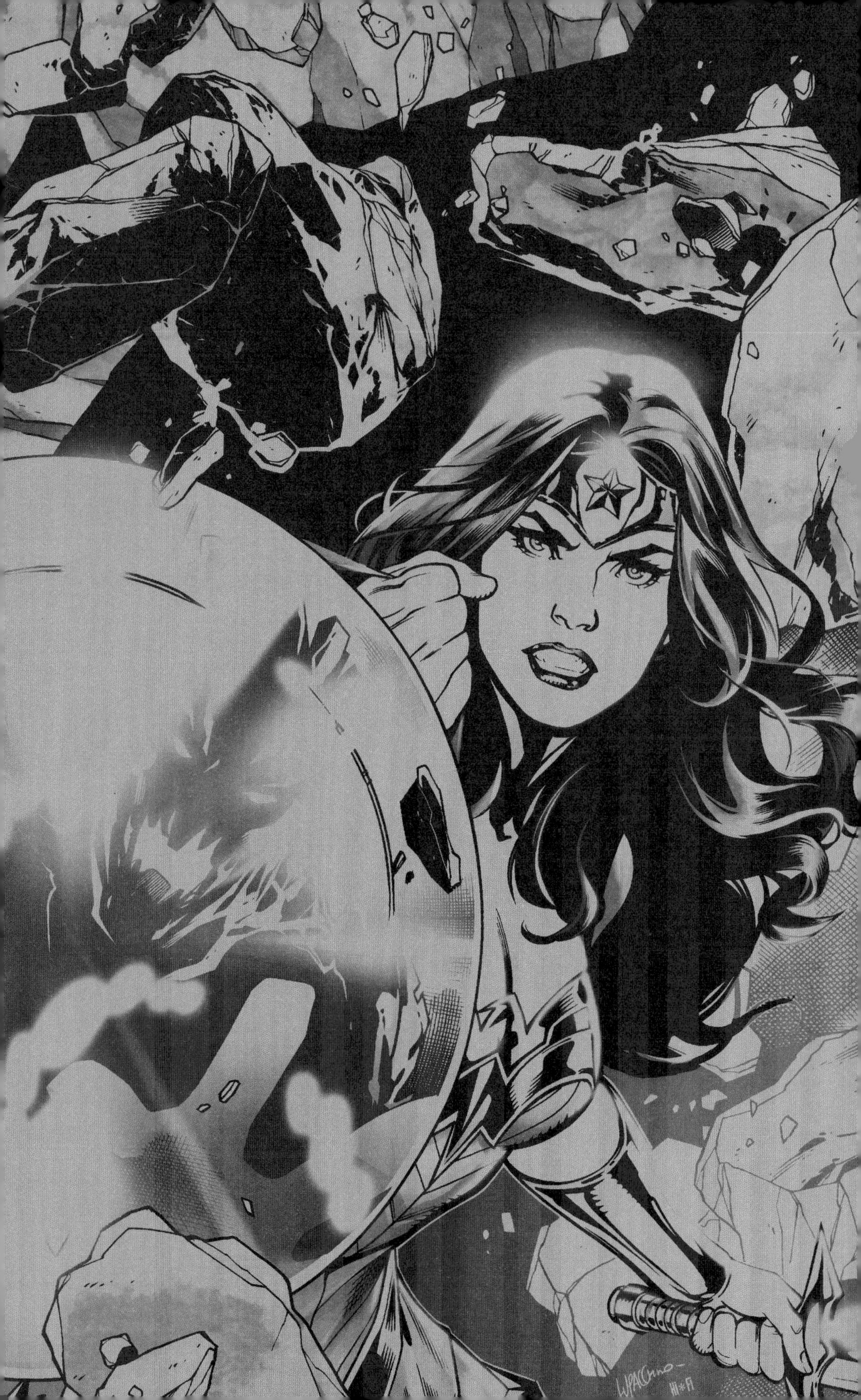

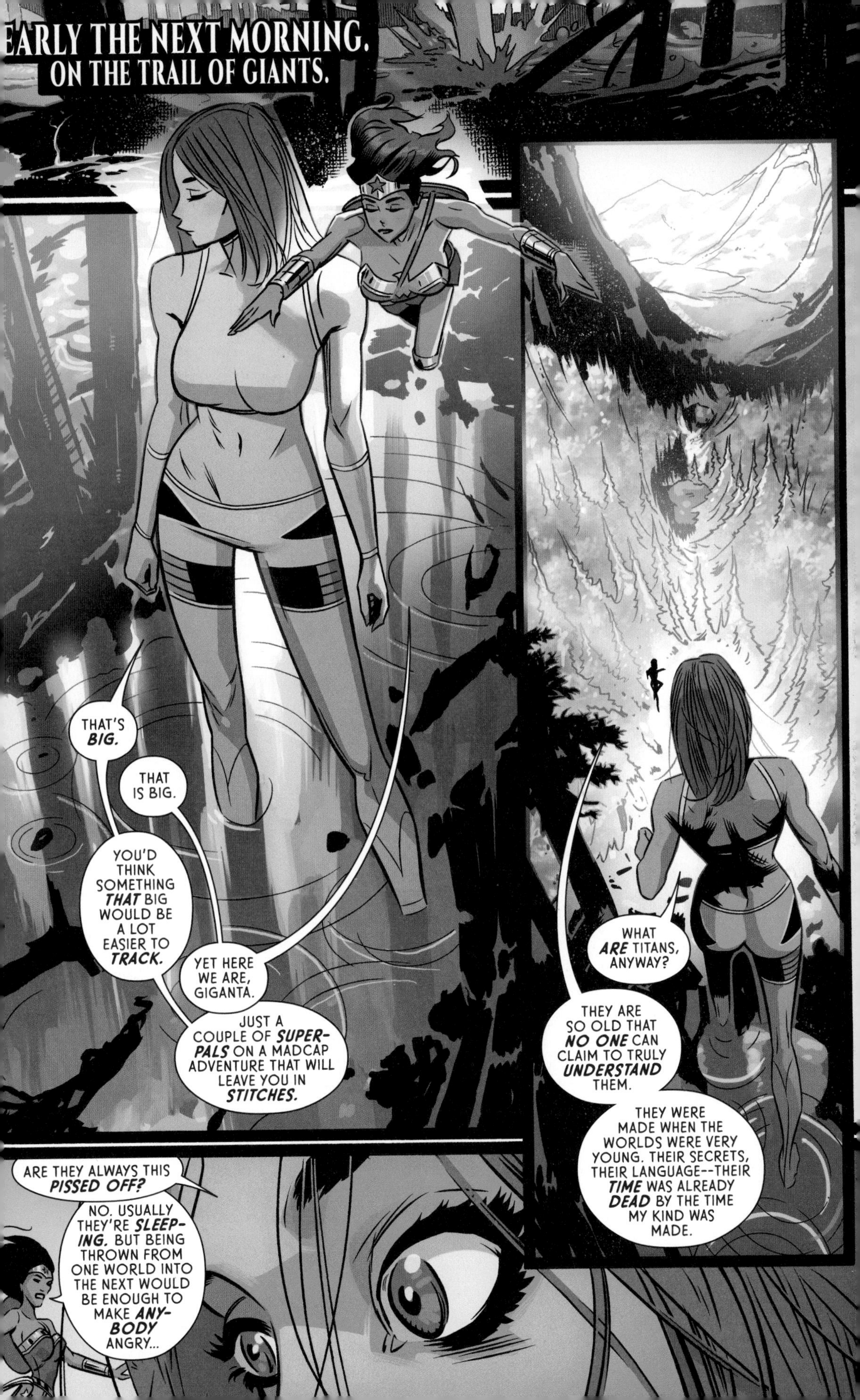
EARLY THE NEXT MORNING. ON THE TRAIL OF GIANTS.
THAT'S BIG.
THAT IS BIG.
YOU'D THINK SOMETHING THAT BIG WOULD BE A LOT EASIER TO TRACK.
YET HERE WE ARE, GIGANTA.
JUST A COUPLE OF SUPER-PALS ON A MADCAP ADVENTURE THAT WILL LEAVE YOU IN STITCHES.
WHAT ARE TITANS, ANYWAY?
THEY ARE SO OLD THAT NO ONE CAN CLAIM TO TRULY UNDERSTAND THEM.
THEY WERE MADE WHEN THE WORLDS WERE VERY YOUNG. THEIR SECRETS, THEIR LANGUAGE--THEIR TIME WAS ALREADY DEAD BY THE TIME MY KIND WAS MADE.
ARE THEY ALWAYS THIS PISSED OFF?
NO. USUALLY THEY'RE SLEEPING. BUT BEING THROWN FROM ONE WORLD INTO THE NEXT WOULD BE ENOUGH TO MAKE ANYBODY ANGRY...

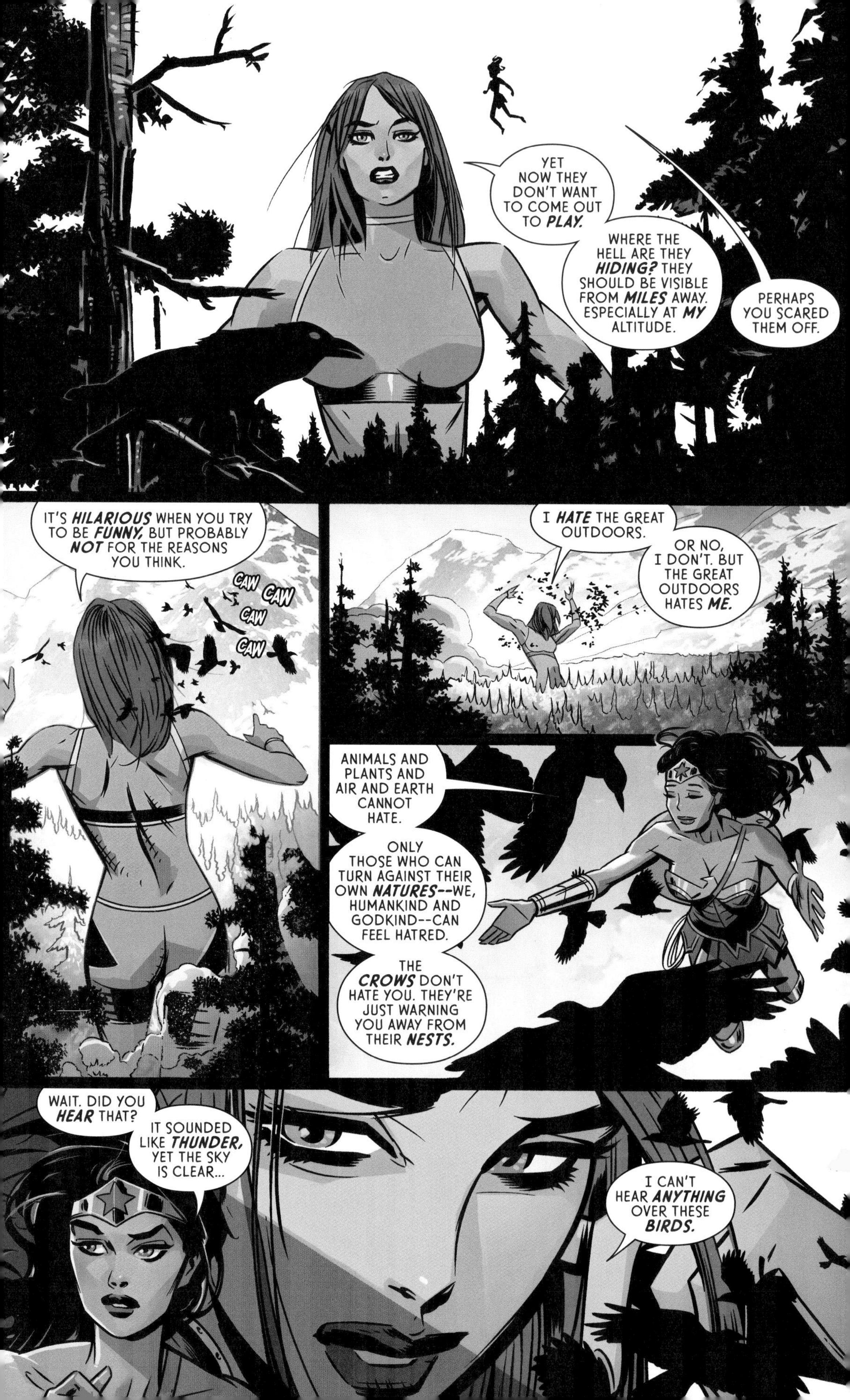
YET NOW THEY DON'T WANT TO COME OUT TO PLAY.
WHERE THE HELL ARE THEY HIDING? THEY SHOULD BE VISIBLE FROM MILES AWAY. ESPECIALLY AT MY ALTITUDE.
PERHAPS YOU SCARED THEM OFF.
IT'S HILARIOUS WHEN YOU TRY TO BE FUNNY, BUT PROBABLY NOT FOR THE REASONS YOU THINK.
CAW CAW
CAW
CAW
I HATE THE GREAT OUTDOORS.
OR NO, I DON'T. BUT THE GREAT OUTDOORS HATES ME.
ANIMALS AND PLANTS AND AIR AND EARTH CANNOT HATE.
ONLY THOSE WHO CAN TURN AGAINST THEIR OWN NATURES--WE, HUMANKIND AND GODKIND--CAN FEEL HATRED.
THE CROWS DON'T HATE YOU. THEY'RE JUST WARNING YOU AWAY FROM THEIR NESTS.
WAIT. DID YOU HEAR THAT?
IT SOUNDED LIKE THUNDER, YET THE SKY IS CLEAR...
I CAN'T HEAR ANYTHING OVER THESE BIRDS.

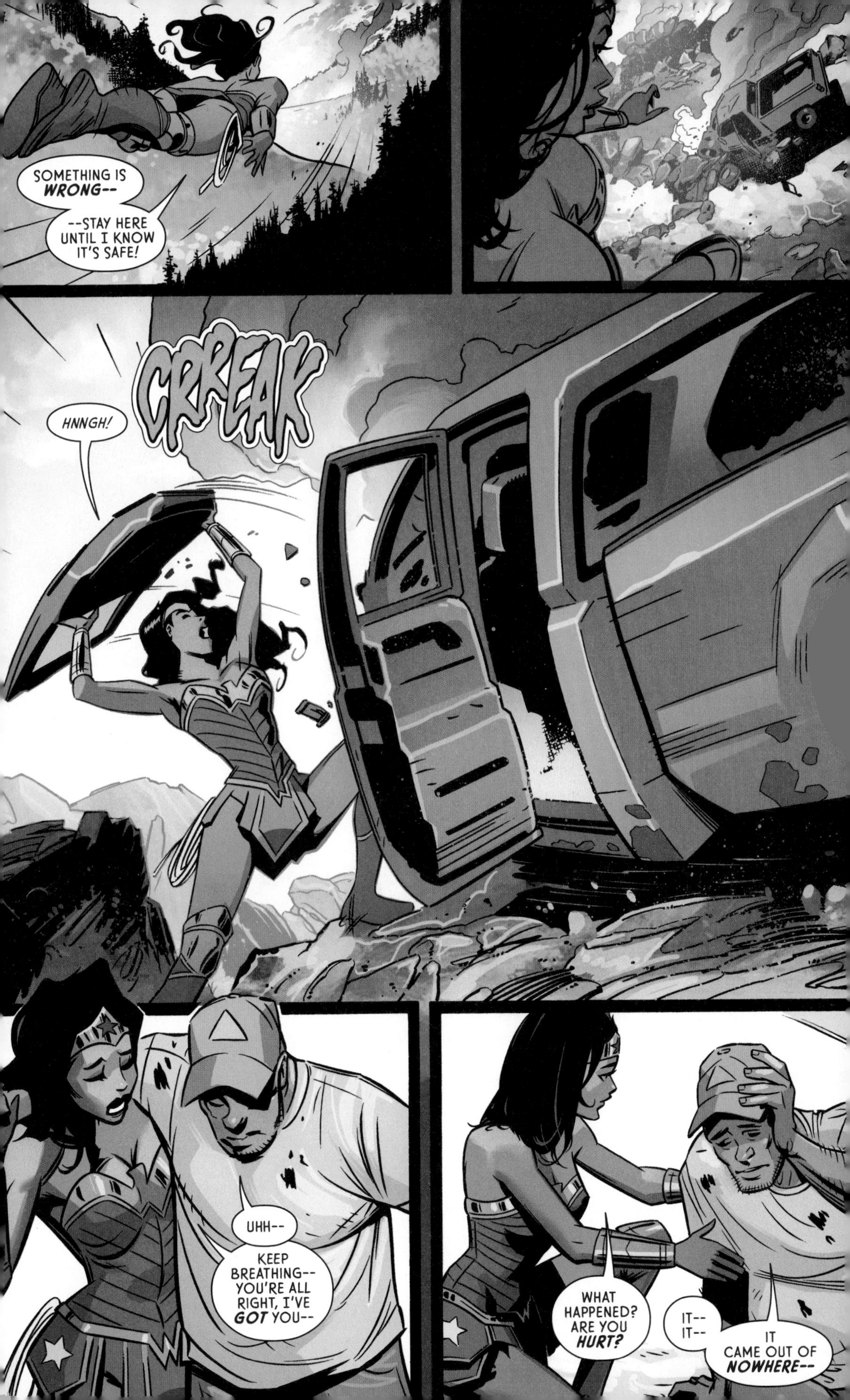
SOMETHING IS **WRONG--**
--STAY HERE UNTIL I KNOW IT'S SAFE!
CRREAK
HNNGH!
UHH--
KEEP BREATHING-- YOU'RE ALL RIGHT, I'VE ***GOT*** YOU--
WHAT HAPPENED? ARE YOU ***HURT?***
IT-- IT--
IT CAME OUT OF ***NOWHERE--***

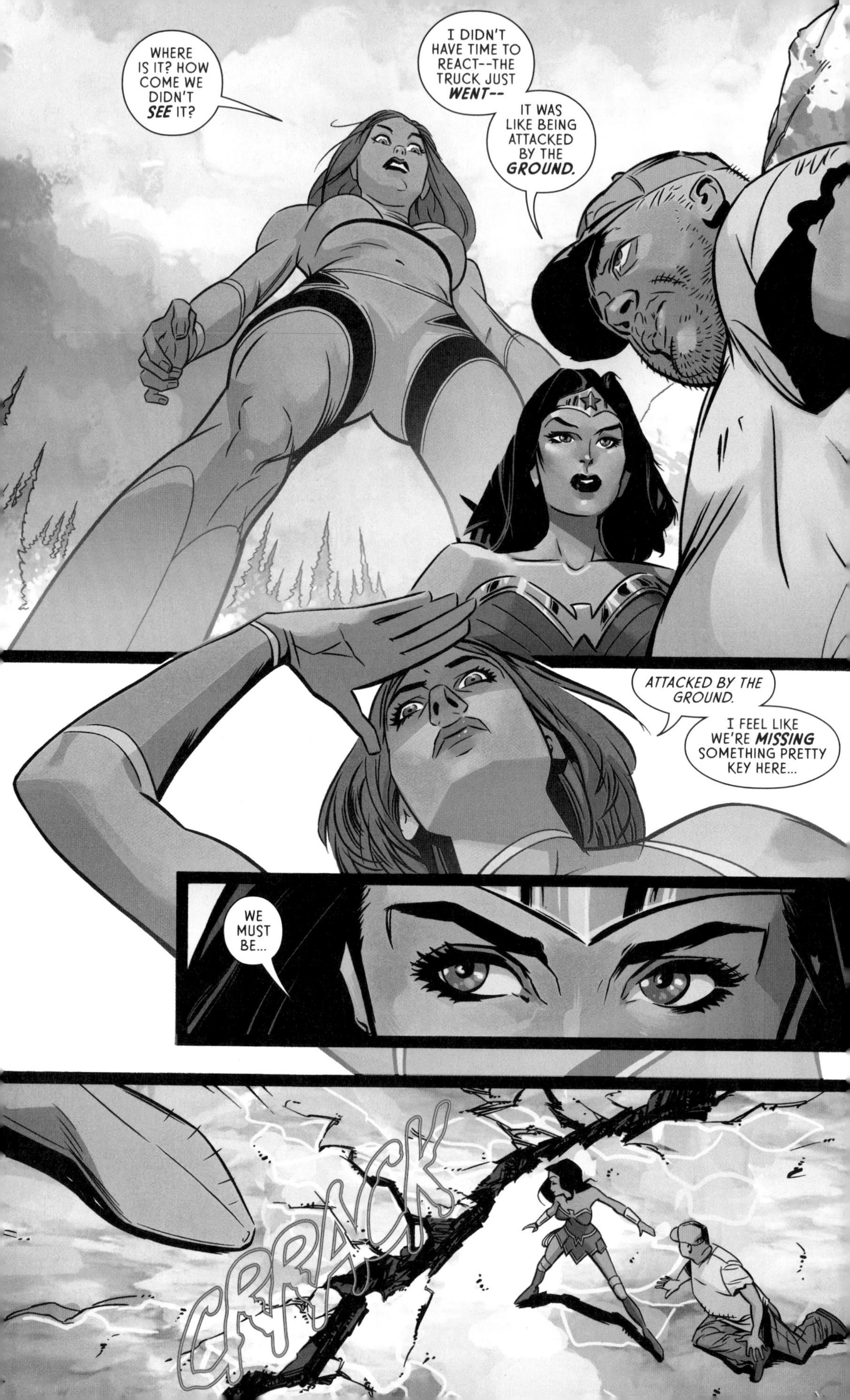
WHERE IS IT? HOW COME WE DIDN'T SEE IT?
I DIDN'T HAVE TIME TO REACT--THE TRUCK JUST WENT--
IT WAS LIKE BEING ATTACKED BY THE GROUND.
ATTACKED BY THE GROUND.
I FEEL LIKE WE'RE MISSING SOMETHING PRETTY KEY HERE...
WE MUST BE...
CRRACK

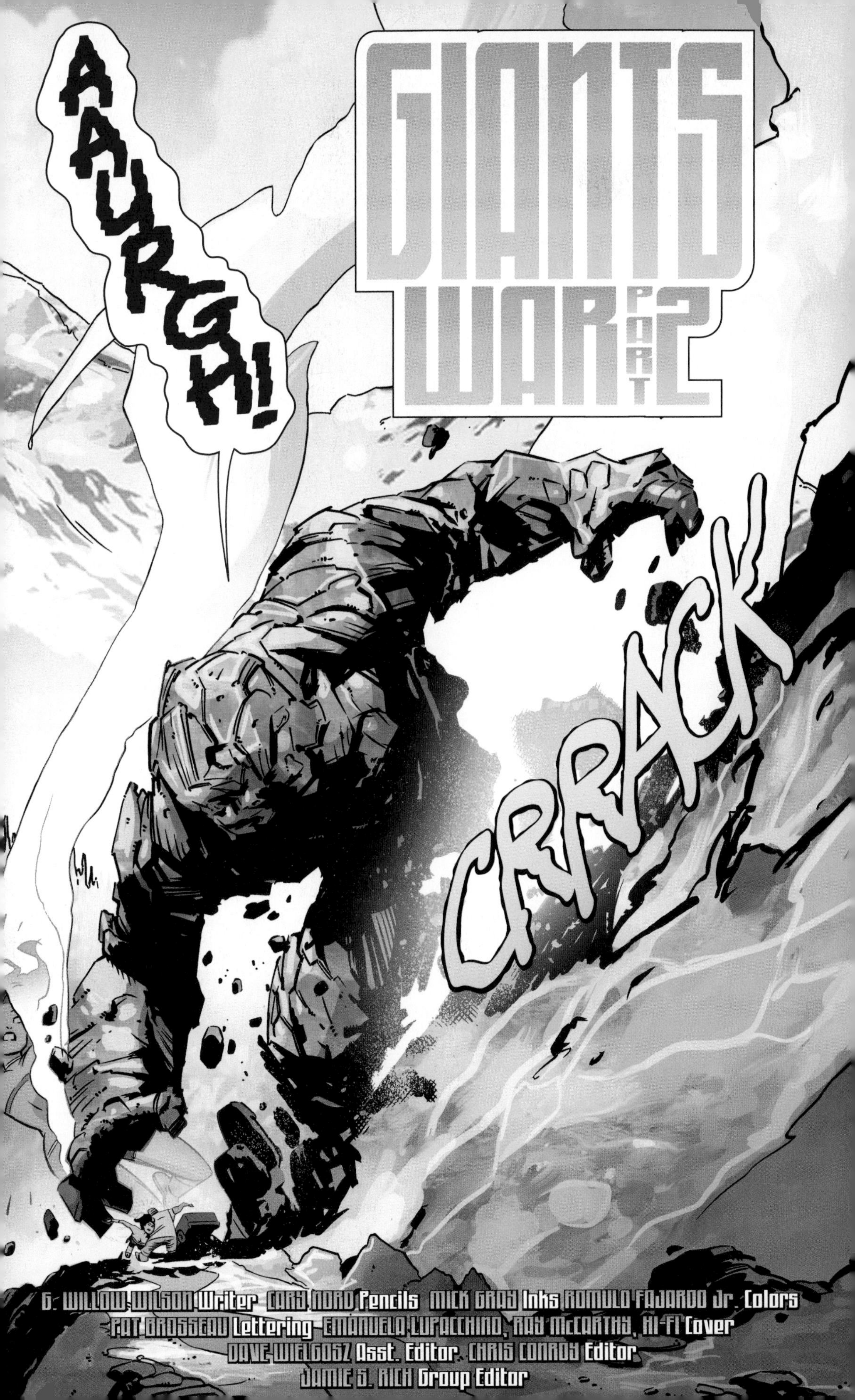
GIANTS WAR PART 2
AAURGH!
CRRACK
G. WILLOW WILSON Writer CARY NORD Pencils MICK GRAY Inks ROMULO FAJARDO Jr. Colors
PAT BROSSEAU Lettering EMANUELA LUPACCHINO, RAY McCARTHY, HI-FI Cover
DAVE WIELGOSZ Asst. Editor CHRIS CONROY Editor
JAMIE S. RICH Group Editor

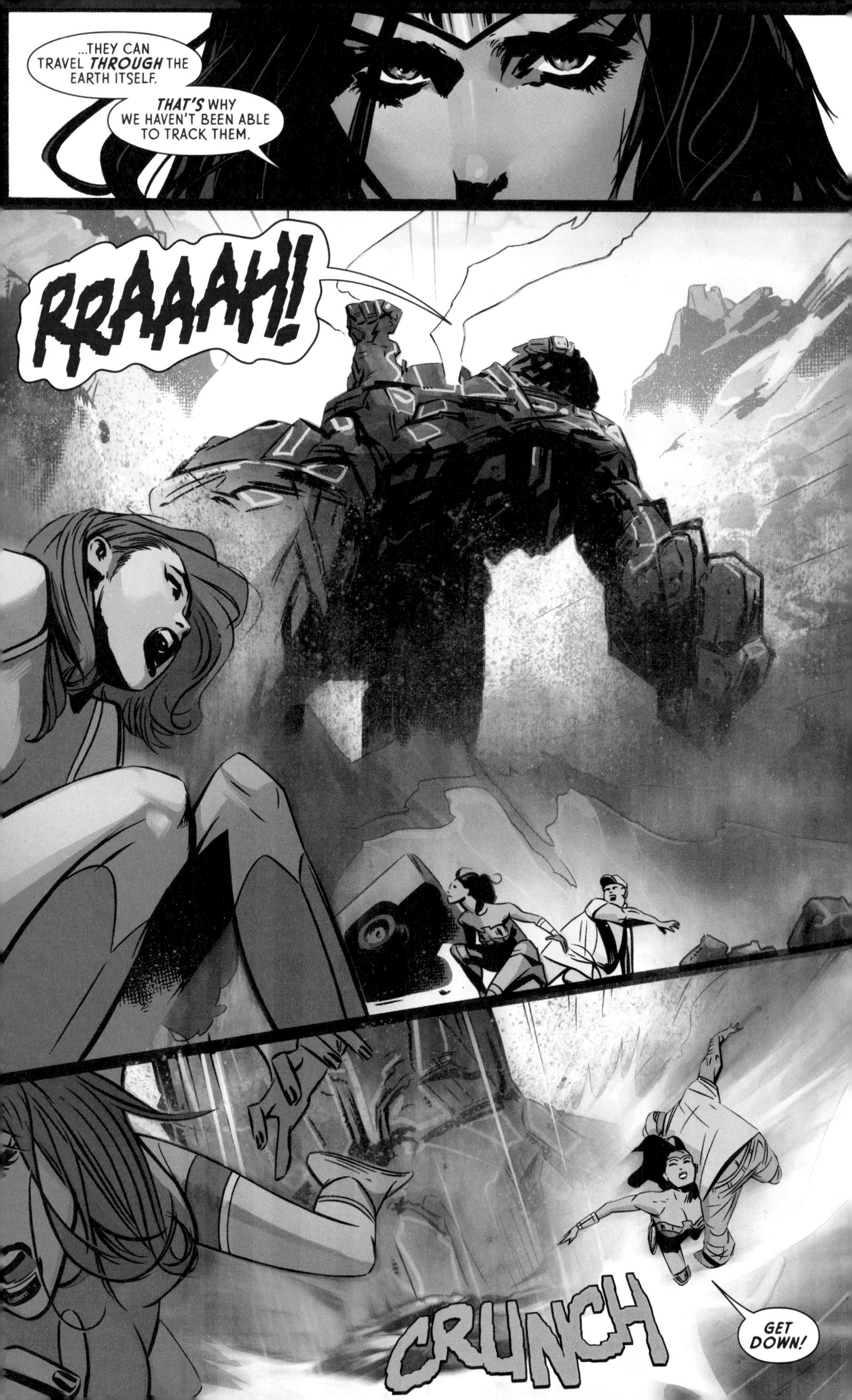
...THEY CAN TRAVEL THROUGH THE EARTH ITSELF.
THAT'S WHY WE HAVEN'T BEEN ABLE TO TRACK THEM.
RRAAAH!
CRUNCH
GET DOWN!

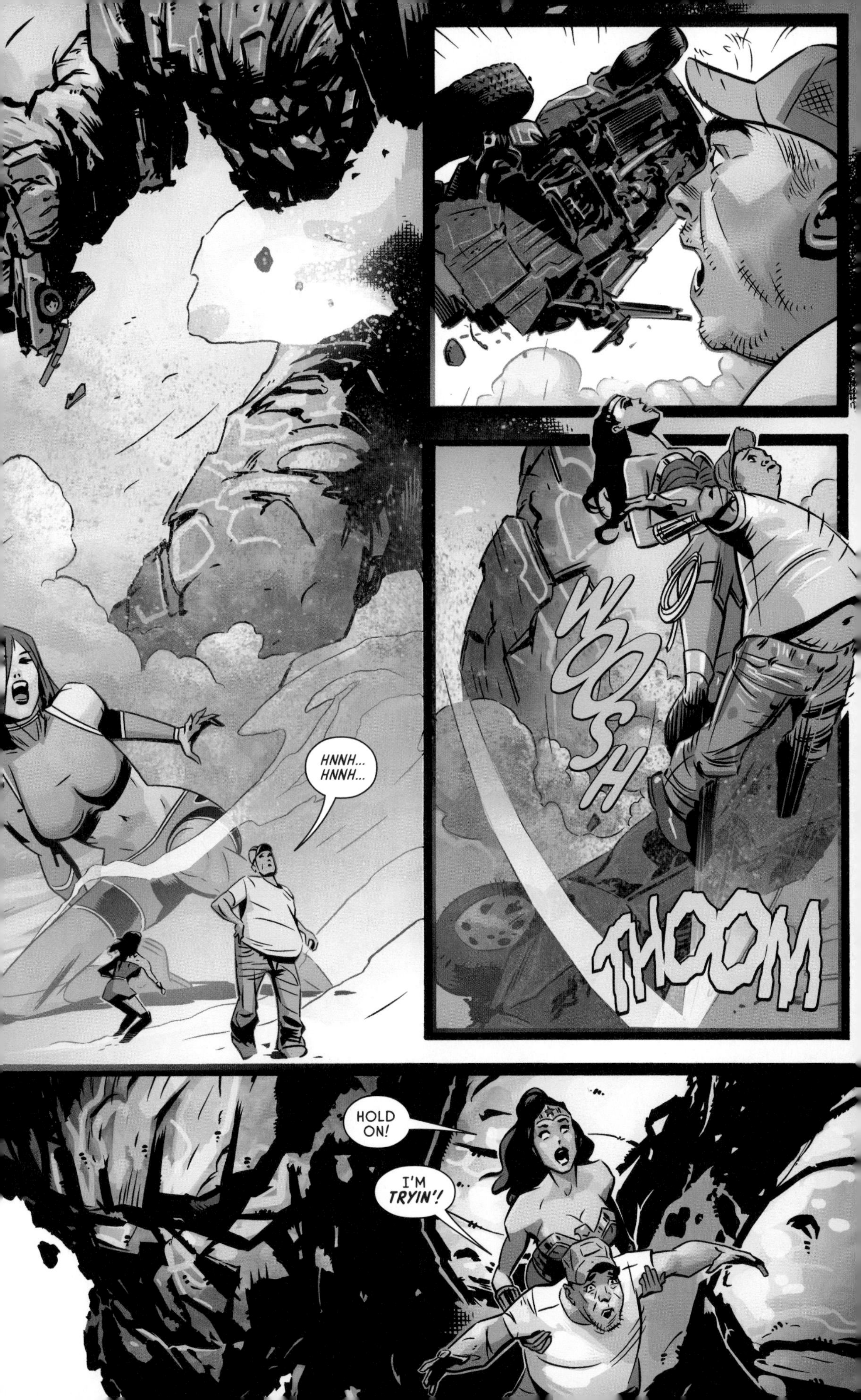
HNNH...
HNNH...
WOOSH
THOOM
HOLD ON!
I'M TRYIN'!

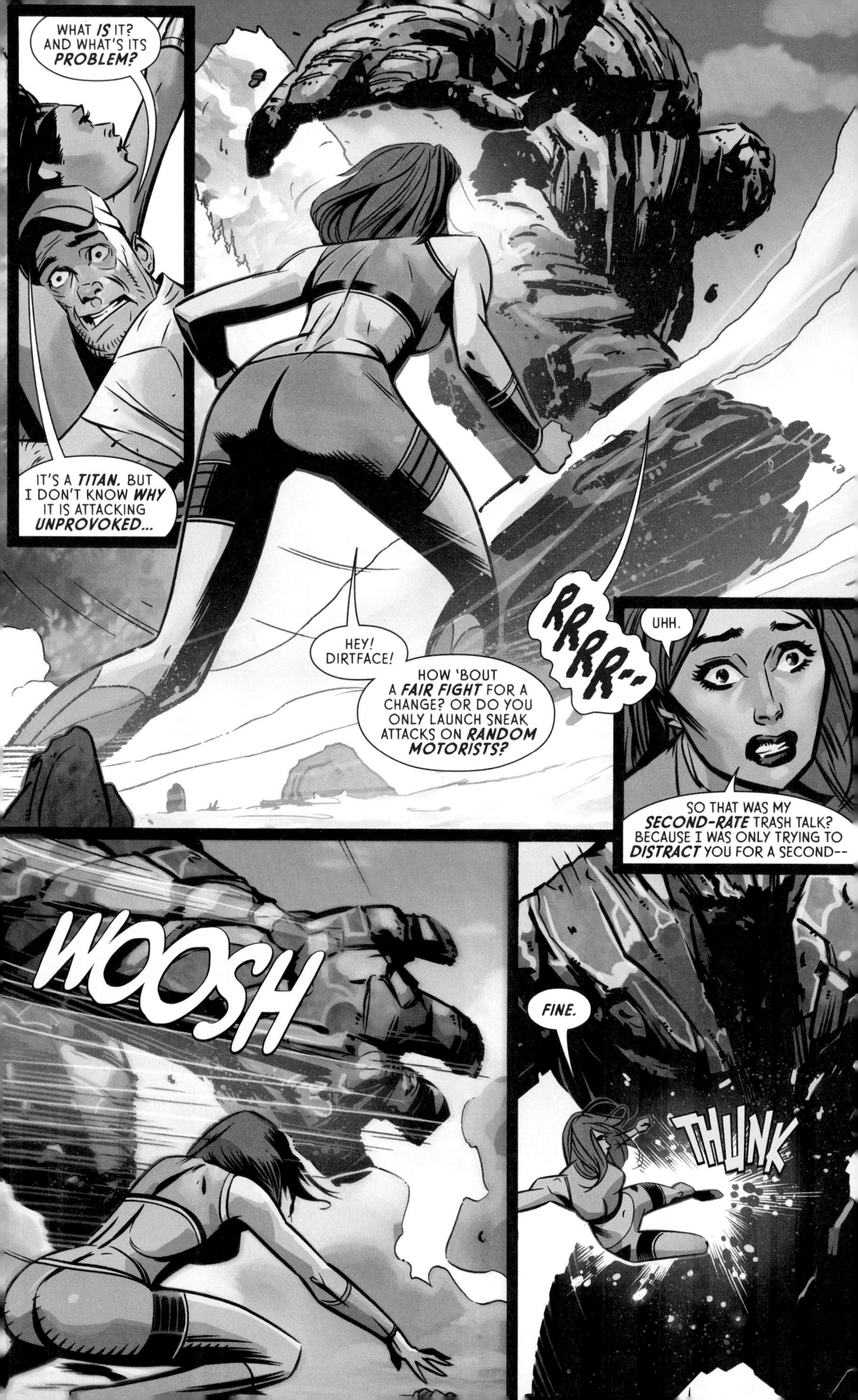

WHAT IS IT? AND WHAT'S ITS PROBLEM?
IT'S A TITAN. BUT I DON'T KNOW WHY IT IS ATTACKING UNPROVOKED...
HEY! DIRTFACE!
HOW 'BOUT A FAIR FIGHT FOR A CHANGE? OR DO YOU ONLY LAUNCH SNEAK ATTACKS ON RANDOM MOTORISTS?
RRRRR--
UHH.
SO THAT WAS MY SECOND-RATE TRASH TALK? BECAUSE I WAS ONLY TRYING TO DISTRACT YOU FOR A SECOND--
WOOSH
FINE.
THUNK

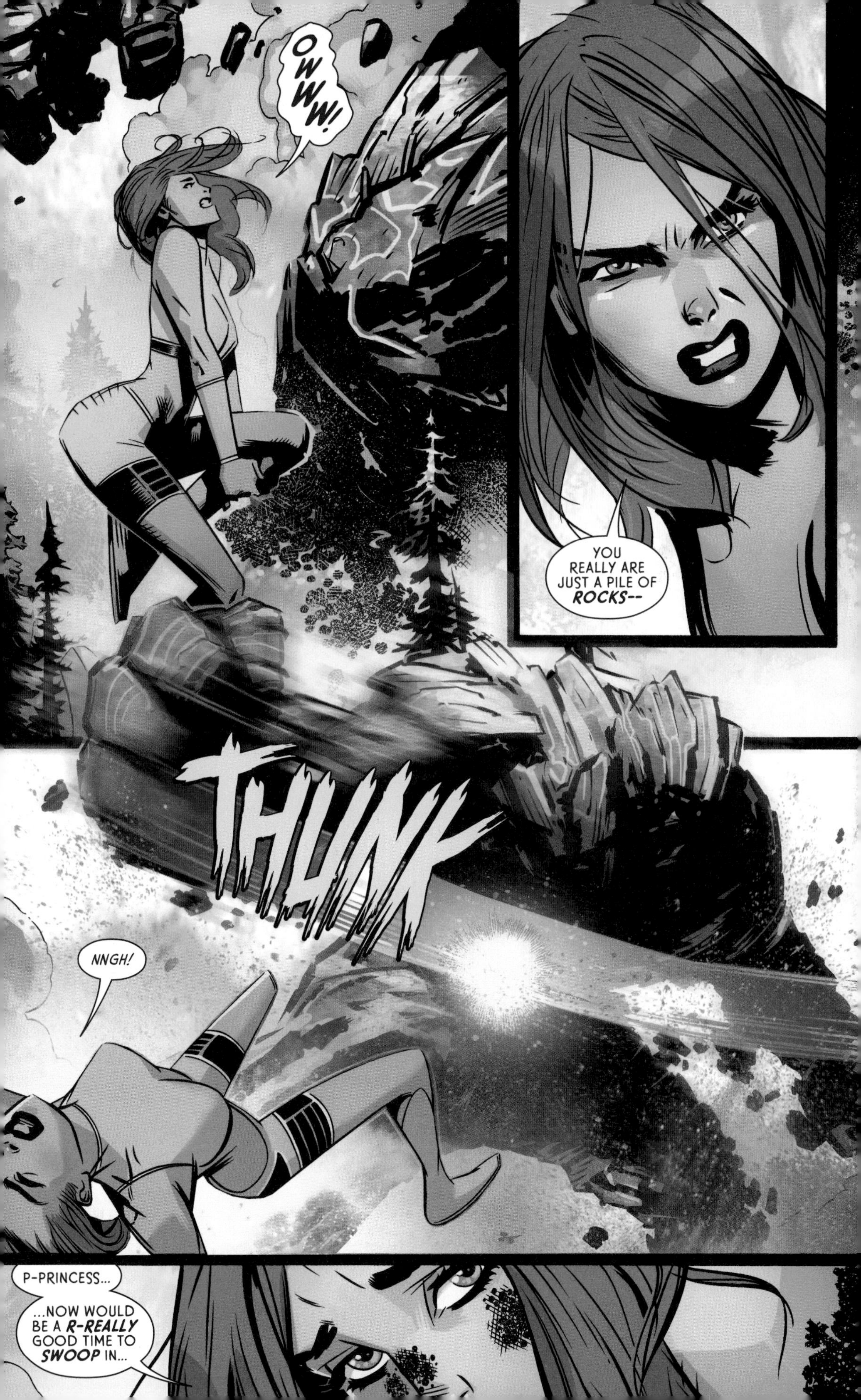
OWWW!
YOU REALLY ARE JUST A PILE OF ROCKS--
THUNK
NNGH!
P-PRINCESS...
...NOW WOULD BE A R-REALLY GOOD TIME TO SWOOP IN...

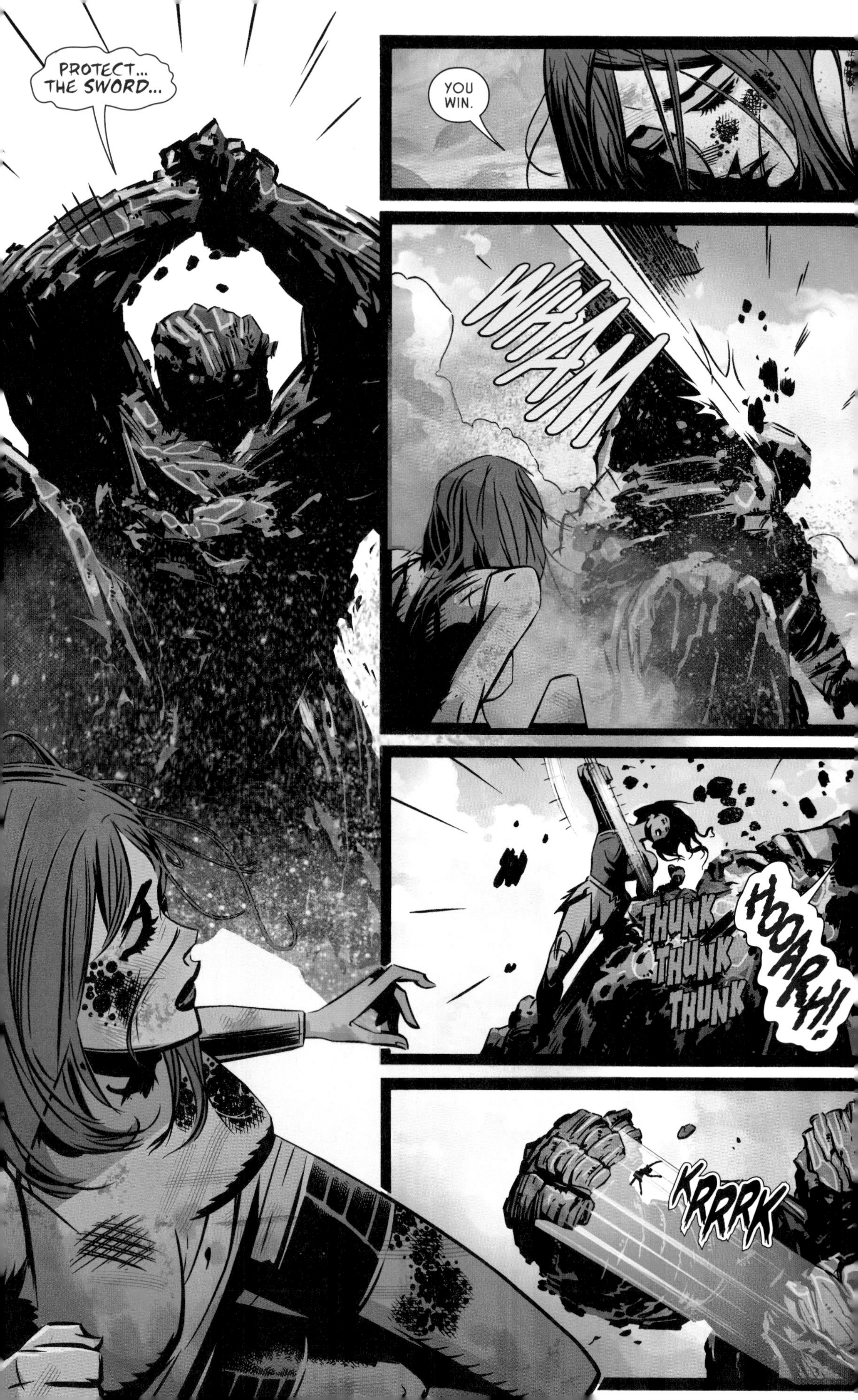

PROTECT... THE SWORD...
YOU WIN.
WHAM
THUNK
THUNK
THUNK
HOOARH!!
KRRRK

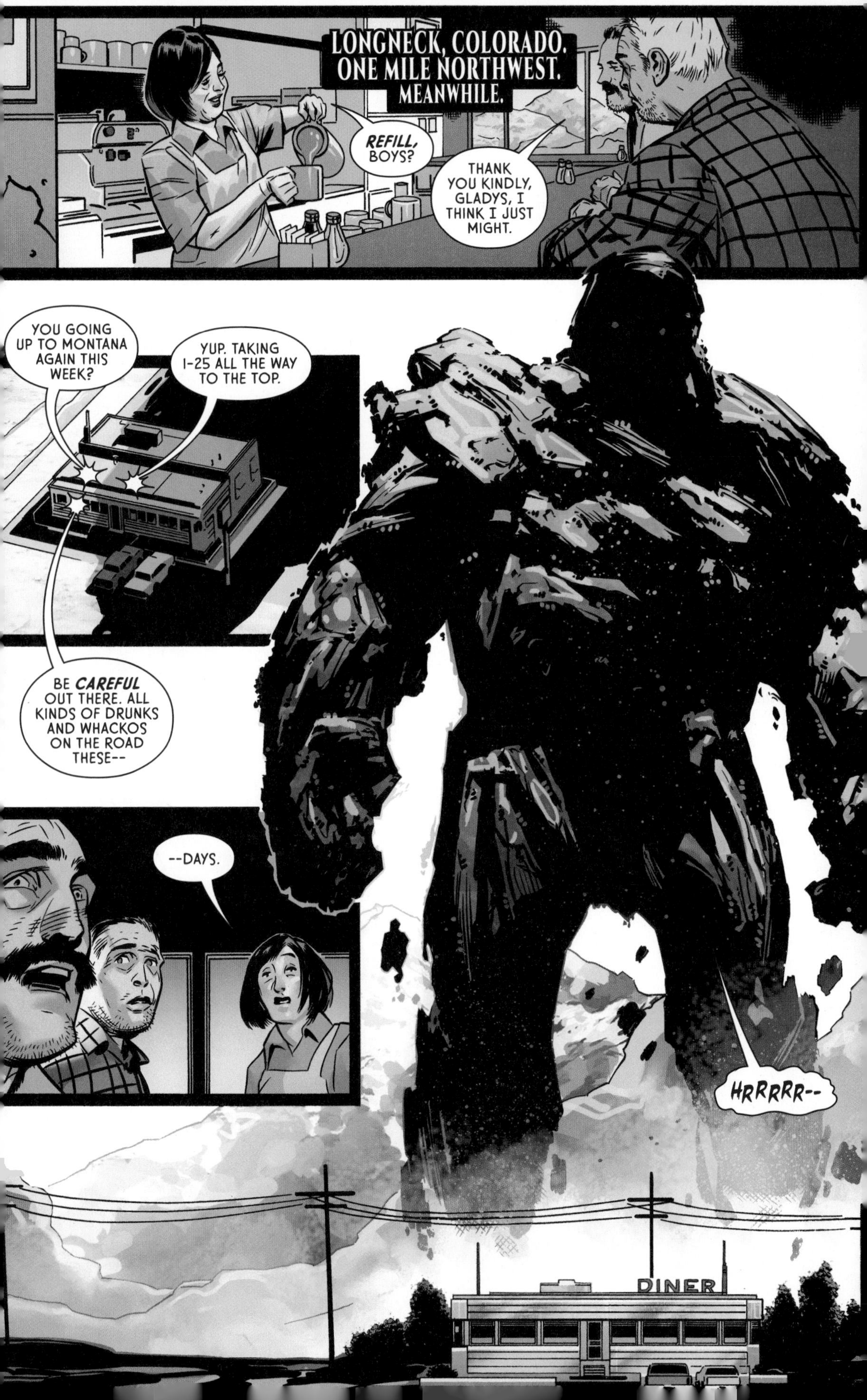
LONGNECK, COLORADO. ONE MILE NORTHWEST. MEANWHILE.
REFILL, BOYS?
THANK YOU KINDLY, GLADYS, I THINK I JUST MIGHT.
YOU GOING UP TO MONTANA AGAIN THIS WEEK?
YUP. TAKING I-25 ALL THE WAY TO THE TOP.
BE CAREFUL OUT THERE. ALL KINDS OF DRUNKS AND WHACKOS ON THE ROAD THESE--
--DAYS.
HRRRRR--
DINER

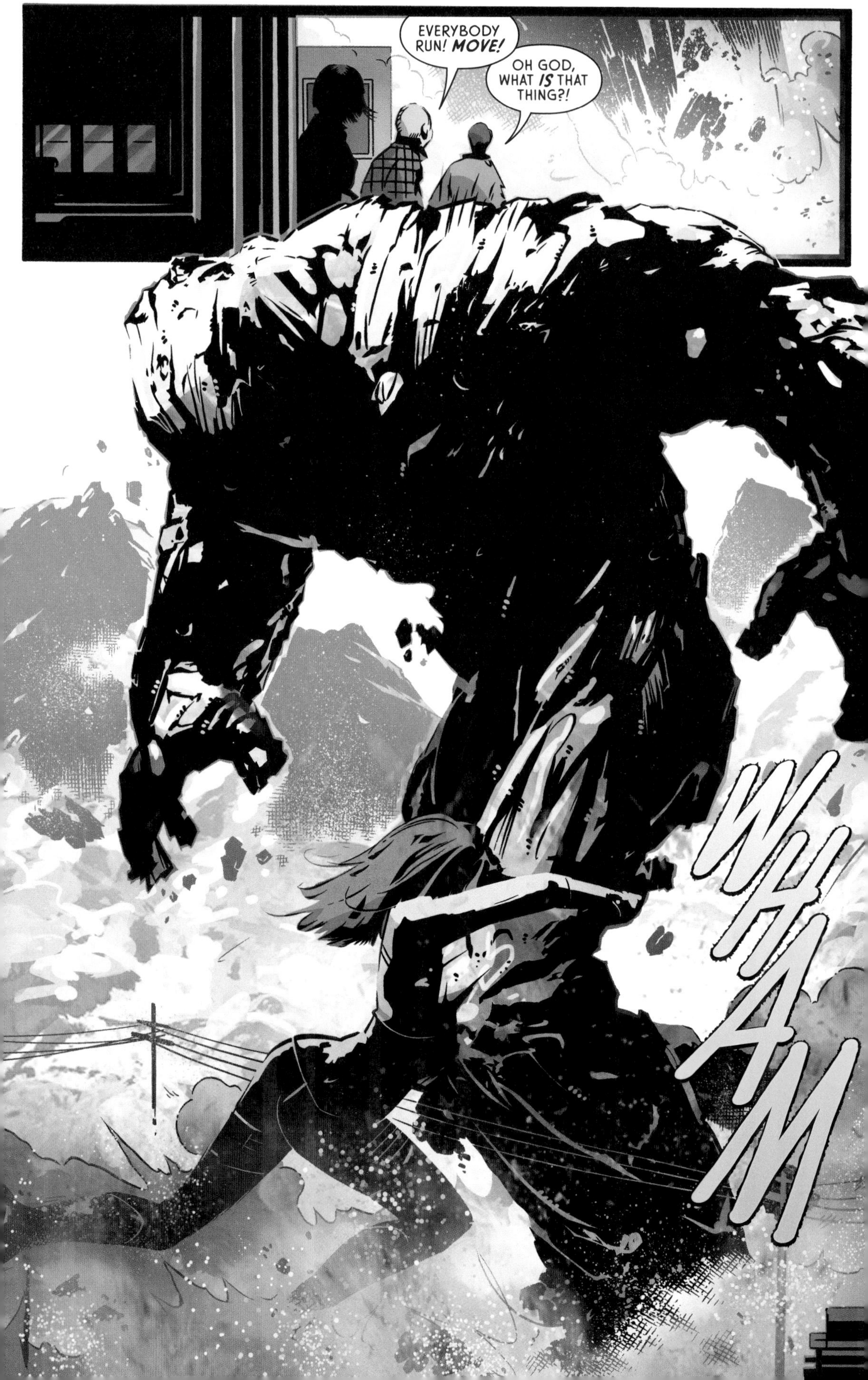
EVERYBODY RUN! MOVE!
OH GOD, WHAT IS THAT THING?!
WHAM

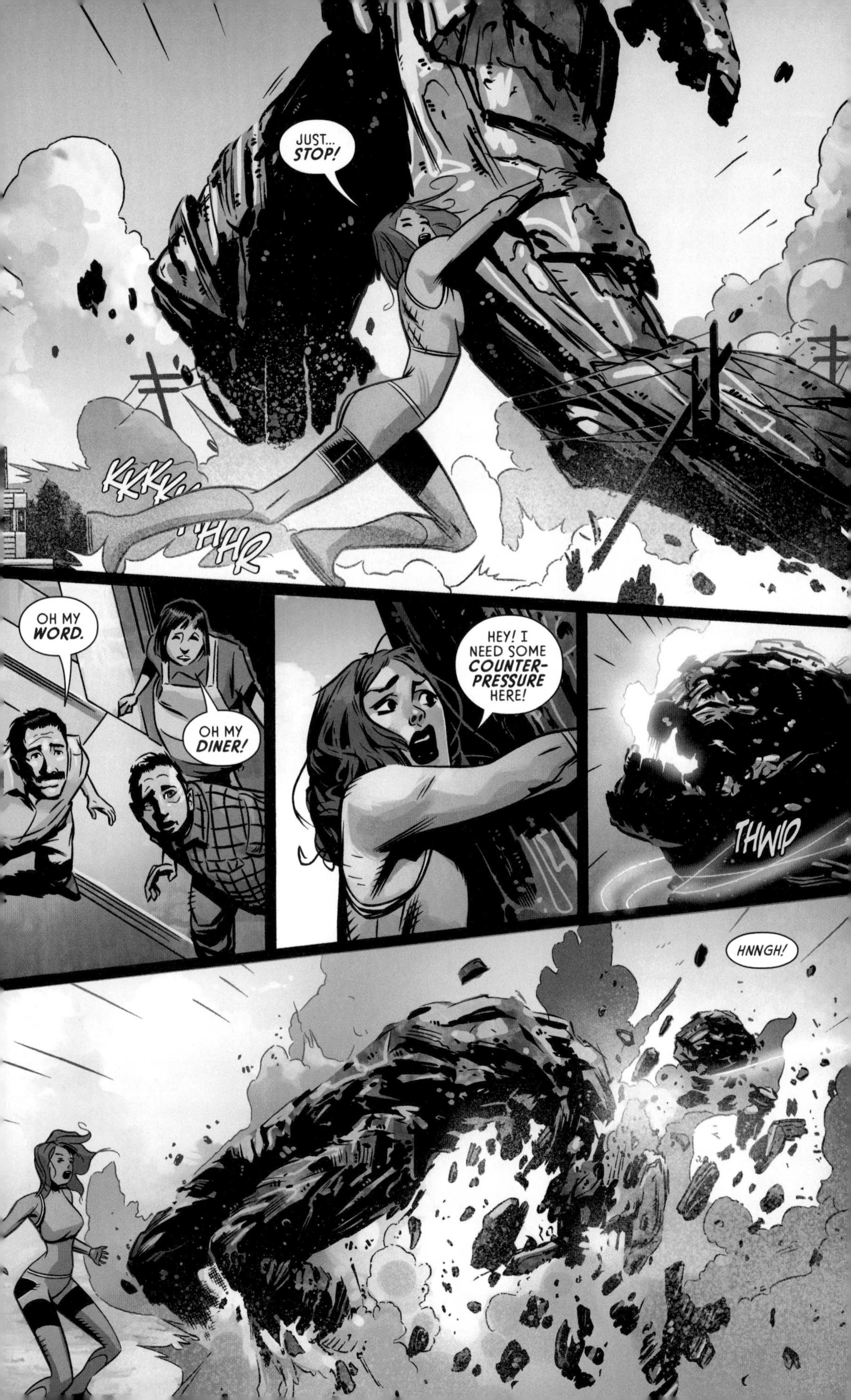
JUST... STOP!
KKKKK
HHR
OH MY WORD.
OH MY DINER!
HEY! I NEED SOME COUNTER-PRESSURE HERE!
THWIP
HNNGH!

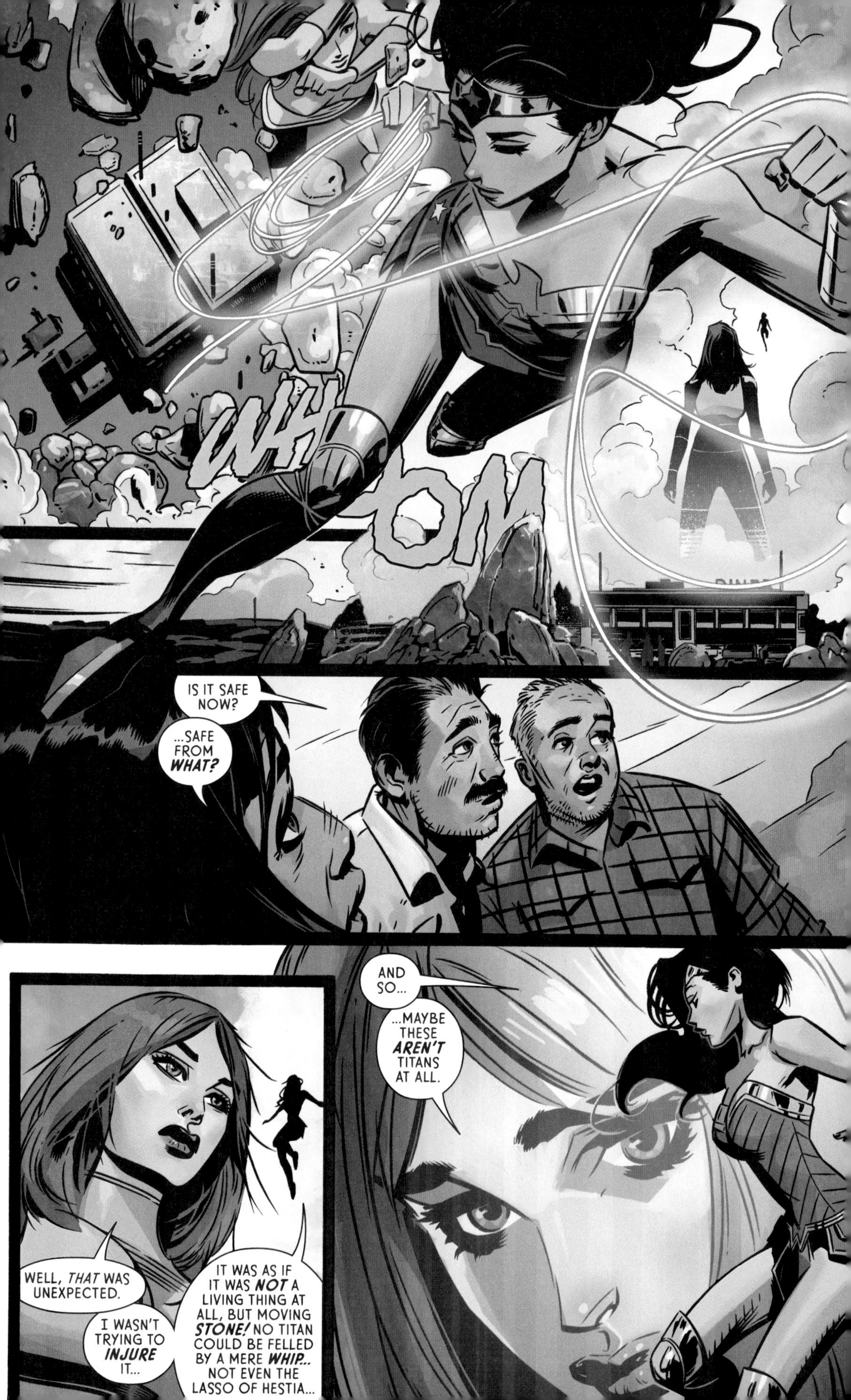
WHOOM
IS IT SAFE NOW?
...SAFE FROM WHAT?
AND SO...
...MAYBE THESE AREN'T TITANS AT ALL.
WELL, THAT WAS UNEXPECTED.
I WASN'T TRYING TO INJURE IT...
IT WAS AS IF IT WAS NOT A LIVING THING AT ALL, BUT MOVING STONE! NO TITAN COULD BE FELLED BY A MERE WHIP... NOT EVEN THE LASSO OF HESTIA...

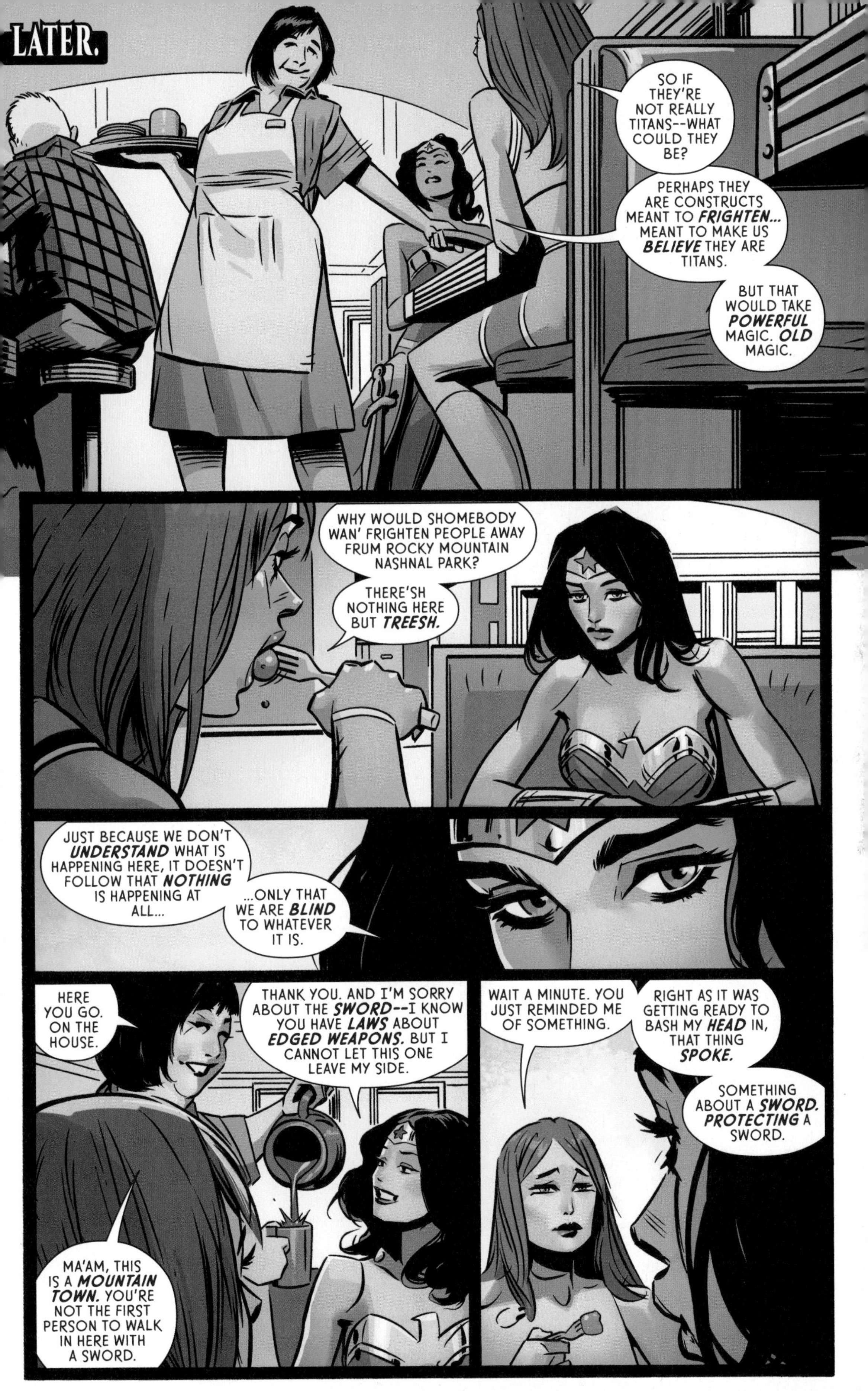
LATER.
SO IF THEY'RE NOT REALLY TITANS--WHAT COULD THEY BE?
PERHAPS THEY ARE CONSTRUCTS MEANT TO *FRIGHTEN...* MEANT TO MAKE US *BELIEVE* THEY ARE TITANS.
BUT THAT WOULD TAKE *POWERFUL* MAGIC. *OLD* MAGIC.
WHY WOULD SHOMEBODY WAN' FRIGHTEN PEOPLE AWAY FRUM ROCKY MOUNTAIN NASHNAL PARK?
THERE'SH NOTHING HERE BUT *TREESH.*
JUST BECAUSE WE DON'T *UNDERSTAND* WHAT IS HAPPENING HERE, IT DOESN'T FOLLOW THAT *NOTHING* IS HAPPENING AT ALL...
...ONLY THAT WE ARE *BLIND* TO WHATEVER IT IS.
HERE YOU GO. ON THE HOUSE.
THANK YOU. AND I'M SORRY ABOUT THE *SWORD*--I KNOW YOU HAVE *LAWS* ABOUT *EDGED WEAPONS.* BUT I CANNOT LET THIS ONE LEAVE MY SIDE.
MA'AM, THIS IS A *MOUNTAIN TOWN.* YOU'RE NOT THE FIRST PERSON TO WALK IN HERE WITH A SWORD.
WAIT A MINUTE. YOU JUST REMINDED ME OF SOMETHING.
RIGHT AS IT WAS GETTING READY TO BASH MY *HEAD* IN, THAT THING *SPOKE.*
SOMETHING ABOUT A *SWORD. PROTECTING* A SWORD.

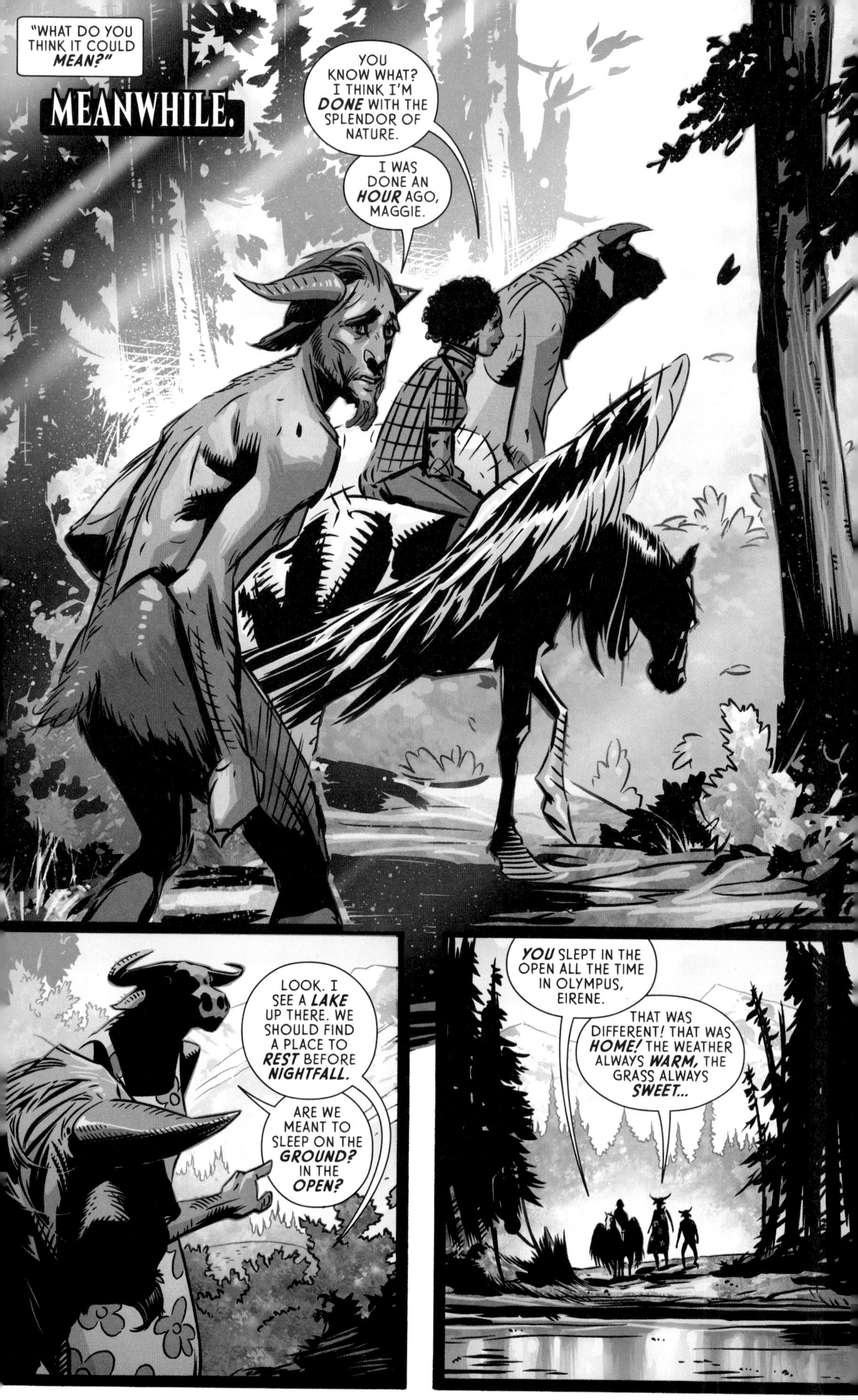
"WHAT DO YOU THINK IT COULD MEAN?"
MEANWHILE.
YOU KNOW WHAT? I THINK I'M DONE WITH THE SPLENDOR OF NATURE.
I WAS DONE AN HOUR AGO, MAGGIE.
LOOK. I SEE A LAKE UP THERE. WE SHOULD FIND A PLACE TO REST BEFORE NIGHTFALL.
ARE WE MEANT TO SLEEP ON THE GROUND? IN THE OPEN?
YOU SLEPT IN THE OPEN ALL THE TIME IN OLYMPUS, EIRENE.
THAT WAS DIFFERENT! THAT WAS HOME! THE WEATHER ALWAYS WARM, THE GRASS ALWAYS SWEET...

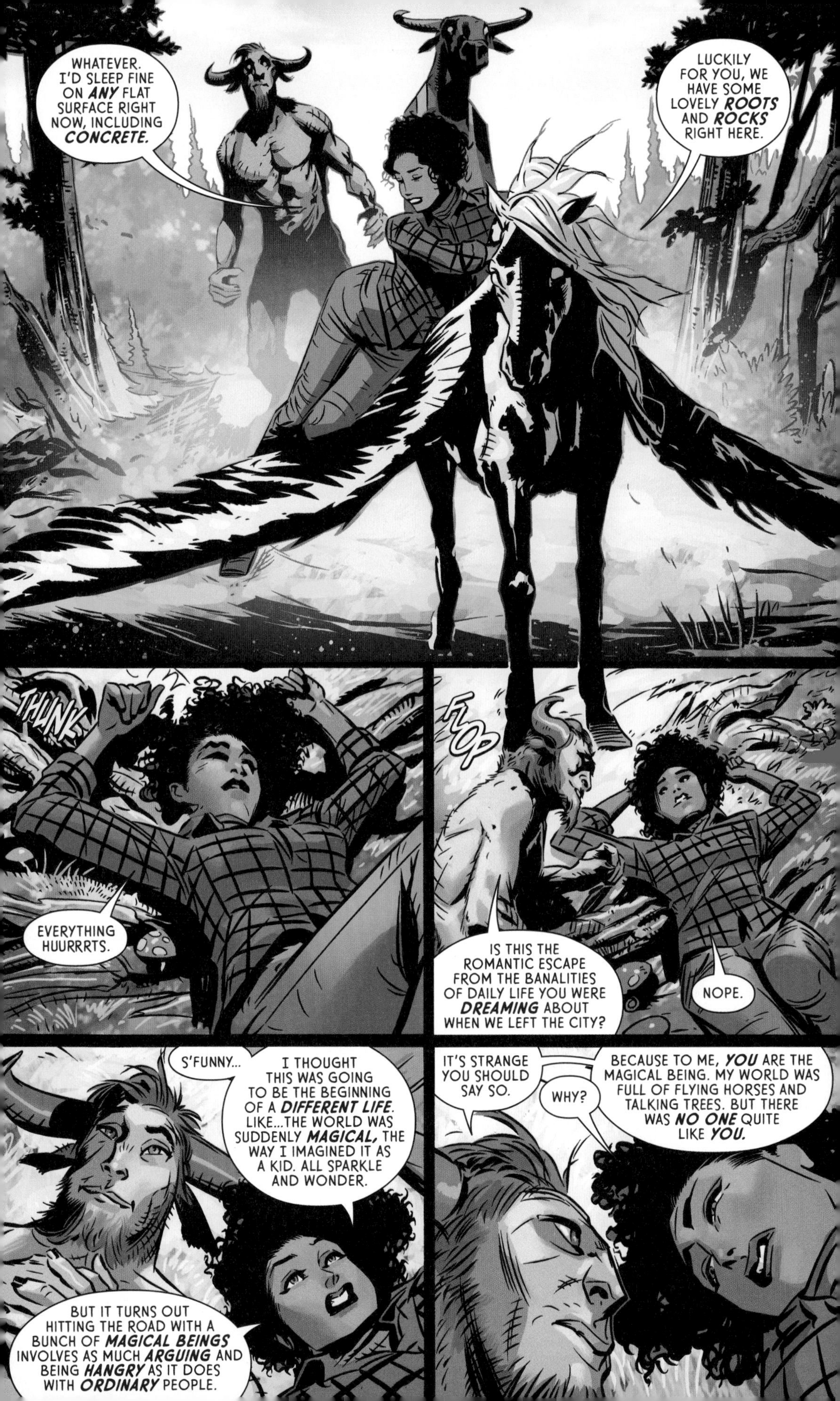
WHATEVER. I'D SLEEP FINE ON ANY FLAT SURFACE RIGHT NOW, INCLUDING CONCRETE.
LUCKILY FOR YOU, WE HAVE SOME LOVELY ROOTS AND ROCKS RIGHT HERE.
THUNK
EVERYTHING HUURRRTS.
FLOP
IS THIS THE ROMANTIC ESCAPE FROM THE BANALITIES OF DAILY LIFE YOU WERE DREAMING ABOUT WHEN WE LEFT THE CITY?
NOPE.
S'FUNNY...
I THOUGHT THIS WAS GOING TO BE THE BEGINNING OF A DIFFERENT LIFE. LIKE...THE WORLD WAS SUDDENLY MAGICAL, THE WAY I IMAGINED IT AS A KID. ALL SPARKLE AND WONDER.
BUT IT TURNS OUT HITTING THE ROAD WITH A BUNCH OF MAGICAL BEINGS INVOLVES AS MUCH ARGUING AND BEING HANGRY AS IT DOES WITH ORDINARY PEOPLE.
IT'S STRANGE YOU SHOULD SAY SO.
WHY?
BECAUSE TO ME, YOU ARE THE MAGICAL BEING. MY WORLD WAS FULL OF FLYING HORSES AND TALKING TREES. BUT THERE WAS NO ONE QUITE LIKE YOU.

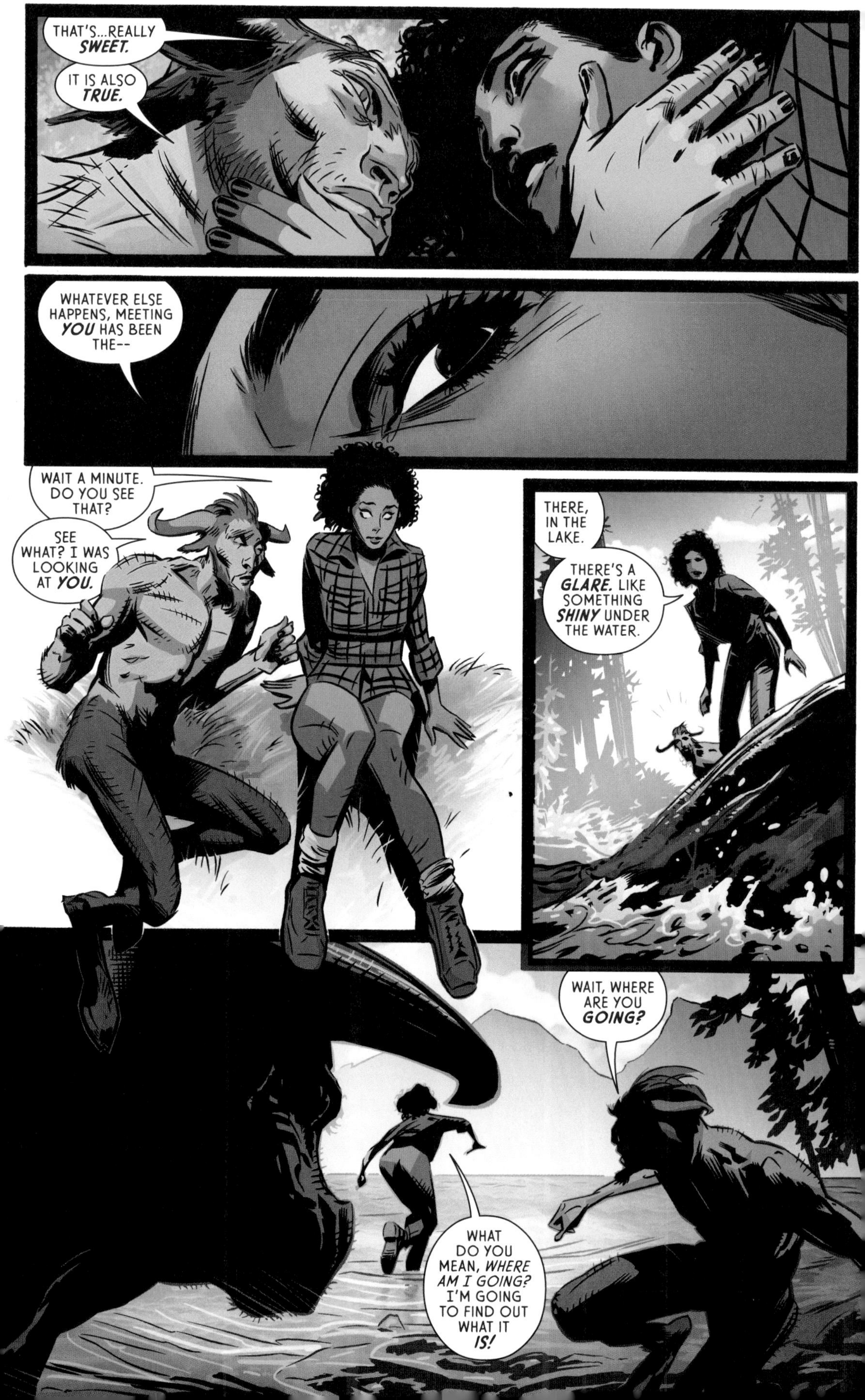
THAT'S...REALLY SWEET.
IT IS ALSO TRUE.
WHATEVER ELSE HAPPENS, MEETING YOU HAS BEEN THE--
WAIT A MINUTE. DO YOU SEE THAT?
SEE WHAT? I WAS LOOKING AT YOU.
THERE, IN THE LAKE.
THERE'S A GLARE. LIKE SOMETHING SHINY UNDER THE WATER.
WAIT, WHERE ARE YOU GOING?
WHAT DO YOU MEAN, WHERE AM I GOING? I'M GOING TO FIND OUT WHAT IT IS!

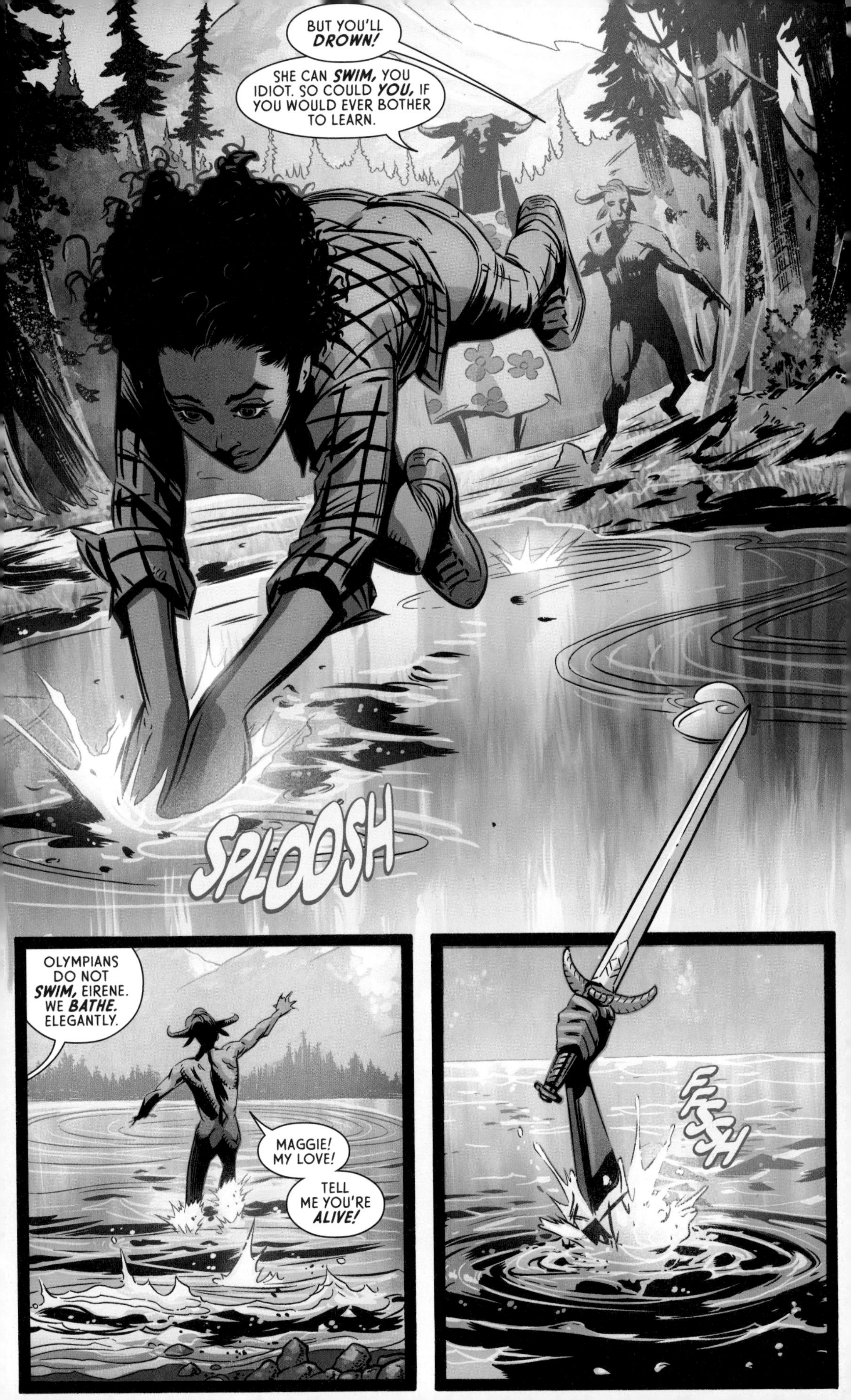
BUT YOU'LL DROWN!
SHE CAN SWIM, YOU IDIOT. SO COULD YOU, IF YOU WOULD EVER BOTHER TO LEARN.
SPLOOSH
OLYMPIANS DO NOT SWIM, EIRENE. WE BATHE. ELEGANTLY.
MAGGIE! MY LOVE!
TELL ME YOU'RE ALIVE!
FSSH

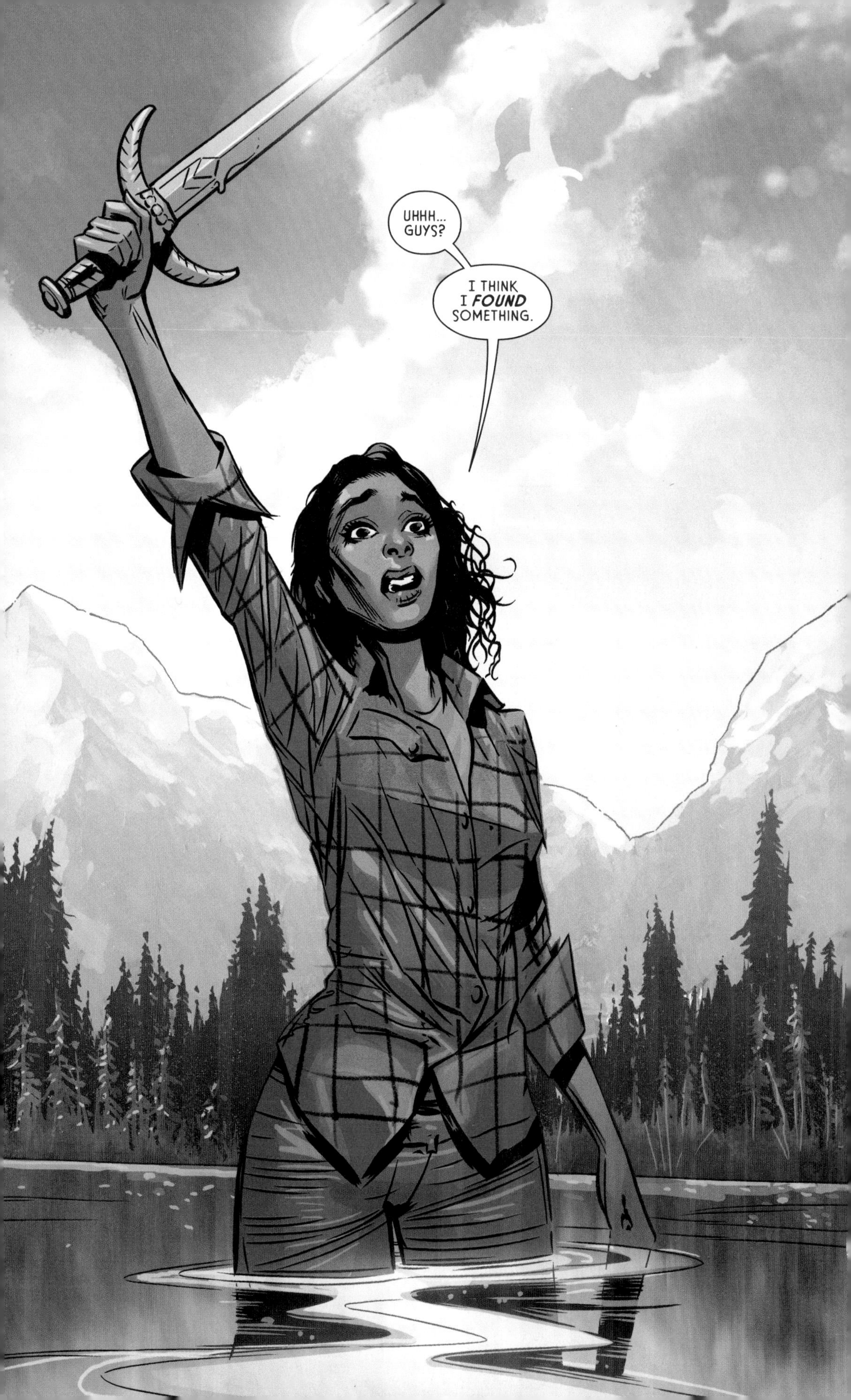
UHHH... GUYS?
I THINK I *FOUND* SOMETHING.

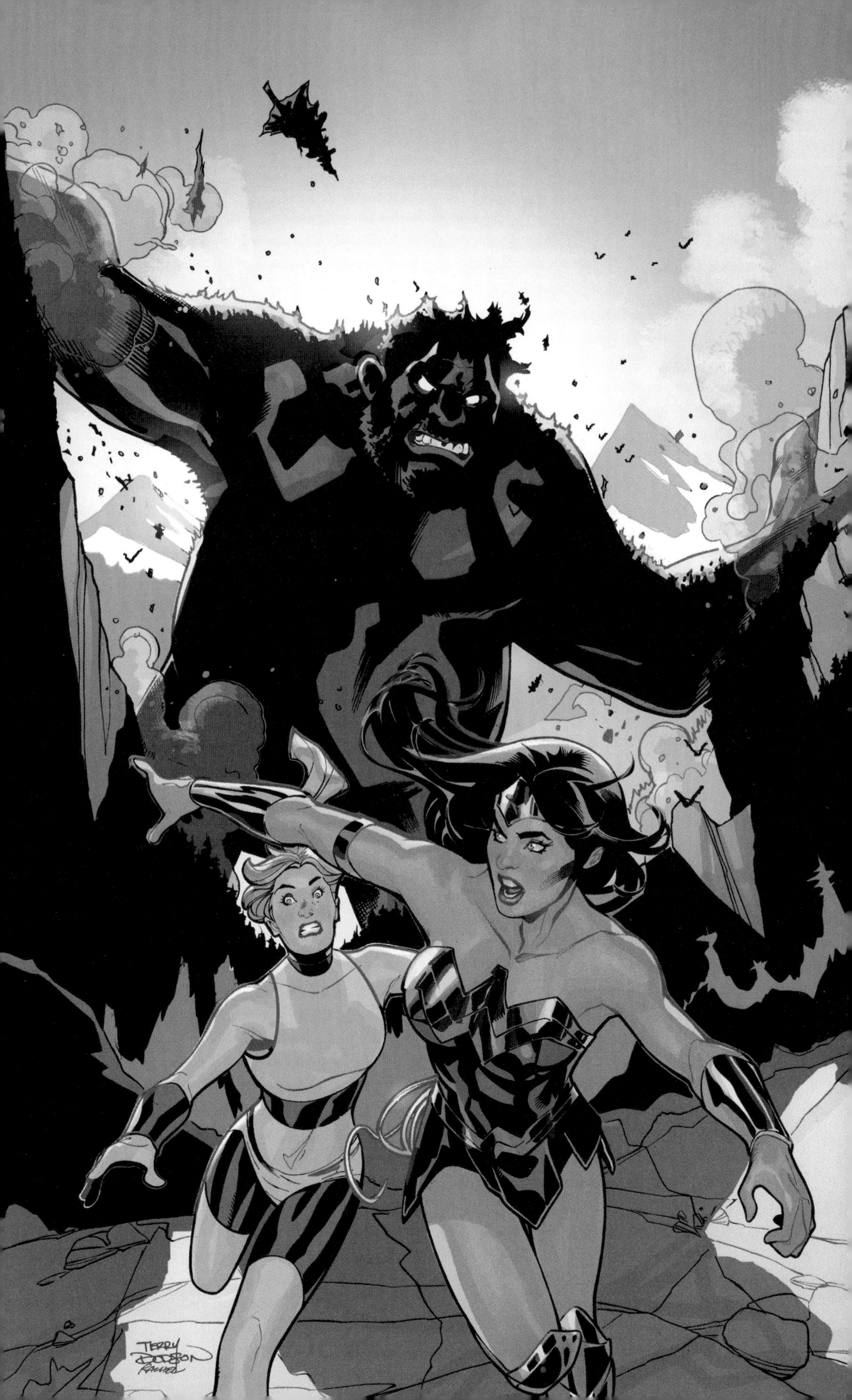
TERRY
DODSON
RACHEL

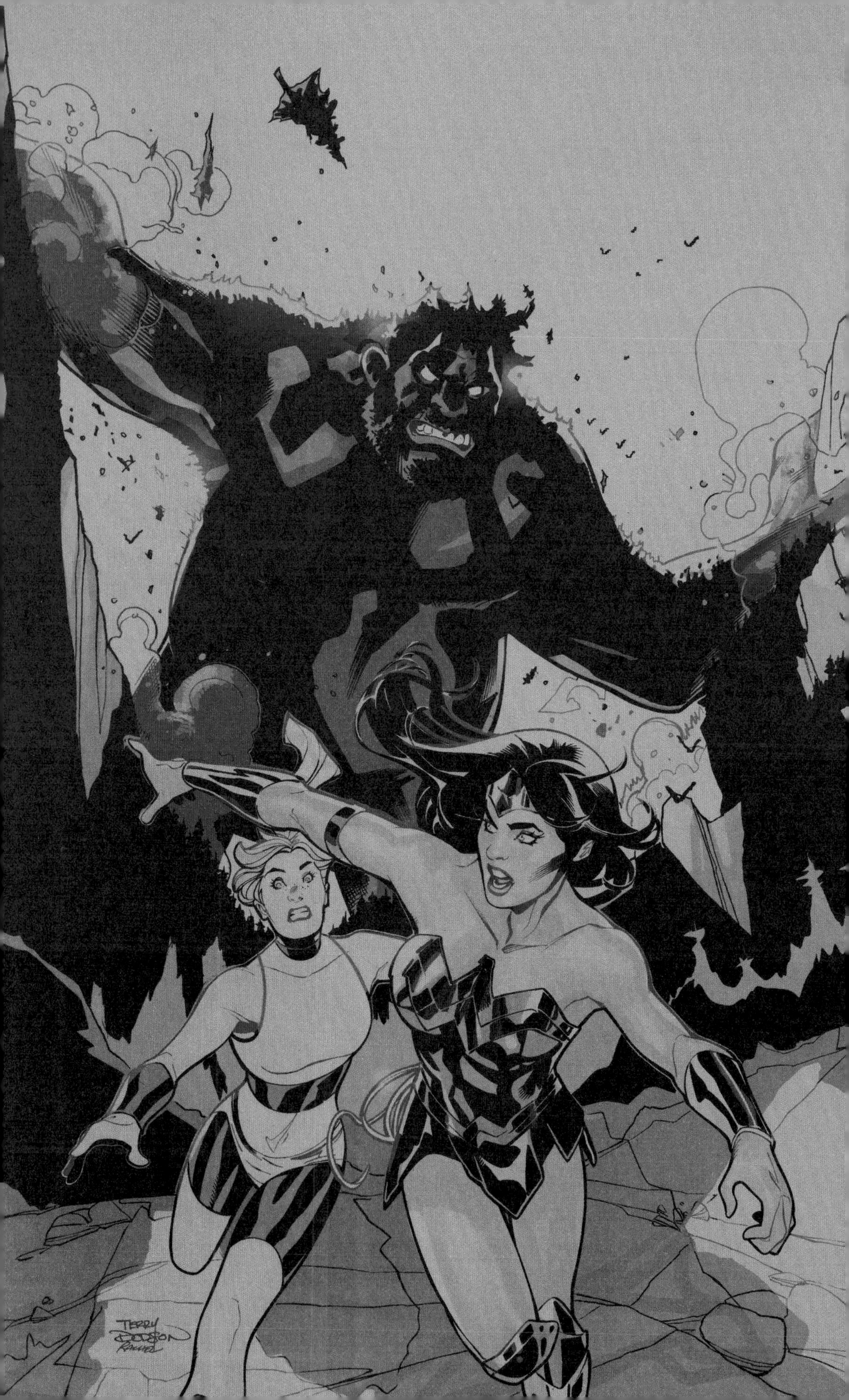
TERRY
DODSON
RACHEL

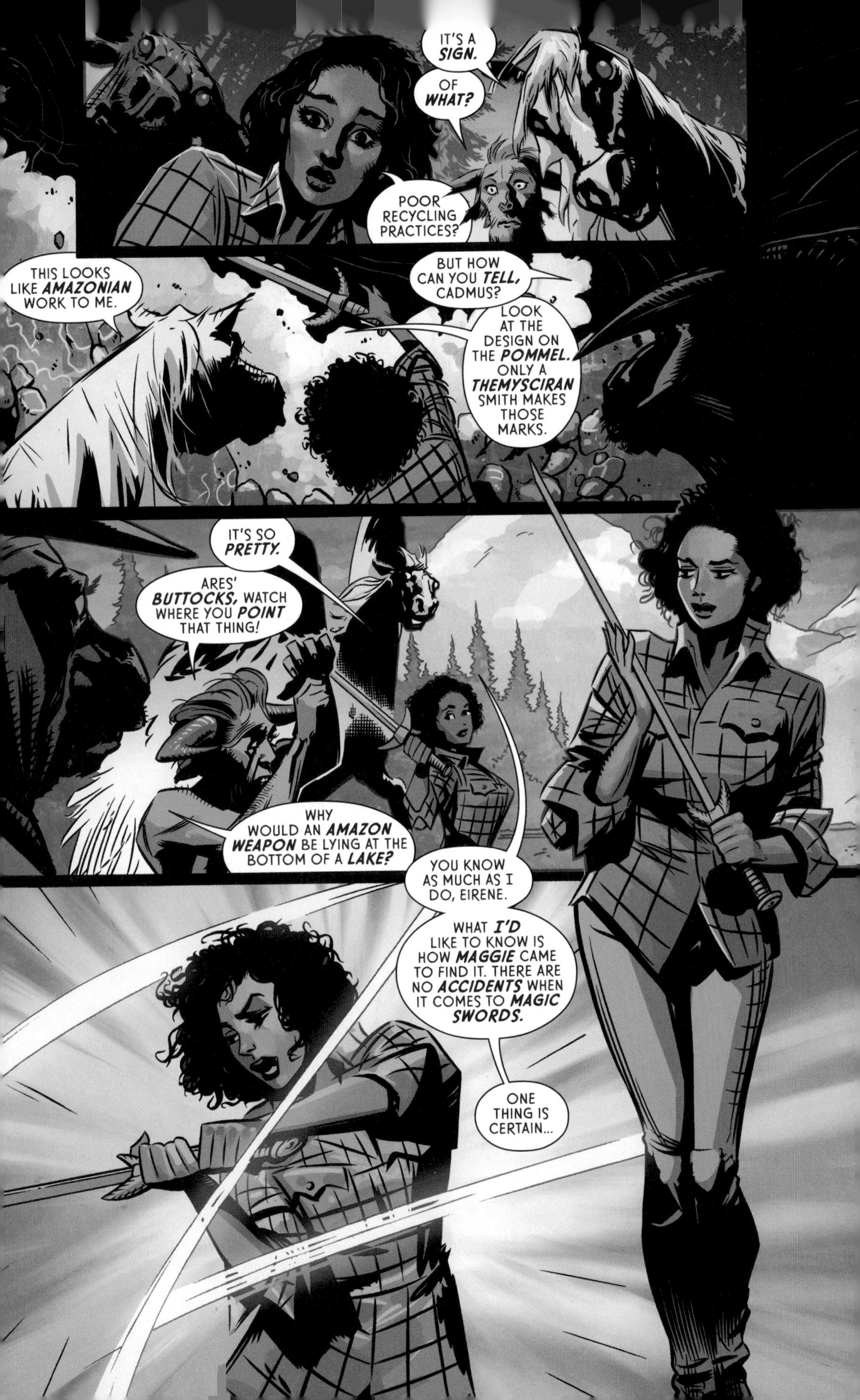
IT'S A SIGN.
OF WHAT?
POOR RECYCLING PRACTICES?
THIS LOOKS LIKE AMAZONIAN WORK TO ME.
BUT HOW CAN YOU TELL, CADMUS?
LOOK AT THE DESIGN ON THE POMMEL. ONLY A THEMYSCIRAN SMITH MAKES THOSE MARKS.
IT'S SO PRETTY.
ARES' BUTTOCKS, WATCH WHERE YOU POINT THAT THING!
WHY WOULD AN AMAZON WEAPON BE LYING AT THE BOTTOM OF A LAKE?
YOU KNOW AS MUCH AS I DO, EIRENE.
WHAT I'D LIKE TO KNOW IS HOW MAGGIE CAME TO FIND IT. THERE ARE NO ACCIDENTS WHEN IT COMES TO MAGIC SWORDS.
ONE THING IS CERTAIN...

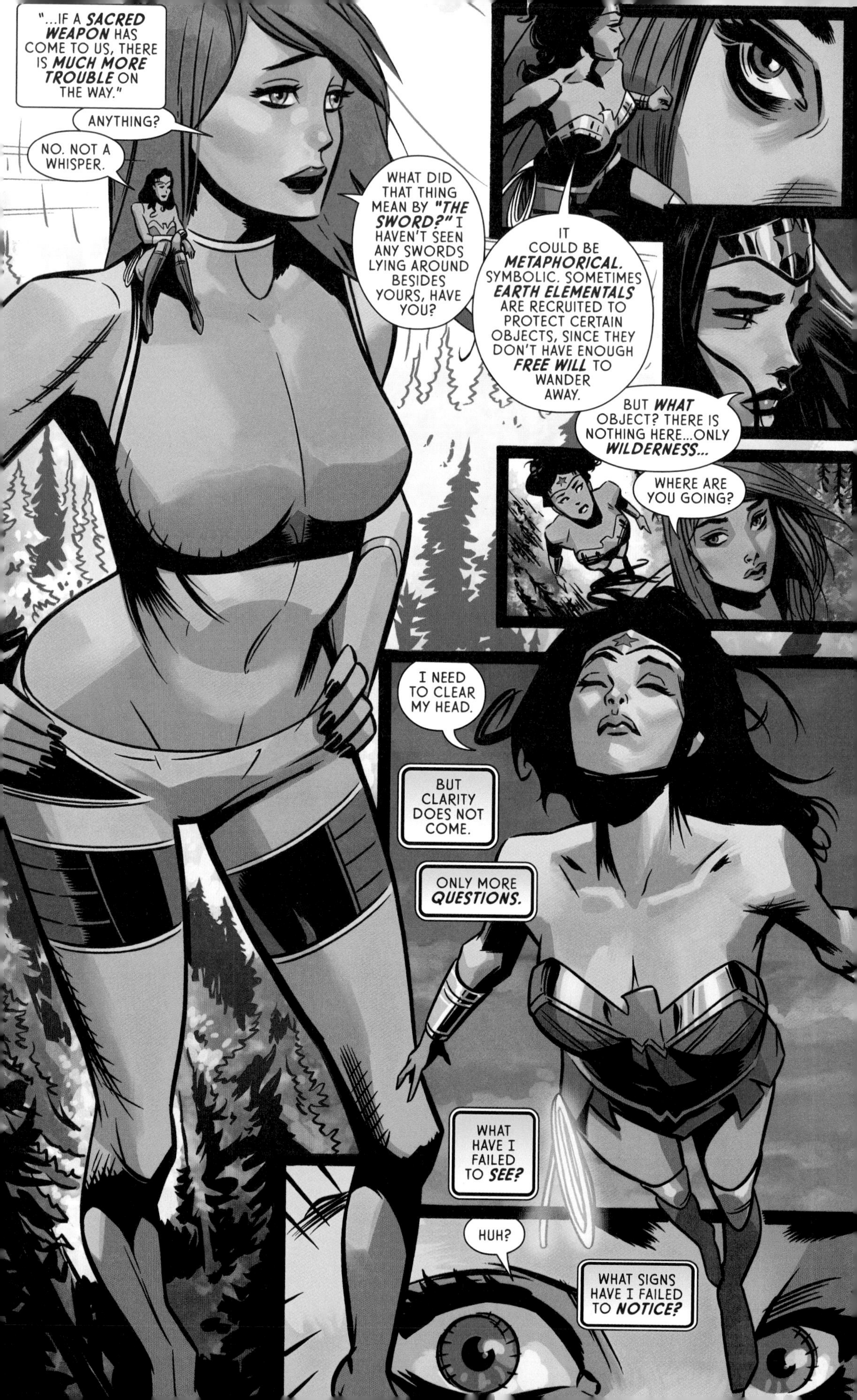
"...IF A SACRED WEAPON HAS COME TO US, THERE IS MUCH MORE TROUBLE ON THE WAY."
ANYTHING?
NO. NOT A WHISPER.
WHAT DID THAT THING MEAN BY "THE SWORD?" I HAVEN'T SEEN ANY SWORDS LYING AROUND BESIDES YOURS, HAVE YOU?
IT COULD BE METAPHORICAL. SYMBOLIC. SOMETIMES EARTH ELEMENTALS ARE RECRUITED TO PROTECT CERTAIN OBJECTS, SINCE THEY DON'T HAVE ENOUGH FREE WILL TO WANDER AWAY.
BUT WHAT OBJECT? THERE IS NOTHING HERE...ONLY WILDERNESS...
WHERE ARE YOU GOING?
I NEED TO CLEAR MY HEAD.
BUT CLARITY DOES NOT COME.
ONLY MORE QUESTIONS.
WHAT HAVE I FAILED TO SEE?
HUH?
WHAT SIGNS HAVE I FAILED TO NOTICE?

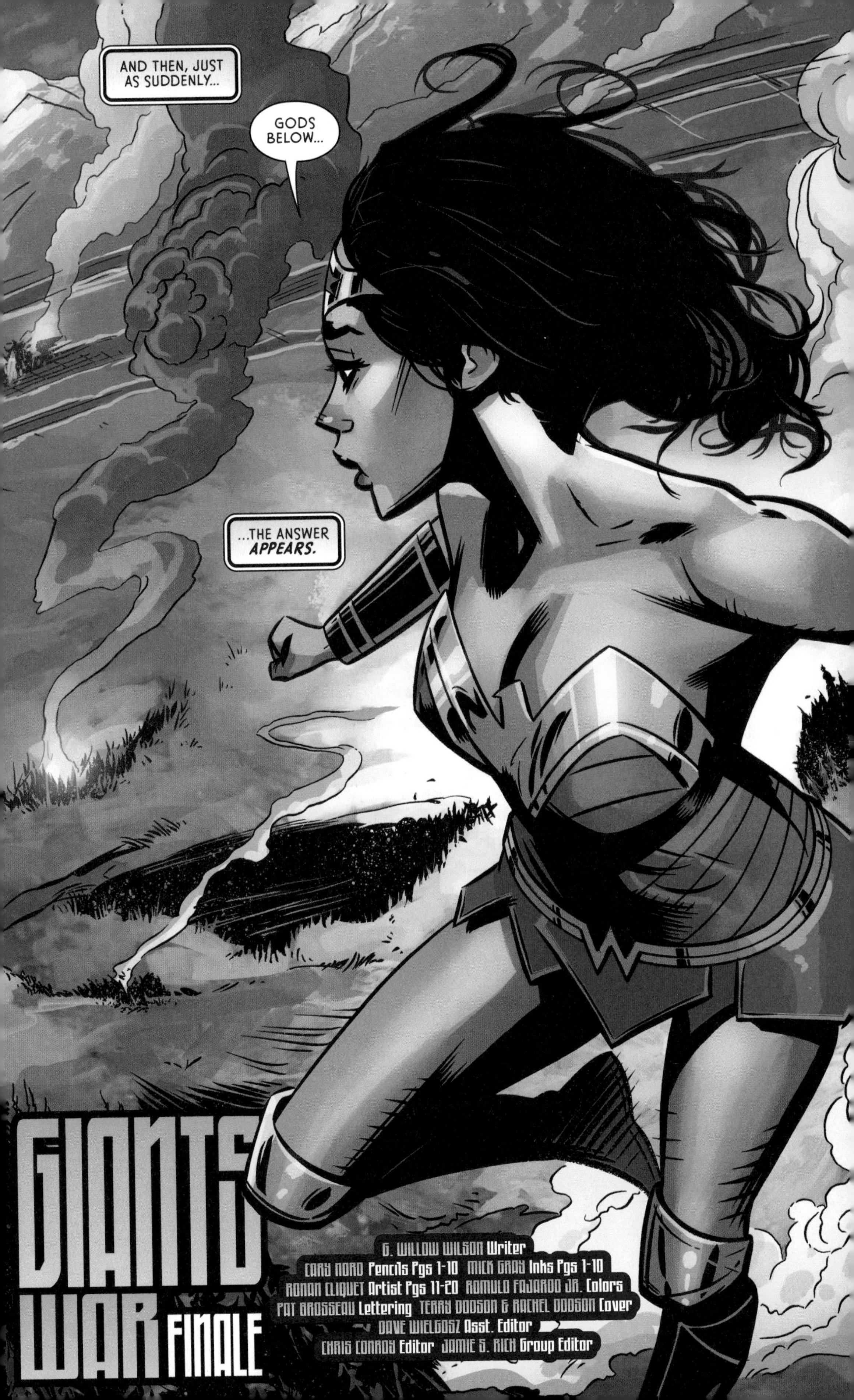
AND THEN, JUST AS SUDDENLY...
GODS BELOW...
...THE ANSWER *APPEARS.*
GIANTS WAR FINALE
G. WILLOW WILSON Writer
CARY NORD Pencils Pgs 1-10 MICK GRAY Inks Pgs 1-10
RONAN CLIQUET Artist Pgs 11-20 ROMULO FAJARDO JR. Colors
PAT BROSSEAU Lettering TERRY DODSON & RACHEL DODSON Cover
DAVE WIELGOSZ Asst. Editor
CHRIS CONROY Editor JAMIE S. RICH Group Editor

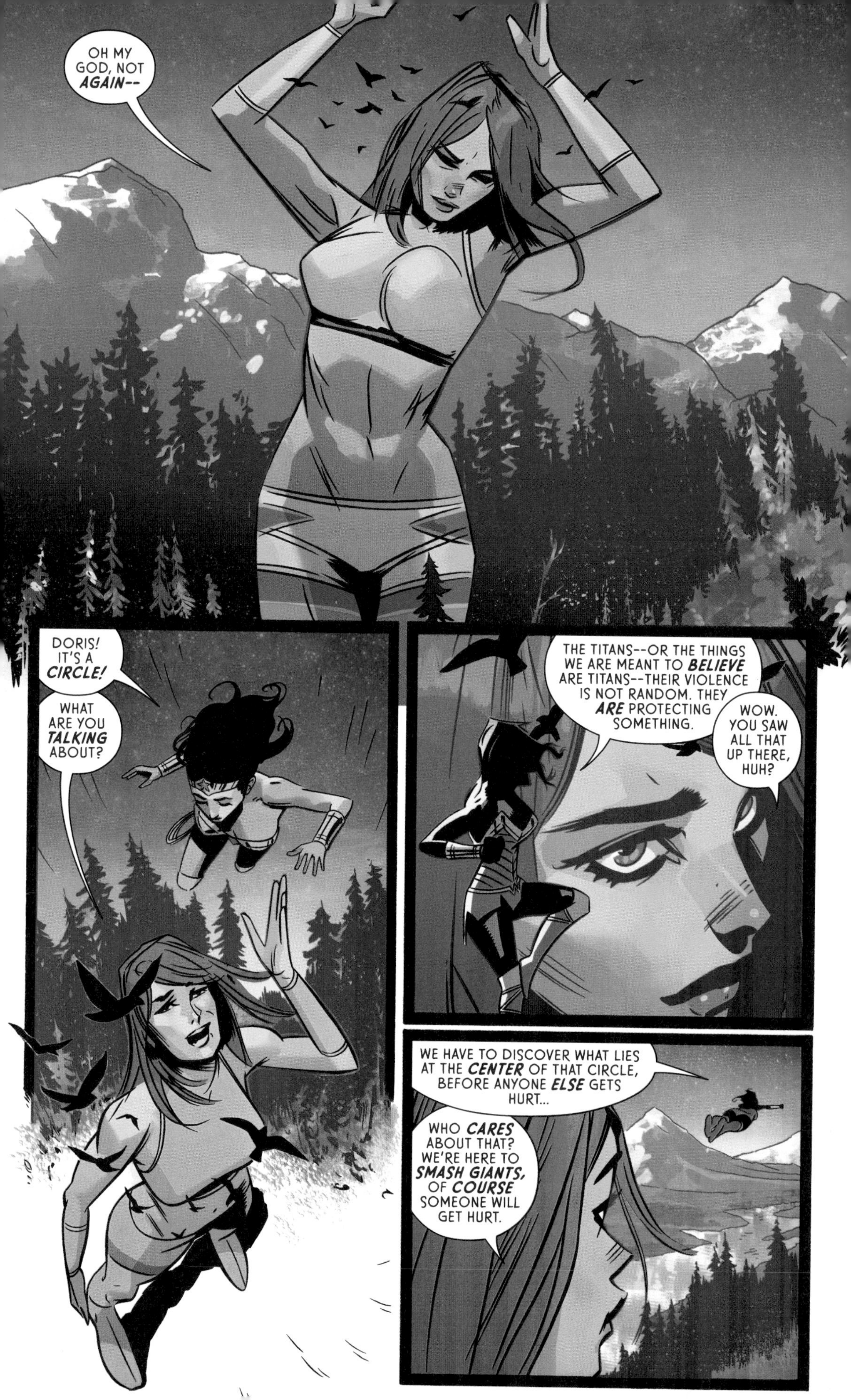
OH MY GOD, NOT AGAIN--
DORIS! IT'S A CIRCLE!
WHAT ARE YOU TALKING ABOUT?
THE TITANS--OR THE THINGS WE ARE MEANT TO BELIEVE ARE TITANS--THEIR VIOLENCE IS NOT RANDOM. THEY ARE PROTECTING SOMETHING.
WOW. YOU SAW ALL THAT UP THERE, HUH?
WE HAVE TO DISCOVER WHAT LIES AT THE CENTER OF THAT CIRCLE, BEFORE ANYONE ELSE GETS HURT...
WHO CARES ABOUT THAT? WE'RE HERE TO SMASH GIANTS, OF COURSE SOMEONE WILL GET HURT.

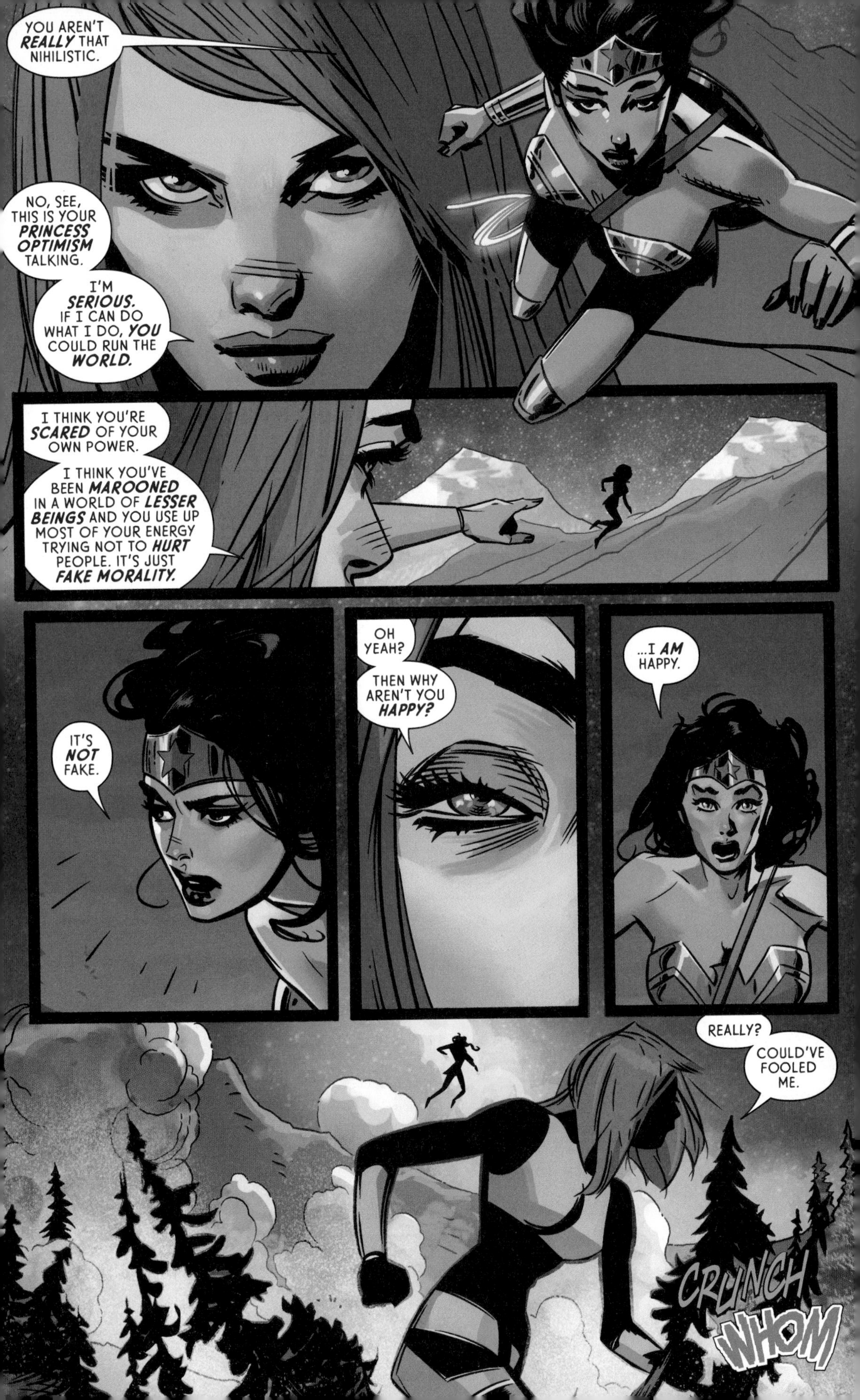
YOU AREN'T *REALLY* THAT NIHILISTIC.
NO, SEE, THIS IS YOUR *PRINCESS OPTIMISM* TALKING.
I'M *SERIOUS.* IF I CAN DO WHAT I DO, *YOU* COULD RUN THE *WORLD.*
I THINK YOU'RE *SCARED* OF YOUR OWN POWER.
I THINK YOU'VE BEEN *MAROONED* IN A WORLD OF *LESSER BEINGS* AND YOU USE UP MOST OF YOUR ENERGY TRYING NOT TO *HURT* PEOPLE. IT'S JUST *FAKE MORALITY.*
IT'S *NOT* FAKE.
OH YEAH?
THEN WHY AREN'T YOU *HAPPY?*
...I *AM* HAPPY.
REALLY?
COULD'VE FOOLED ME.
CRUNCH
WHOM

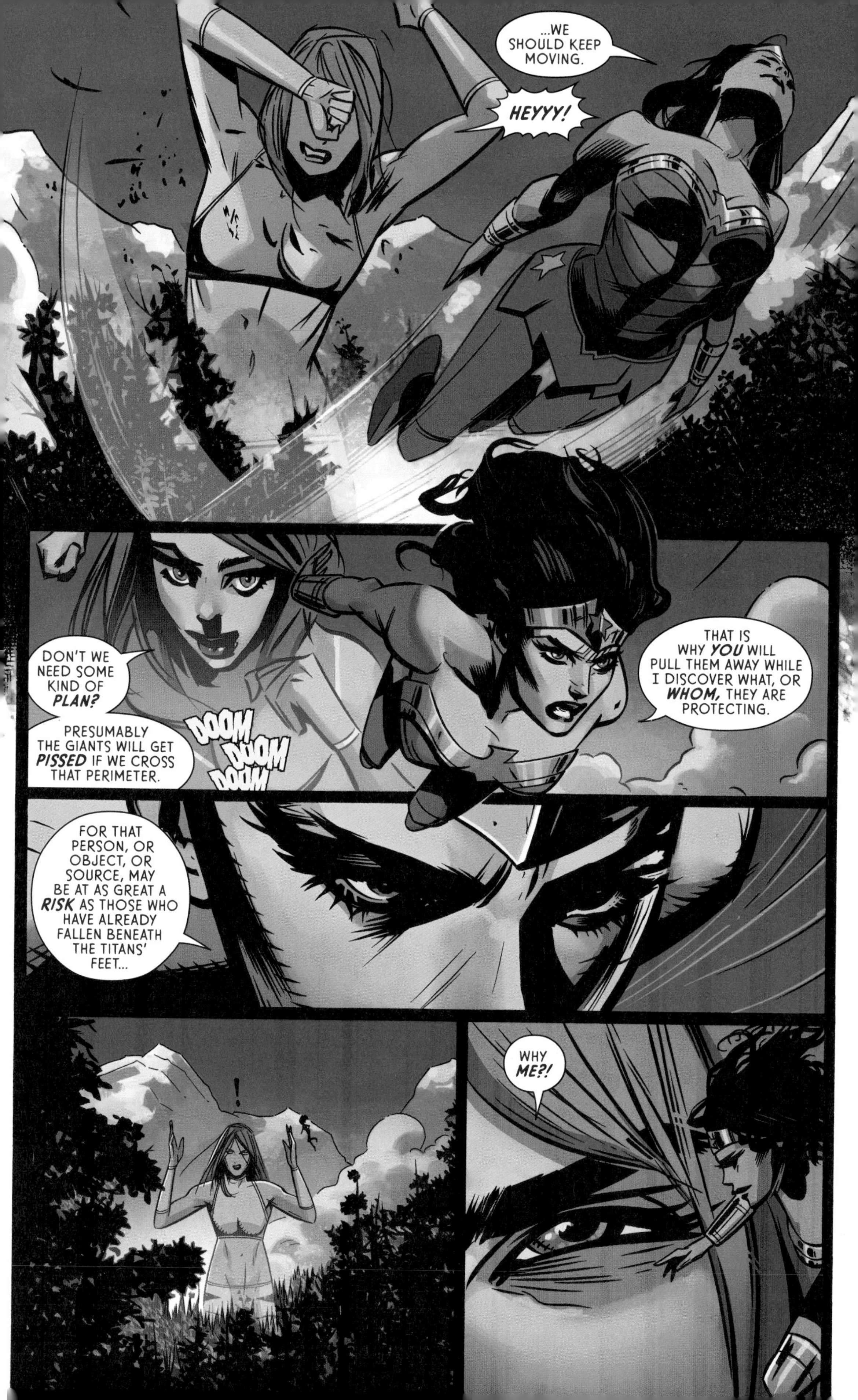
...WE SHOULD KEEP MOVING.
HEYYY!
DON'T WE NEED SOME KIND OF PLAN?
PRESUMABLY THE GIANTS WILL GET PISSED IF WE CROSS THAT PERIMETER.
DOOM DOOM DOOM
THAT IS WHY YOU WILL PULL THEM AWAY WHILE I DISCOVER WHAT, OR WHOM, THEY ARE PROTECTING.
FOR THAT PERSON, OR OBJECT, OR SOURCE, MAY BE AT AS GREAT A RISK AS THOSE WHO HAVE ALREADY FALLEN BENEATH THE TITANS' FEET...
!
WHY ME?!

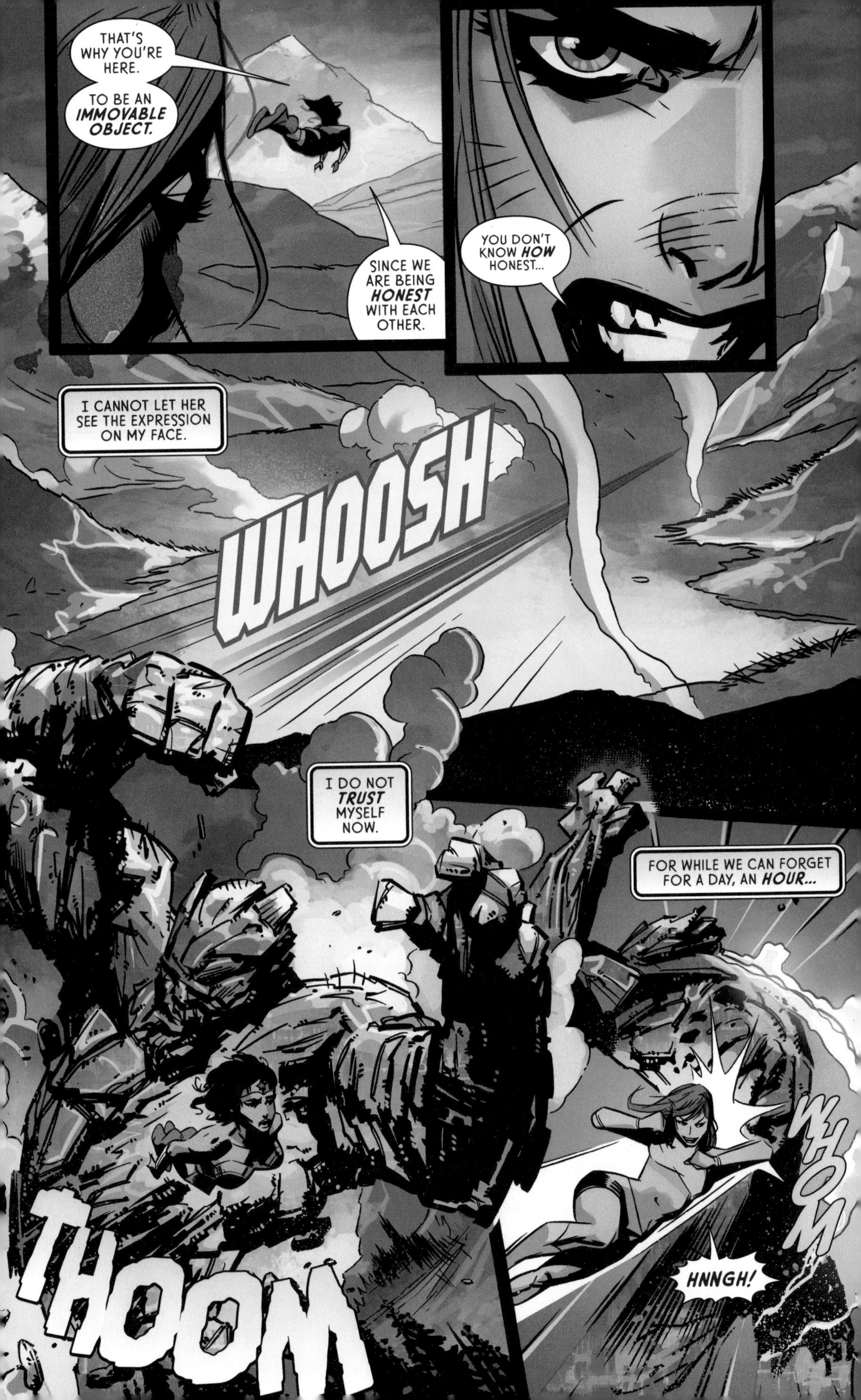
THAT'S WHY YOU'RE HERE.
TO BE AN *IMMOVABLE OBJECT.*
SINCE WE ARE BEING *HONEST* WITH EACH OTHER.
YOU DON'T KNOW *HOW* HONEST...
I CANNOT LET HER SEE THE EXPRESSION ON MY FACE.
WHOOSH
I DO NOT *TRUST* MYSELF NOW.
FOR WHILE WE CAN FORGET FOR A DAY, AN *HOUR*...
THOOM
WHOOM
HNNGH!

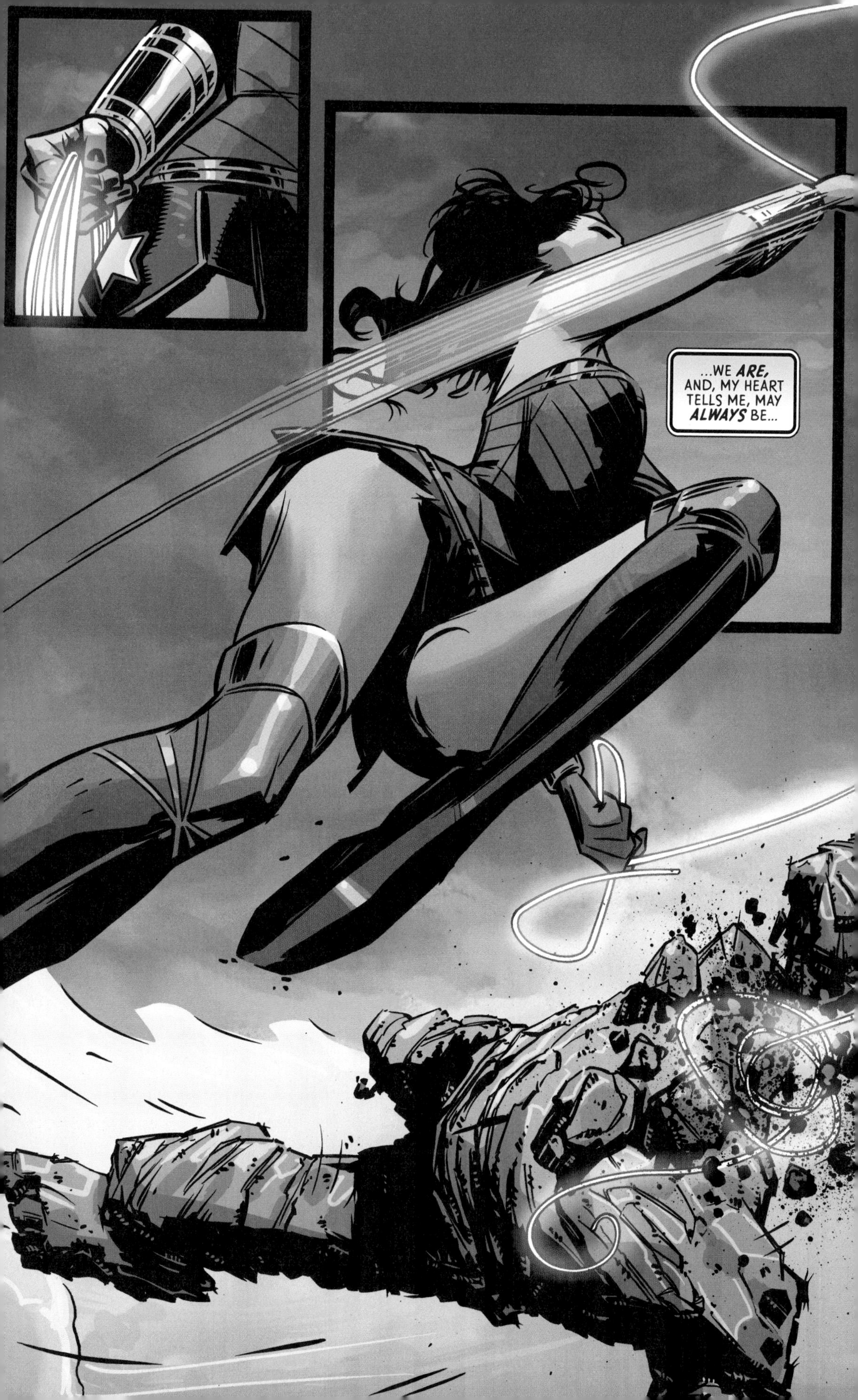
...WE *ARE,* AND, MY HEART TELLS ME, MAY *ALWAYS* BE...

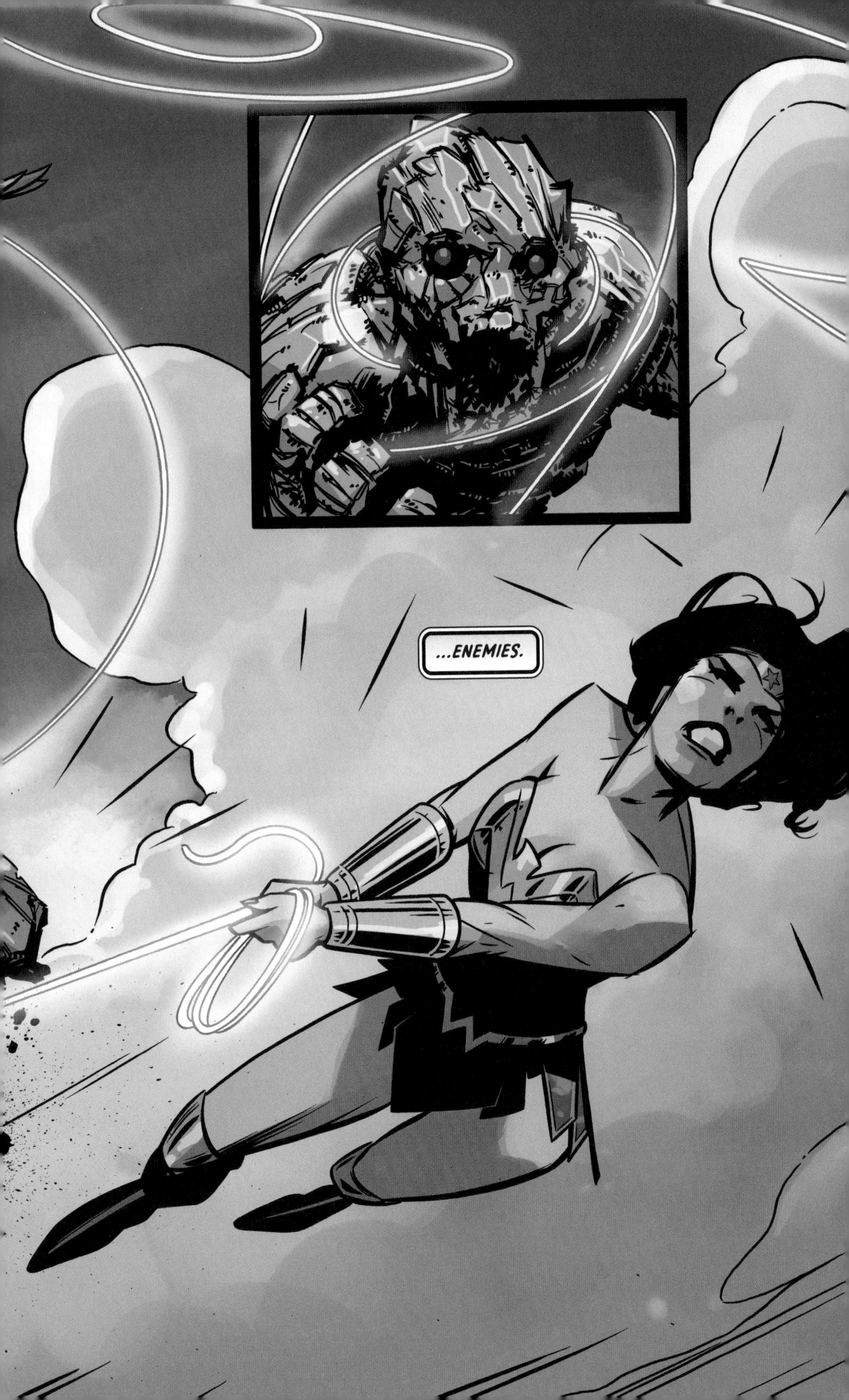
...ENEMIES.

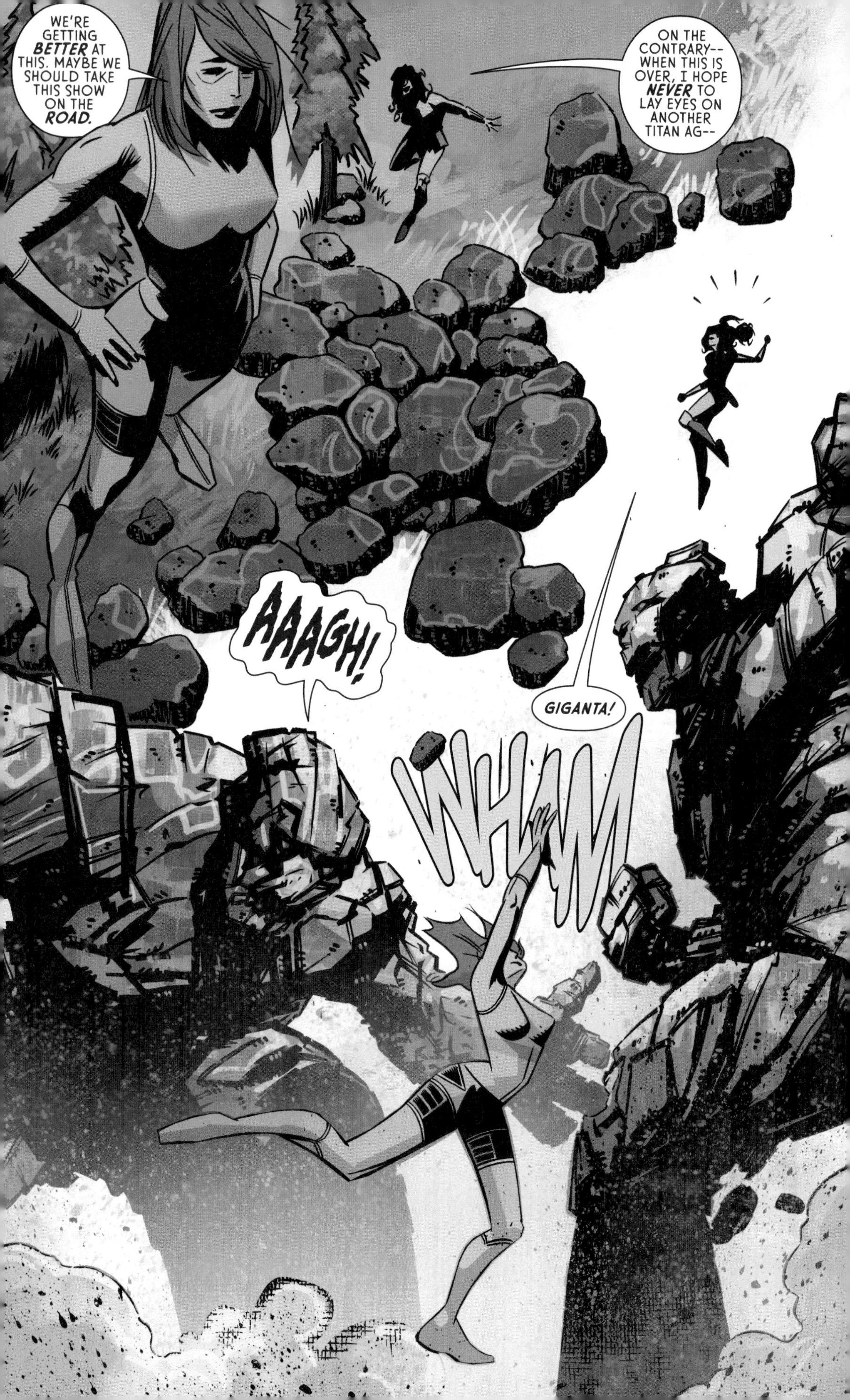
WE'RE GETTING BETTER AT THIS. MAYBE WE SHOULD TAKE THIS SHOW ON THE ROAD.
ON THE CONTRARY-- WHEN THIS IS OVER, I HOPE NEVER TO LAY EYES ON ANOTHER TITAN AG--
AAAGH!
GIGANTA!
WHAM

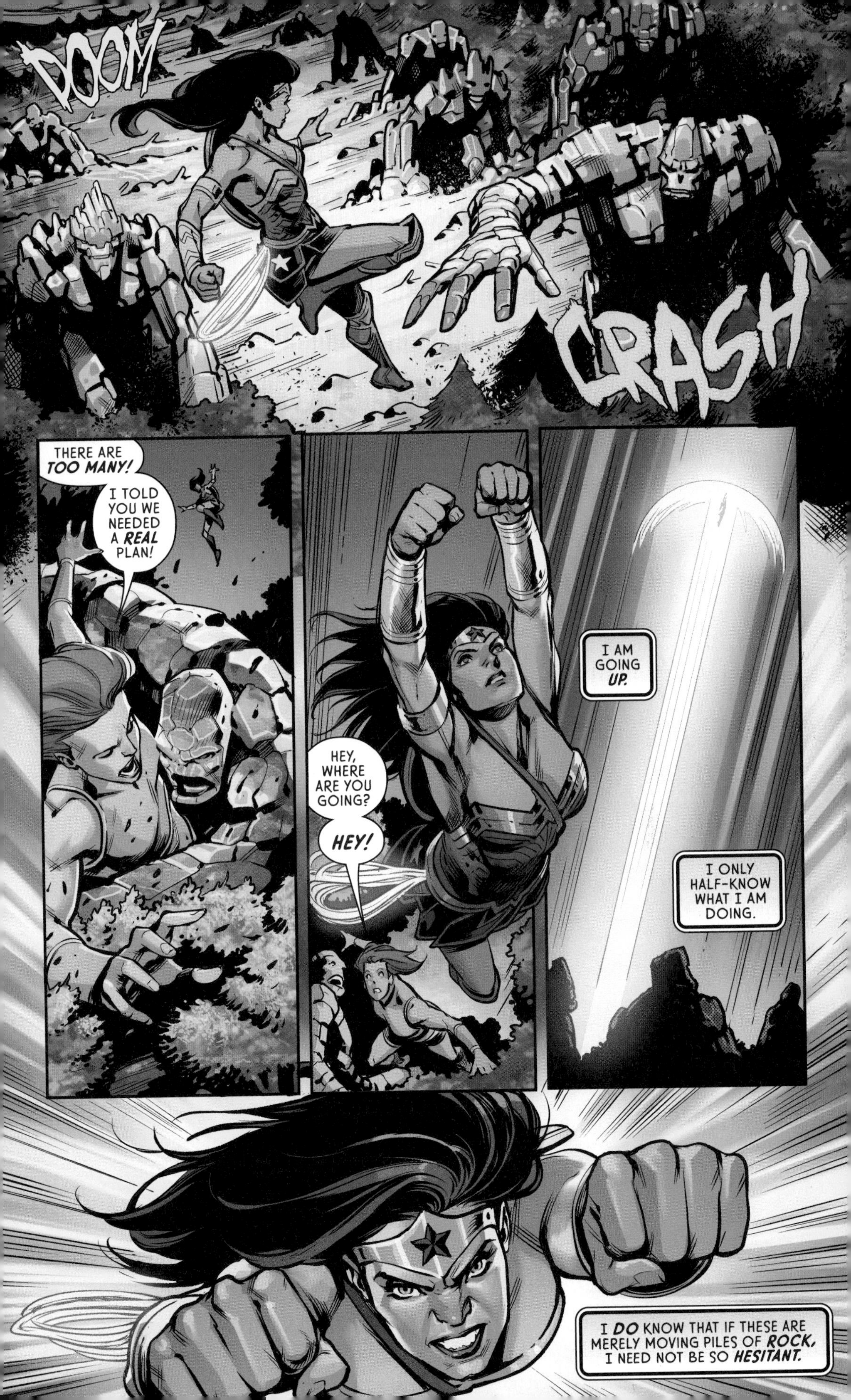
DOOM
CRASH
THERE ARE TOO MANY!
I TOLD YOU WE NEEDED A REAL PLAN!
HEY, WHERE ARE YOU GOING?
HEY!
I AM GOING UP.
I ONLY HALF-KNOW WHAT I AM DOING.
I DO KNOW THAT IF THESE ARE MERELY MOVING PILES OF ROCK, I NEED NOT BE SO HESITANT.

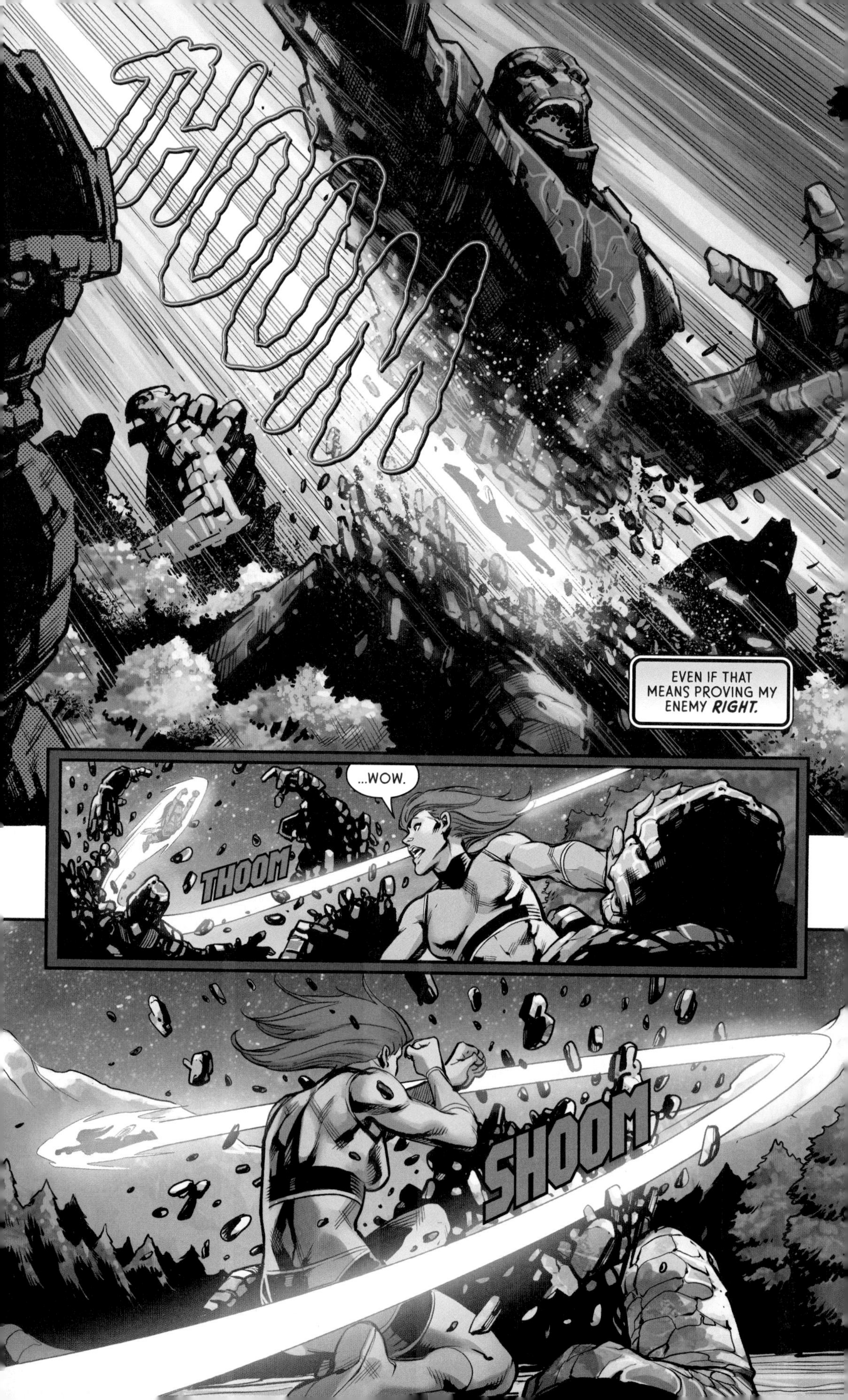
THOOM
EVEN IF THAT MEANS PROVING MY ENEMY *RIGHT.*
...WOW.
THOOM
SHOOM

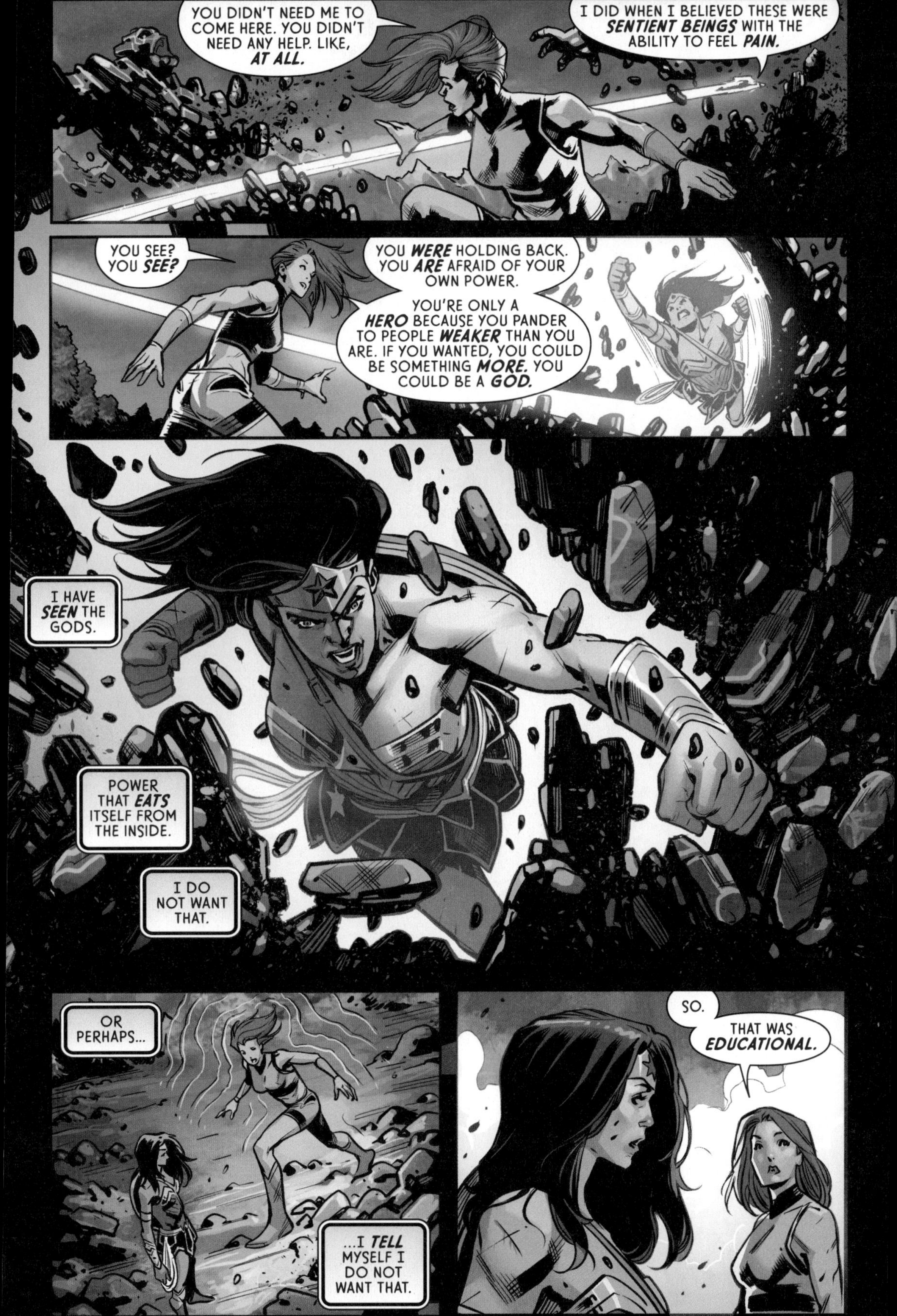
YOU DIDN'T NEED ME TO COME HERE. YOU DIDN'T NEED ANY HELP. LIKE, AT ALL.
I DID WHEN I BELIEVED THESE WERE SENTIENT BEINGS WITH THE ABILITY TO FEEL PAIN.
YOU SEE? YOU SEE?
YOU WERE HOLDING BACK. YOU ARE AFRAID OF YOUR OWN POWER.
YOU'RE ONLY A HERO BECAUSE YOU PANDER TO PEOPLE WEAKER THAN YOU ARE. IF YOU WANTED, YOU COULD BE SOMETHING MORE. YOU COULD BE A GOD.
I HAVE SEEN THE GODS.
POWER THAT EATS ITSELF FROM THE INSIDE.
I DO NOT WANT THAT.
OR PERHAPS...
...I TELL MYSELF I DO NOT WANT THAT.
SO.
THAT WAS EDUCATIONAL.

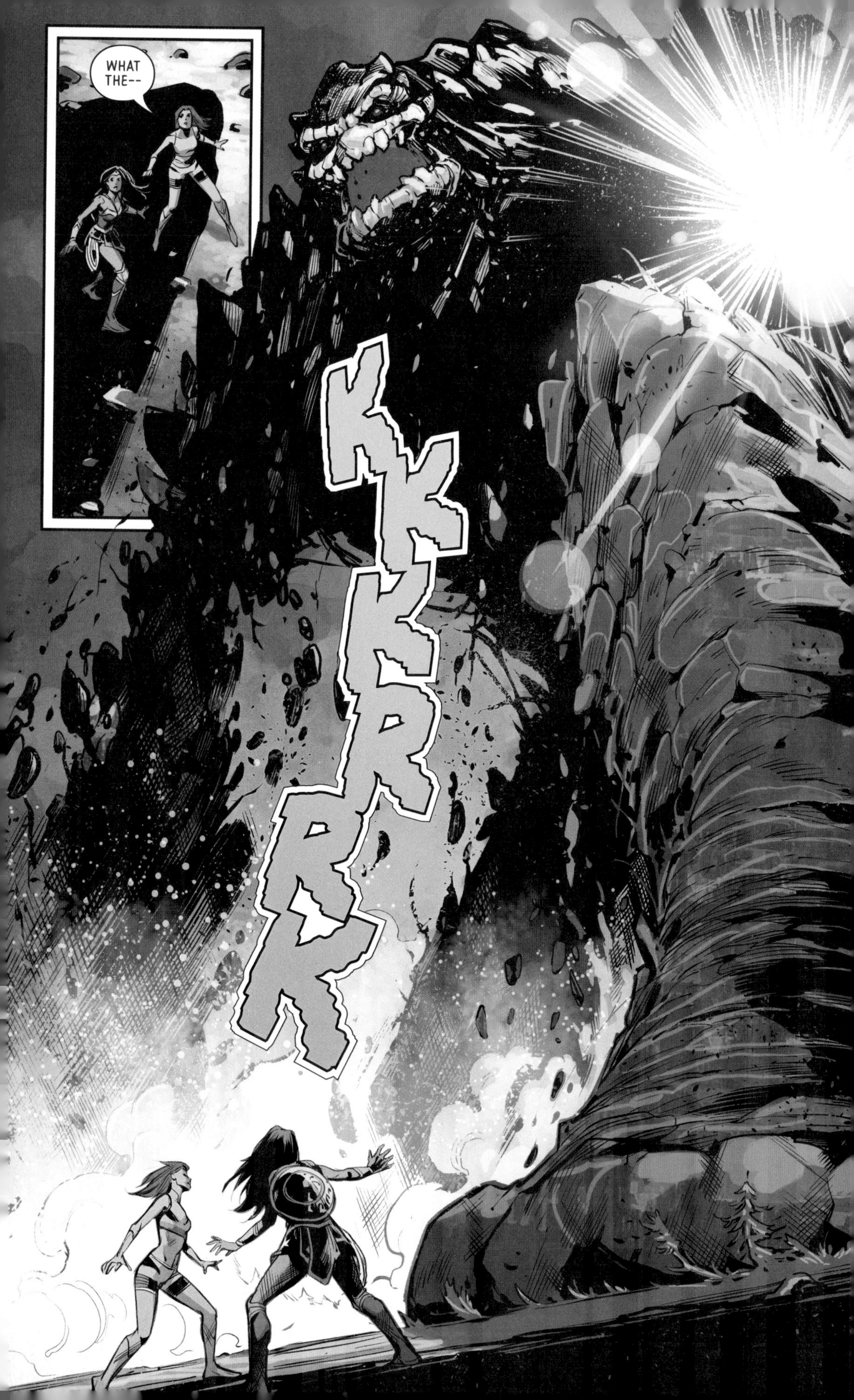
WHAT THE--
KKRRR

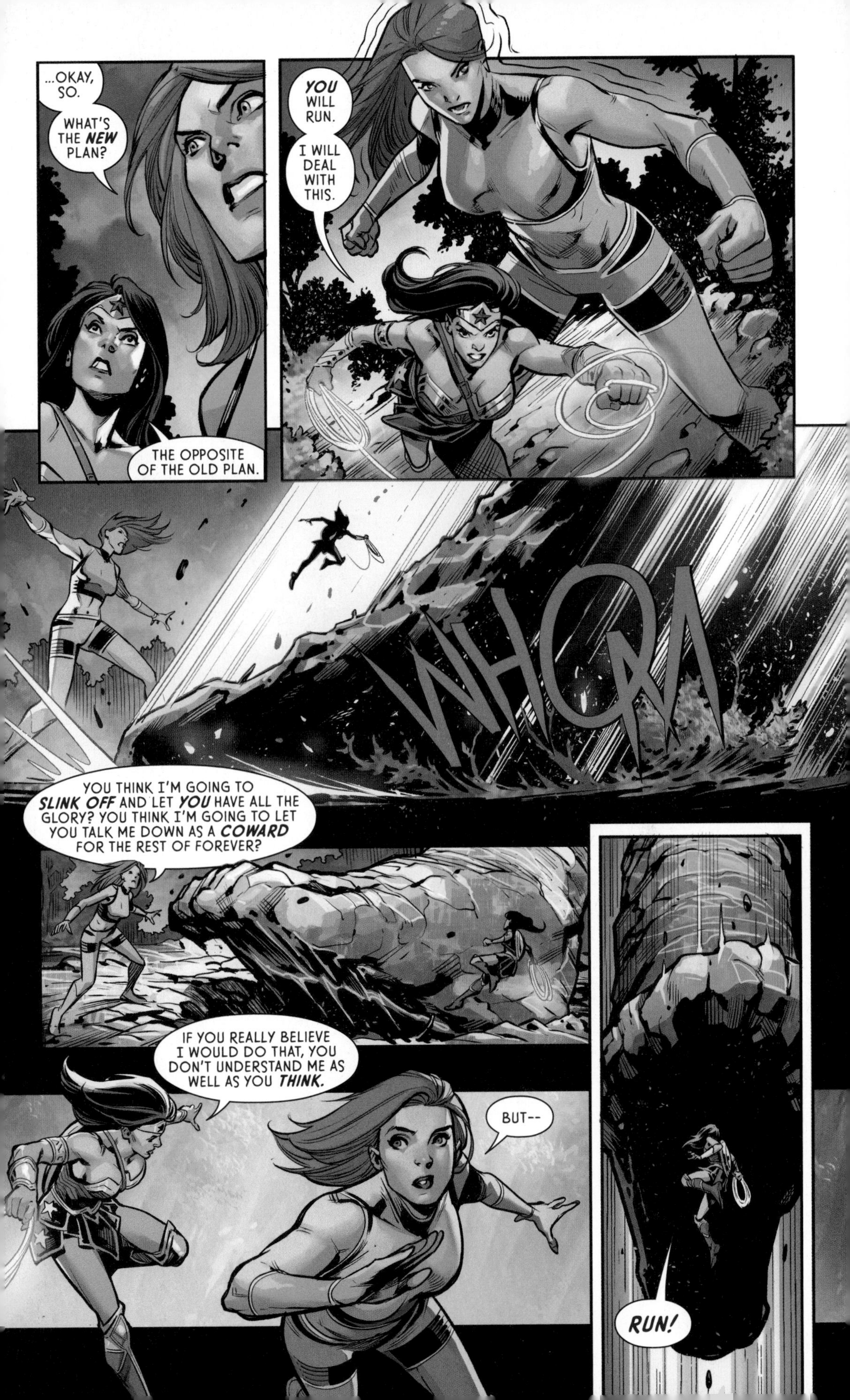
...OKAY, SO.
WHAT'S THE **NEW** PLAN?
THE OPPOSITE OF THE OLD PLAN.
YOU WILL RUN.
I WILL DEAL WITH THIS.
WHOA
YOU THINK I'M GOING TO **SLINK OFF** AND LET **YOU** HAVE ALL THE GLORY? YOU THINK I'M GOING TO LET YOU TALK ME DOWN AS A **COWARD** FOR THE REST OF FOREVER?
IF YOU REALLY BELIEVE I WOULD DO THAT, YOU DON'T UNDERSTAND ME AS WELL AS YOU **THINK.**
BUT--
RUN!

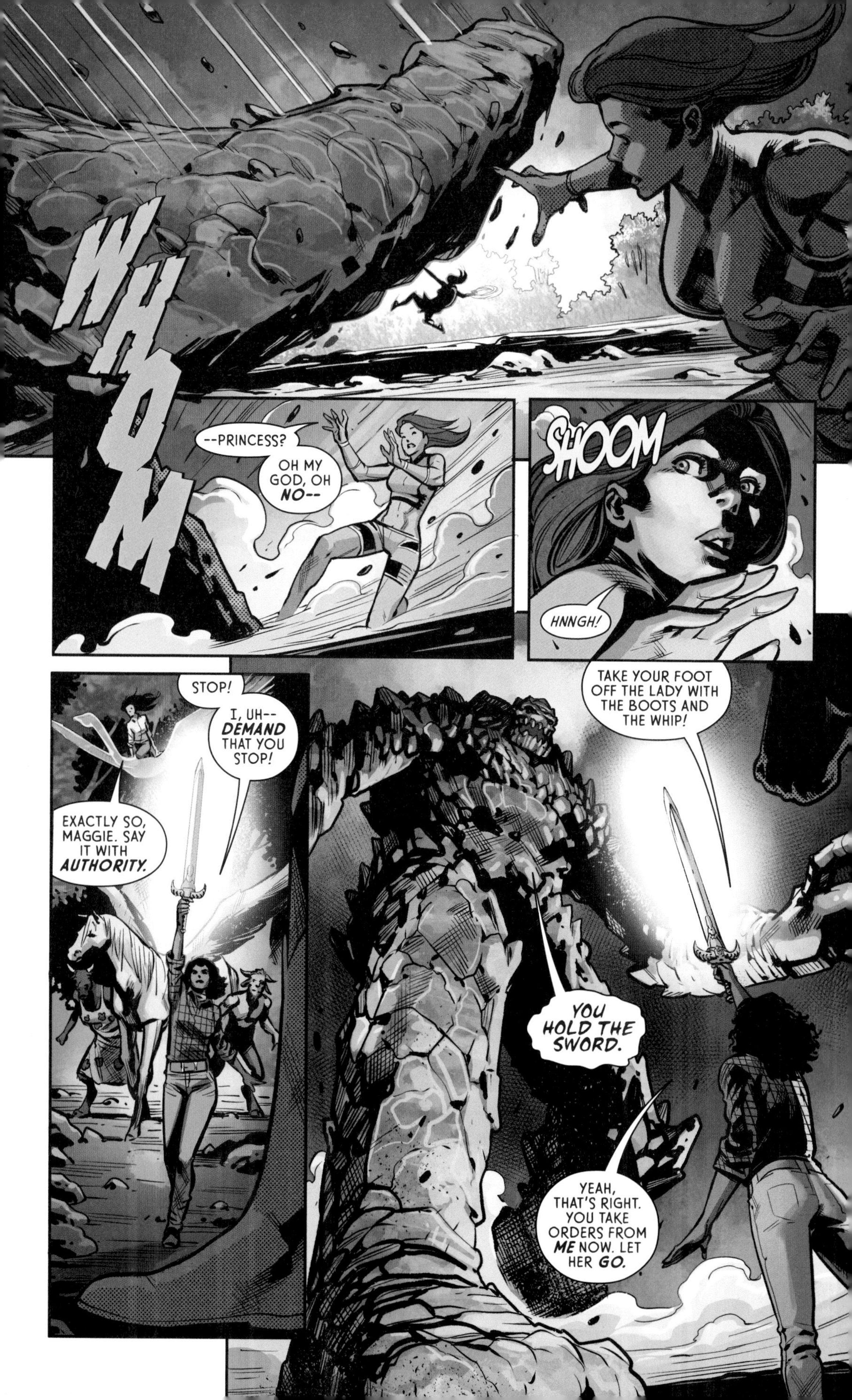

WHOOM
--PRINCESS?
OH MY GOD, OH NO--
SHOOM
HNNGH!
STOP!
I, UH-- DEMAND THAT YOU STOP!
EXACTLY SO, MAGGIE. SAY IT WITH AUTHORITY.
TAKE YOUR FOOT OFF THE LADY WITH THE BOOTS AND THE WHIP!
YOU HOLD THE SWORD.
YEAH, THAT'S RIGHT. YOU TAKE ORDERS FROM ME NOW. LET HER GO.

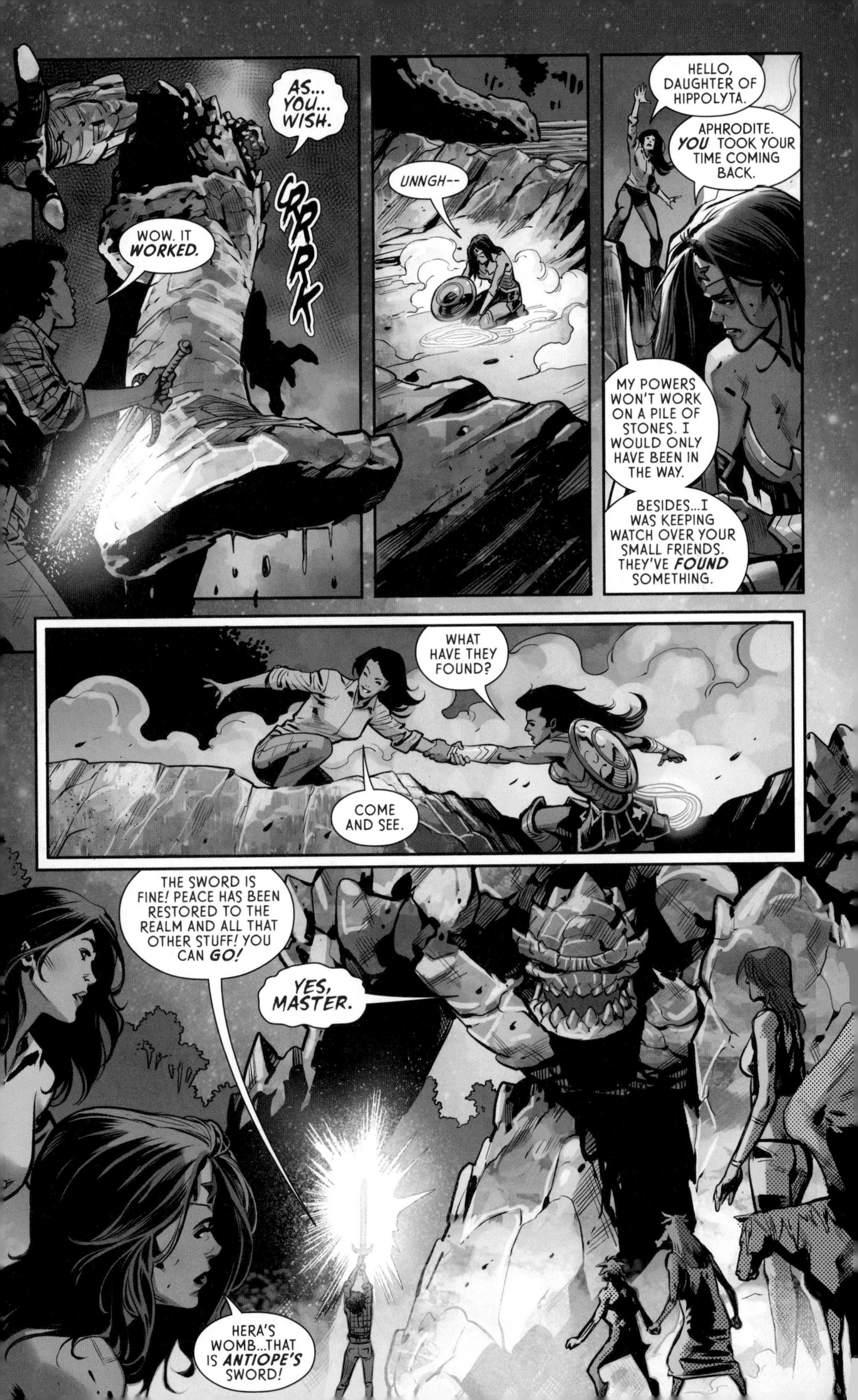
AS... YOU... WISH.
CRRRK
WOW. IT WORKED.
UNNGH--
HELLO, DAUGHTER OF HIPPOLYTA.
APHRODITE. YOU TOOK YOUR TIME COMING BACK.
MY POWERS WON'T WORK ON A PILE OF STONES. I WOULD ONLY HAVE BEEN IN THE WAY.
BESIDES...I WAS KEEPING WATCH OVER YOUR SMALL FRIENDS. THEY'VE FOUND SOMETHING.
WHAT HAVE THEY FOUND?
COME AND SEE.
THE SWORD IS FINE! PEACE HAS BEEN RESTORED TO THE REALM AND ALL THAT OTHER STUFF! YOU CAN GO!
YES, MASTER.
HERA'S WOMB...THAT IS ANTIOPE'S SWORD!

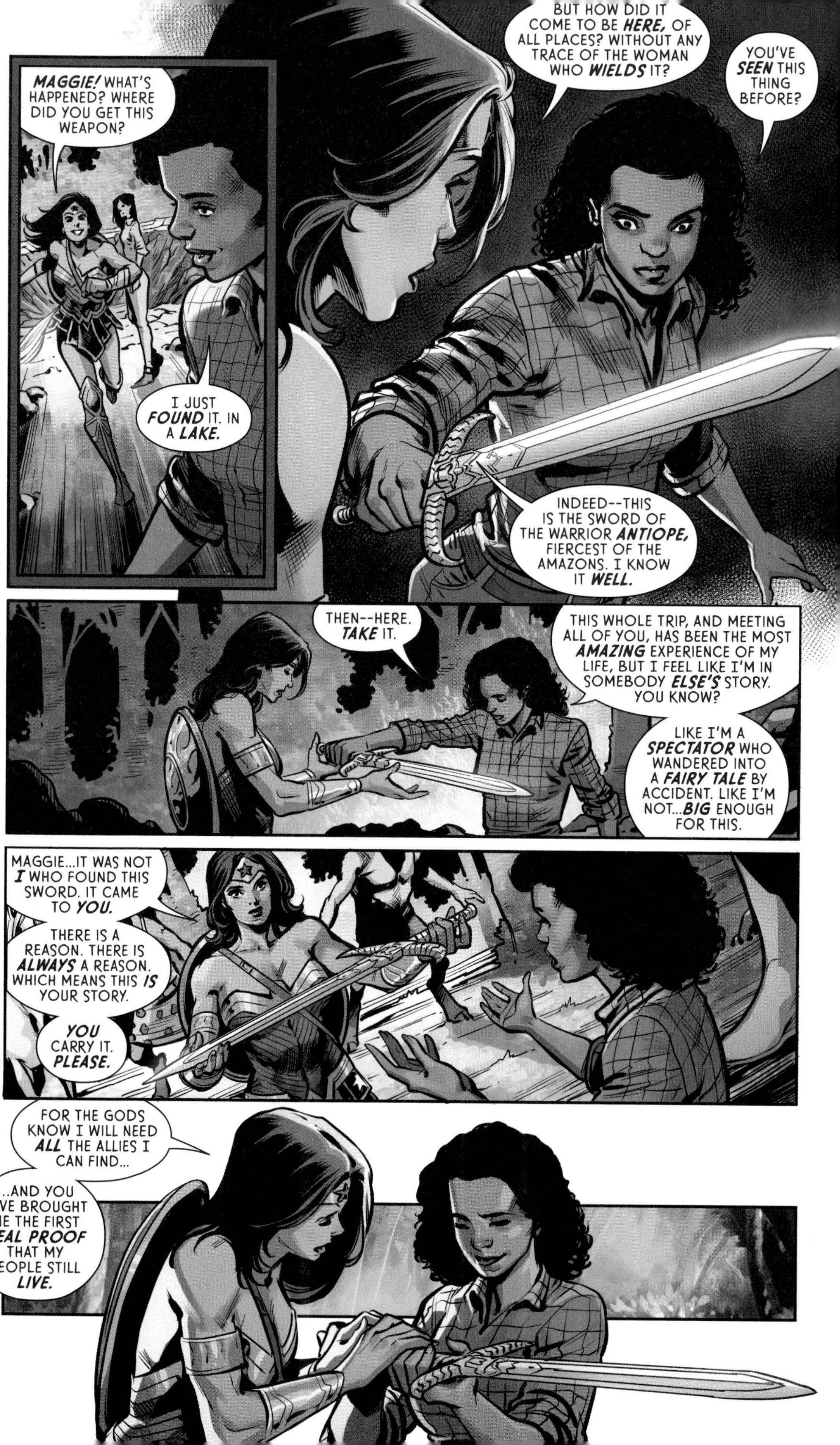

MAGGIE! WHAT'S HAPPENED? WHERE DID YOU GET THIS WEAPON?
I JUST FOUND IT. IN A LAKE.
BUT HOW DID IT COME TO BE HERE, OF ALL PLACES? WITHOUT ANY TRACE OF THE WOMAN WHO WIELDS IT?
YOU'VE SEEN THIS THING BEFORE?
INDEED--THIS IS THE SWORD OF THE WARRIOR ANTIOPE, FIERCEST OF THE AMAZONS. I KNOW IT WELL.
THEN--HERE. TAKE IT.
THIS WHOLE TRIP, AND MEETING ALL OF YOU, HAS BEEN THE MOST AMAZING EXPERIENCE OF MY LIFE, BUT I FEEL LIKE I'M IN SOMEBODY ELSE'S STORY. YOU KNOW?
LIKE I'M A SPECTATOR WHO WANDERED INTO A FAIRY TALE BY ACCIDENT. LIKE I'M NOT...BIG ENOUGH FOR THIS.
MAGGIE...IT WAS NOT I WHO FOUND THIS SWORD. IT CAME TO YOU.
THERE IS A REASON. THERE IS ALWAYS A REASON. WHICH MEANS THIS IS YOUR STORY.
YOU CARRY IT. PLEASE.
FOR THE GODS KNOW I WILL NEED ALL THE ALLIES I CAN FIND...
...AND YOU HAVE BROUGHT ME THE FIRST REAL PROOF THAT MY PEOPLE STILL LIVE.

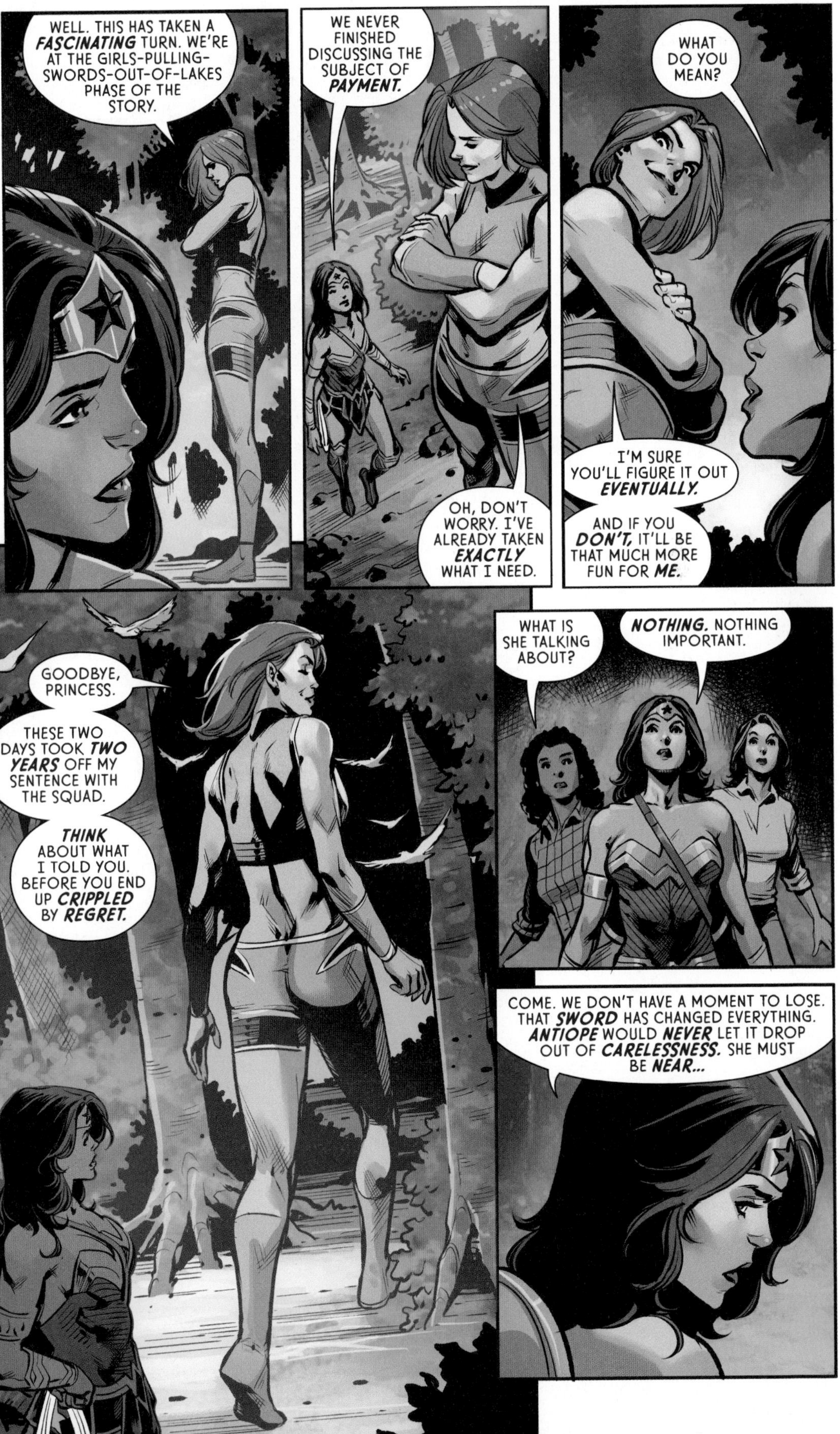

WELL. THIS HAS TAKEN A FASCINATING TURN. WE'RE AT THE GIRLS-PULLING-SWORDS-OUT-OF-LAKES PHASE OF THE STORY.
WE NEVER FINISHED DISCUSSING THE SUBJECT OF PAYMENT.
OH, DON'T WORRY. I'VE ALREADY TAKEN EXACTLY WHAT I NEED.
WHAT DO YOU MEAN?
I'M SURE YOU'LL FIGURE IT OUT EVENTUALLY.
AND IF YOU DON'T, IT'LL BE THAT MUCH MORE FUN FOR ME.
GOODBYE, PRINCESS.
THESE TWO DAYS TOOK TWO YEARS OFF MY SENTENCE WITH THE SQUAD.
THINK ABOUT WHAT I TOLD YOU. BEFORE YOU END UP CRIPPLED BY REGRET.
WHAT IS SHE TALKING ABOUT?
NOTHING. NOTHING IMPORTANT.
COME. WE DON'T HAVE A MOMENT TO LOSE. THAT SWORD HAS CHANGED EVERYTHING. ANTIOPE WOULD NEVER LET IT DROP OUT OF CARELESSNESS. SHE MUST BE NEAR...

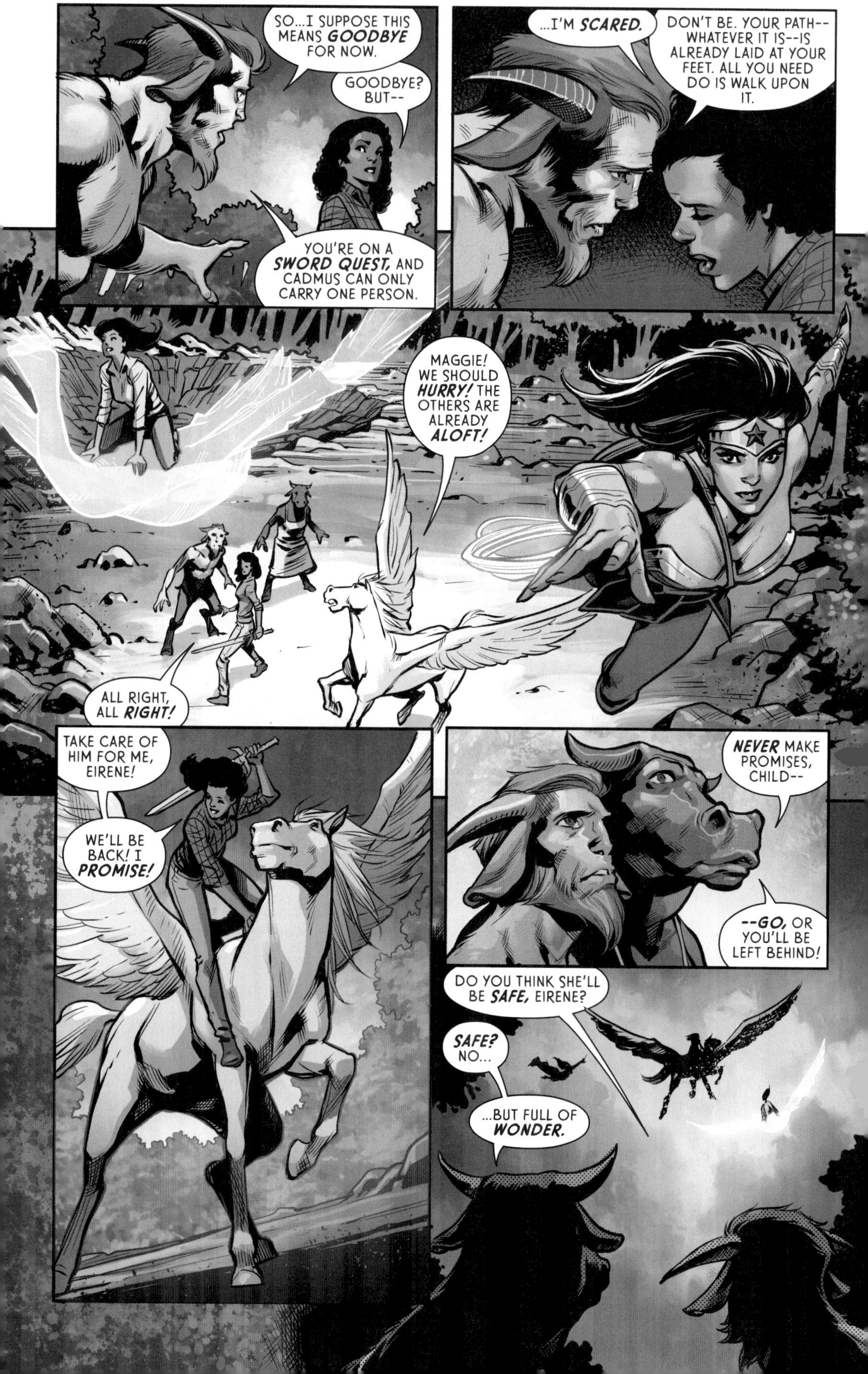

SO...I SUPPOSE THIS MEANS GOODBYE FOR NOW.
GOODBYE? BUT--
YOU'RE ON A SWORD QUEST, AND CADMUS CAN ONLY CARRY ONE PERSON.
...I'M SCARED.
DON'T BE. YOUR PATH--WHATEVER IT IS--IS ALREADY LAID AT YOUR FEET. ALL YOU NEED DO IS WALK UPON IT.
MAGGIE! WE SHOULD HURRY! THE OTHERS ARE ALREADY ALOFT!
ALL RIGHT, ALL RIGHT!
TAKE CARE OF HIM FOR ME, EIRENE!
WE'LL BE BACK! I PROMISE!
NEVER MAKE PROMISES, CHILD--
--GO, OR YOU'LL BE LEFT BEHIND!
DO YOU THINK SHE'LL BE SAFE, EIRENE?
SAFE? NO...
...BUT FULL OF WONDER.

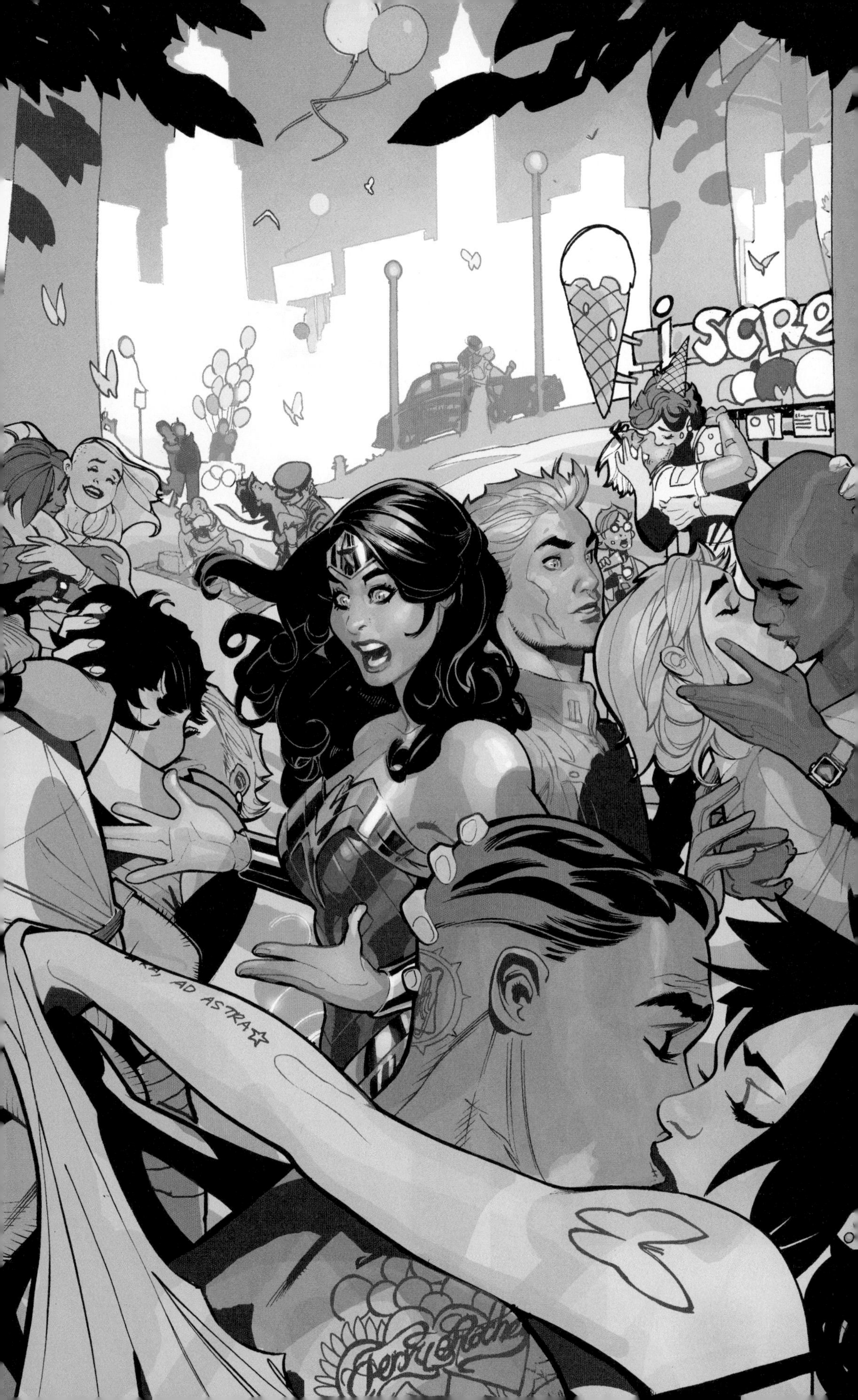
AD ASTRA

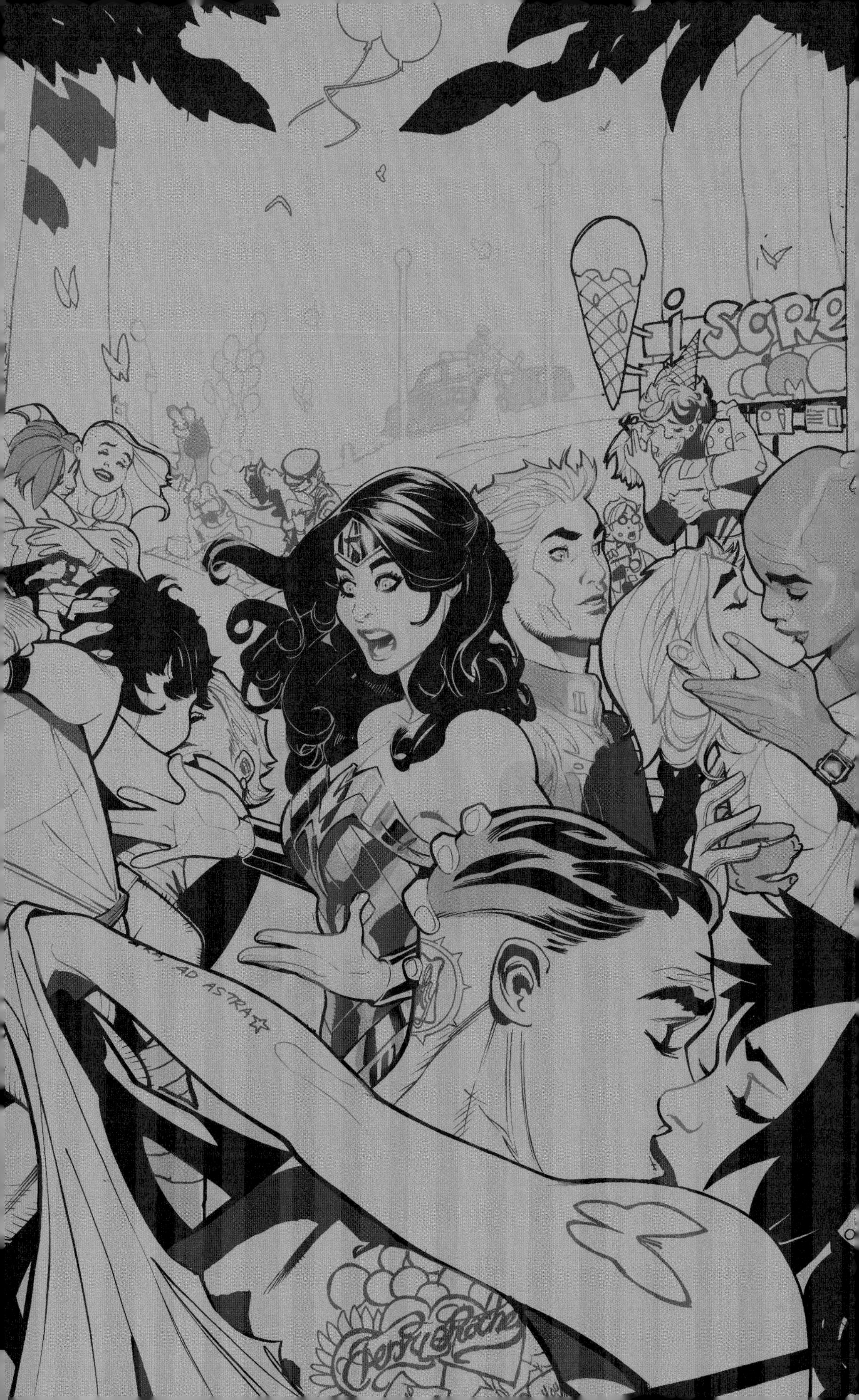
AD ASTRA

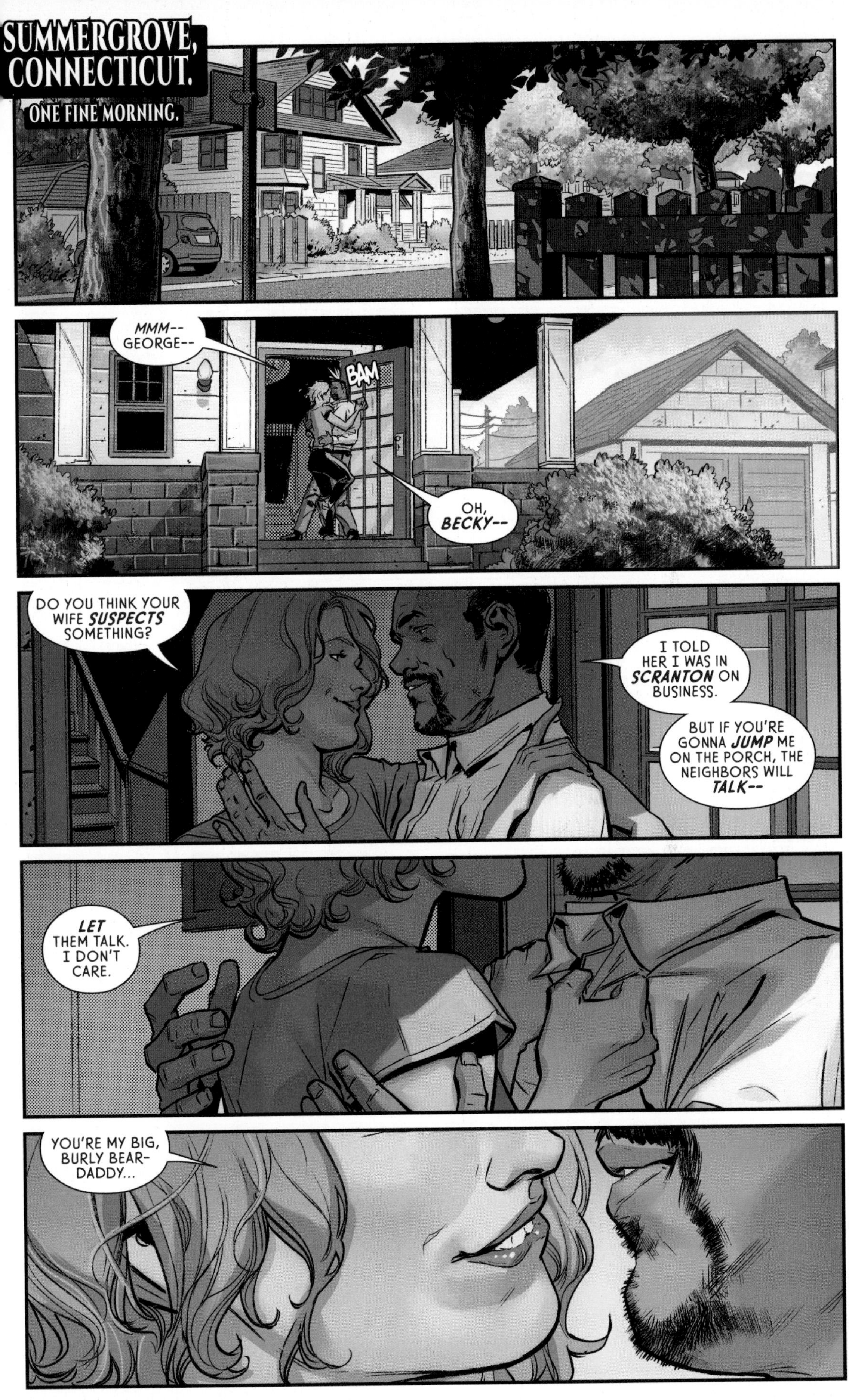
SUMMERGROVE, CONNECTICUT.
ONE FINE MORNING.
MMM-- GEORGE--
BAM
OH, BECKY--
DO YOU THINK YOUR WIFE SUSPECTS SOMETHING?
I TOLD HER I WAS IN SCRANTON ON BUSINESS.
BUT IF YOU'RE GONNA JUMP ME ON THE PORCH, THE NEIGHBORS WILL TALK--
LET THEM TALK. I DON'T CARE.
YOU'RE MY BIG, BURLY BEAR-DADDY...

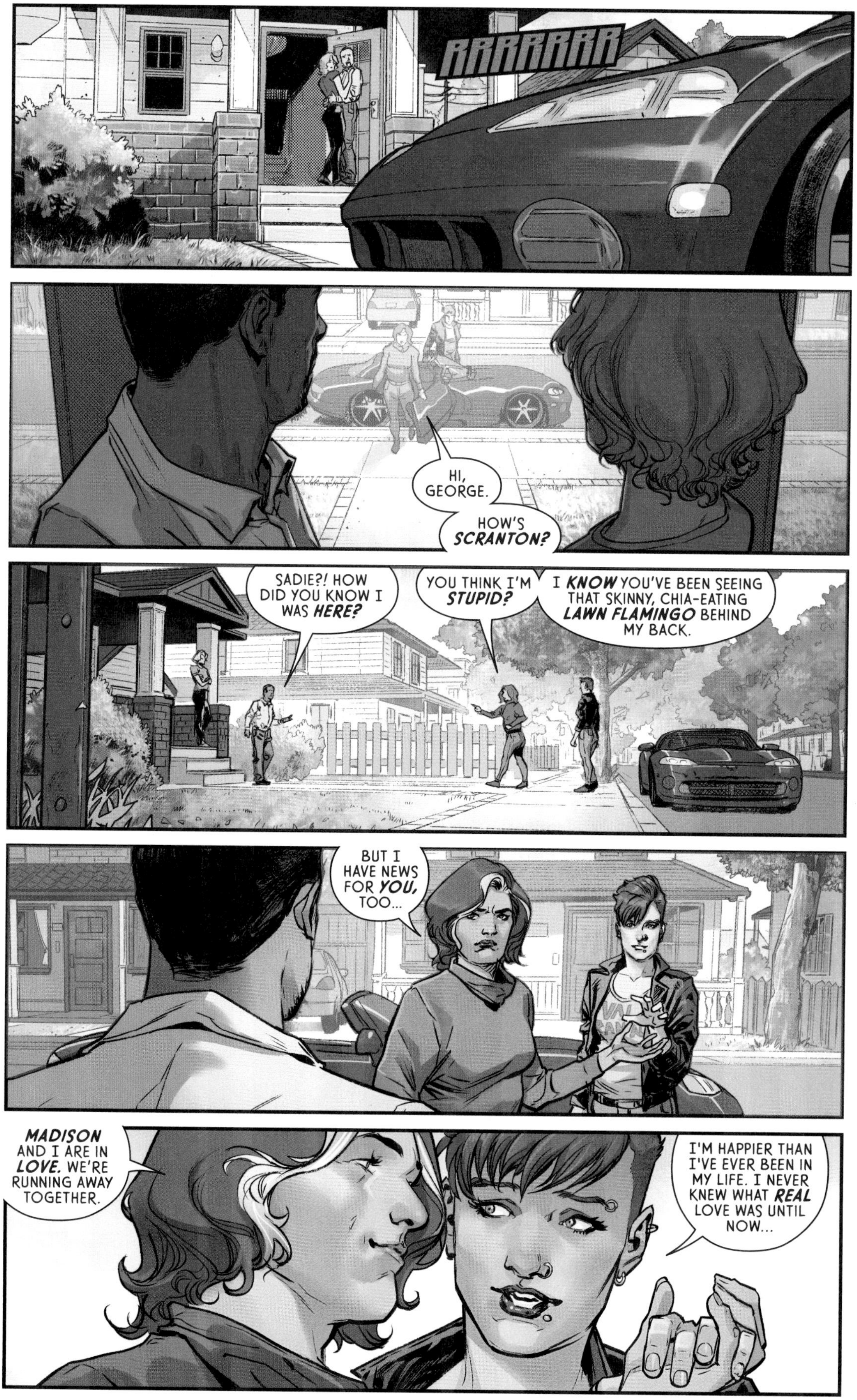
RRRRRRR
HI, GEORGE.
HOW'S SCRANTON?
SADIE?! HOW DID YOU KNOW I WAS HERE?
YOU THINK I'M STUPID?
I KNOW YOU'VE BEEN SEEING THAT SKINNY, CHIA-EATING LAWN FLAMINGO BEHIND MY BACK.
BUT I HAVE NEWS FOR YOU, TOO...
MADISON AND I ARE IN LOVE. WE'RE RUNNING AWAY TOGETHER.
I'M HAPPIER THAN I'VE EVER BEEN IN MY LIFE. I NEVER KNEW WHAT REAL LOVE WAS UNTIL NOW...

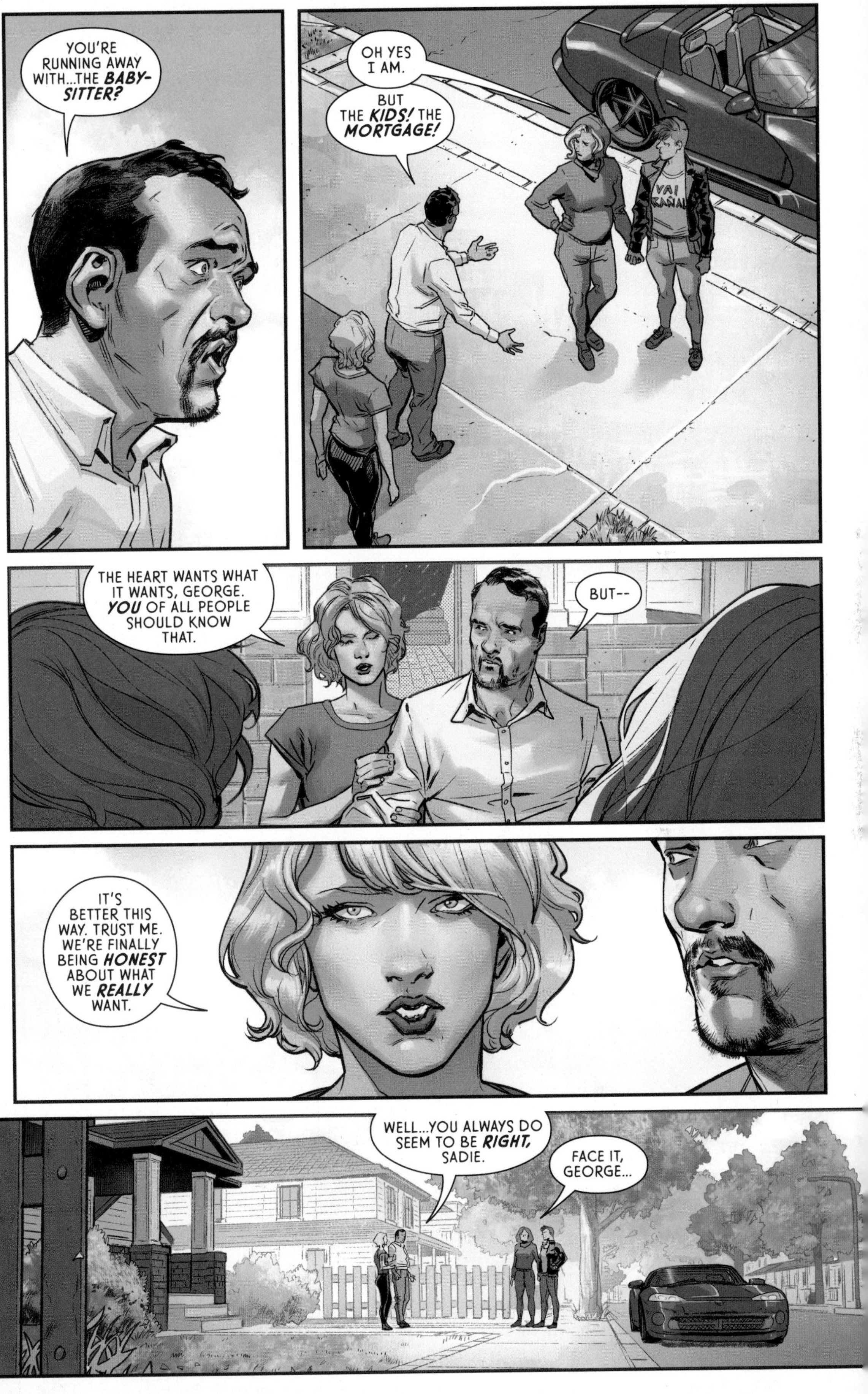
YOU'RE RUNNING AWAY WITH...THE BABY-SITTER?
OH YES I AM.
BUT THE KIDS! THE MORTGAGE!
VAI CAÑAL
THE HEART WANTS WHAT IT WANTS, GEORGE. YOU OF ALL PEOPLE SHOULD KNOW THAT.
BUT--
IT'S BETTER THIS WAY. TRUST ME. WE'RE FINALLY BEING HONEST ABOUT WHAT WE REALLY WANT.
WELL...YOU ALWAYS DO SEEM TO BE RIGHT, SADIE.
FACE IT, GEORGE...

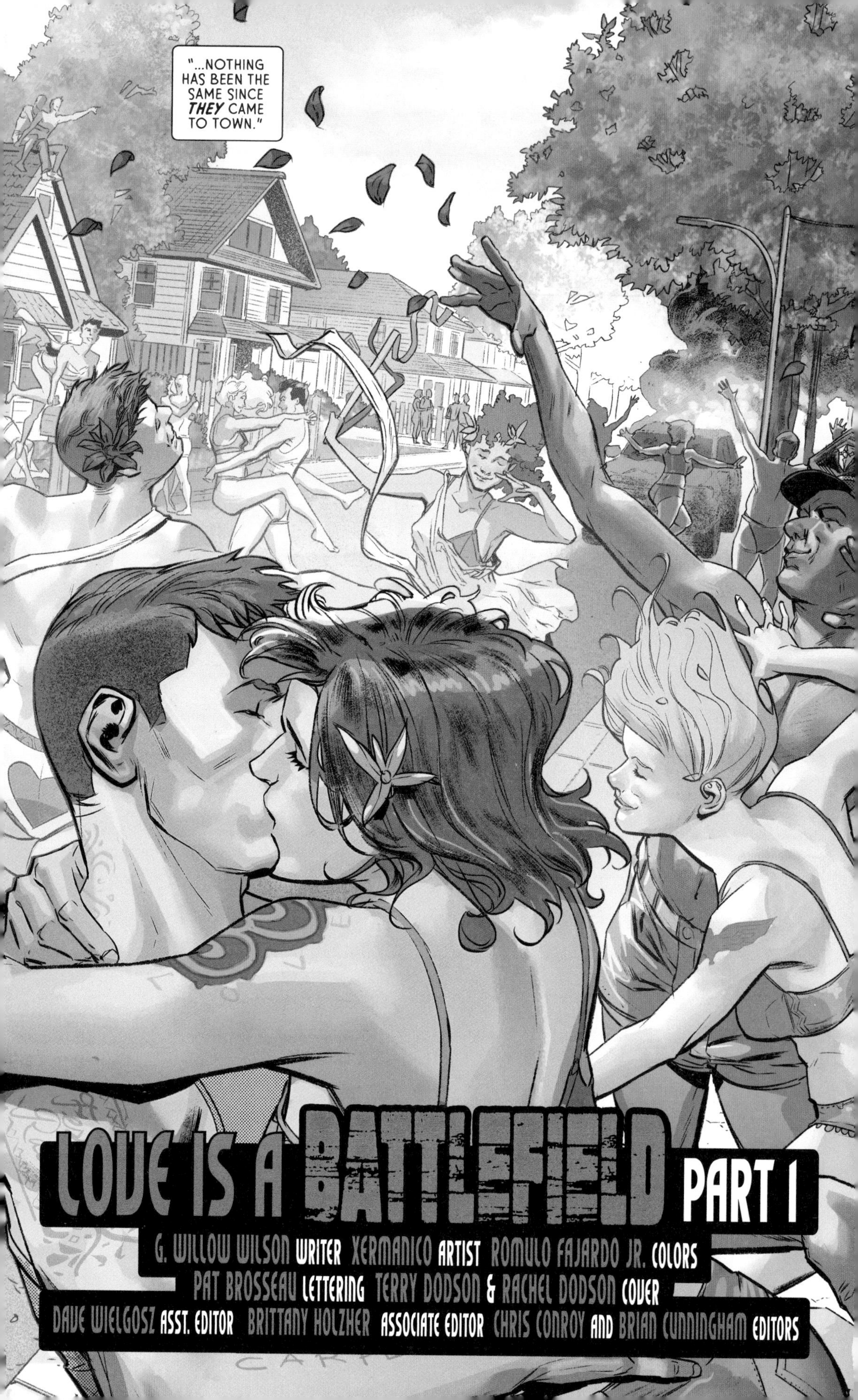
"...NOTHING HAS BEEN THE SAME SINCE *THEY* CAME TO TOWN."
LOVE IS A BATTLEFIELD PART 1
G. WILLOW WILSON WRITER XERMANICO ARTIST ROMULO FAJARDO JR. COLORS
PAT BROSSEAU LETTERING TERRY DODSON & RACHEL DODSON COVER
DAVE WIELGOSZ ASST. EDITOR BRITTANY HOLZHER ASSOCIATE EDITOR CHRIS CONROY AND BRIAN CUNNINGHAM EDITORS

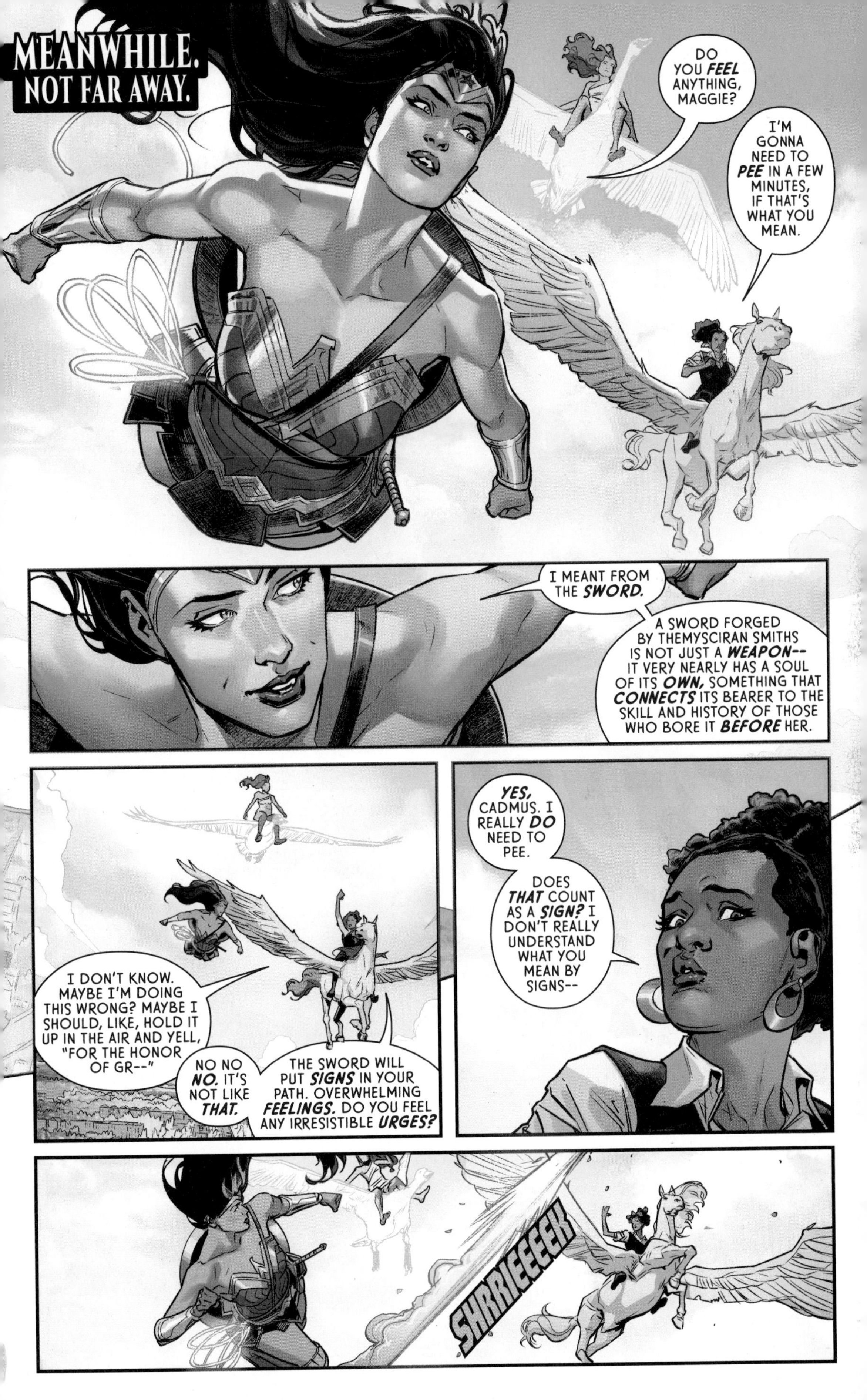
MEANWHILE. NOT FAR AWAY.
DO YOU FEEL ANYTHING, MAGGIE?
I'M GONNA NEED TO PEE IN A FEW MINUTES, IF THAT'S WHAT YOU MEAN.
I MEANT FROM THE SWORD.
A SWORD FORGED BY THEMYSCIRAN SMITHS IS NOT JUST A WEAPON-- IT VERY NEARLY HAS A SOUL OF ITS OWN, SOMETHING THAT CONNECTS ITS BEARER TO THE SKILL AND HISTORY OF THOSE WHO BORE IT BEFORE HER.
I DON'T KNOW. MAYBE I'M DOING THIS WRONG? MAYBE I SHOULD, LIKE, HOLD IT UP IN THE AIR AND YELL, "FOR THE HONOR OF GR--"
NO NO NO. IT'S NOT LIKE THAT.
THE SWORD WILL PUT SIGNS IN YOUR PATH. OVERWHELMING FEELINGS. DO YOU FEEL ANY IRRESISTIBLE URGES?
YES, CADMUS. I REALLY DO NEED TO PEE.
DOES THAT COUNT AS A SIGN? I DON'T REALLY UNDERSTAND WHAT YOU MEAN BY SIGNS--
SHRIEEEEK

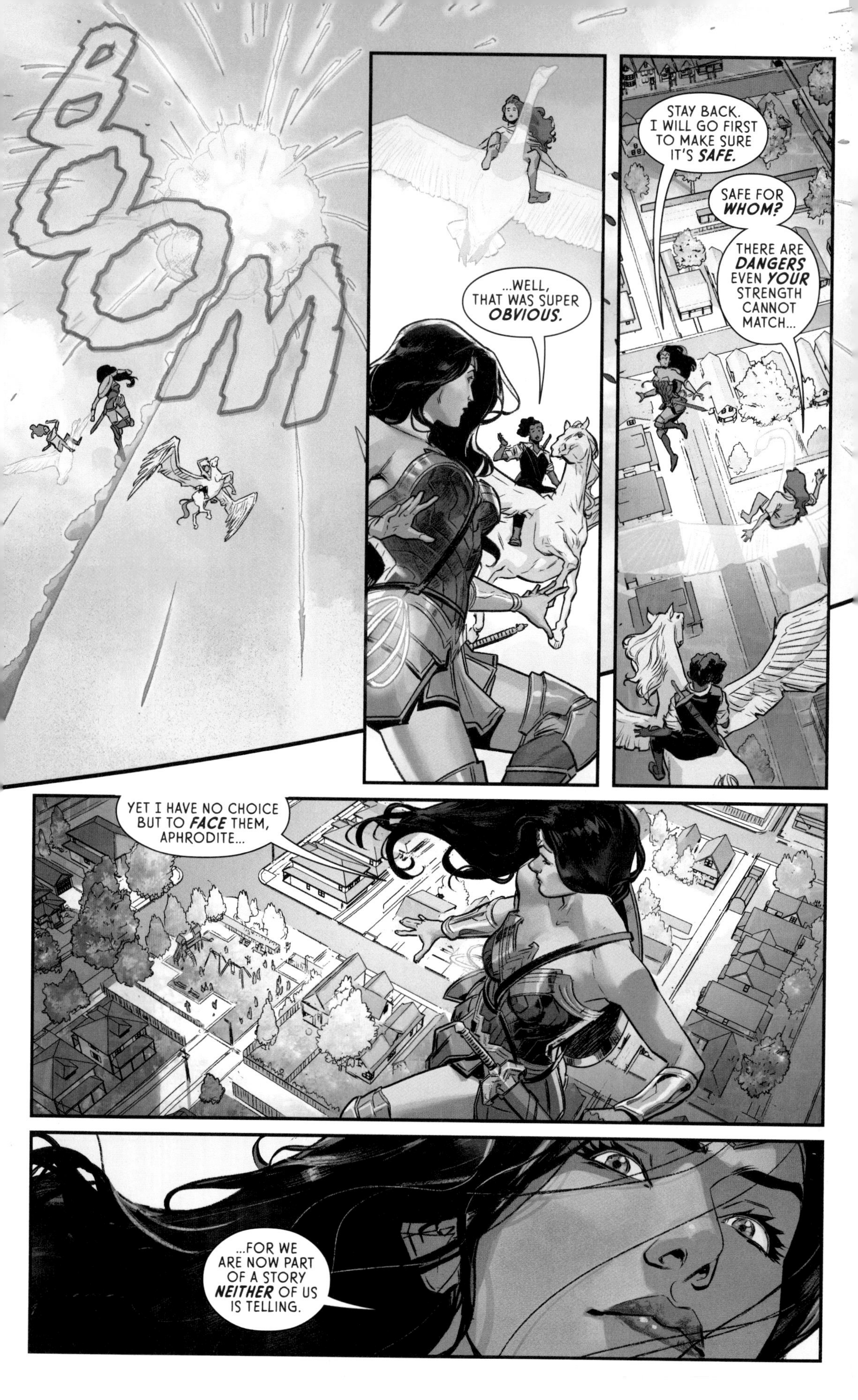
BOOM
...WELL, THAT WAS SUPER OBVIOUS.
STAY BACK. I WILL GO FIRST TO MAKE SURE IT'S SAFE.
SAFE FOR WHOM?
THERE ARE DANGERS EVEN YOUR STRENGTH CANNOT MATCH...
YET I HAVE NO CHOICE BUT TO FACE THEM, APHRODITE...
...FOR WE ARE NOW PART OF A STORY NEITHER OF US IS TELLING.

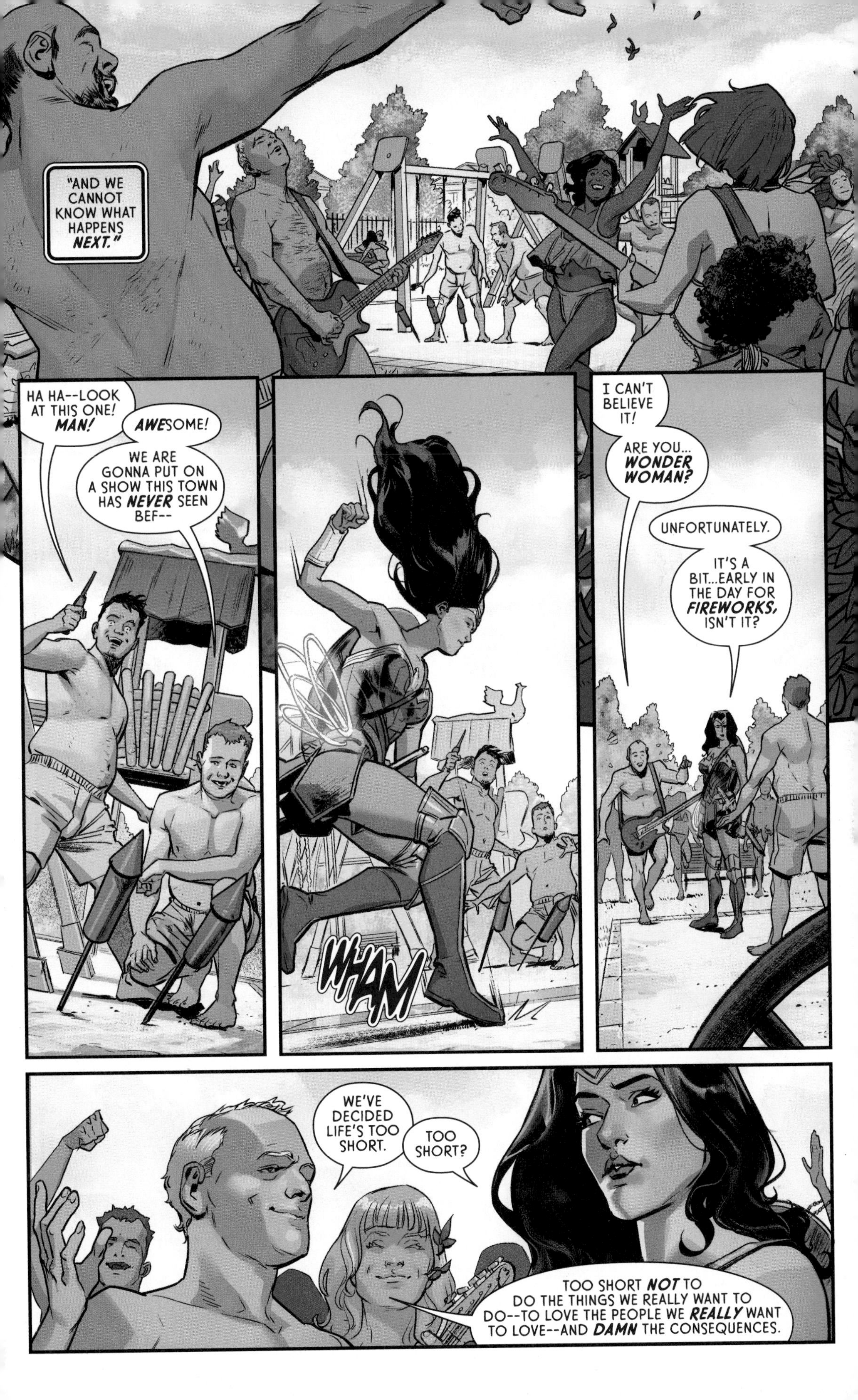
"AND WE CANNOT KNOW WHAT HAPPENS *NEXT.*"
HA HA--LOOK AT THIS ONE! *MAN!*
*AWE*SOME!
WE ARE GONNA PUT ON A SHOW THIS TOWN HAS *NEVER* SEEN BEF--
WHAM
I CAN'T BELIEVE IT!
ARE YOU... *WONDER WOMAN?*
UNFORTUNATELY.
IT'S A BIT...EARLY IN THE DAY FOR *FIREWORKS,* ISN'T IT?
WE'VE DECIDED LIFE'S TOO SHORT.
TOO SHORT?
TOO SHORT *NOT* TO DO THE THINGS WE REALLY WANT TO DO--TO LOVE THE PEOPLE WE *REALLY* WANT TO LOVE--AND *DAMN* THE CONSEQUENCES.

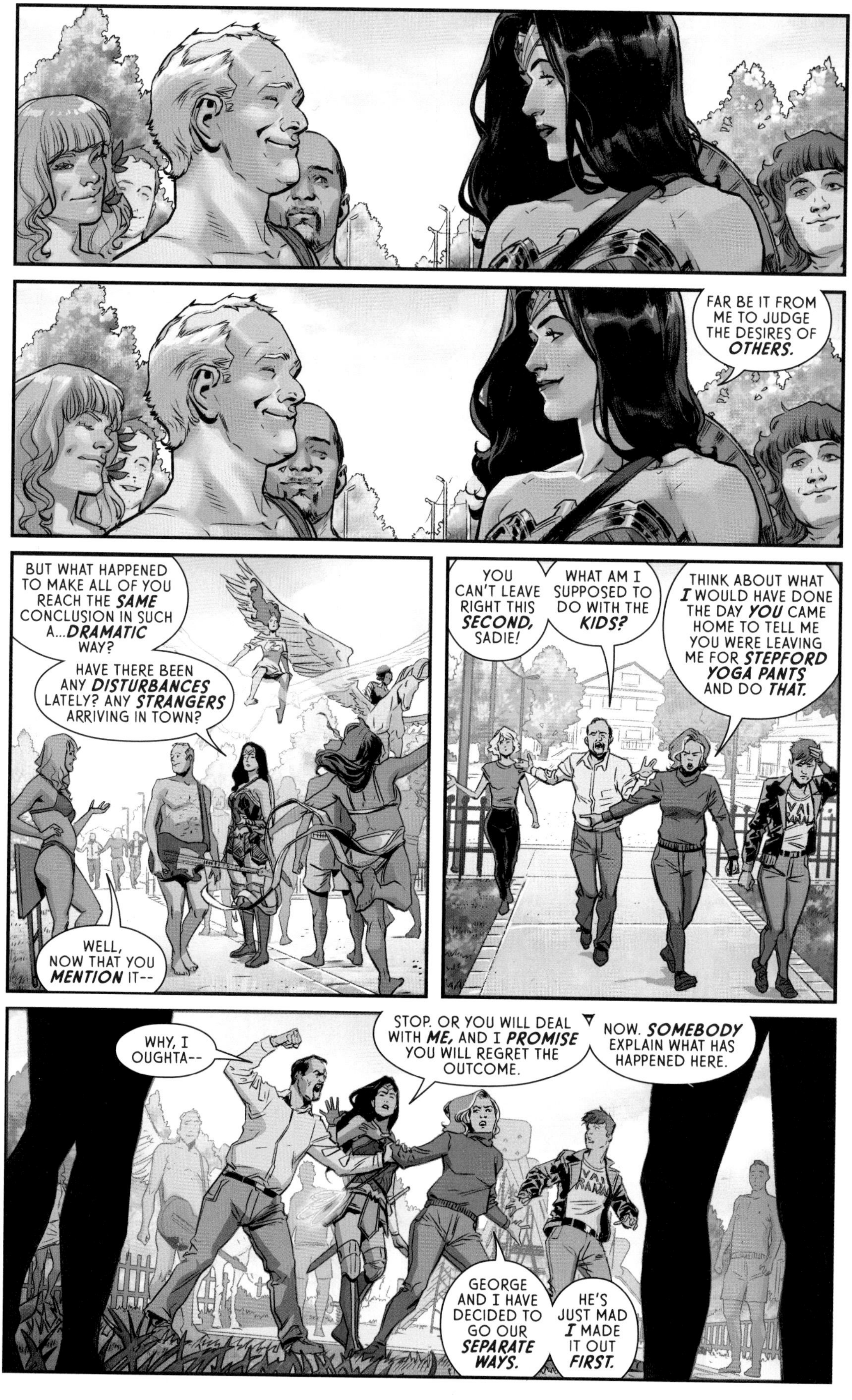
FAR BE IT FROM ME TO JUDGE THE DESIRES OF OTHERS.
BUT WHAT HAPPENED TO MAKE ALL OF YOU REACH THE SAME CONCLUSION IN SUCH A...DRAMATIC WAY?
HAVE THERE BEEN ANY DISTURBANCES LATELY? ANY STRANGERS ARRIVING IN TOWN?
WELL, NOW THAT YOU MENTION IT--
YOU CAN'T LEAVE RIGHT THIS SECOND, SADIE!
WHAT AM I SUPPOSED TO DO WITH THE KIDS?
THINK ABOUT WHAT I WOULD HAVE DONE THE DAY YOU CAME HOME TO TELL ME YOU WERE LEAVING ME FOR STEPFORD YOGA PANTS AND DO THAT.
WHY, I OUGHTA--
STOP. OR YOU WILL DEAL WITH ME, AND I PROMISE YOU WILL REGRET THE OUTCOME.
NOW. SOMEBODY EXPLAIN WHAT HAS HAPPENED HERE.
GEORGE AND I HAVE DECIDED TO GO OUR SEPARATE WAYS.
HE'S JUST MAD I MADE IT OUT FIRST.

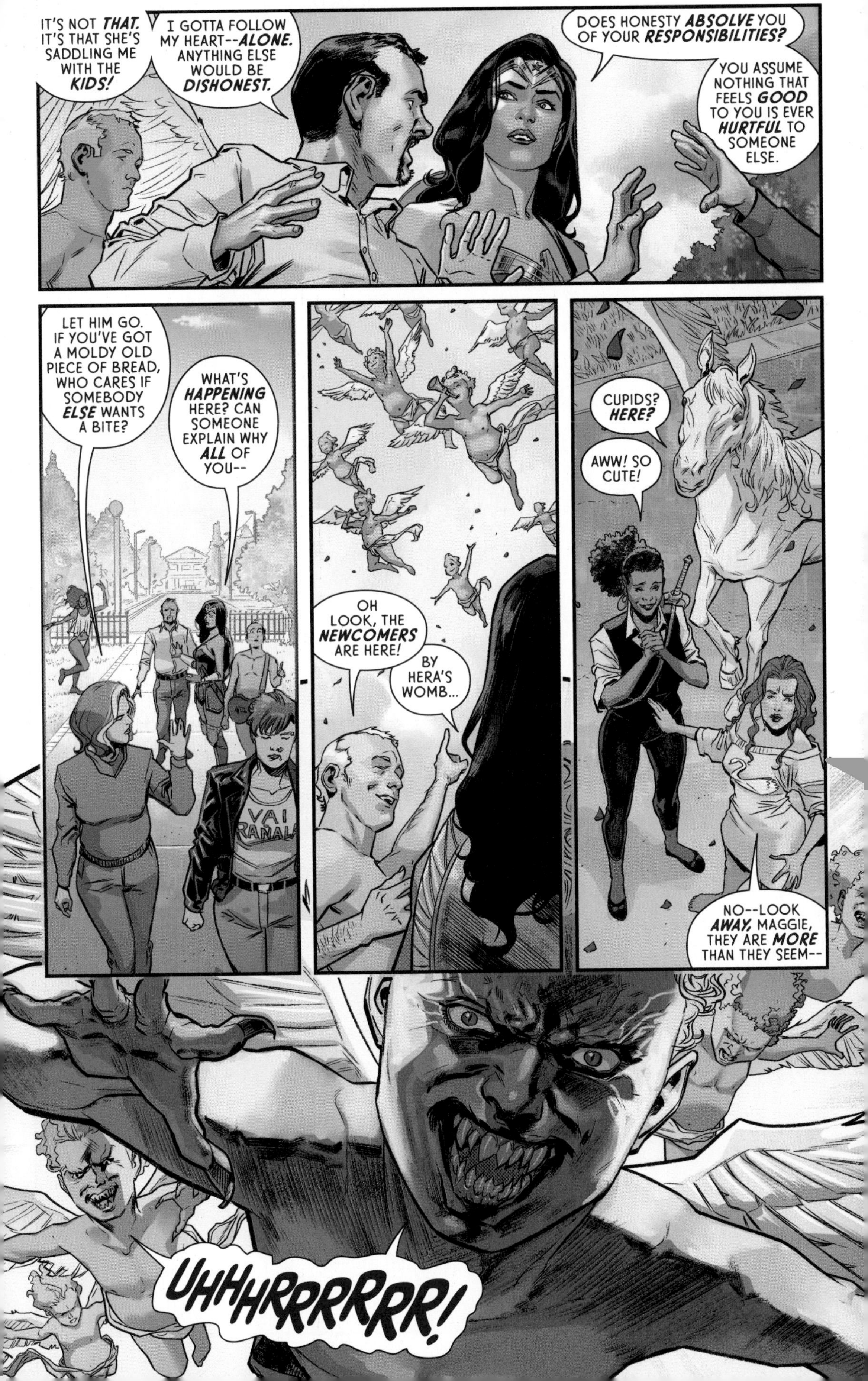
IT'S NOT THAT. IT'S THAT SHE'S SADDLING ME WITH THE KIDS!
I GOTTA FOLLOW MY HEART--ALONE. ANYTHING ELSE WOULD BE DISHONEST.
DOES HONESTY ABSOLVE YOU OF YOUR RESPONSIBILITIES?
YOU ASSUME NOTHING THAT FEELS GOOD TO YOU IS EVER HURTFUL TO SOMEONE ELSE.
LET HIM GO. IF YOU'VE GOT A MOLDY OLD PIECE OF BREAD, WHO CARES IF SOMEBODY ELSE WANTS A BITE?
WHAT'S HAPPENING HERE? CAN SOMEONE EXPLAIN WHY ALL OF YOU--
VAI RAÑALA
OH LOOK, THE NEWCOMERS ARE HERE!
BY HERA'S WOMB...
CUPIDS? HERE?
AWW! SO CUTE!
NO--LOOK AWAY, MAGGIE, THEY ARE MORE THAN THEY SEEM--
UHHHRRRRRR!

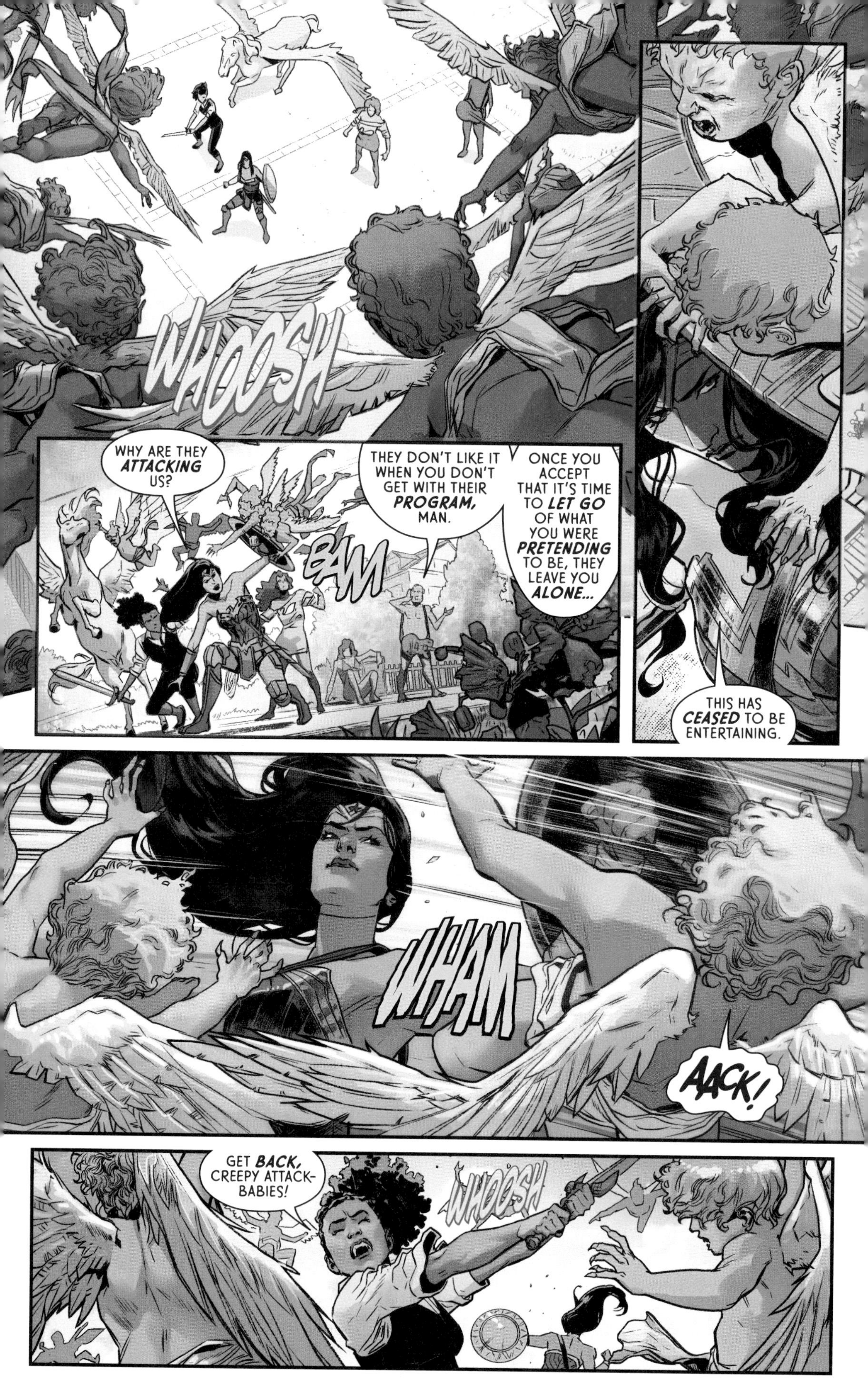
WHOOSH
WHY ARE THEY ATTACKING US?
THEY DON'T LIKE IT WHEN YOU DON'T GET WITH THEIR PROGRAM, MAN.
ONCE YOU ACCEPT THAT IT'S TIME TO LET GO OF WHAT YOU WERE PRETENDING TO BE, THEY LEAVE YOU ALONE...
BAM
THIS HAS CEASED TO BE ENTERTAINING.
WHAM
AACK!
GET BACK, CREEPY ATTACK-BABIES!
WHOOSH

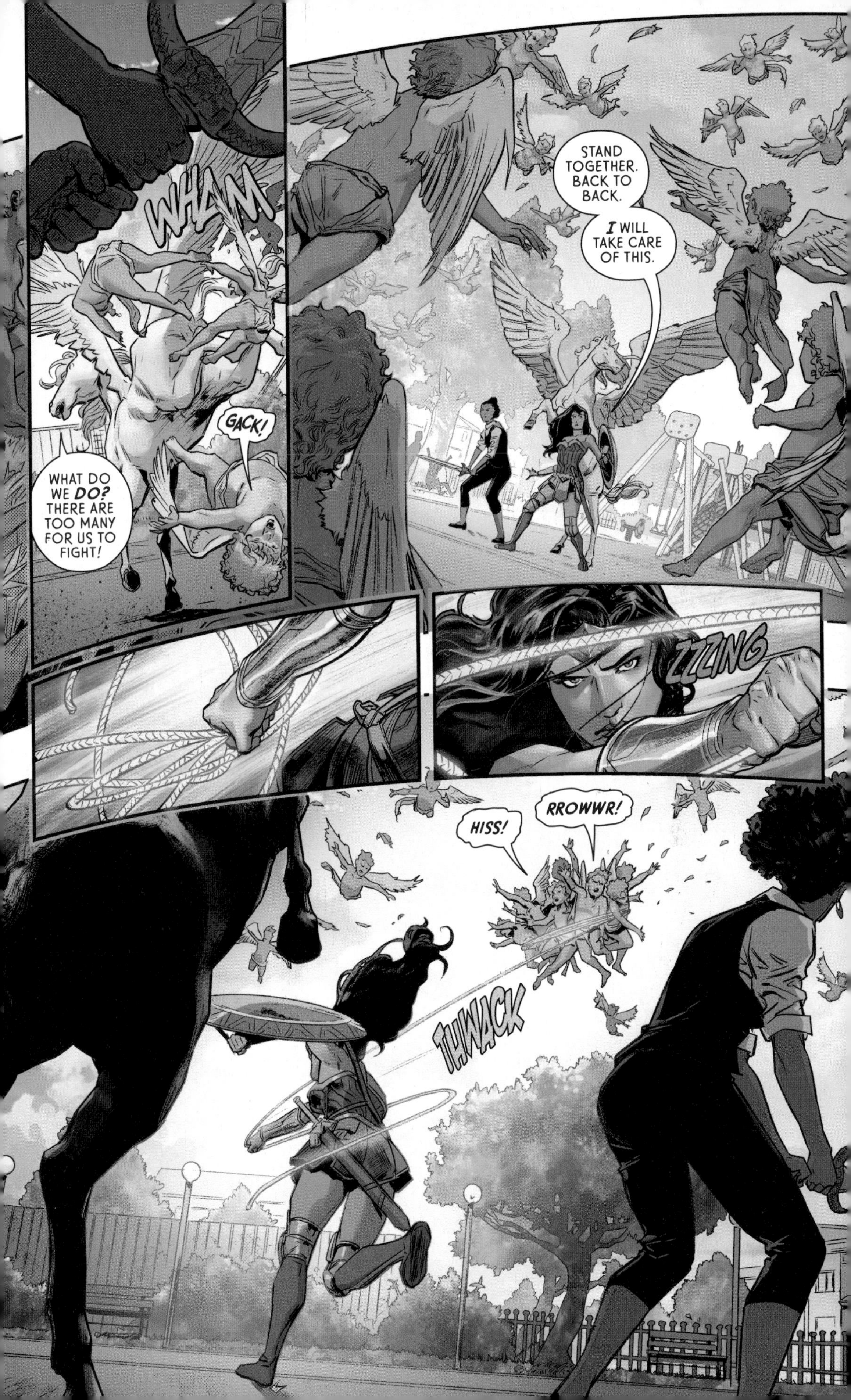
WHAM
GACK!
WHAT DO WE DO? THERE ARE TOO MANY FOR US TO FIGHT!
STAND TOGETHER. BACK TO BACK.
I WILL TAKE CARE OF THIS.
ZZZING
HISS!
RROWWR!
THWACK

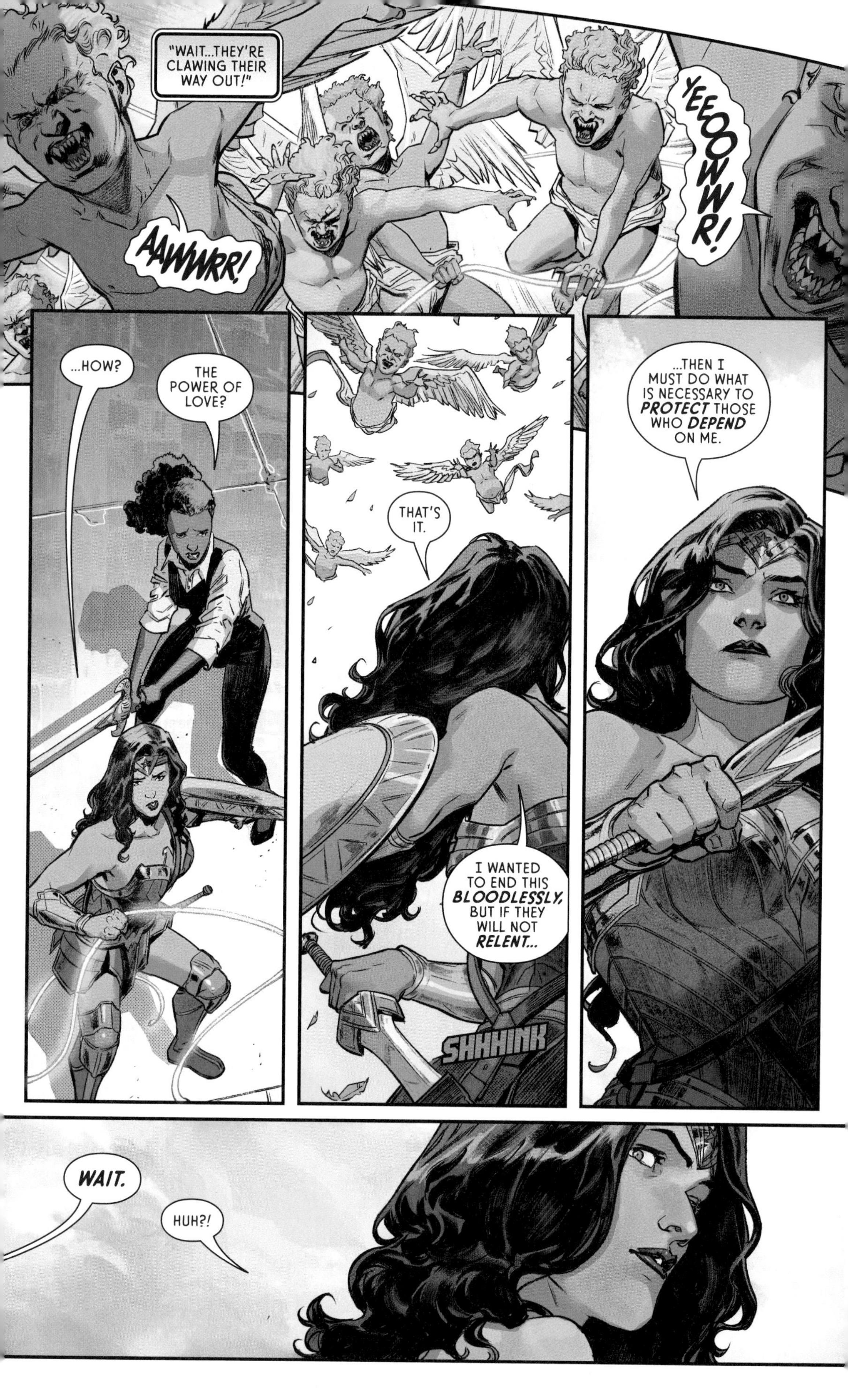
"WAIT...THEY'RE CLAWING THEIR WAY OUT!"
AAWWRR!
YEEOOWWR!
...HOW?
THE POWER OF LOVE?
THAT'S IT.
I WANTED TO END THIS BLOODLESSLY, BUT IF THEY WILL NOT RELENT...
SHHHINK
...THEN I MUST DO WHAT IS NECESSARY TO PROTECT THOSE WHO DEPEND ON ME.
WAIT.
HUH?!

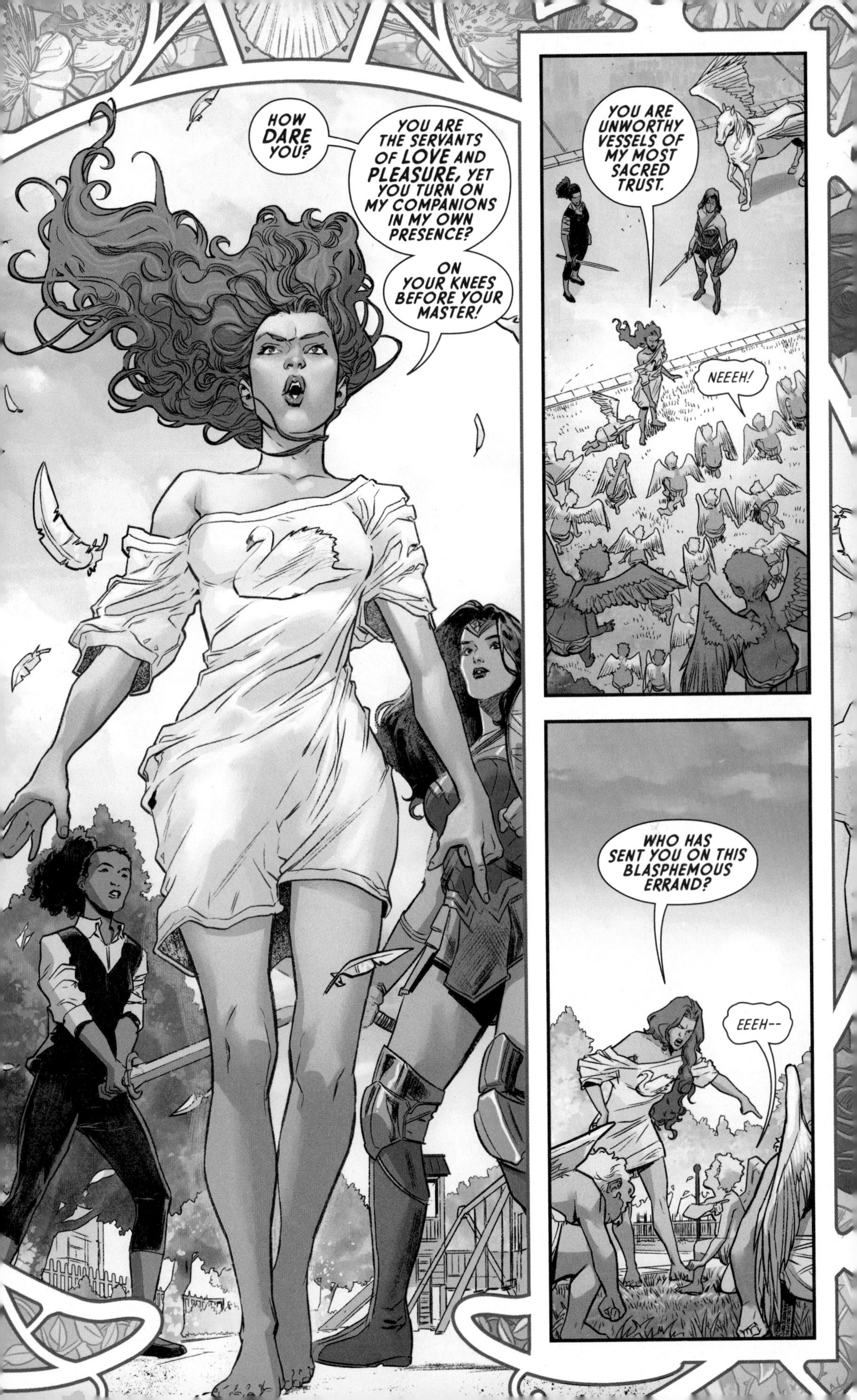
HOW DARE YOU?
YOU ARE THE SERVANTS OF LOVE AND PLEASURE, YET YOU TURN ON MY COMPANIONS IN MY OWN PRESENCE?
ON YOUR KNEES BEFORE YOUR MASTER!
YOU ARE UNWORTHY VESSELS OF MY MOST SACRED TRUST.
NEEEH!
WHO HAS SENT YOU ON THIS BLASPHEMOUS ERRAND?
EEEH--

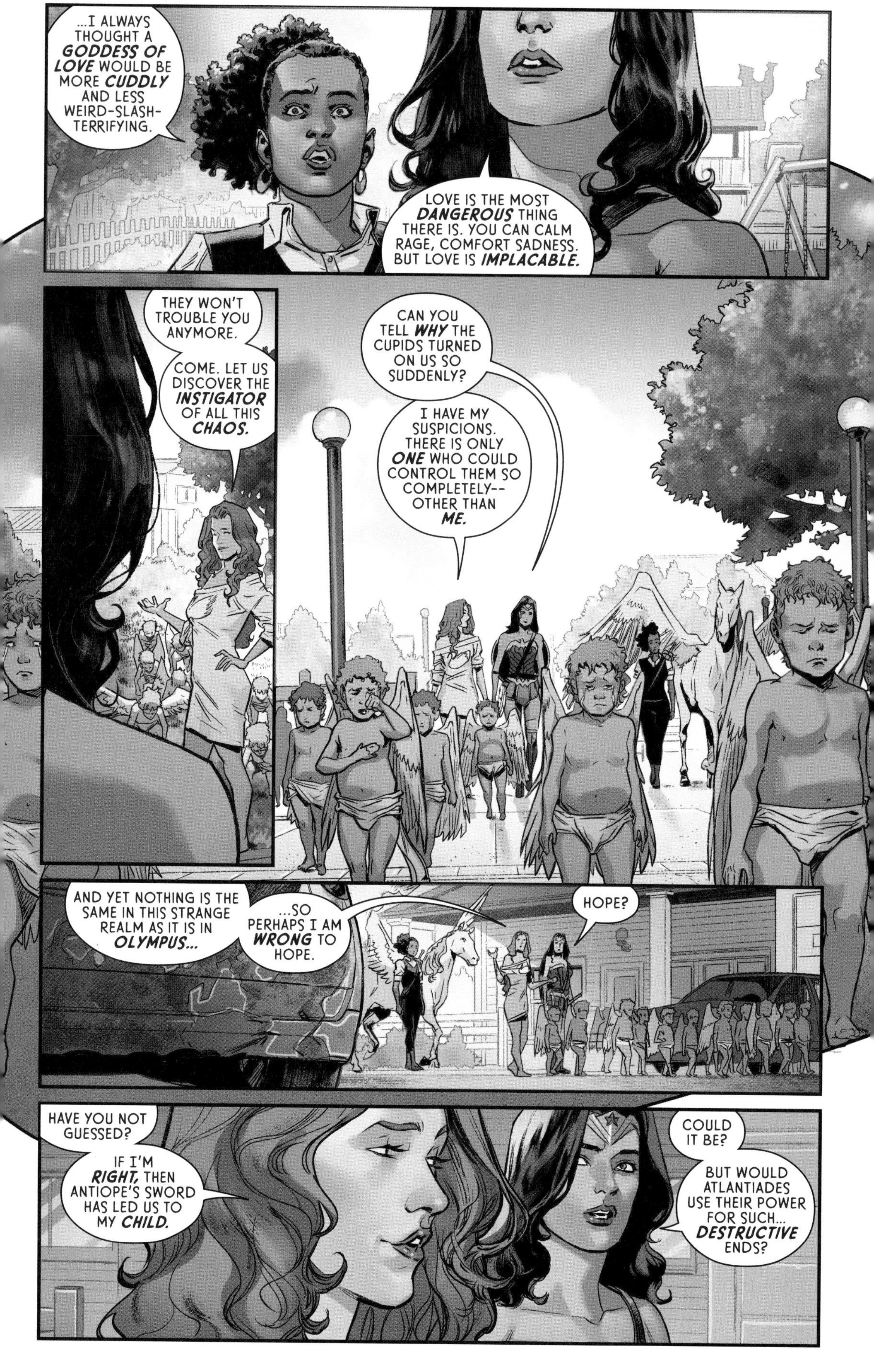
...I ALWAYS THOUGHT A GODDESS OF LOVE WOULD BE MORE CUDDLY AND LESS WEIRD-SLASH-TERRIFYING.
LOVE IS THE MOST DANGEROUS THING THERE IS. YOU CAN CALM RAGE, COMFORT SADNESS. BUT LOVE IS IMPLACABLE.
THEY WON'T TROUBLE YOU ANYMORE.
COME. LET US DISCOVER THE INSTIGATOR OF ALL THIS CHAOS.
CAN YOU TELL WHY THE CUPIDS TURNED ON US SO SUDDENLY?
I HAVE MY SUSPICIONS. THERE IS ONLY ONE WHO COULD CONTROL THEM SO COMPLETELY-- OTHER THAN ME.
AND YET NOTHING IS THE SAME IN THIS STRANGE REALM AS IT IS IN OLYMPUS...
...SO PERHAPS I AM WRONG TO HOPE.
HOPE?
HAVE YOU NOT GUESSED?
IF I'M RIGHT, THEN ANTIOPE'S SWORD HAS LED US TO MY CHILD.
COULD IT BE?
BUT WOULD ATLANTIADES USE THEIR POWER FOR SUCH... DESTRUCTIVE ENDS?

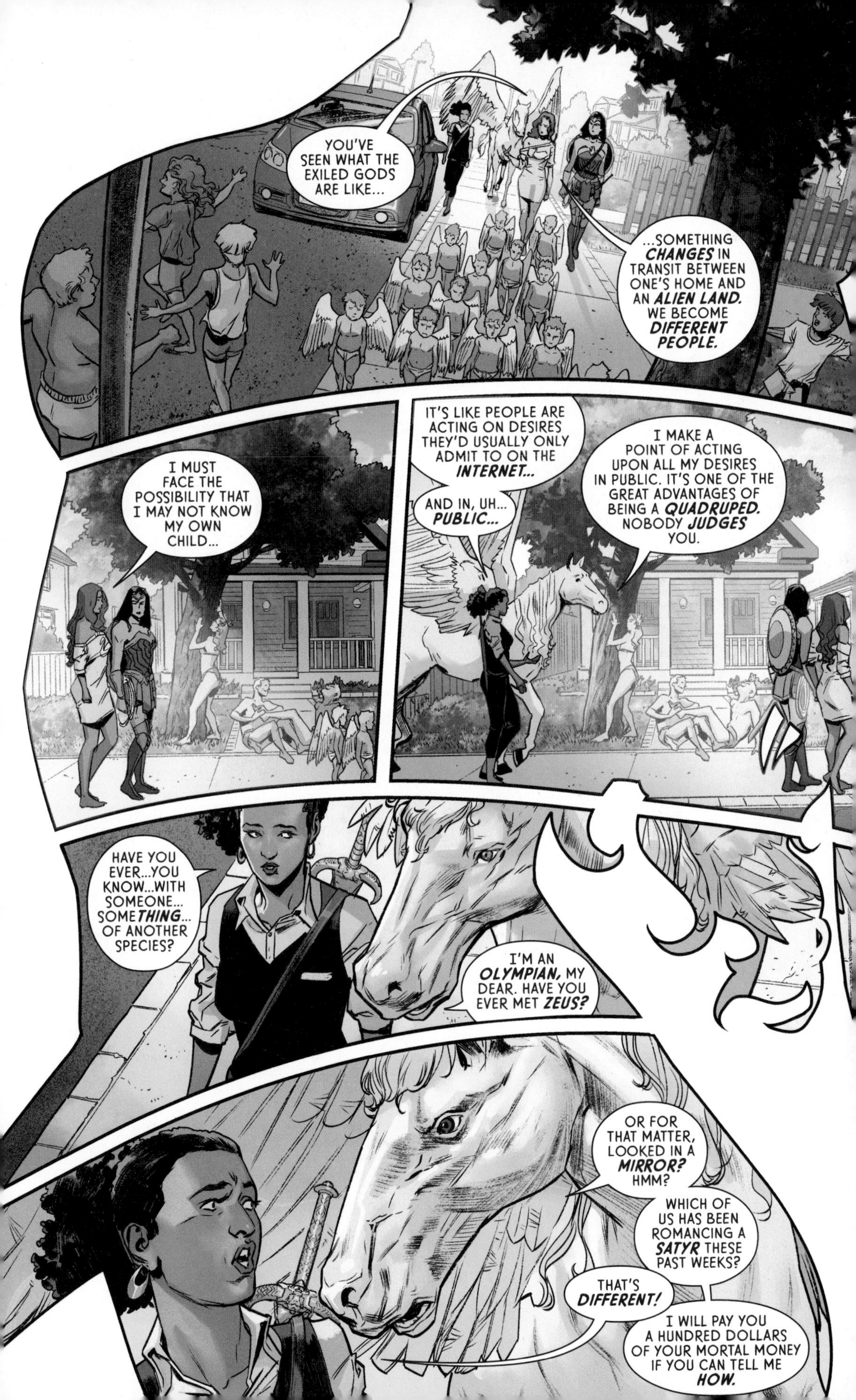

YOU'VE SEEN WHAT THE EXILED GODS ARE LIKE...
...SOMETHING **CHANGES** IN TRANSIT BETWEEN ONE'S HOME AND AN **ALIEN LAND.** WE BECOME **DIFFERENT PEOPLE.**
I MUST FACE THE POSSIBILITY THAT I MAY NOT KNOW MY OWN CHILD...
IT'S LIKE PEOPLE ARE ACTING ON DESIRES THEY'D USUALLY ONLY ADMIT TO ON THE **INTERNET...**
AND IN, UH... **PUBLIC...**
I MAKE A POINT OF ACTING UPON ALL MY DESIRES IN PUBLIC. IT'S ONE OF THE GREAT ADVANTAGES OF BEING A **QUADRUPED.** NOBODY **JUDGES** YOU.
HAVE YOU EVER...YOU KNOW...WITH SOMEONE... SOME**THING**... OF ANOTHER SPECIES?
I'M AN **OLYMPIAN,** MY DEAR. HAVE YOU EVER MET **ZEUS?**
OR FOR THAT MATTER, LOOKED IN A **MIRROR?** HMM?
WHICH OF US HAS BEEN ROMANCING A **SATYR** THESE PAST WEEKS?
THAT'S **DIFFERENT!**
I WILL PAY YOU A HUNDRED DOLLARS OF YOUR MORTAL MONEY IF YOU CAN TELL ME **HOW.**

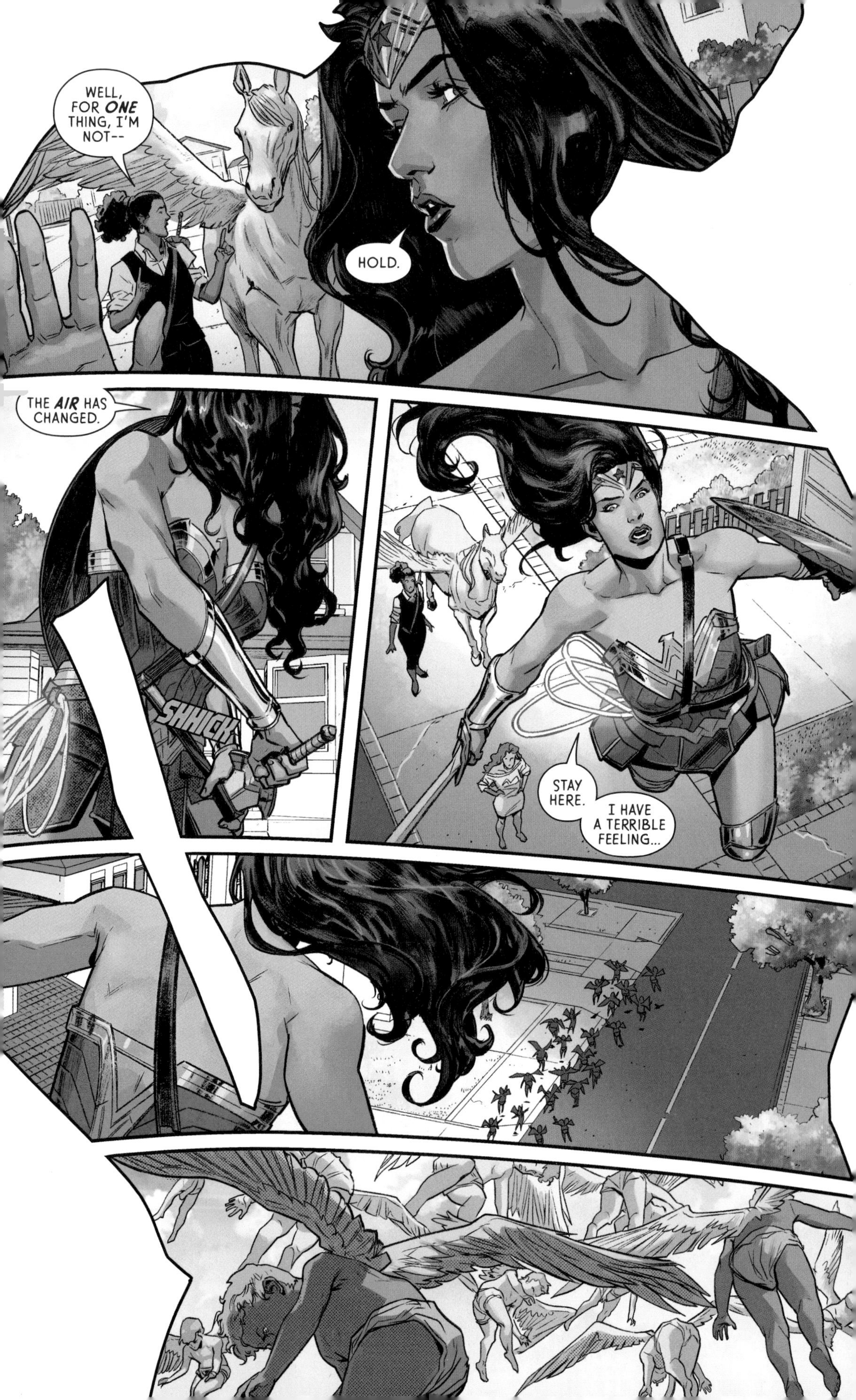
WELL, FOR ONE THING, I'M NOT--
HOLD.
THE AIR HAS CHANGED.
SHHICK
STAY HERE.
I HAVE A TERRIBLE FEELING...

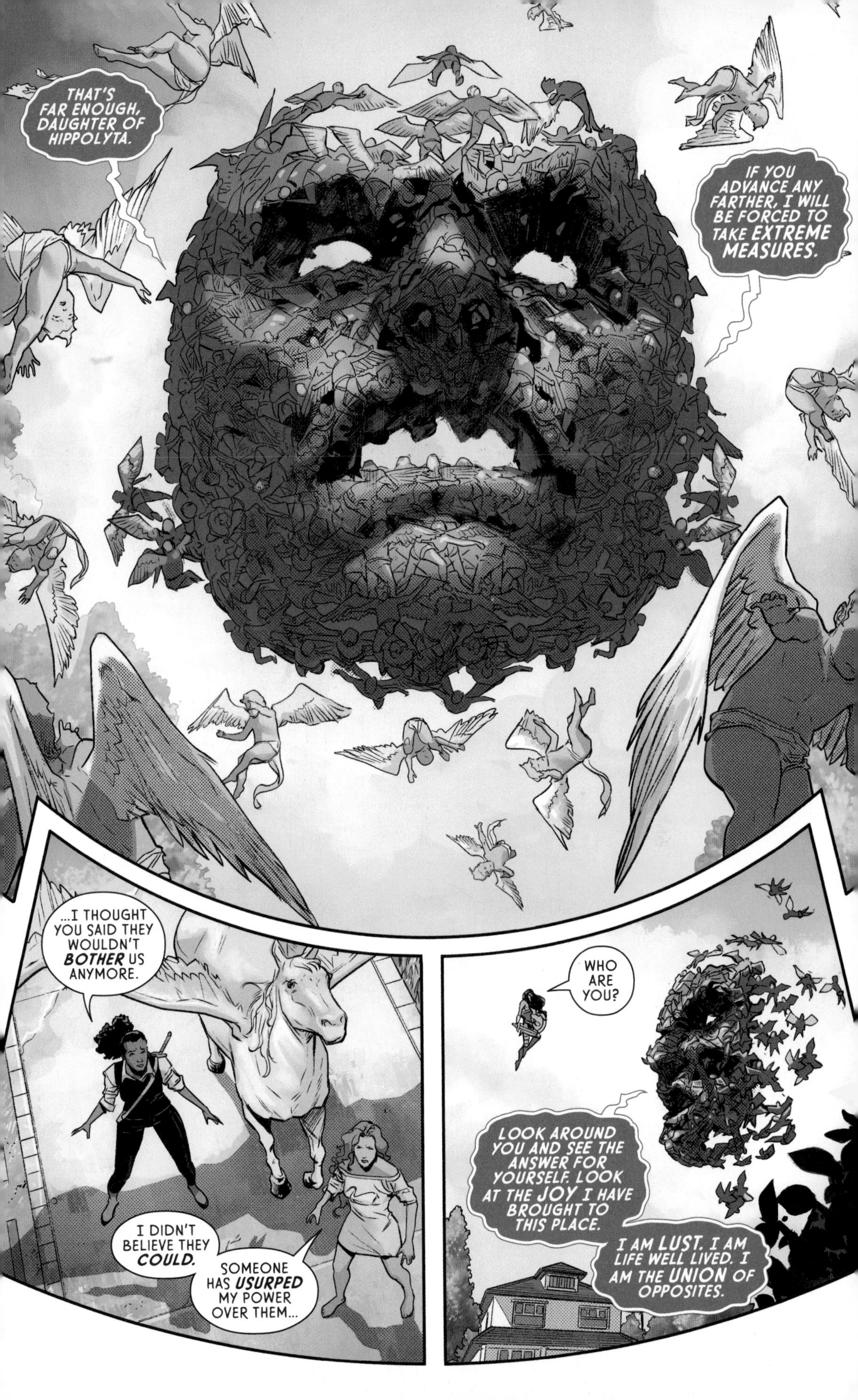

THAT'S FAR ENOUGH, DAUGHTER OF HIPPOLYTA.
IF YOU ADVANCE ANY FARTHER, I WILL BE FORCED TO TAKE EXTREME MEASURES.
...I THOUGHT YOU SAID THEY WOULDN'T BOTHER US ANYMORE.
I DIDN'T BELIEVE THEY COULD.
SOMEONE HAS USURPED MY POWER OVER THEM...
WHO ARE YOU?
LOOK AROUND YOU AND SEE THE ANSWER FOR YOURSELF. LOOK AT THE JOY I HAVE BROUGHT TO THIS PLACE.
I AM LUST. I AM LIFE WELL LIVED. I AM THE UNION OF OPPOSITES.

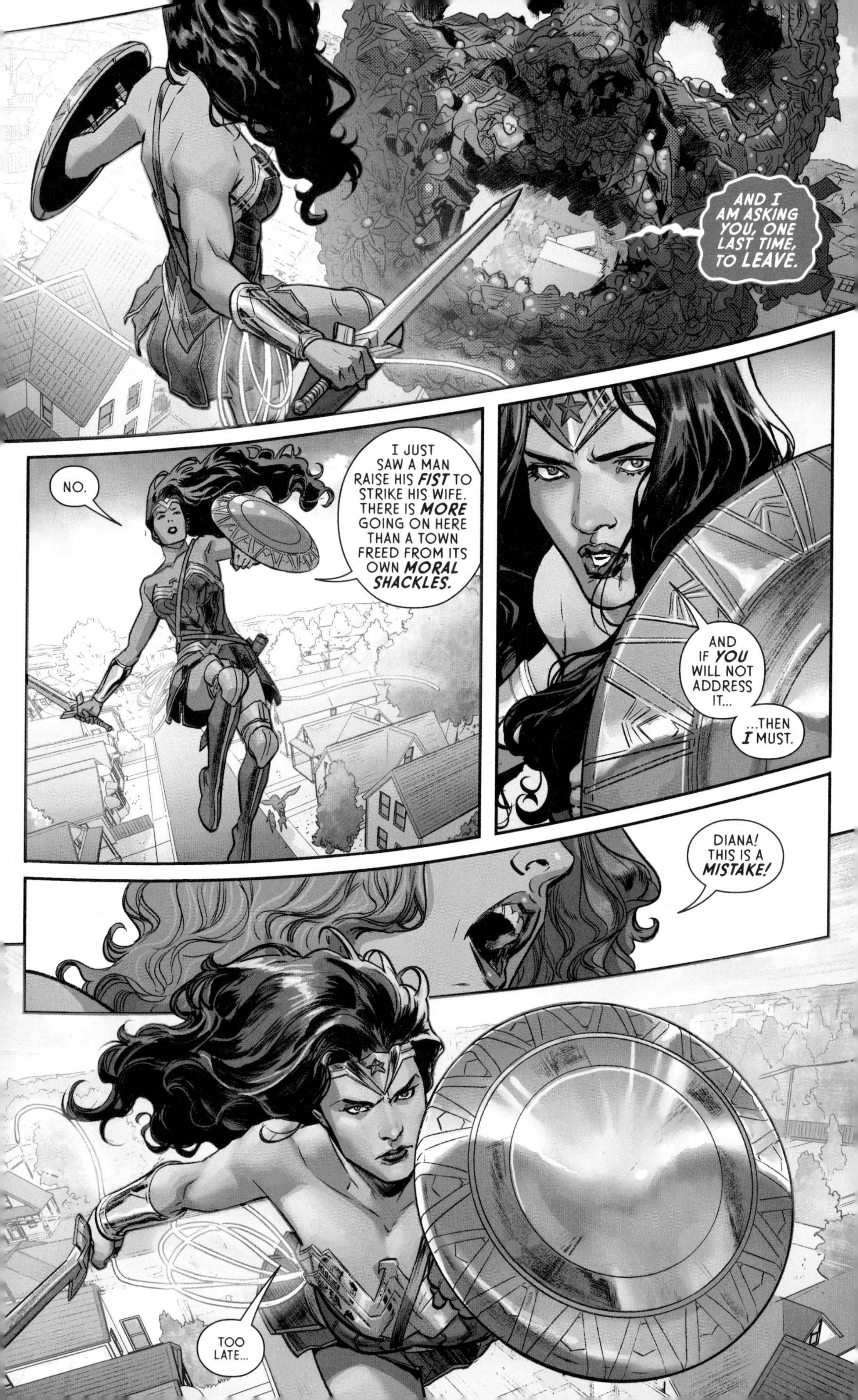

AND I AM ASKING YOU, ONE LAST TIME, TO LEAVE.
NO.
I JUST SAW A MAN RAISE HIS FIST TO STRIKE HIS WIFE. THERE IS MORE GOING ON HERE THAN A TOWN FREED FROM ITS OWN MORAL SHACKLES.
AND IF YOU WILL NOT ADDRESS IT...
...THEN I MUST.
DIANA! THIS IS A MISTAKE!
TOO LATE...

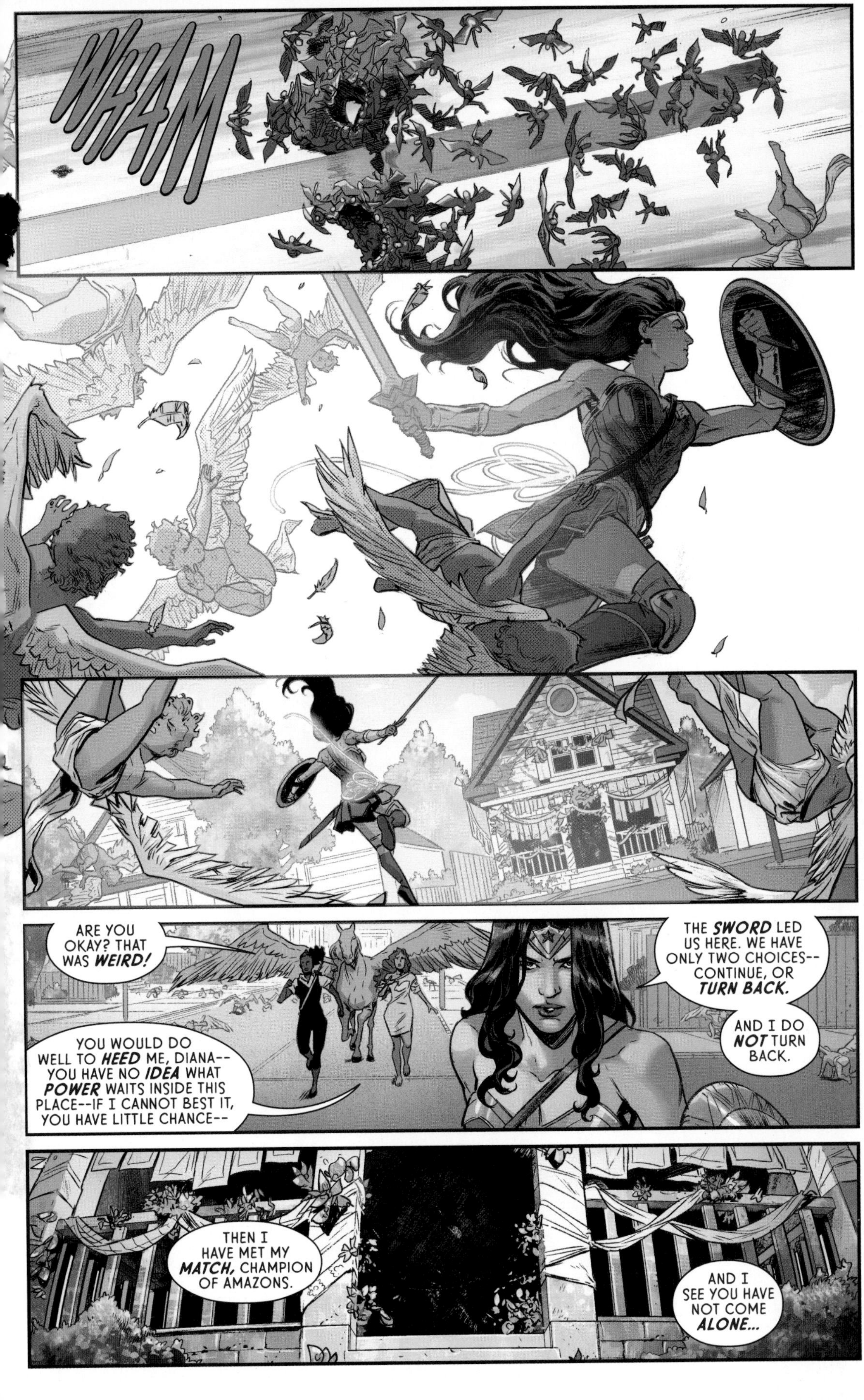
WHAM
ARE YOU OKAY? THAT WAS WEIRD!
YOU WOULD DO WELL TO HEED ME, DIANA-- YOU HAVE NO IDEA WHAT POWER WAITS INSIDE THIS PLACE--IF I CANNOT BEST IT, YOU HAVE LITTLE CHANCE--
THE SWORD LED US HERE. WE HAVE ONLY TWO CHOICES-- CONTINUE, OR TURN BACK.
AND I DO NOT TURN BACK.
THEN I HAVE MET MY MATCH, CHAMPION OF AMAZONS.
AND I SEE YOU HAVE NOT COME ALONE...

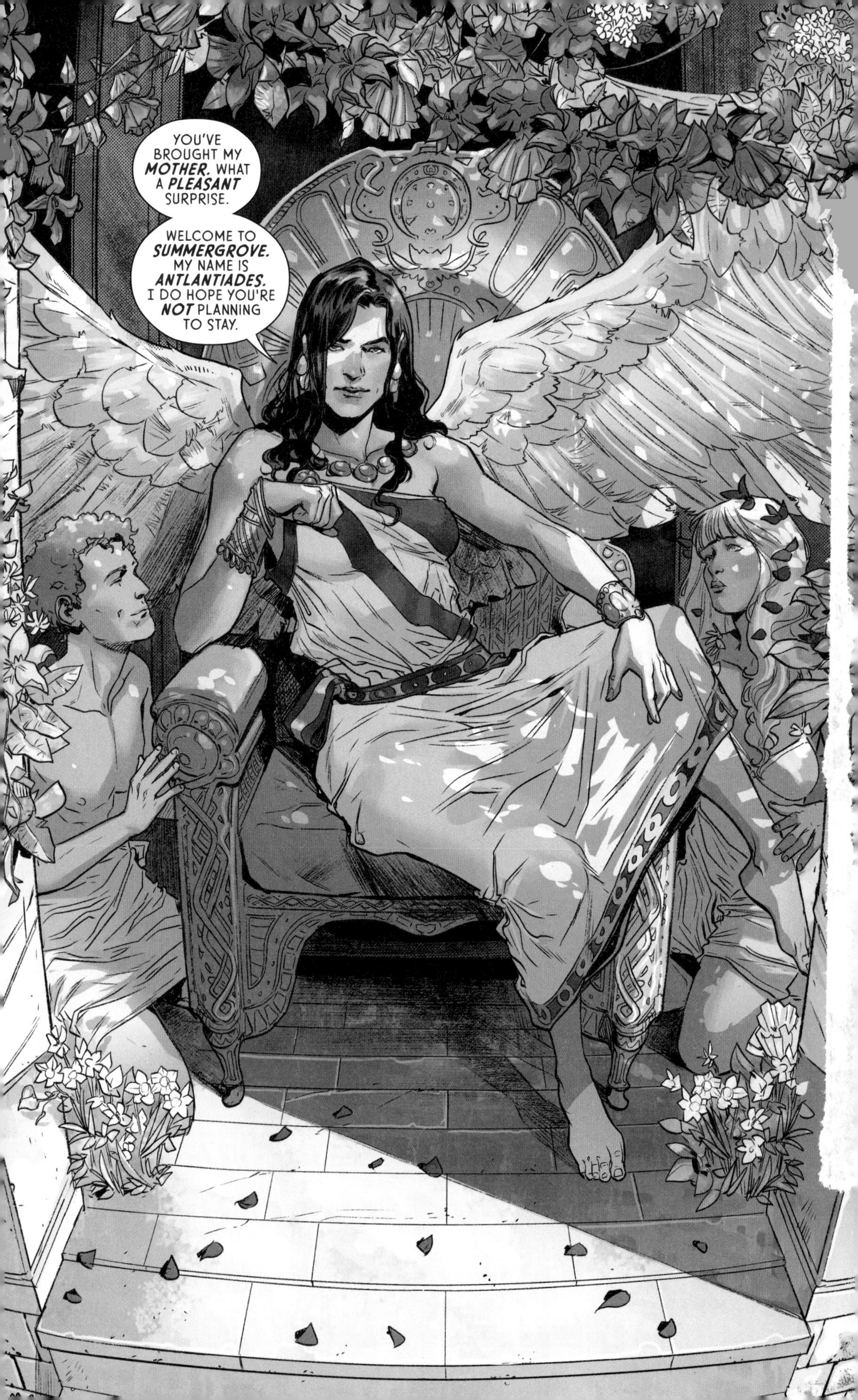
YOU'VE BROUGHT MY **MOTHER.** WHAT A **PLEASANT** SURPRISE.
WELCOME TO **SUMMERGROVE.** MY NAME IS **ANTLANTIADES.** I DO HOPE YOU'RE **NOT** PLANNING TO STAY.

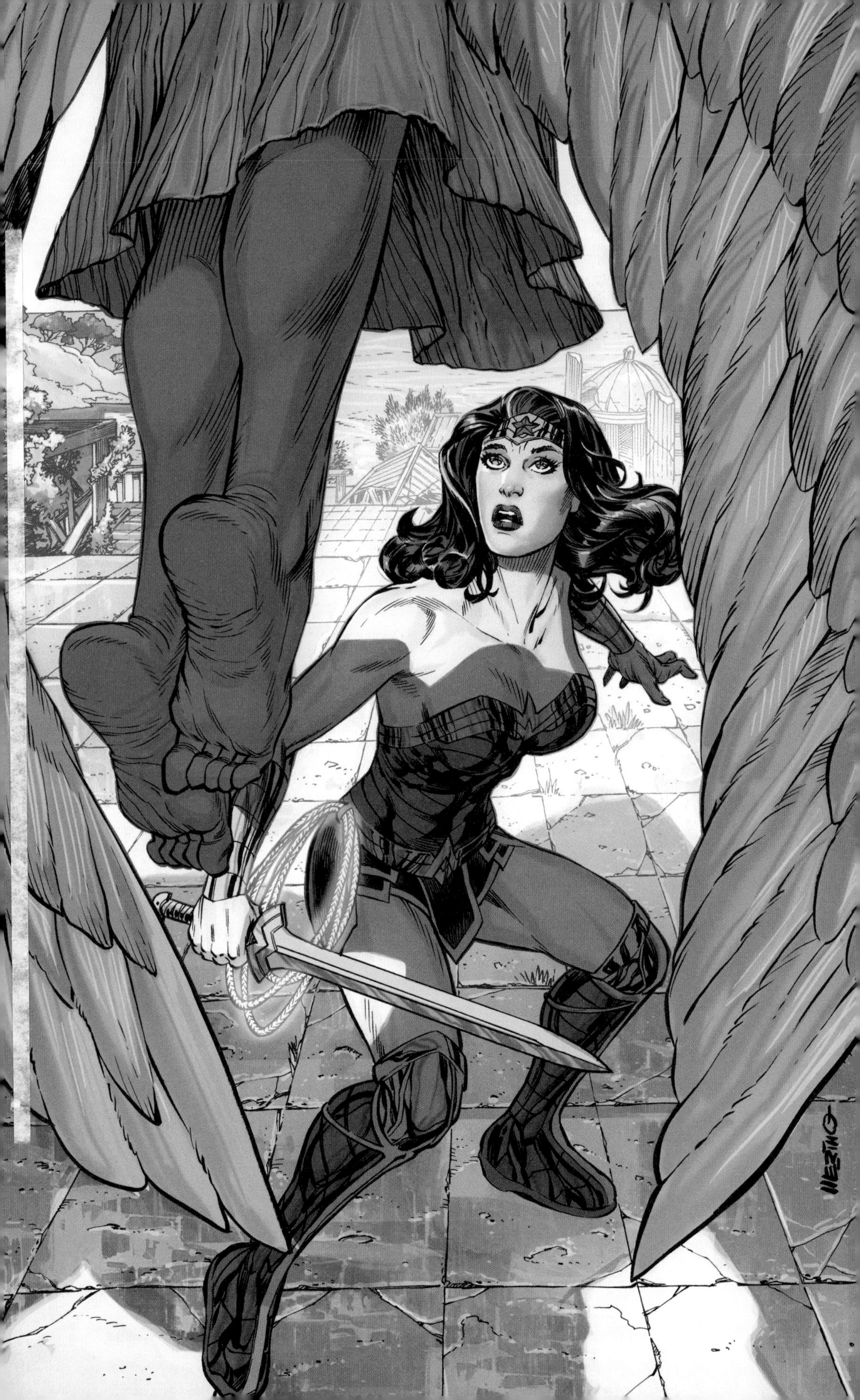

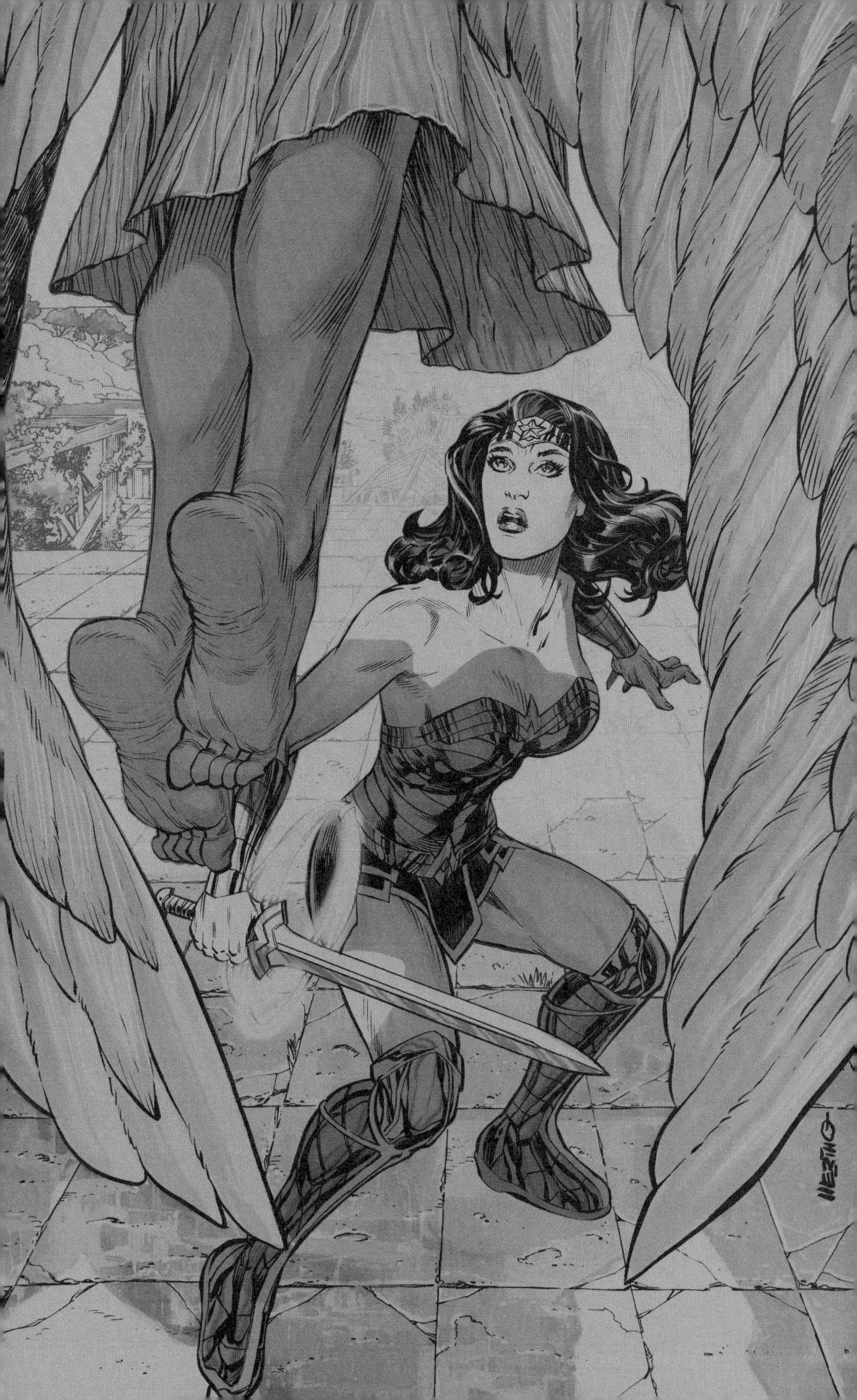

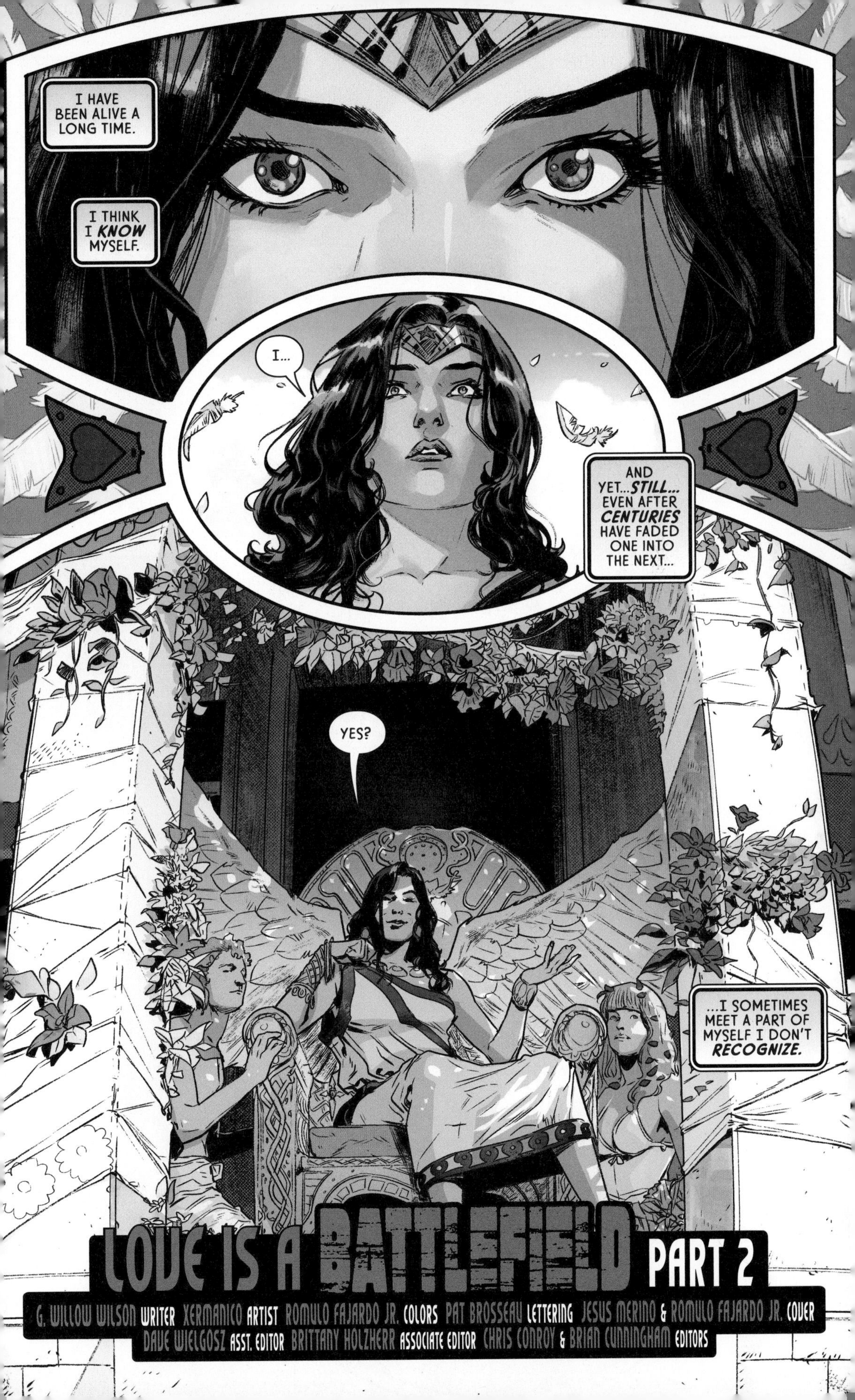

I HAVE BEEN ALIVE A LONG TIME.
I THINK I KNOW MYSELF.
I...
AND YET...STILL... EVEN AFTER CENTURIES HAVE FADED ONE INTO THE NEXT...
YES?
...I SOMETIMES MEET A PART OF MYSELF I DON'T RECOGNIZE.
LOVE IS A BATTLEFIELD PART 2
G. WILLOW WILSON WRITER XERMANICO ARTIST ROMULO FAJARDO JR. COLORS PAT BROSSEAU LETTERING JESUS MERINO & ROMULO FAJARDO JR. COVER
DAVE WIELGOSZ ASST. EDITOR BRITTANY HOLZHERR ASSOCIATE EDITOR CHRIS CONROY & BRIAN CUNNINGHAM EDITORS

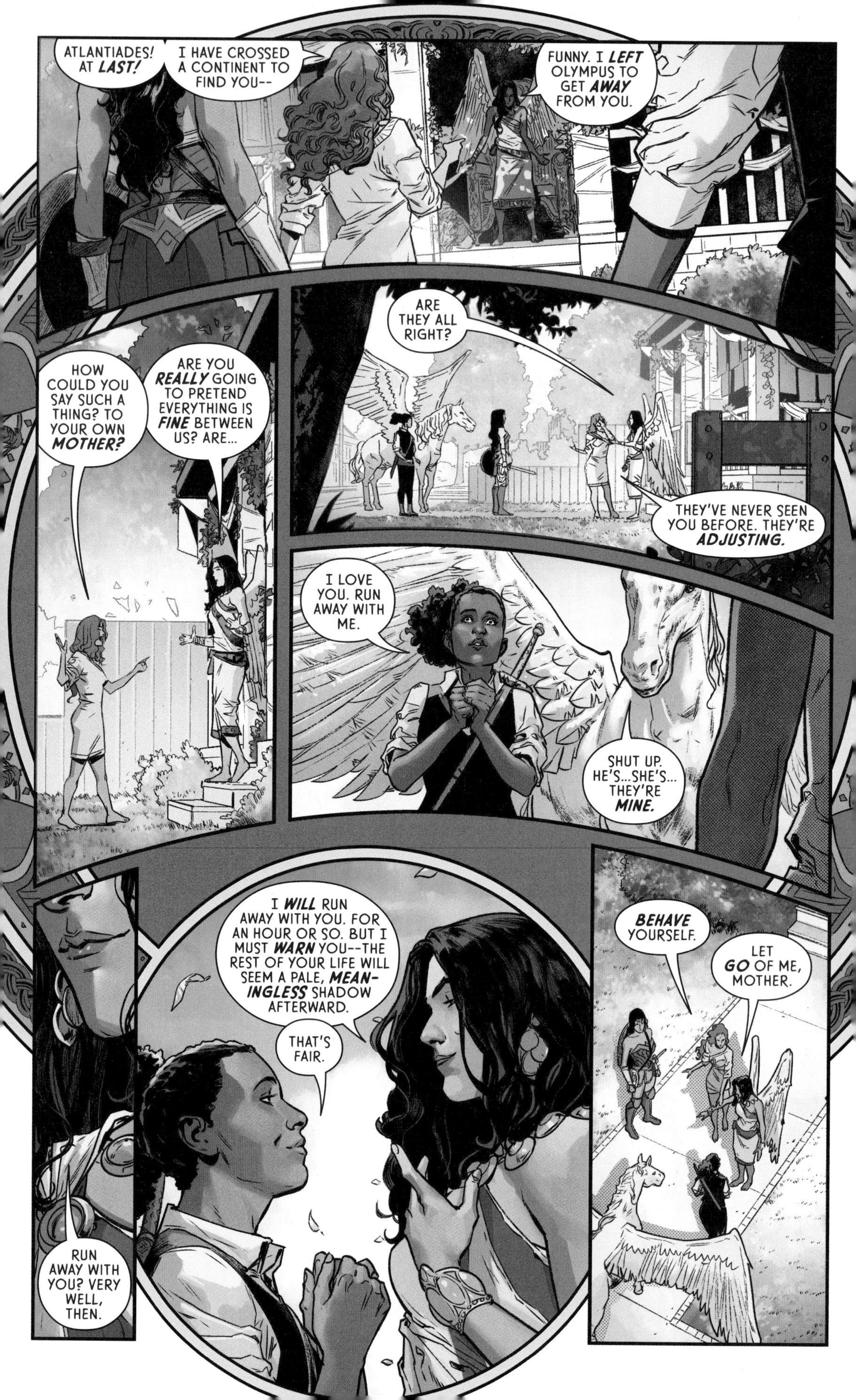
ATLANTIADES! AT LAST!
I HAVE CROSSED A CONTINENT TO FIND YOU--
FUNNY. I LEFT OLYMPUS TO GET AWAY FROM YOU.
HOW COULD YOU SAY SUCH A THING? TO YOUR OWN MOTHER?
ARE YOU REALLY GOING TO PRETEND EVERYTHING IS FINE BETWEEN US? ARE...
ARE THEY ALL RIGHT?
THEY'VE NEVER SEEN YOU BEFORE. THEY'RE ADJUSTING.
I LOVE YOU. RUN AWAY WITH ME.
SHUT UP. HE'S...SHE'S... THEY'RE MINE.
RUN AWAY WITH YOU? VERY WELL, THEN.
I WILL RUN AWAY WITH YOU. FOR AN HOUR OR SO. BUT I MUST WARN YOU--THE REST OF YOUR LIFE WILL SEEM A PALE, MEAN-INGLESS SHADOW AFTERWARD.
THAT'S FAIR.
BEHAVE YOURSELF.
LET GO OF ME, MOTHER.

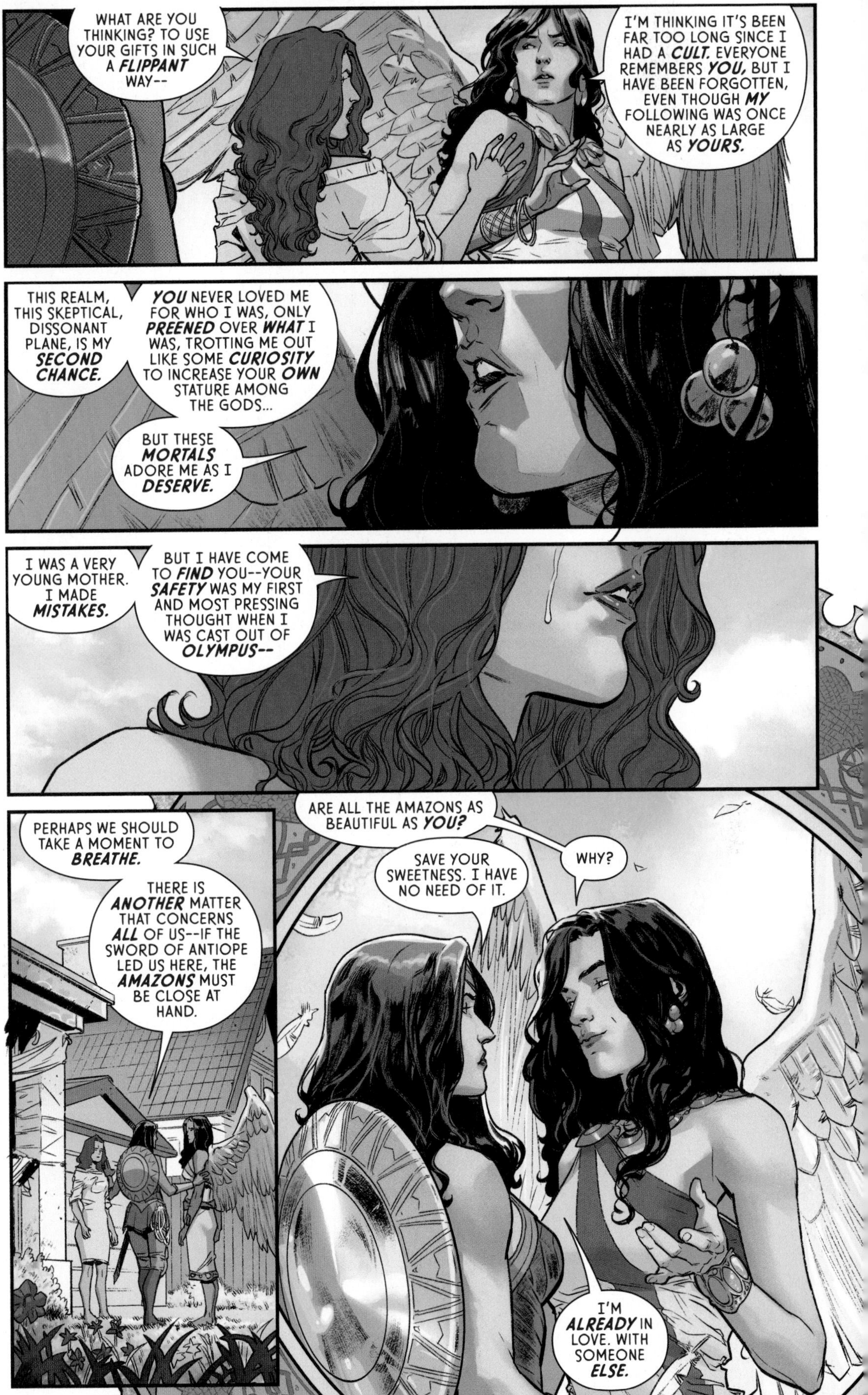
WHAT ARE YOU THINKING? TO USE YOUR GIFTS IN SUCH A FLIPPANT WAY--
I'M THINKING IT'S BEEN FAR TOO LONG SINCE I HAD A CULT. EVERYONE REMEMBERS YOU, BUT I HAVE BEEN FORGOTTEN, EVEN THOUGH MY FOLLOWING WAS ONCE NEARLY AS LARGE AS YOURS.
THIS REALM, THIS SKEPTICAL, DISSONANT PLANE, IS MY SECOND CHANCE.
YOU NEVER LOVED ME FOR WHO I WAS, ONLY PREENED OVER WHAT I WAS, TROTTING ME OUT LIKE SOME CURIOSITY TO INCREASE YOUR OWN STATURE AMONG THE GODS...
BUT THESE MORTALS ADORE ME AS I DESERVE.
I WAS A VERY YOUNG MOTHER. I MADE MISTAKES.
BUT I HAVE COME TO FIND YOU--YOUR SAFETY WAS MY FIRST AND MOST PRESSING THOUGHT WHEN I WAS CAST OUT OF OLYMPUS--
PERHAPS WE SHOULD TAKE A MOMENT TO BREATHE.
THERE IS ANOTHER MATTER THAT CONCERNS ALL OF US--IF THE SWORD OF ANTIOPE LED US HERE, THE AMAZONS MUST BE CLOSE AT HAND.
ARE ALL THE AMAZONS AS BEAUTIFUL AS YOU?
WHY?
SAVE YOUR SWEETNESS. I HAVE NO NEED OF IT.
I'M ALREADY IN LOVE. WITH SOMEONE ELSE.

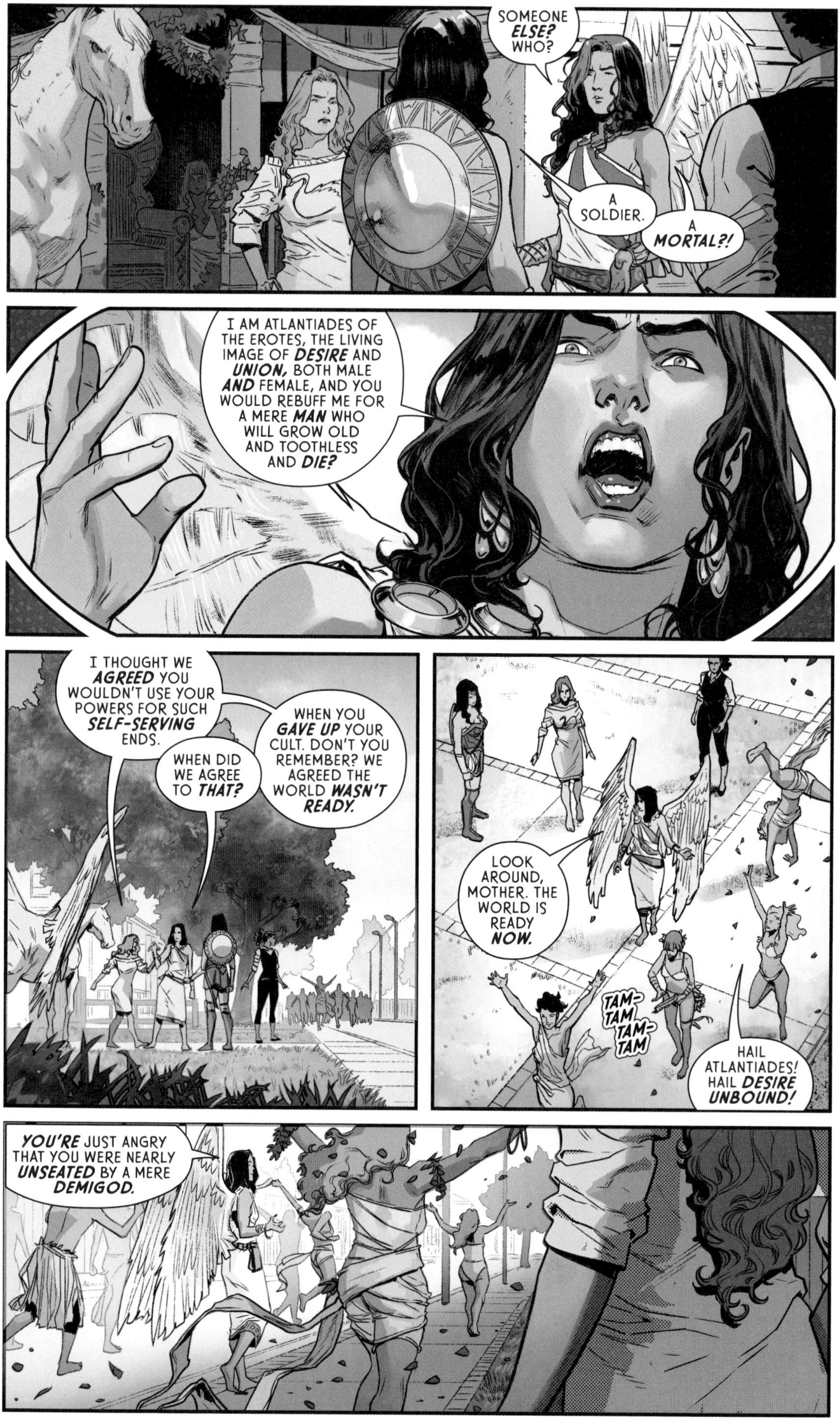
SOMEONE ELSE? WHO?
A SOLDIER.
A MORTAL?!
I AM ATLANTIADES OF THE EROTES, THE LIVING IMAGE OF DESIRE AND UNION, BOTH MALE AND FEMALE, AND YOU WOULD REBUFF ME FOR A MERE MAN WHO WILL GROW OLD AND TOOTHLESS AND DIE?
I THOUGHT WE AGREED YOU WOULDN'T USE YOUR POWERS FOR SUCH SELF-SERVING ENDS.
WHEN DID WE AGREE TO THAT?
WHEN YOU GAVE UP YOUR CULT. DON'T YOU REMEMBER? WE AGREED THE WORLD WASN'T READY.
LOOK AROUND, MOTHER. THE WORLD IS READY NOW.
TAM-TAM-TAM-TAM
HAIL ATLANTIADES! HAIL DESIRE UNBOUND!
YOU'RE JUST ANGRY THAT YOU WERE NEARLY UNSEATED BY A MERE DEMIGOD.

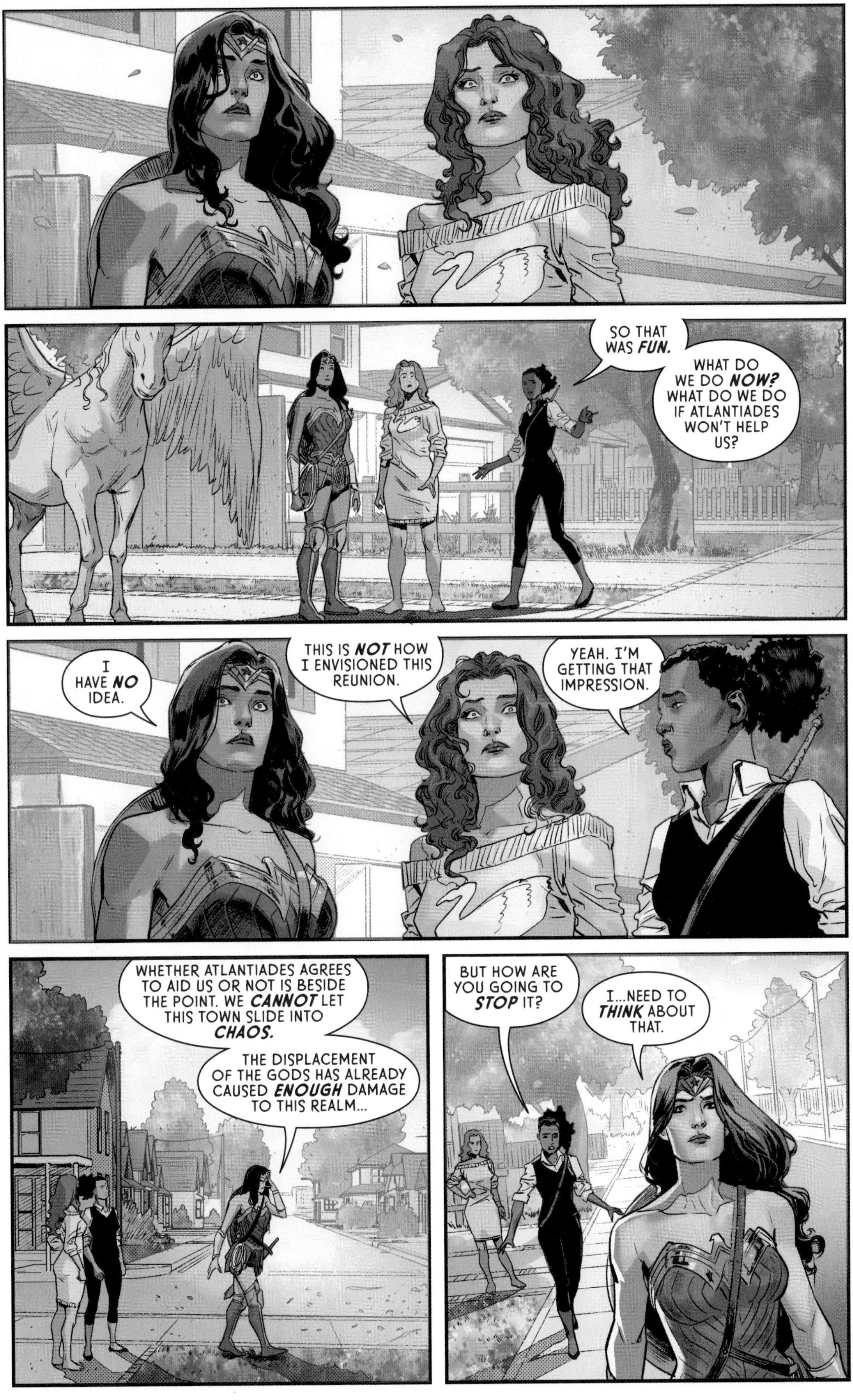
SO THAT WAS FUN.
WHAT DO WE DO NOW? WHAT DO WE DO IF ATLANTIADES WON'T HELP US?
I HAVE NO IDEA.
THIS IS NOT HOW I ENVISIONED THIS REUNION.
YEAH. I'M GETTING THAT IMPRESSION.
WHETHER ATLANTIADES AGREES TO AID US OR NOT IS BESIDE THE POINT. WE CANNOT LET THIS TOWN SLIDE INTO CHAOS.
THE DISPLACEMENT OF THE GODS HAS ALREADY CAUSED ENOUGH DAMAGE TO THIS REALM...
BUT HOW ARE YOU GOING TO STOP IT?
I...NEED TO THINK ABOUT THAT.

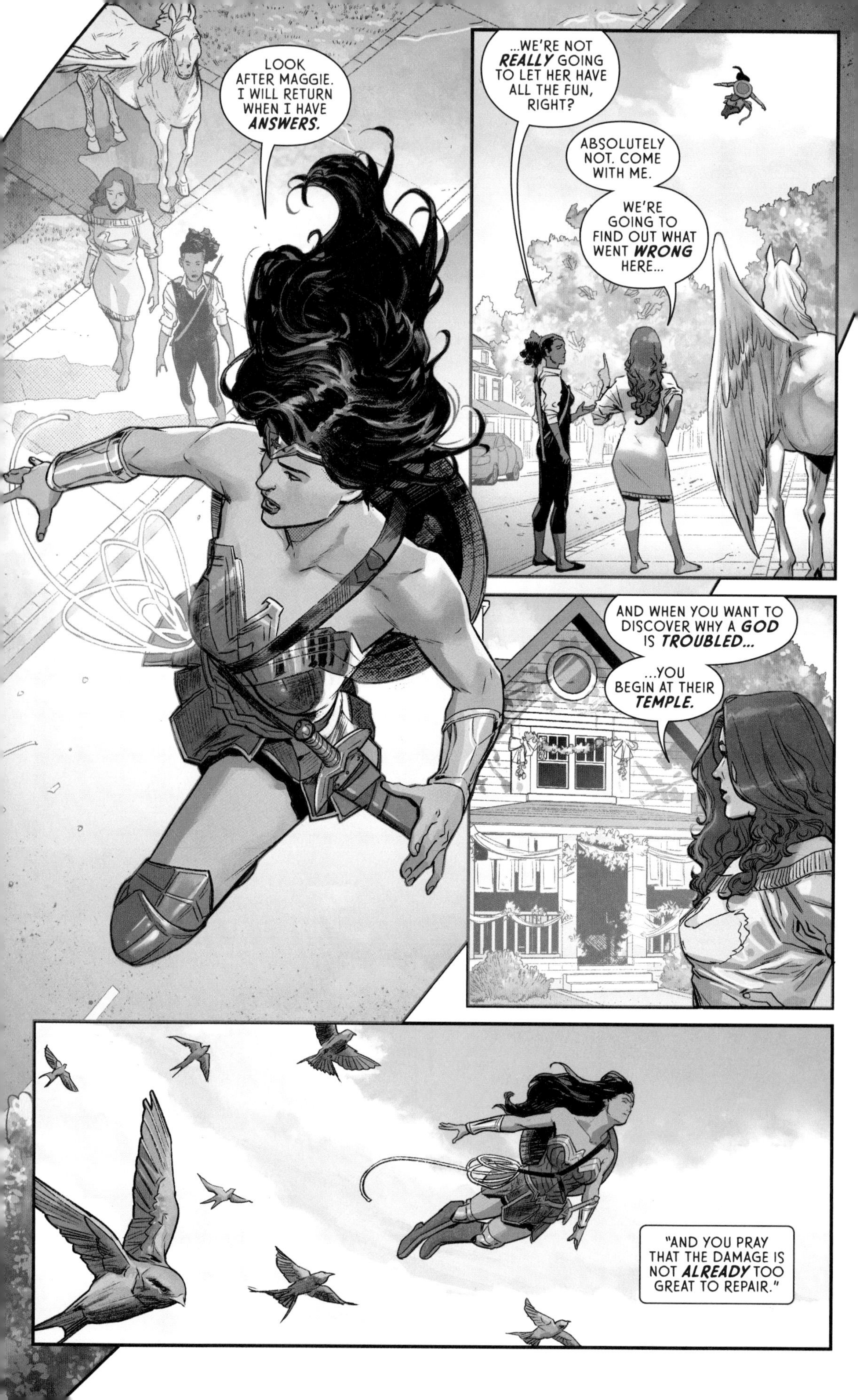
LOOK AFTER MAGGIE. I WILL RETURN WHEN I HAVE ANSWERS.
...WE'RE NOT REALLY GOING TO LET HER HAVE ALL THE FUN, RIGHT?
ABSOLUTELY NOT. COME WITH ME.
WE'RE GOING TO FIND OUT WHAT WENT WRONG HERE...
AND WHEN YOU WANT TO DISCOVER WHY A GOD IS TROUBLED...
...YOU BEGIN AT THEIR TEMPLE.
"AND YOU PRAY THAT THE DAMAGE IS NOT ALREADY TOO GREAT TO REPAIR."

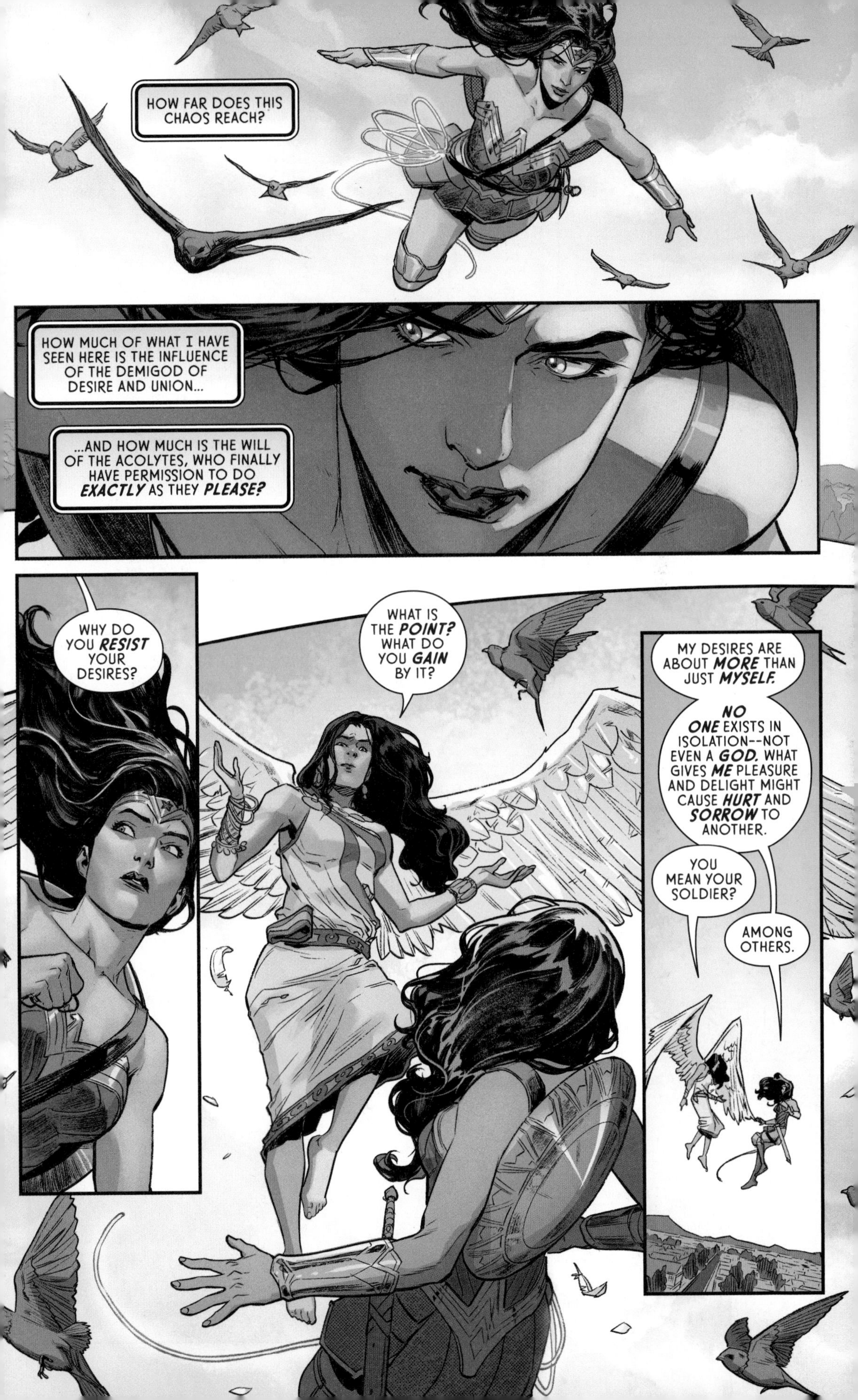

HOW FAR DOES THIS CHAOS REACH?
HOW MUCH OF WHAT I HAVE SEEN HERE IS THE INFLUENCE OF THE DEMIGOD OF DESIRE AND UNION...
...AND HOW MUCH IS THE WILL OF THE ACOLYTES, WHO FINALLY HAVE PERMISSION TO DO EXACTLY AS THEY PLEASE?
WHY DO YOU RESIST YOUR DESIRES?
WHAT IS THE POINT? WHAT DO YOU GAIN BY IT?
MY DESIRES ARE ABOUT MORE THAN JUST MYSELF.
NO ONE EXISTS IN ISOLATION--NOT EVEN A GOD. WHAT GIVES ME PLEASURE AND DELIGHT MIGHT CAUSE HURT AND SORROW TO ANOTHER.
YOU MEAN YOUR SOLDIER?
AMONG OTHERS.

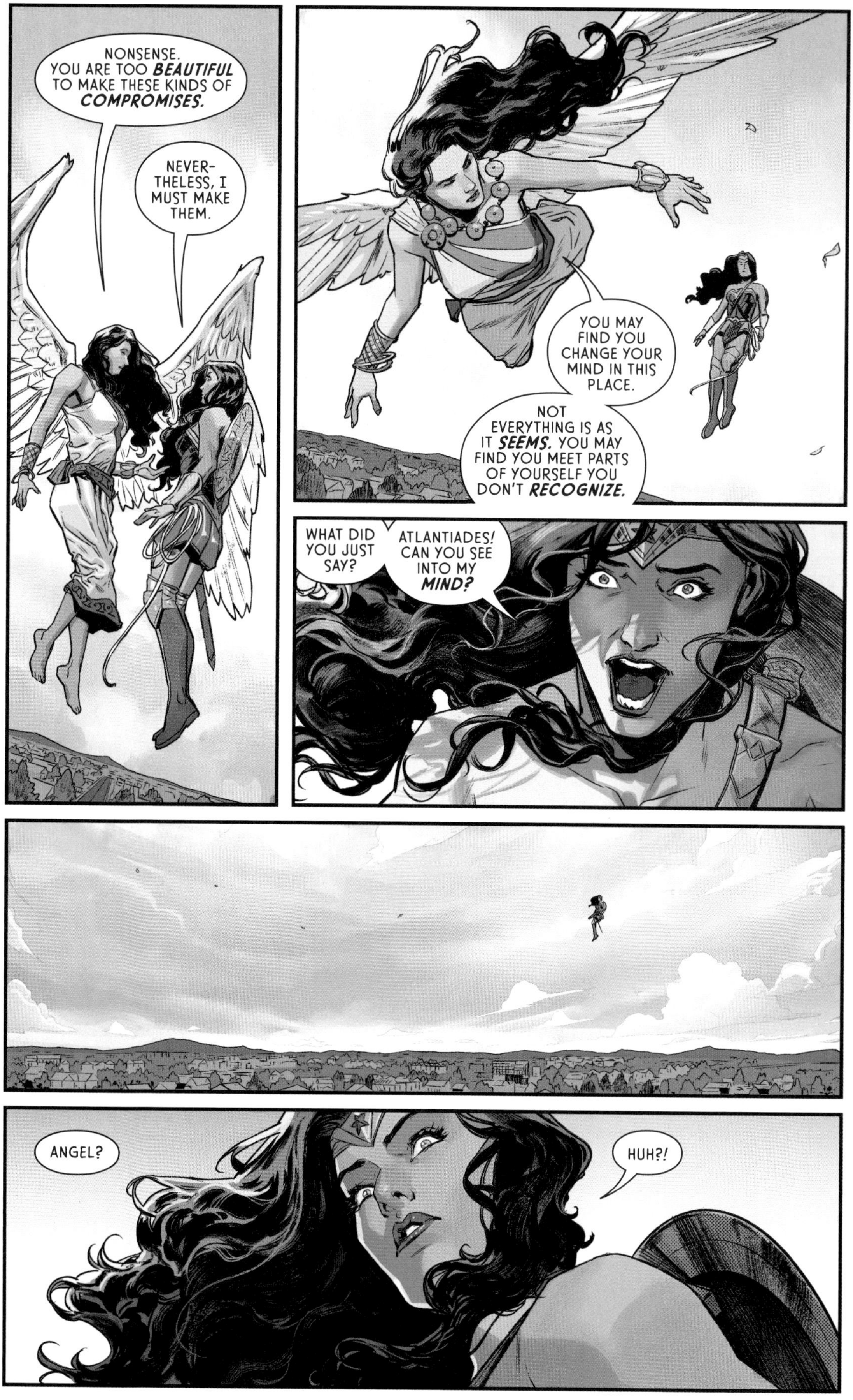
NONSENSE. YOU ARE TOO BEAUTIFUL TO MAKE THESE KINDS OF COMPROMISES.
NEVER-THELESS, I MUST MAKE THEM.
YOU MAY FIND YOU CHANGE YOUR MIND IN THIS PLACE.
NOT EVERYTHING IS AS IT SEEMS. YOU MAY FIND YOU MEET PARTS OF YOURSELF YOU DON'T RECOGNIZE.
WHAT DID YOU JUST SAY?
ATLANTIADES! CAN YOU SEE INTO MY MIND?
ANGEL?
HUH?!

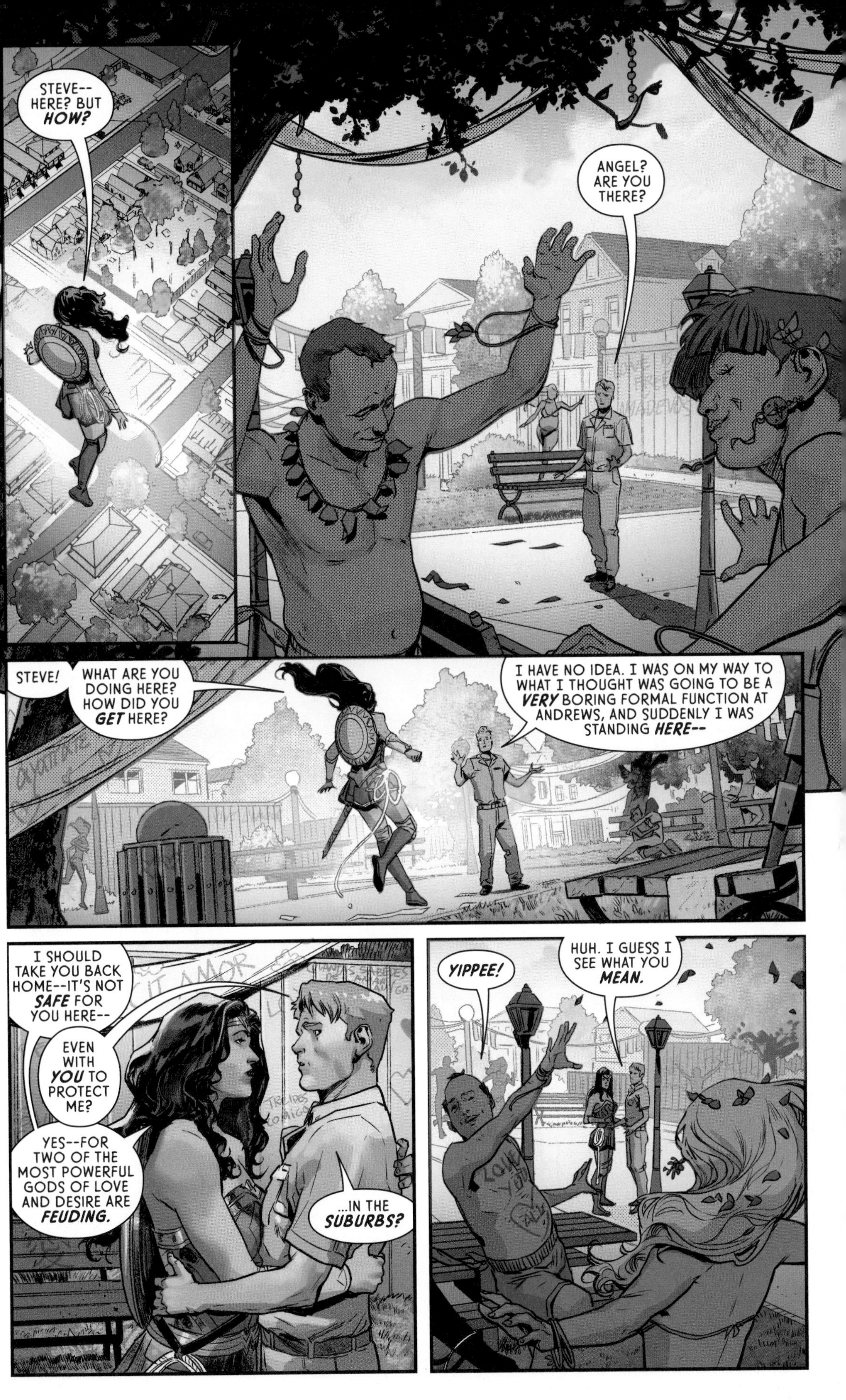

STEVE-- HERE? BUT HOW?
ANGEL? ARE YOU THERE?
STEVE!
WHAT ARE YOU DOING HERE? HOW DID YOU GET HERE?
I HAVE NO IDEA. I WAS ON MY WAY TO WHAT I THOUGHT WAS GOING TO BE A VERY BORING FORMAL FUNCTION AT ANDREWS, AND SUDDENLY I WAS STANDING HERE--
I SHOULD TAKE YOU BACK HOME--IT'S NOT SAFE FOR YOU HERE--
EVEN WITH YOU TO PROTECT ME?
YES--FOR TWO OF THE MOST POWERFUL GODS OF LOVE AND DESIRE ARE FEUDING.
...IN THE SUBURBS?
YIPPEE!
HUH. I GUESS I SEE WHAT YOU MEAN.

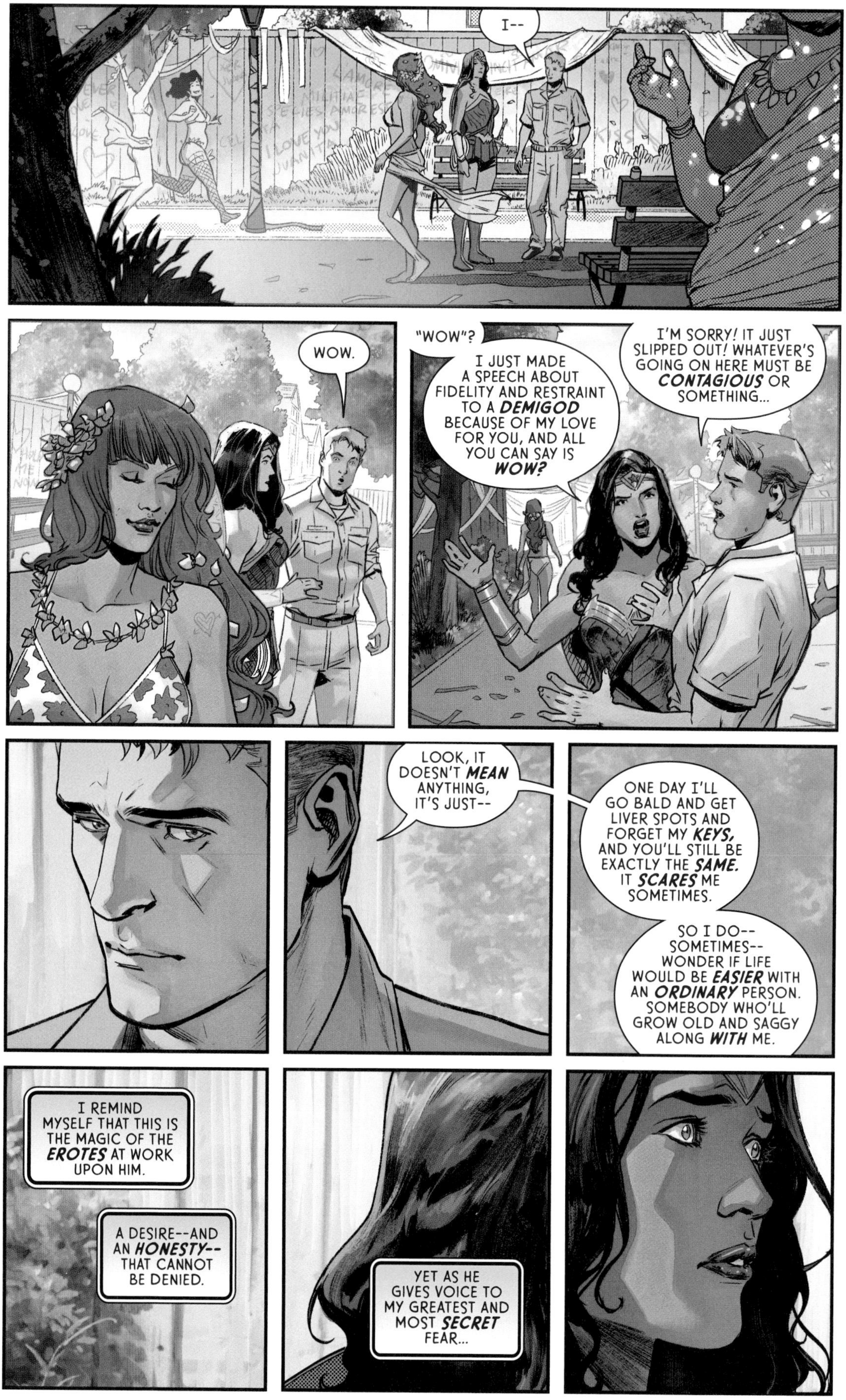
I--
WOW.
"WOW"? I JUST MADE A SPEECH ABOUT FIDELITY AND RESTRAINT TO A DEMIGOD BECAUSE OF MY LOVE FOR YOU, AND ALL YOU CAN SAY IS WOW?
I'M SORRY! IT JUST SLIPPED OUT! WHATEVER'S GOING ON HERE MUST BE CONTAGIOUS OR SOMETHING...
LOOK, IT DOESN'T MEAN ANYTHING, IT'S JUST--
ONE DAY I'LL GO BALD AND GET LIVER SPOTS AND FORGET MY KEYS, AND YOU'LL STILL BE EXACTLY THE SAME. IT SCARES ME SOMETIMES.
SO I DO--SOMETIMES--WONDER IF LIFE WOULD BE EASIER WITH AN ORDINARY PERSON. SOMEBODY WHO'LL GROW OLD AND SAGGY ALONG WITH ME.
I REMIND MYSELF THAT THIS IS THE MAGIC OF THE EROTES AT WORK UPON HIM.
A DESIRE--AND AN HONESTY--THAT CANNOT BE DENIED.
YET AS HE GIVES VOICE TO MY GREATEST AND MOST SECRET FEAR...

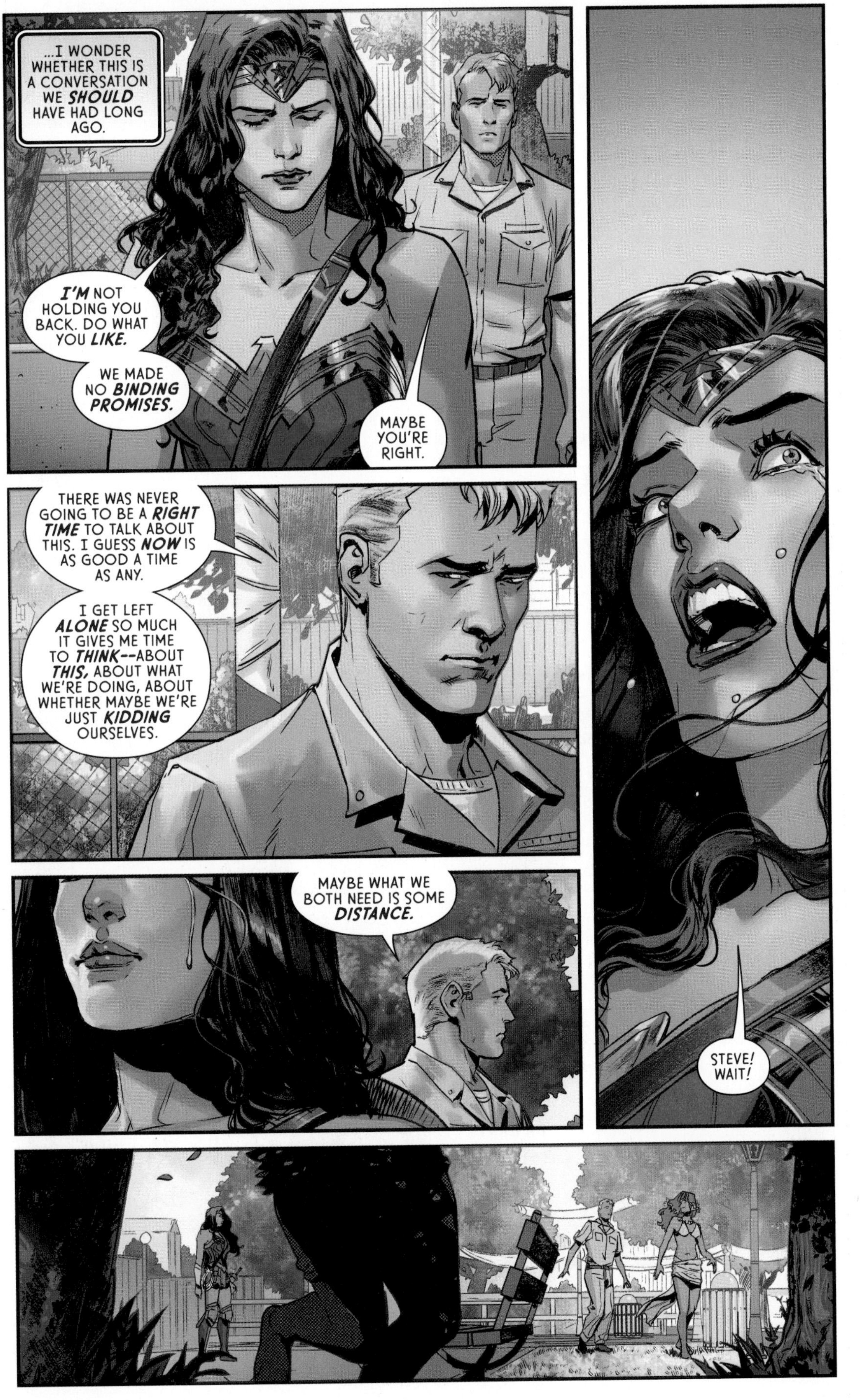

...I WONDER WHETHER THIS IS A CONVERSATION WE *SHOULD* HAVE HAD LONG AGO.
I'M NOT HOLDING YOU BACK. DO WHAT YOU *LIKE.*
WE MADE NO *BINDING PROMISES.*
MAYBE YOU'RE RIGHT.
THERE WAS NEVER GOING TO BE A *RIGHT TIME* TO TALK ABOUT THIS. I GUESS *NOW* IS AS GOOD A TIME AS ANY.
I GET LEFT *ALONE* SO MUCH IT GIVES ME TIME TO *THINK*--ABOUT *THIS,* ABOUT WHAT WE'RE DOING, ABOUT WHETHER MAYBE WE'RE JUST *KIDDING* OURSELVES.
MAYBE WHAT WE BOTH NEED IS SOME *DISTANCE.*
STEVE! WAIT!

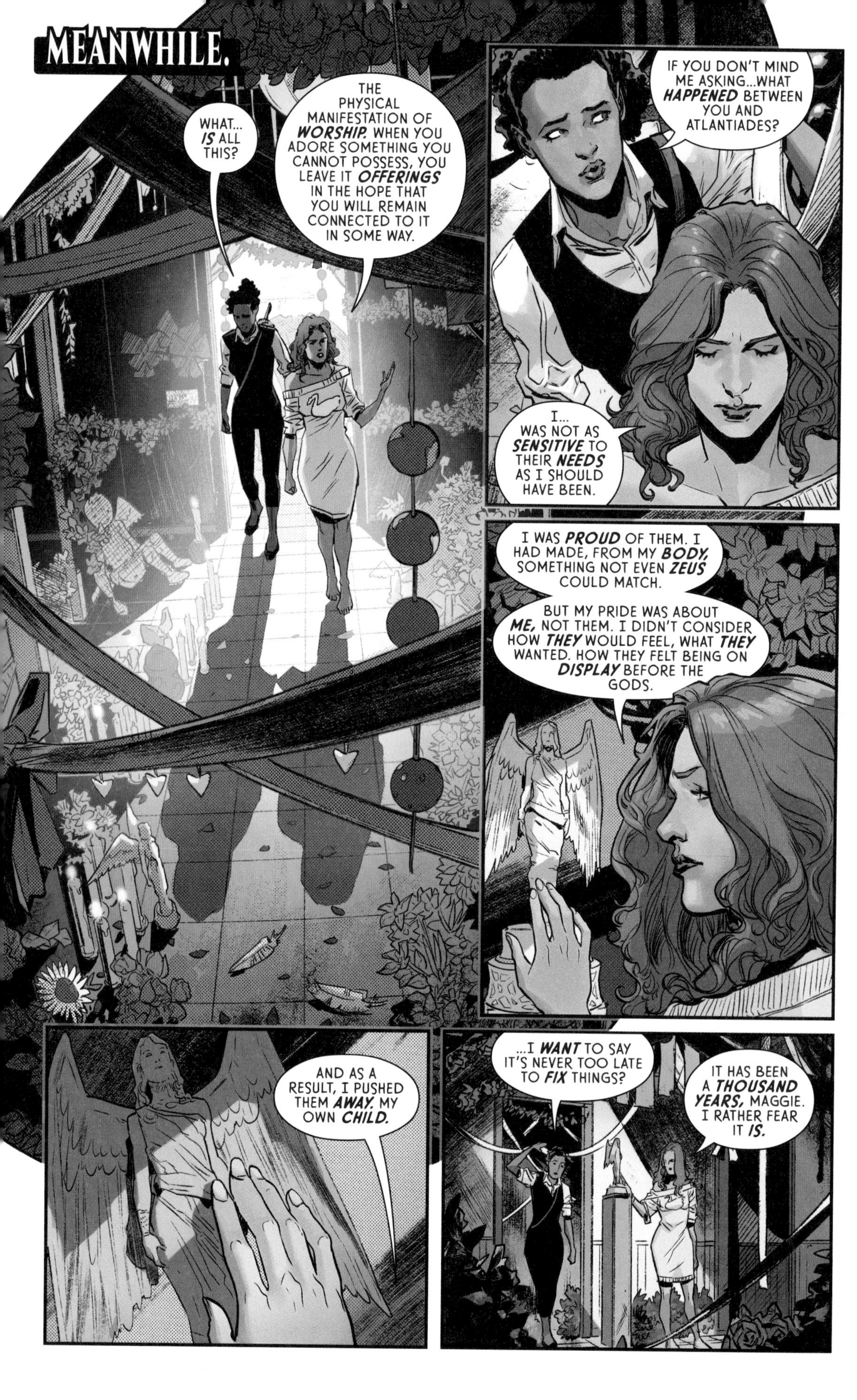
MEANWHILE.
WHAT... IS ALL THIS?
THE PHYSICAL MANIFESTATION OF WORSHIP. WHEN YOU ADORE SOMETHING YOU CANNOT POSSESS, YOU LEAVE IT OFFERINGS IN THE HOPE THAT YOU WILL REMAIN CONNECTED TO IT IN SOME WAY.
IF YOU DON'T MIND ME ASKING...WHAT HAPPENED BETWEEN YOU AND ATLANTIADES?
I... WAS NOT AS SENSITIVE TO THEIR NEEDS AS I SHOULD HAVE BEEN.
I WAS PROUD OF THEM. I HAD MADE, FROM MY BODY, SOMETHING NOT EVEN ZEUS COULD MATCH.
BUT MY PRIDE WAS ABOUT ME, NOT THEM. I DIDN'T CONSIDER HOW THEY WOULD FEEL, WHAT THEY WANTED. HOW THEY FELT BEING ON DISPLAY BEFORE THE GODS.
AND AS A RESULT, I PUSHED THEM AWAY. MY OWN CHILD.
...I WANT TO SAY IT'S NEVER TOO LATE TO FIX THINGS?
IT HAS BEEN A THOUSAND YEARS, MAGGIE. I RATHER FEAR IT IS.

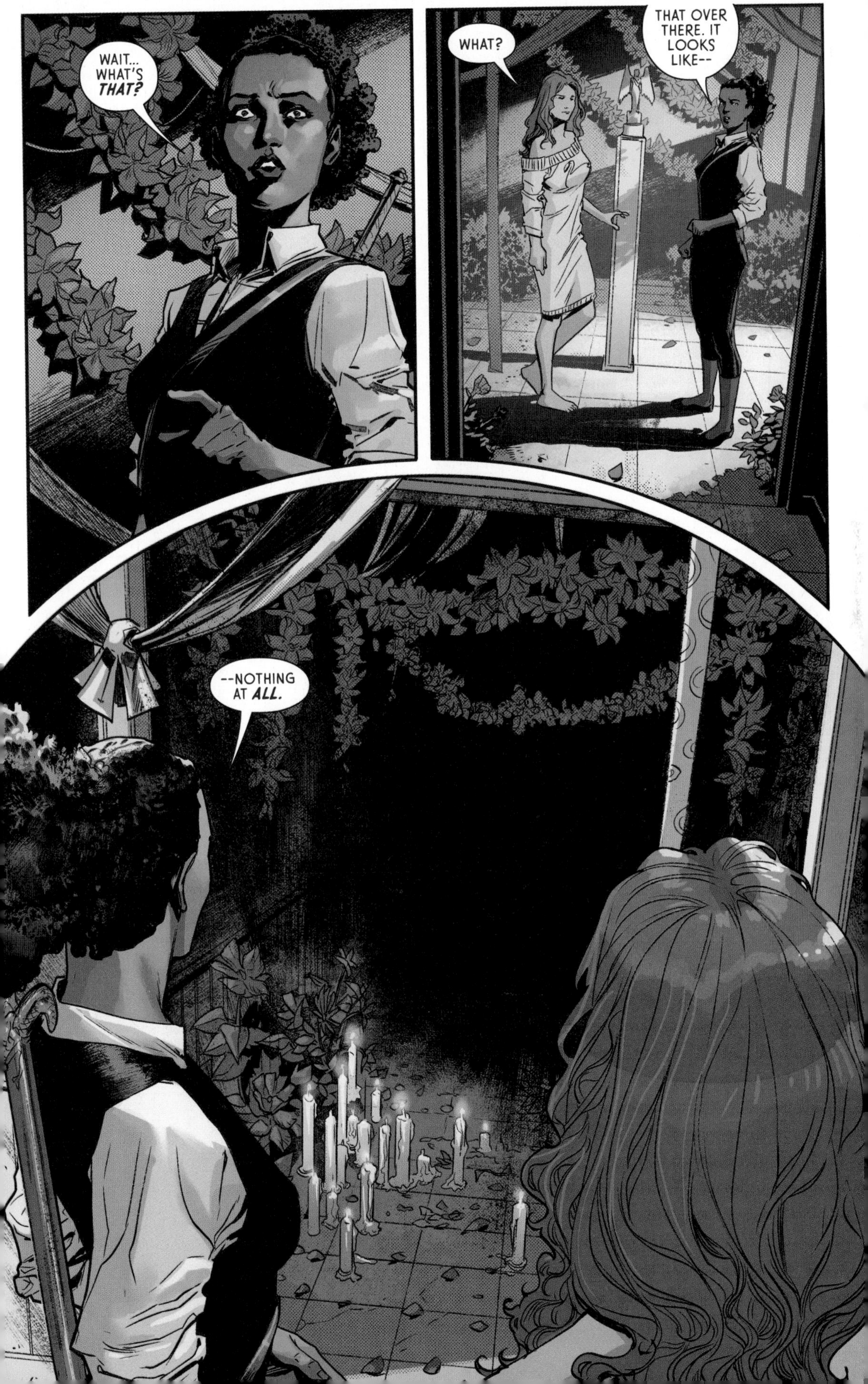
WAIT... WHAT'S *THAT?*
WHAT?
THAT OVER THERE. IT LOOKS LIKE--
--NOTHING AT *ALL.*

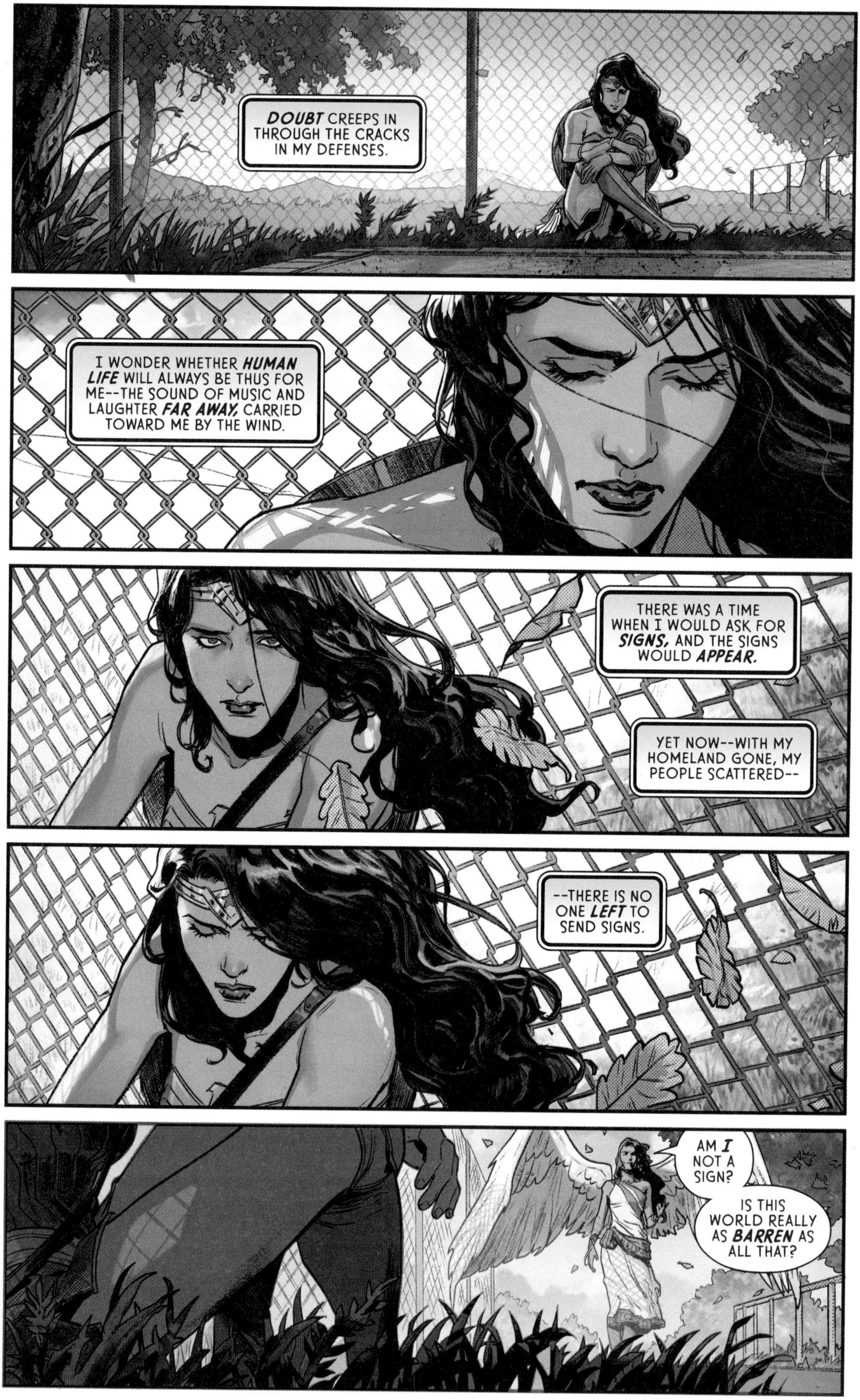
DOUBT CREEPS IN THROUGH THE CRACKS IN MY DEFENSES.
I WONDER WHETHER HUMAN LIFE WILL ALWAYS BE THUS FOR ME--THE SOUND OF MUSIC AND LAUGHTER FAR AWAY, CARRIED TOWARD ME BY THE WIND.
THERE WAS A TIME WHEN I WOULD ASK FOR SIGNS, AND THE SIGNS WOULD APPEAR.
YET NOW--WITH MY HOMELAND GONE, MY PEOPLE SCATTERED--
--THERE IS NO ONE LEFT TO SEND SIGNS.
AM I NOT A SIGN?
IS THIS WORLD REALLY AS BARREN AS ALL THAT?

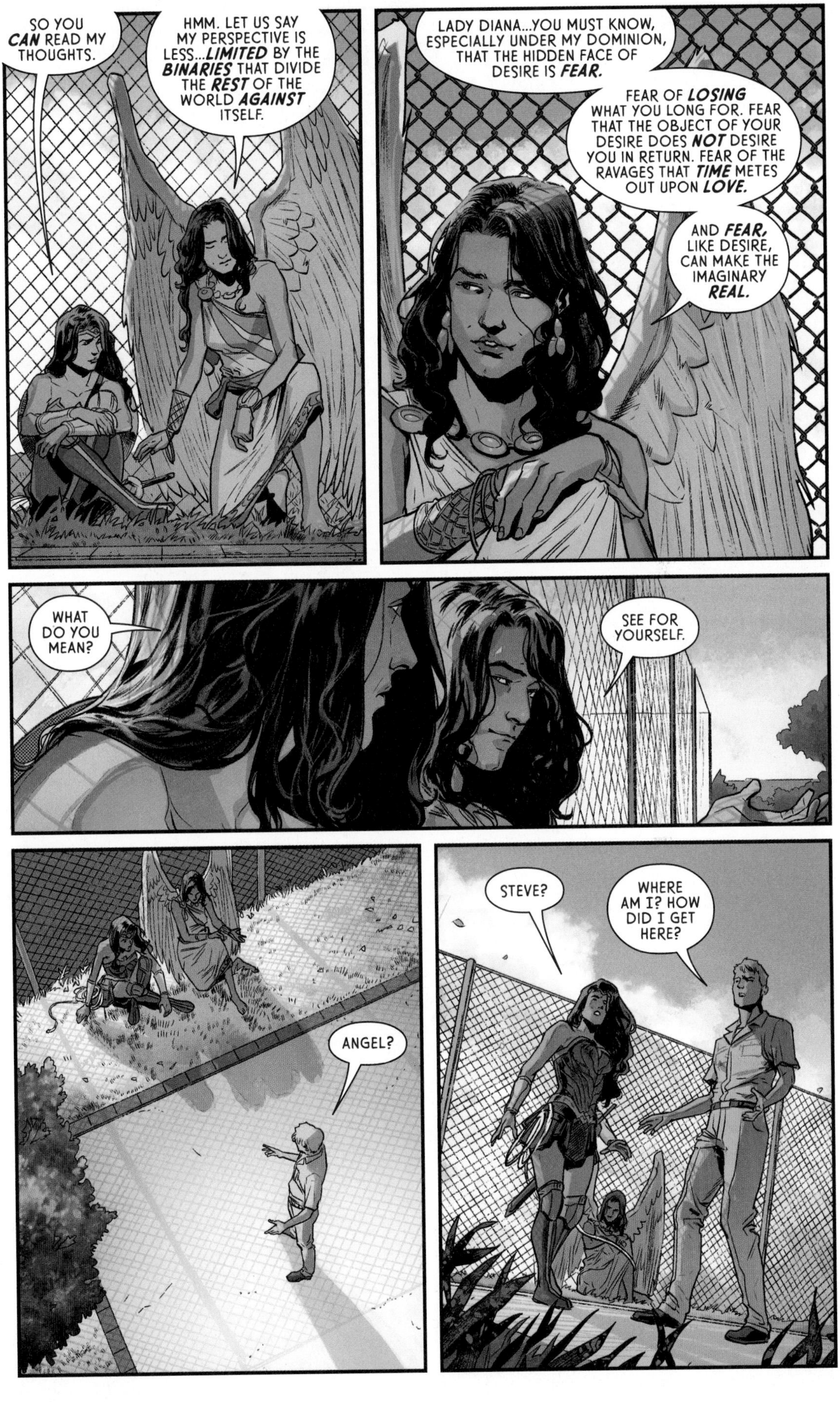

SO YOU CAN READ MY THOUGHTS.
HMM. LET US SAY MY PERSPECTIVE IS LESS...LIMITED BY THE BINARIES THAT DIVIDE THE REST OF THE WORLD AGAINST ITSELF.
LADY DIANA...YOU MUST KNOW, ESPECIALLY UNDER MY DOMINION, THAT THE HIDDEN FACE OF DESIRE IS FEAR.
FEAR OF LOSING WHAT YOU LONG FOR. FEAR THAT THE OBJECT OF YOUR DESIRE DOES NOT DESIRE YOU IN RETURN. FEAR OF THE RAVAGES THAT TIME METES OUT UPON LOVE.
AND FEAR, LIKE DESIRE, CAN MAKE THE IMAGINARY REAL.
WHAT DO YOU MEAN?
SEE FOR YOURSELF.
ANGEL?
STEVE?
WHERE AM I? HOW DID I GET HERE?

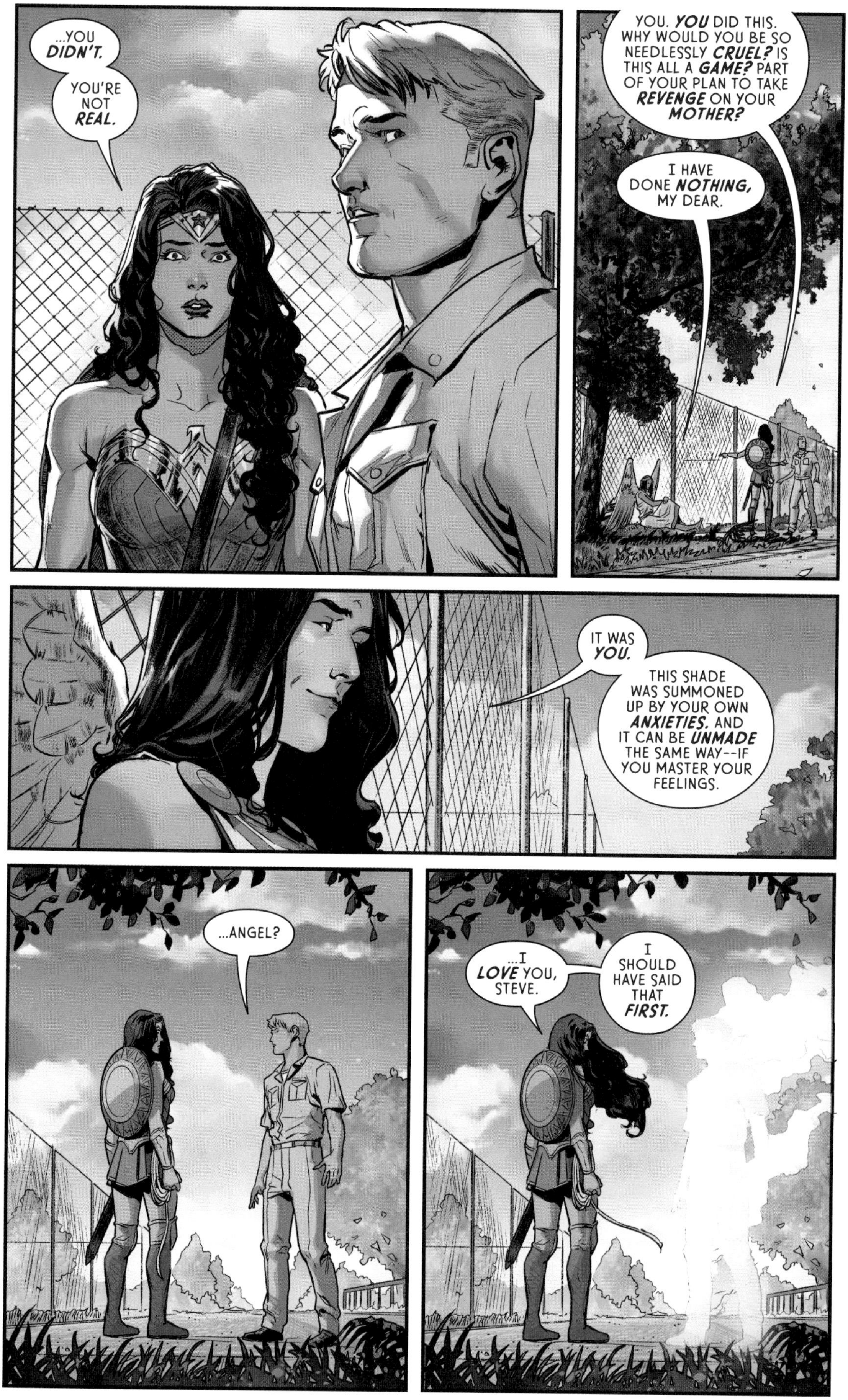
...YOU DIDN'T.
YOU'RE NOT REAL.
YOU. YOU DID THIS. WHY WOULD YOU BE SO NEEDLESSLY CRUEL? IS THIS ALL A GAME? PART OF YOUR PLAN TO TAKE REVENGE ON YOUR MOTHER?
I HAVE DONE NOTHING, MY DEAR.
IT WAS YOU.
THIS SHADE WAS SUMMONED UP BY YOUR OWN ANXIETIES. AND IT CAN BE UNMADE THE SAME WAY--IF YOU MASTER YOUR FEELINGS.
...ANGEL?
...I LOVE YOU, STEVE.
I SHOULD HAVE SAID THAT FIRST.

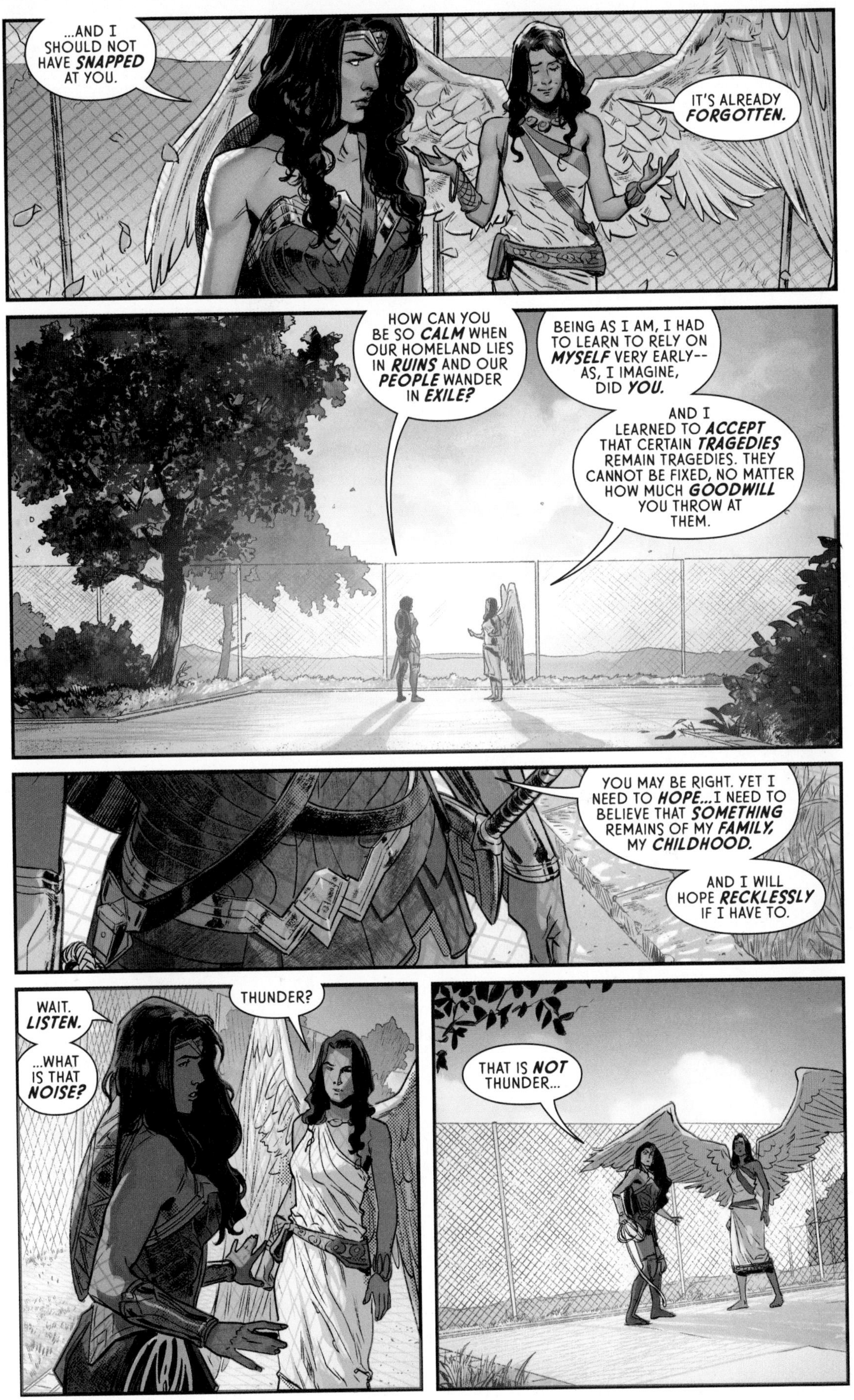
...AND I SHOULD NOT HAVE SNAPPED AT YOU.
IT'S ALREADY FORGOTTEN.
HOW CAN YOU BE SO CALM WHEN OUR HOMELAND LIES IN RUINS AND OUR PEOPLE WANDER IN EXILE?
BEING AS I AM, I HAD TO LEARN TO RELY ON MYSELF VERY EARLY-- AS, I IMAGINE, DID YOU.
AND I LEARNED TO ACCEPT THAT CERTAIN TRAGEDIES REMAIN TRAGEDIES. THEY CANNOT BE FIXED, NO MATTER HOW MUCH GOODWILL YOU THROW AT THEM.
YOU MAY BE RIGHT. YET I NEED TO HOPE...I NEED TO BELIEVE THAT SOMETHING REMAINS OF MY FAMILY, MY CHILDHOOD.
AND I WILL HOPE RECKLESSLY IF I HAVE TO.
WAIT. LISTEN.
THUNDER?
...WHAT IS THAT NOISE?
THAT IS NOT THUNDER...

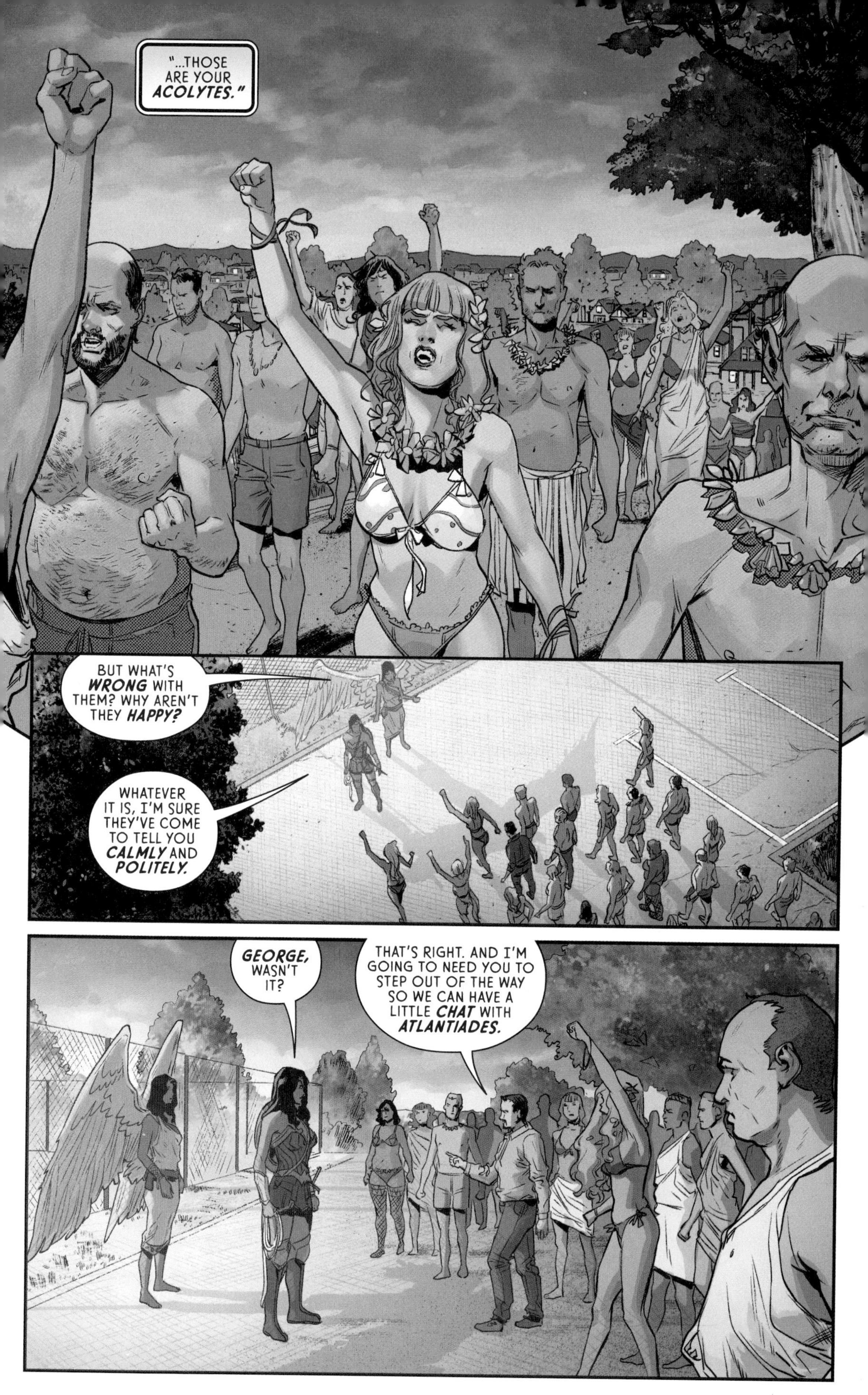
"...THOSE ARE YOUR ACOLYTES."
BUT WHAT'S WRONG WITH THEM? WHY AREN'T THEY HAPPY?
WHATEVER IT IS, I'M SURE THEY'VE COME TO TELL YOU CALMLY AND POLITELY.
GEORGE, WASN'T IT?
THAT'S RIGHT. AND I'M GOING TO NEED YOU TO STEP OUT OF THE WAY SO WE CAN HAVE A LITTLE CHAT WITH ATLANTIADES.

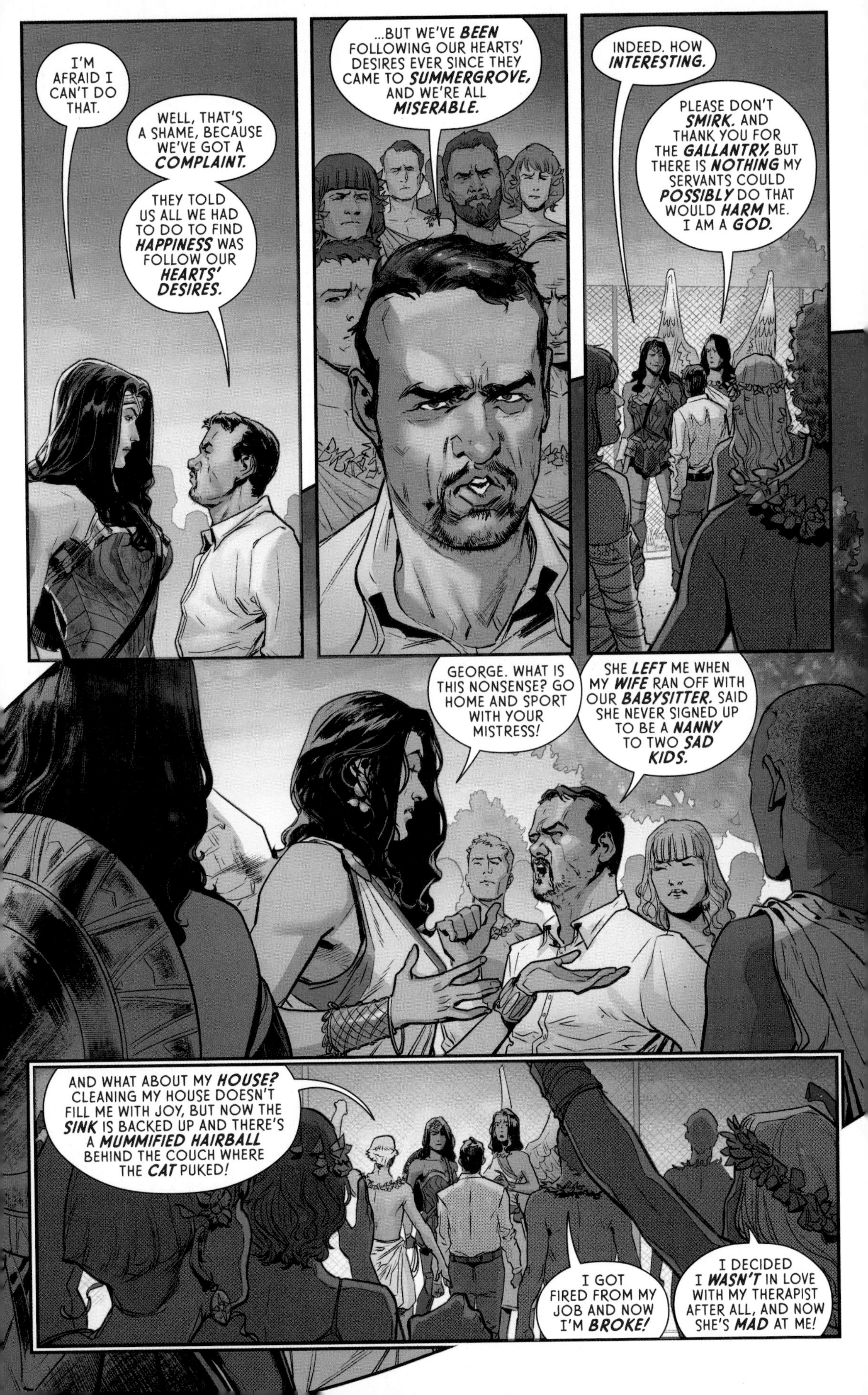
I'M AFRAID I CAN'T DO THAT.
WELL, THAT'S A SHAME, BECAUSE WE'VE GOT A COMPLAINT.
THEY TOLD US ALL WE HAD TO DO TO FIND HAPPINESS WAS FOLLOW OUR HEARTS' DESIRES.
...BUT WE'VE BEEN FOLLOWING OUR HEARTS' DESIRES EVER SINCE THEY CAME TO SUMMERGROVE, AND WE'RE ALL MISERABLE.
INDEED. HOW INTERESTING.
PLEASE DON'T SMIRK. AND THANK YOU FOR THE GALLANTRY, BUT THERE IS NOTHING MY SERVANTS COULD POSSIBLY DO THAT WOULD HARM ME. I AM A GOD.
GEORGE. WHAT IS THIS NONSENSE? GO HOME AND SPORT WITH YOUR MISTRESS!
SHE LEFT ME WHEN MY WIFE RAN OFF WITH OUR BABYSITTER. SAID SHE NEVER SIGNED UP TO BE A NANNY TO TWO SAD KIDS.
AND WHAT ABOUT MY HOUSE? CLEANING MY HOUSE DOESN'T FILL ME WITH JOY, BUT NOW THE SINK IS BACKED UP AND THERE'S A MUMMIFIED HAIRBALL BEHIND THE COUCH WHERE THE CAT PUKED!
I GOT FIRED FROM MY JOB AND NOW I'M BROKE!
I DECIDED I WASN'T IN LOVE WITH MY THERAPIST AFTER ALL, AND NOW SHE'S MAD AT ME!

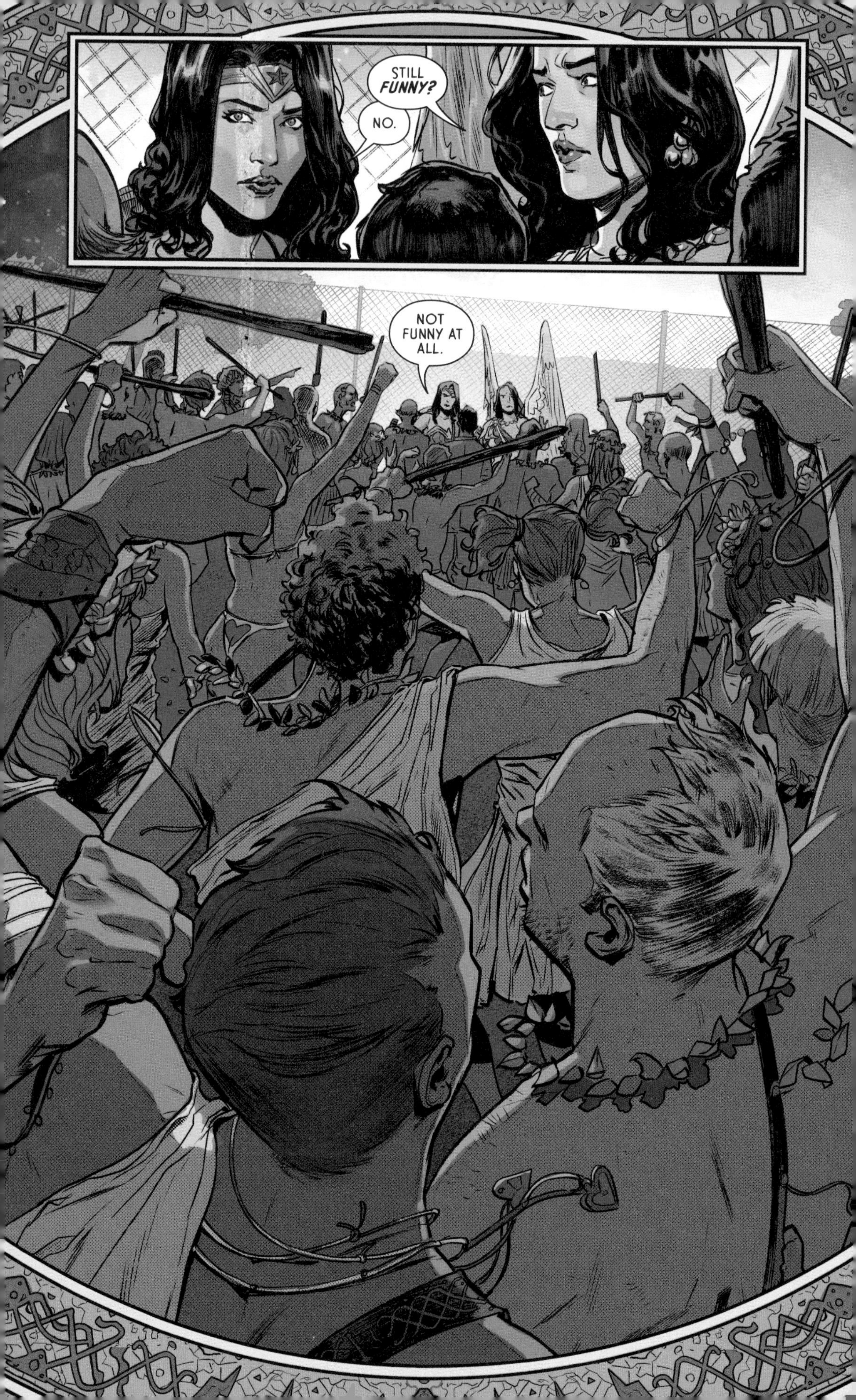
STILL FUNNY?
NO.
NOT FUNNY AT ALL.

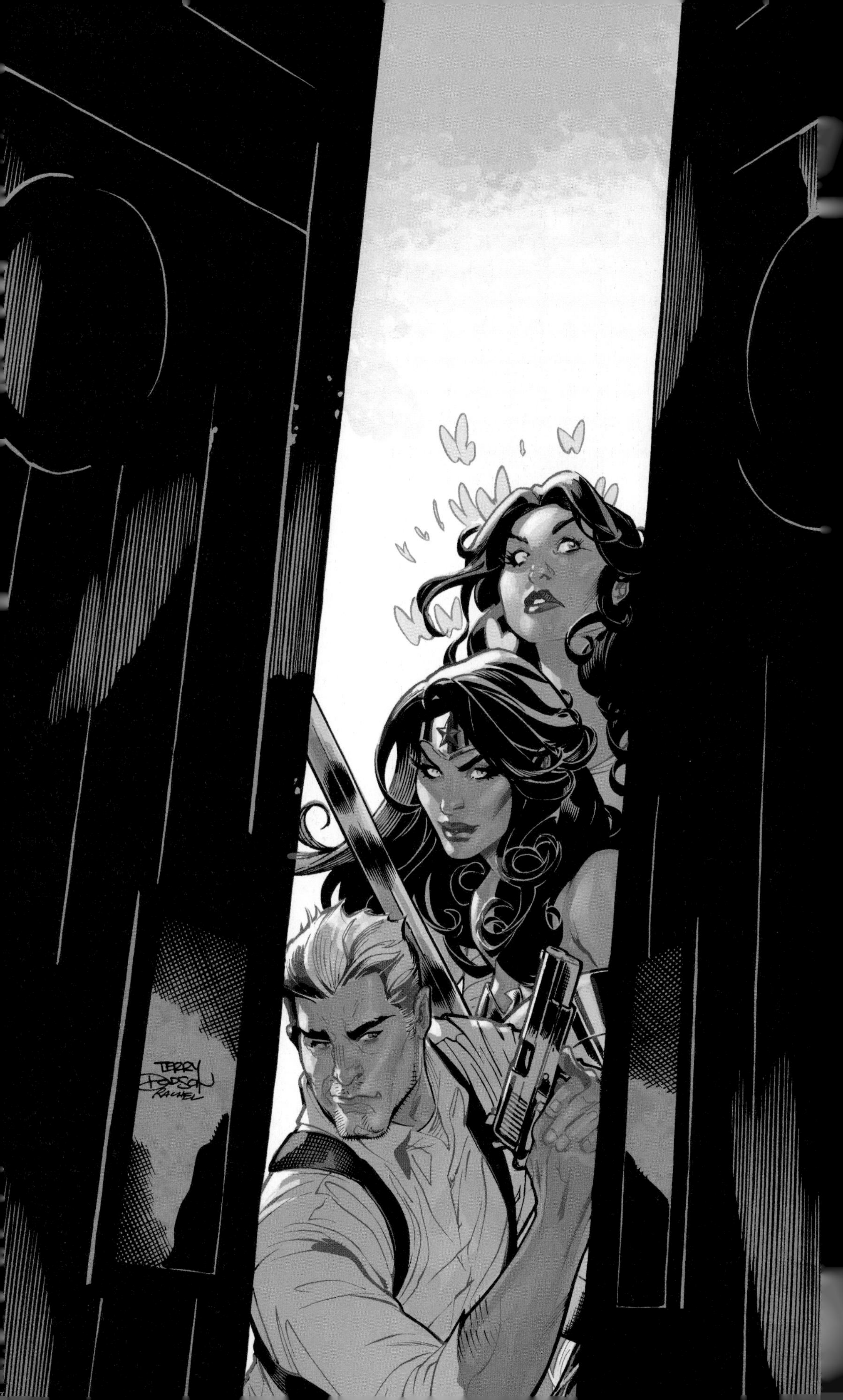
TERRY
DODSON
RACHEL

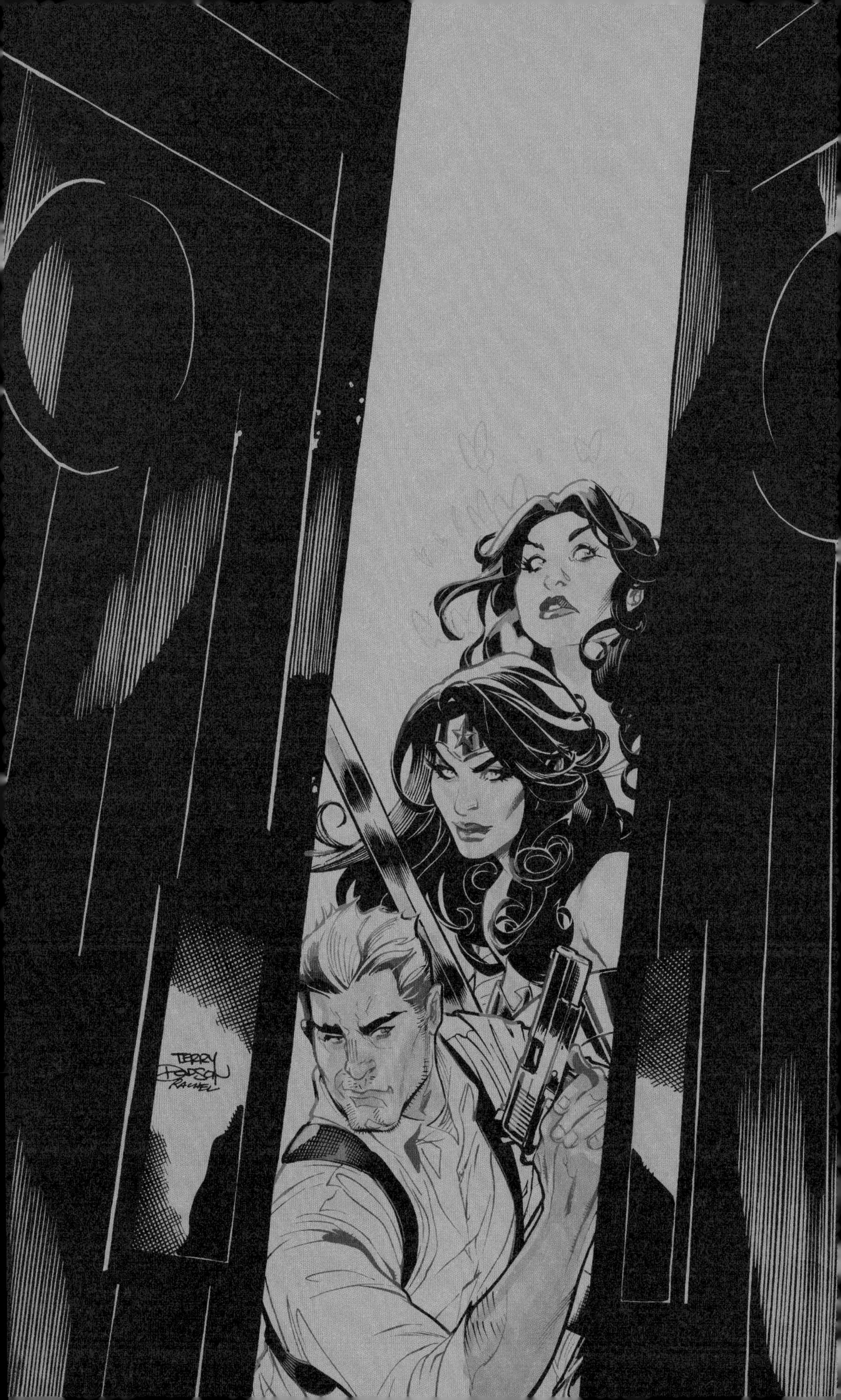
TERRY
DODSON
RACHEL

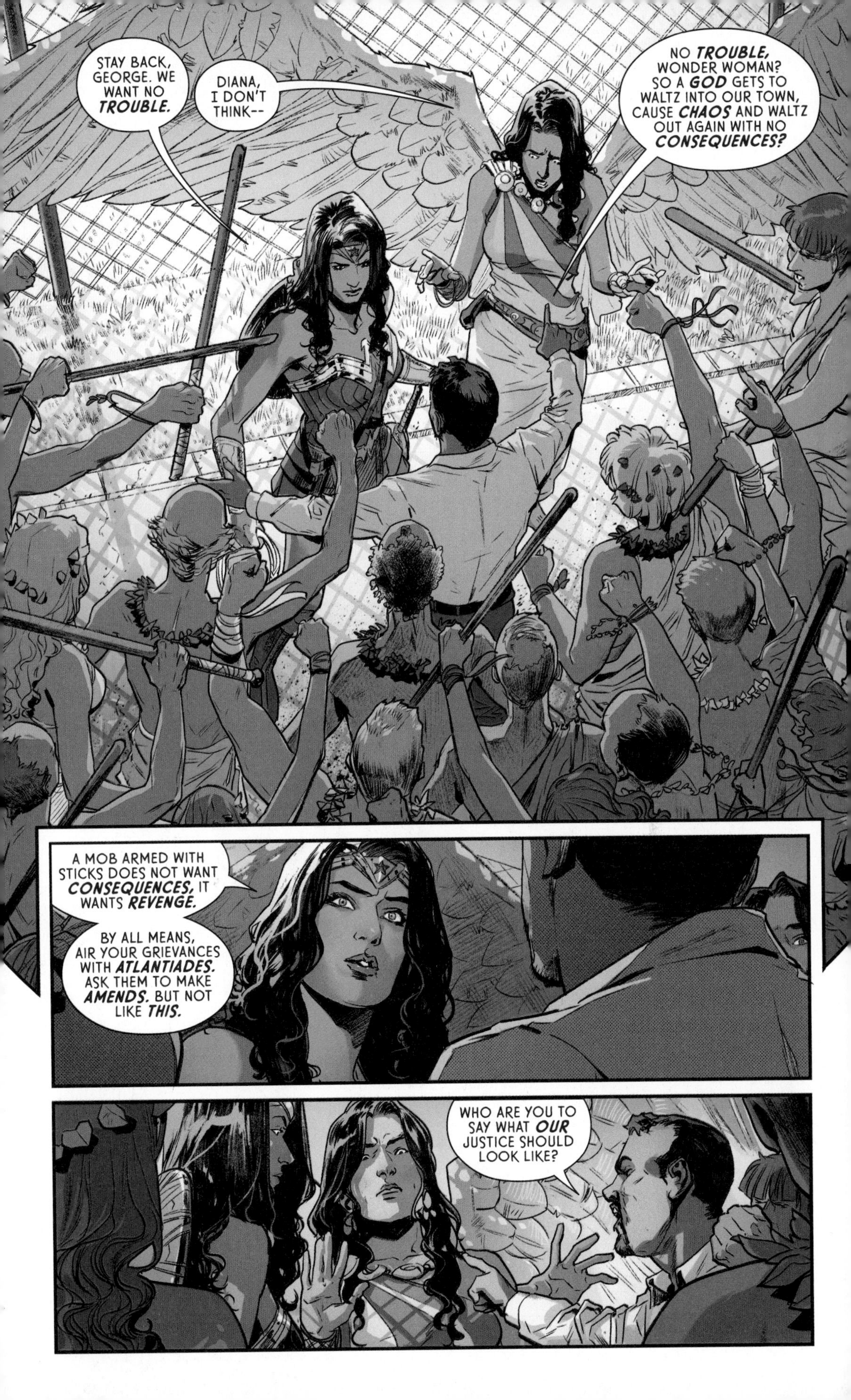
STAY BACK, GEORGE. WE WANT NO TROUBLE.
DIANA, I DON'T THINK--
NO TROUBLE, WONDER WOMAN? SO A GOD GETS TO WALTZ INTO OUR TOWN, CAUSE CHAOS AND WALTZ OUT AGAIN WITH NO CONSEQUENCES?
A MOB ARMED WITH STICKS DOES NOT WANT CONSEQUENCES, IT WANTS REVENGE.
BY ALL MEANS, AIR YOUR GRIEVANCES WITH ATLANTIADES. ASK THEM TO MAKE AMENDS. BUT NOT LIKE THIS.
WHO ARE YOU TO SAY WHAT OUR JUSTICE SHOULD LOOK LIKE?

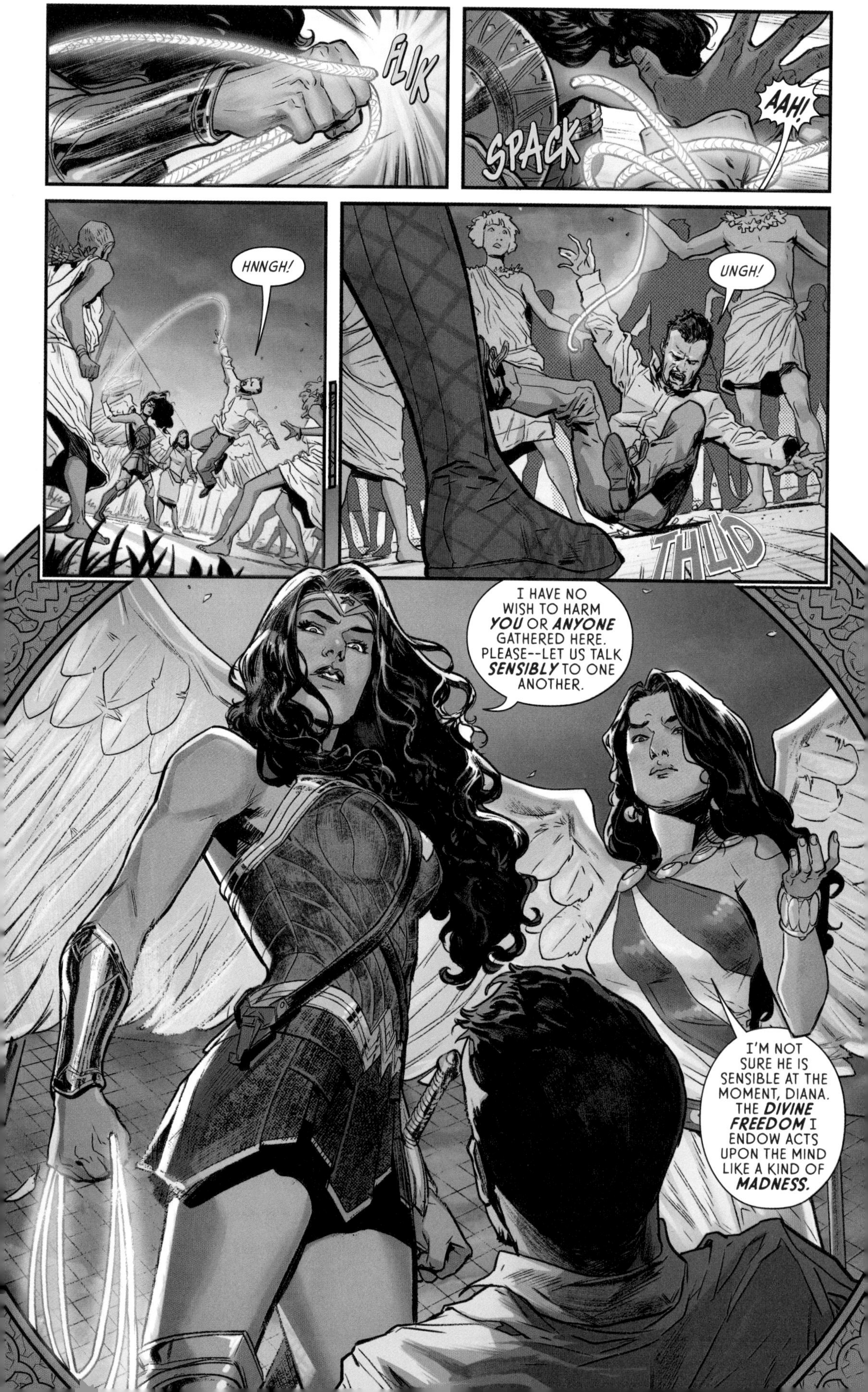
FLIK
SPACK
AAH!
HNNGH!
UNGH!
THUD
I HAVE NO WISH TO HARM *YOU* OR *ANYONE* GATHERED HERE. PLEASE--LET US TALK *SENSIBLY* TO ONE ANOTHER.
I'M NOT SURE HE IS SENSIBLE AT THE MOMENT, DIANA. THE *DIVINE FREEDOM* I ENDOW ACTS UPON THE MIND LIKE A KIND OF *MADNESS.*

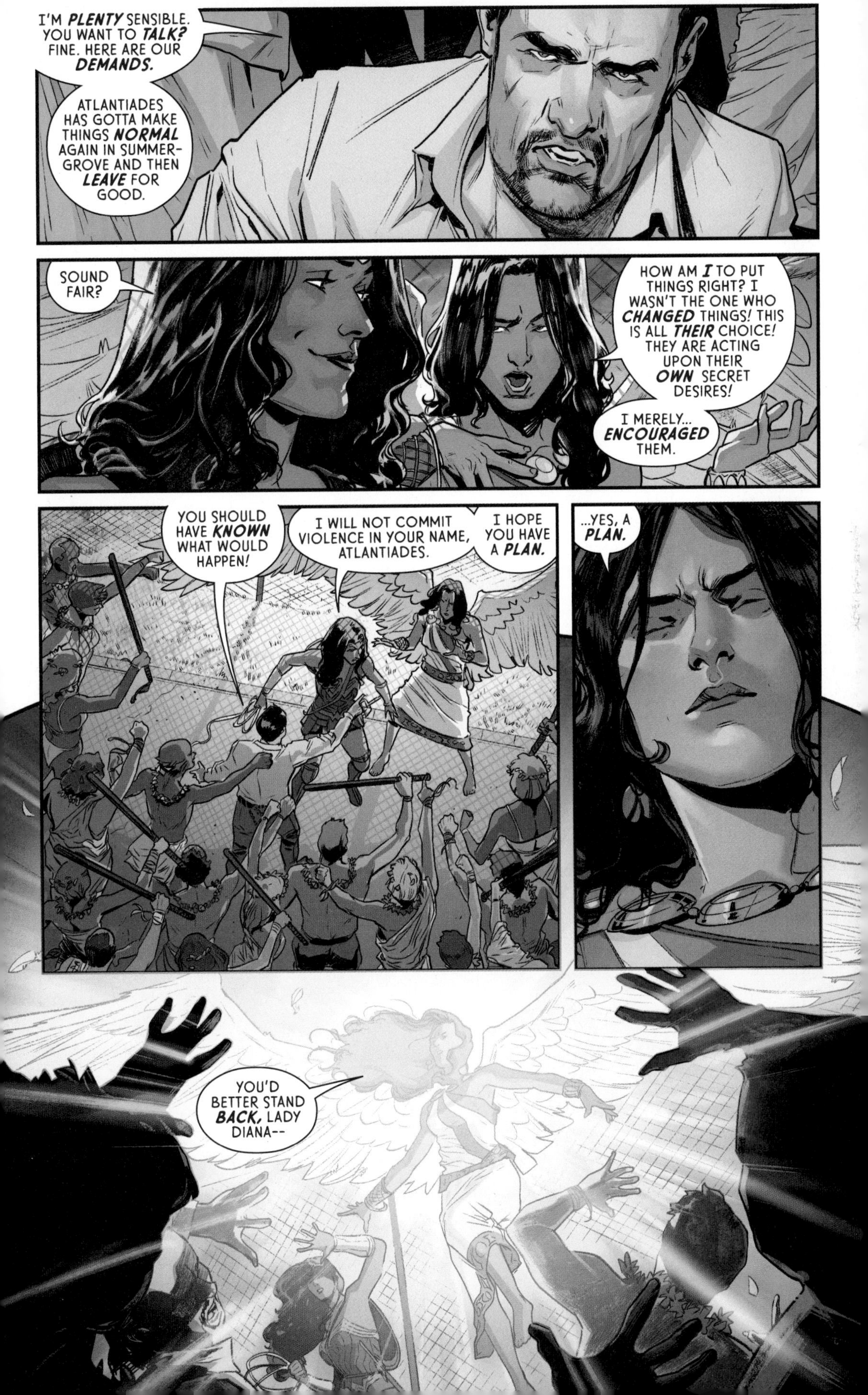
I'M PLENTY SENSIBLE. YOU WANT TO TALK? FINE. HERE ARE OUR DEMANDS.
ATLANTIADES HAS GOTTA MAKE THINGS NORMAL AGAIN IN SUMMER-GROVE AND THEN LEAVE FOR GOOD.
SOUND FAIR?
HOW AM I TO PUT THINGS RIGHT? I WASN'T THE ONE WHO CHANGED THINGS! THIS IS ALL THEIR CHOICE! THEY ARE ACTING UPON THEIR OWN SECRET DESIRES!
I MERELY... ENCOURAGED THEM.
YOU SHOULD HAVE KNOWN WHAT WOULD HAPPEN!
I WILL NOT COMMIT VIOLENCE IN YOUR NAME, ATLANTIADES.
I HOPE YOU HAVE A PLAN.
...YES, A PLAN.
YOU'D BETTER STAND BACK, LADY DIANA--

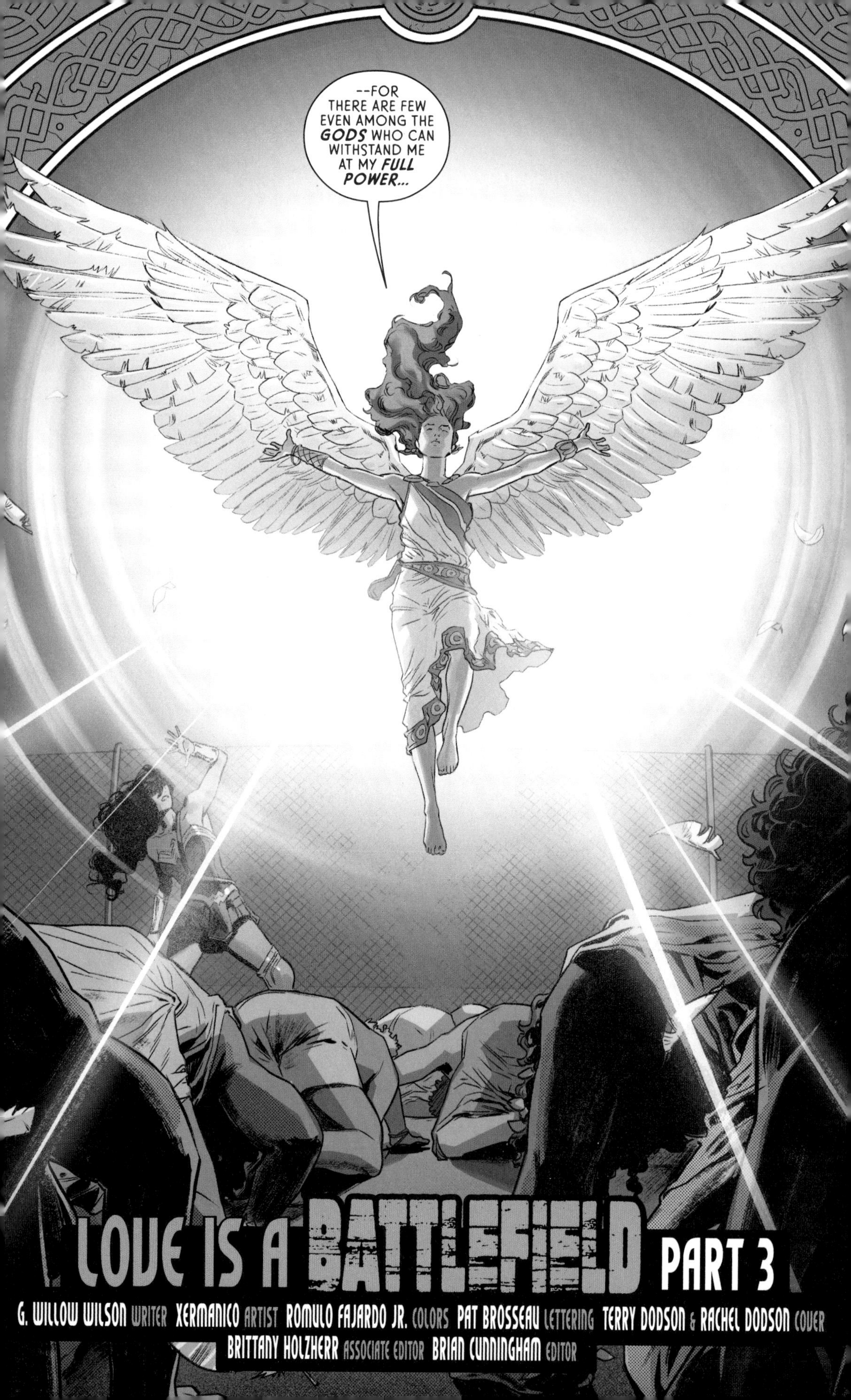
--FOR THERE ARE FEW EVEN AMONG THE GODS WHO CAN WITHSTAND ME AT MY FULL POWER...
LOVE IS A BATTLEFIELD PART 3
G. WILLOW WILSON WRITER XERMANICO ARTIST ROMULO FAJARDO JR. COLORS PAT BROSSEAU LETTERING TERRY DODSON & RACHEL DODSON COVER
BRITTANY HOLZHERR ASSOCIATE EDITOR BRIAN CUNNINGHAM EDITOR

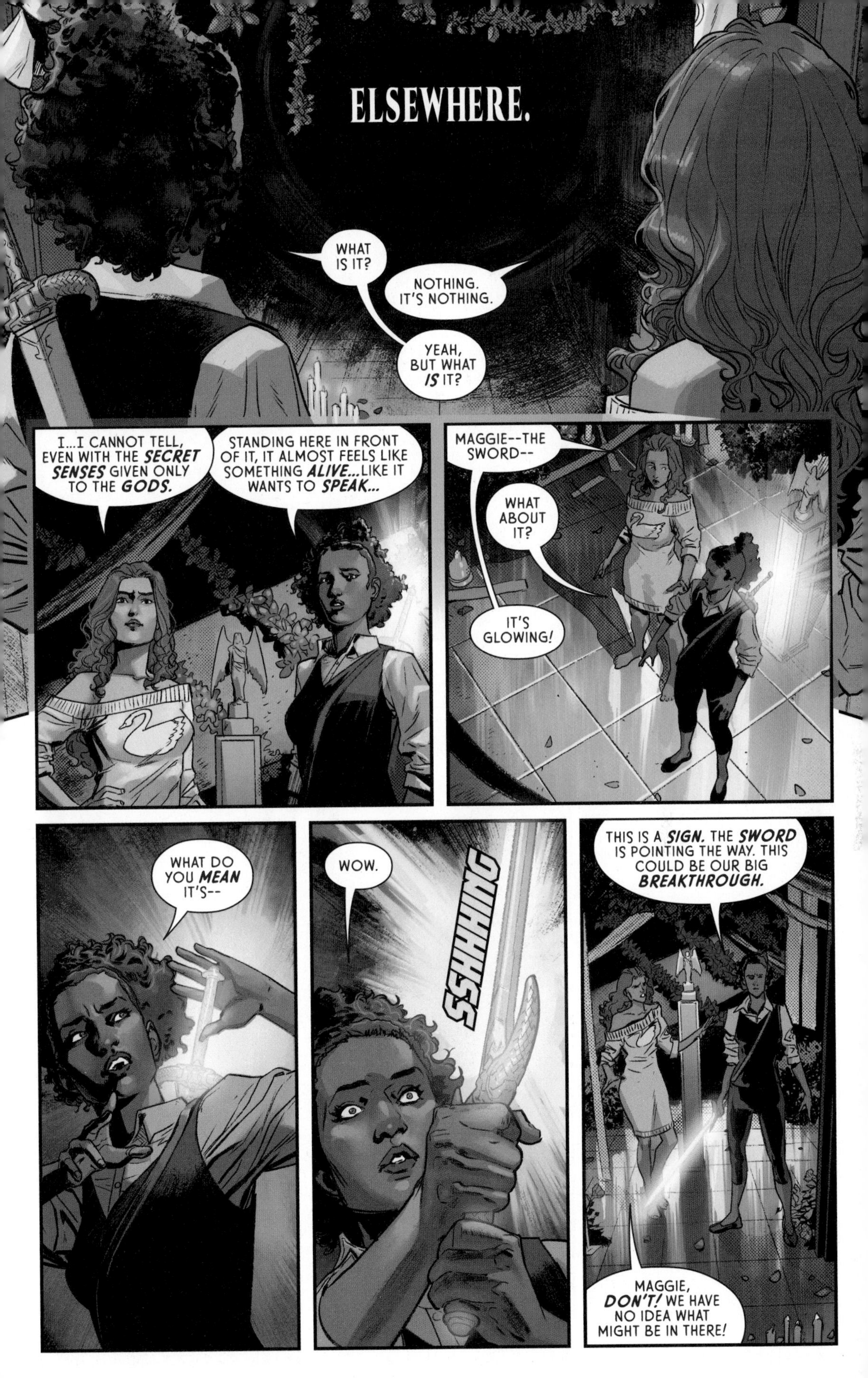
ELSEWHERE.
WHAT IS IT?
NOTHING. IT'S NOTHING.
YEAH, BUT WHAT IS IT?
I...I CANNOT TELL, EVEN WITH THE SECRET SENSES GIVEN ONLY TO THE GODS.
STANDING HERE IN FRONT OF IT, IT ALMOST FEELS LIKE SOMETHING ALIVE...LIKE IT WANTS TO SPEAK...
MAGGIE--THE SWORD--
WHAT ABOUT IT?
IT'S GLOWING!
WHAT DO YOU MEAN IT'S--
WOW.
SSHHHING
THIS IS A SIGN. THE SWORD IS POINTING THE WAY. THIS COULD BE OUR BIG BREAKTHROUGH.
MAGGIE, DON'T! WE HAVE NO IDEA WHAT MIGHT BE IN THERE!

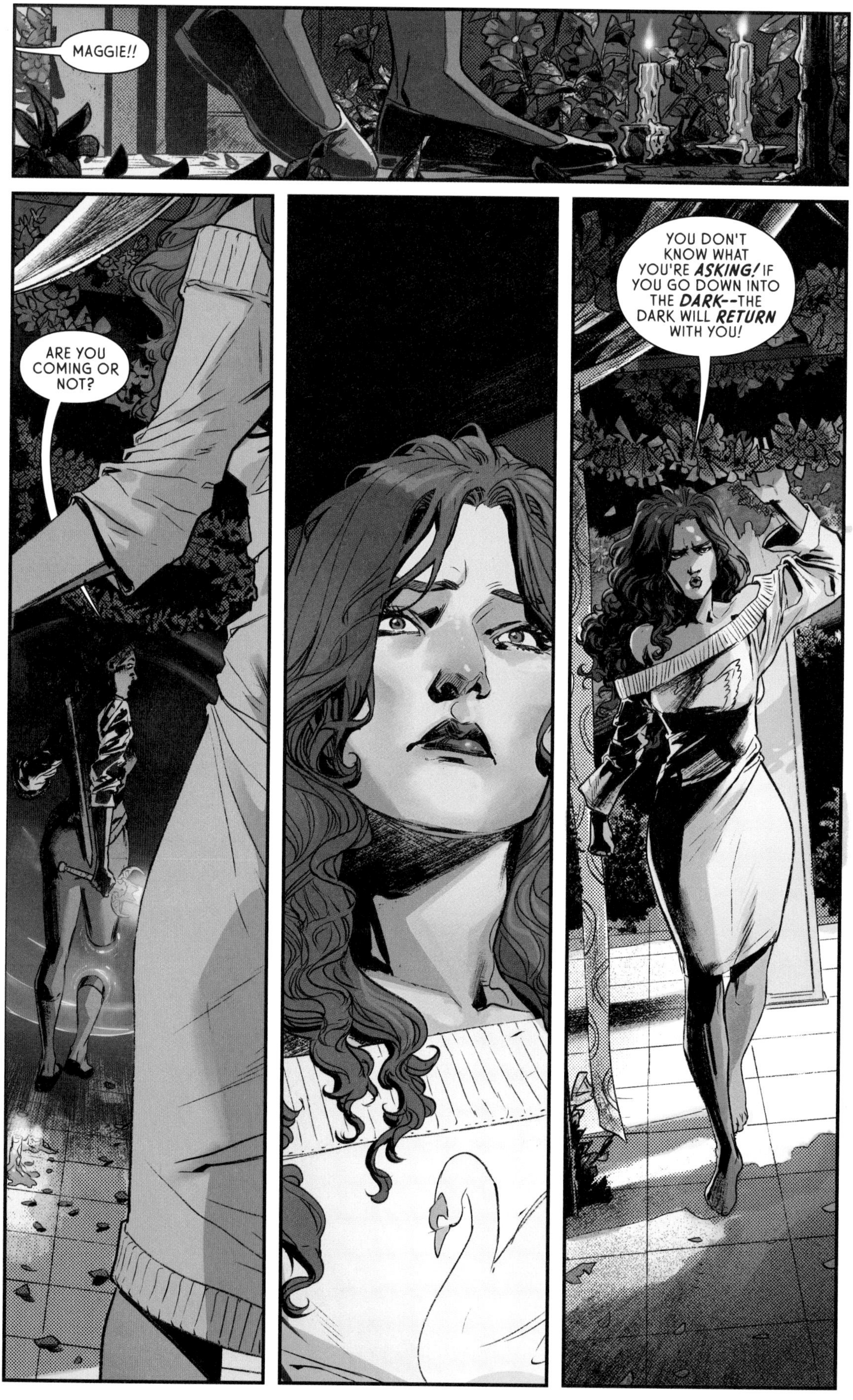
MAGGIE!!
ARE YOU COMING OR NOT?
YOU DON'T KNOW WHAT YOU'RE ASKING! IF YOU GO DOWN INTO THE DARK--THE DARK WILL RETURN WITH YOU!

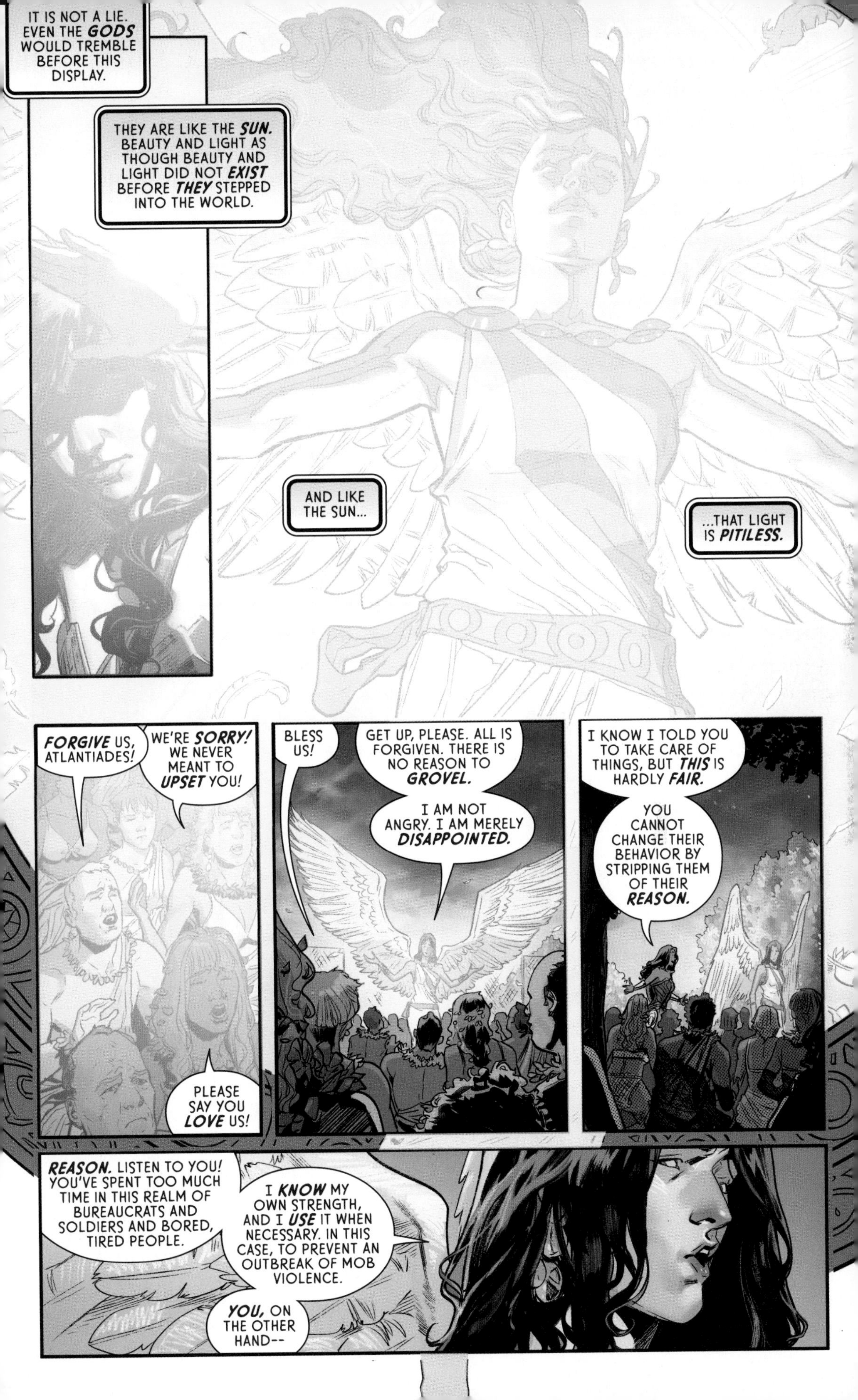
IT IS NOT A LIE. EVEN THE GODS WOULD TREMBLE BEFORE THIS DISPLAY.
THEY ARE LIKE THE SUN. BEAUTY AND LIGHT AS THOUGH BEAUTY AND LIGHT DID NOT EXIST BEFORE THEY STEPPED INTO THE WORLD.
AND LIKE THE SUN...
...THAT LIGHT IS PITILESS.
FORGIVE US, ATLANTIADES!
WE'RE SORRY! WE NEVER MEANT TO UPSET YOU!
PLEASE SAY YOU LOVE US!
BLESS US!
GET UP, PLEASE. ALL IS FORGIVEN. THERE IS NO REASON TO GROVEL.
I AM NOT ANGRY. I AM MERELY DISAPPOINTED.
I KNOW I TOLD YOU TO TAKE CARE OF THINGS, BUT THIS IS HARDLY FAIR.
YOU CANNOT CHANGE THEIR BEHAVIOR BY STRIPPING THEM OF THEIR REASON.
REASON. LISTEN TO YOU! YOU'VE SPENT TOO MUCH TIME IN THIS REALM OF BUREAUCRATS AND SOLDIERS AND BORED, TIRED PEOPLE.
I KNOW MY OWN STRENGTH, AND I USE IT WHEN NECESSARY. IN THIS CASE, TO PREVENT AN OUTBREAK OF MOB VIOLENCE.
YOU, ON THE OTHER HAND--

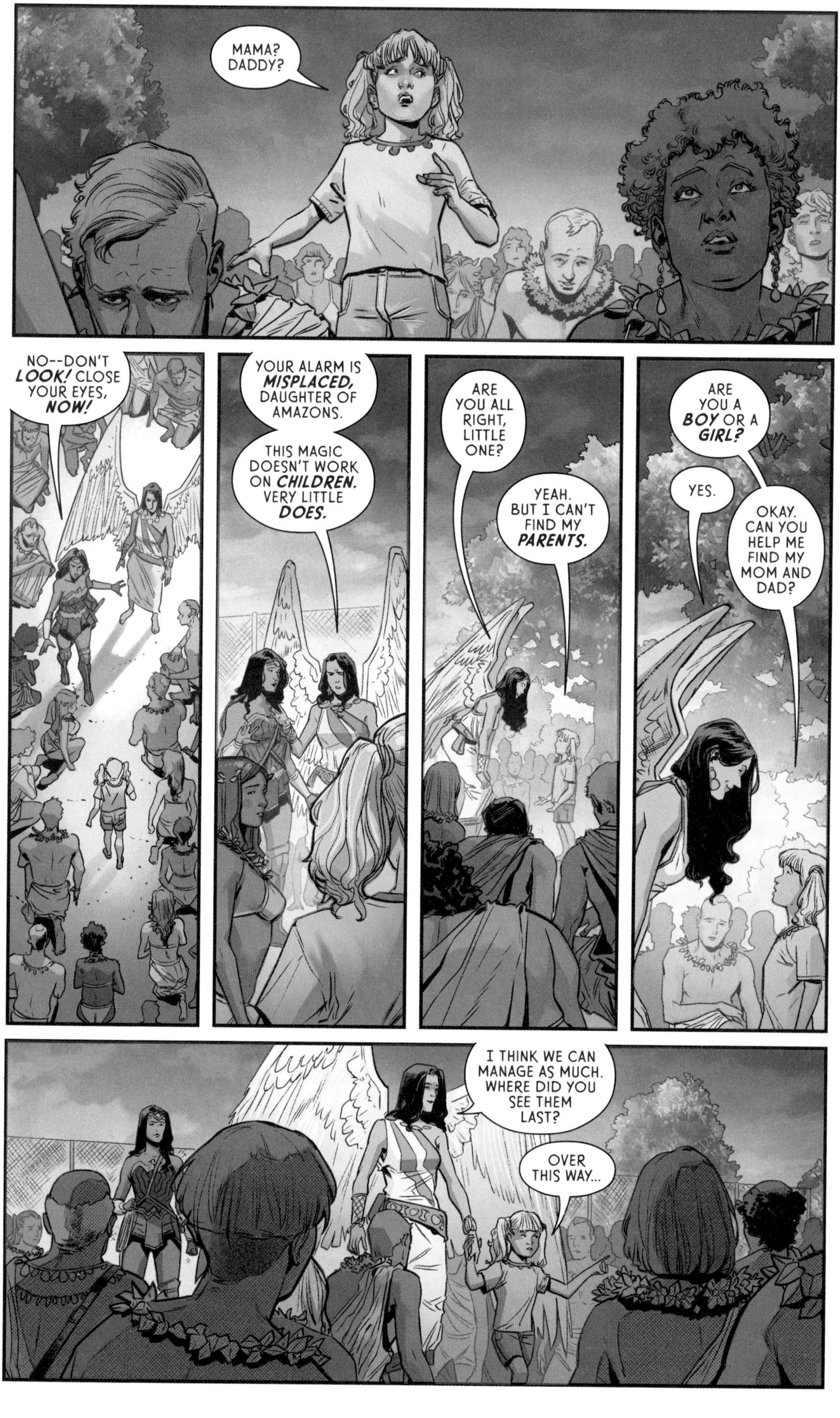
MAMA? DADDY?
NO--DON'T LOOK! CLOSE YOUR EYES, NOW!
YOUR ALARM IS MISPLACED, DAUGHTER OF AMAZONS.
THIS MAGIC DOESN'T WORK ON CHILDREN. VERY LITTLE DOES.
ARE YOU ALL RIGHT, LITTLE ONE?
YEAH. BUT I CAN'T FIND MY PARENTS.
ARE YOU A BOY OR A GIRL?
YES.
OKAY. CAN YOU HELP ME FIND MY MOM AND DAD?
I THINK WE CAN MANAGE AS MUCH. WHERE DID YOU SEE THEM LAST?
OVER THIS WAY...

YOU LOOK *SAD.*

THIS IS NOT TURNING OUT THE WAY I *WISHED.*

I THOUGHT I COULD *FREE* THESE PEOPLE FROM THE SHACKLES OF THEIR *ORDINARY LIVES.* GIVE THEM A CHANCE TO START OVER AND INDULGE THEIR MOST *ARDENT* DESIRES.

BUT LIFE ISN'T LIKE THAT. THE CHOICES WE MAKE *FOLLOW* US. OUR DESIRES BEGET *CHILDREN,* LITERAL AND FIGURATIVE...

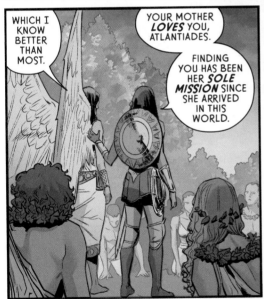

WHICH I KNOW BETTER THAN MOST.

YOUR MOTHER *LOVES* YOU, ATLANTIADES.

FINDING YOU HAS BEEN HER *SOLE MISSION* SINCE SHE ARRIVED IN THIS WORLD.

MUCH IS STILL... *UNRESOLVED* BETWEEN ME AND MY MOTHER.

BUT WHATEVER ELSE HAPPENS, IT IS BECAUSE OF *HER* THAT I MET YOU, AND FOR *THAT,* I AM GRATEFUL.

I--

I HAVE TOLD YOU THAT MY HEART IS NOT *FREE.*

LOOKING AT ME *SOULFULLY* WILL NOT CHANGE THAT.

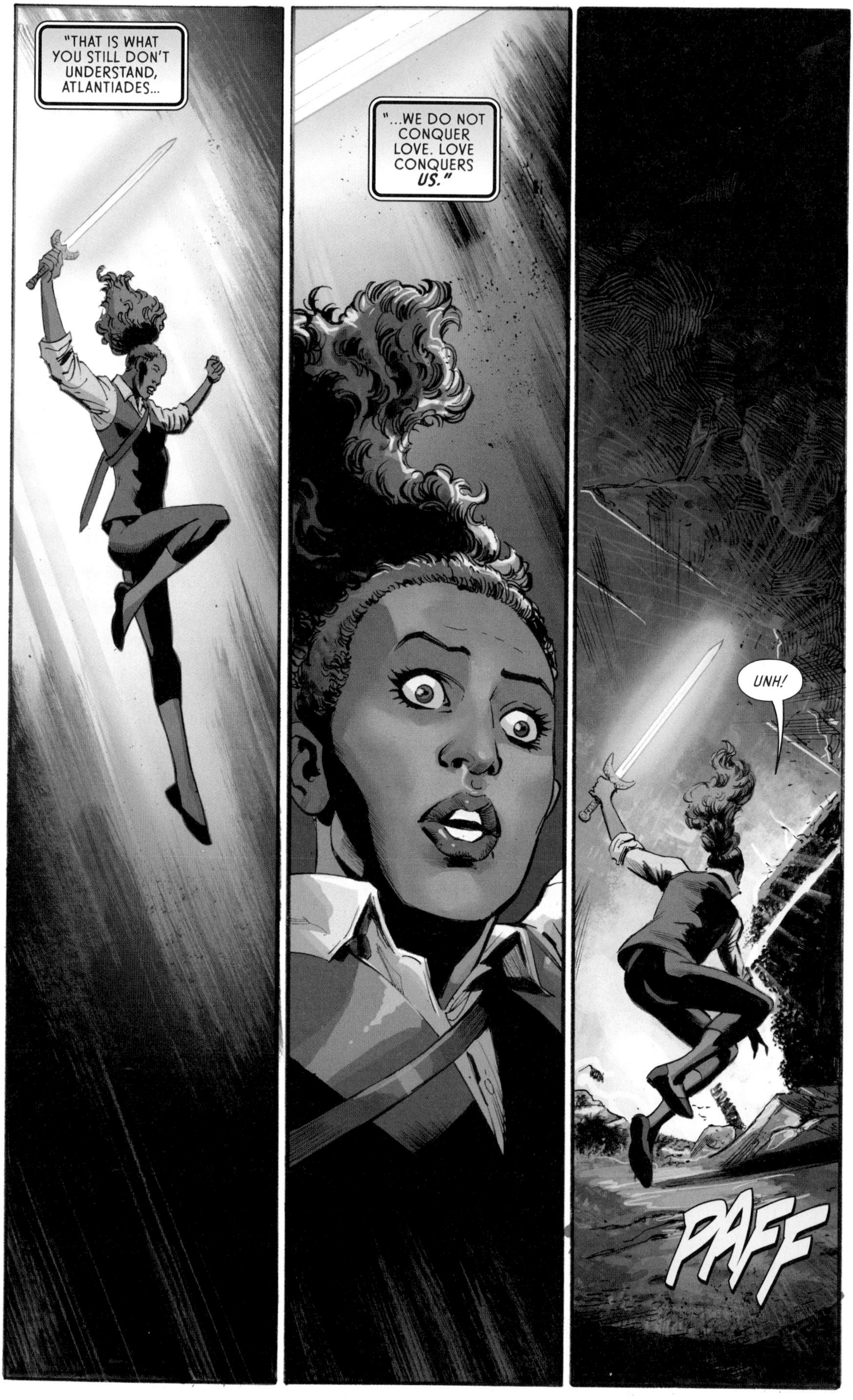
"THAT IS WHAT YOU STILL DON'T UNDERSTAND, ATLANTIADES...
"...WE DO NOT CONQUER LOVE. LOVE CONQUERS *US.*"
UNH!
PAFF

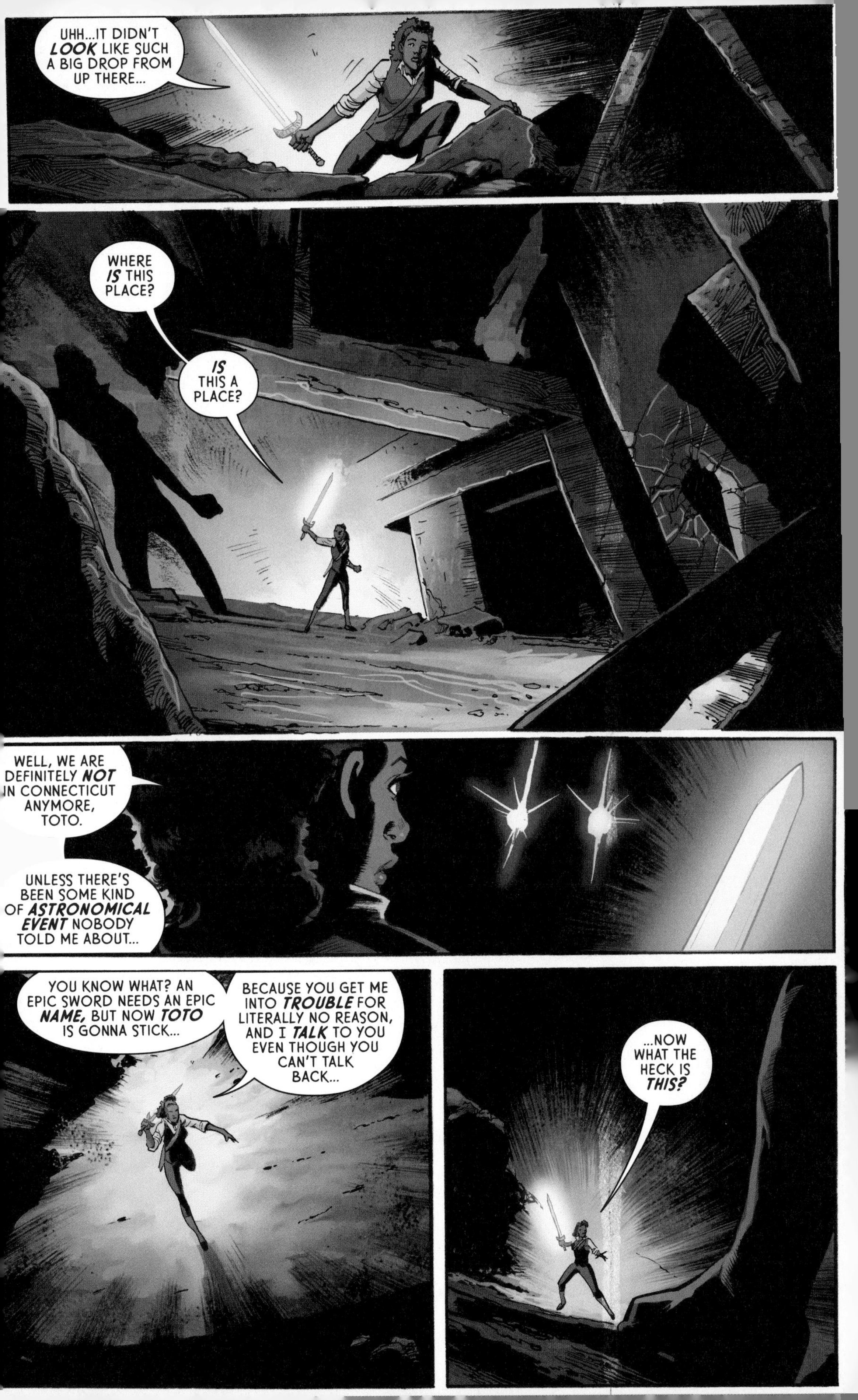
UHH...IT DIDN'T LOOK LIKE SUCH A BIG DROP FROM UP THERE...
WHERE IS THIS PLACE?
IS THIS A PLACE?
WELL, WE ARE DEFINITELY NOT IN CONNECTICUT ANYMORE, TOTO.
UNLESS THERE'S BEEN SOME KIND OF ASTRONOMICAL EVENT NOBODY TOLD ME ABOUT...
YOU KNOW WHAT? AN EPIC SWORD NEEDS AN EPIC NAME, BUT NOW TOTO IS GONNA STICK...
BECAUSE YOU GET ME INTO TROUBLE FOR LITERALLY NO REASON, AND I TALK TO YOU EVEN THOUGH YOU CAN'T TALK BACK...
...NOW WHAT THE HECK IS THIS?

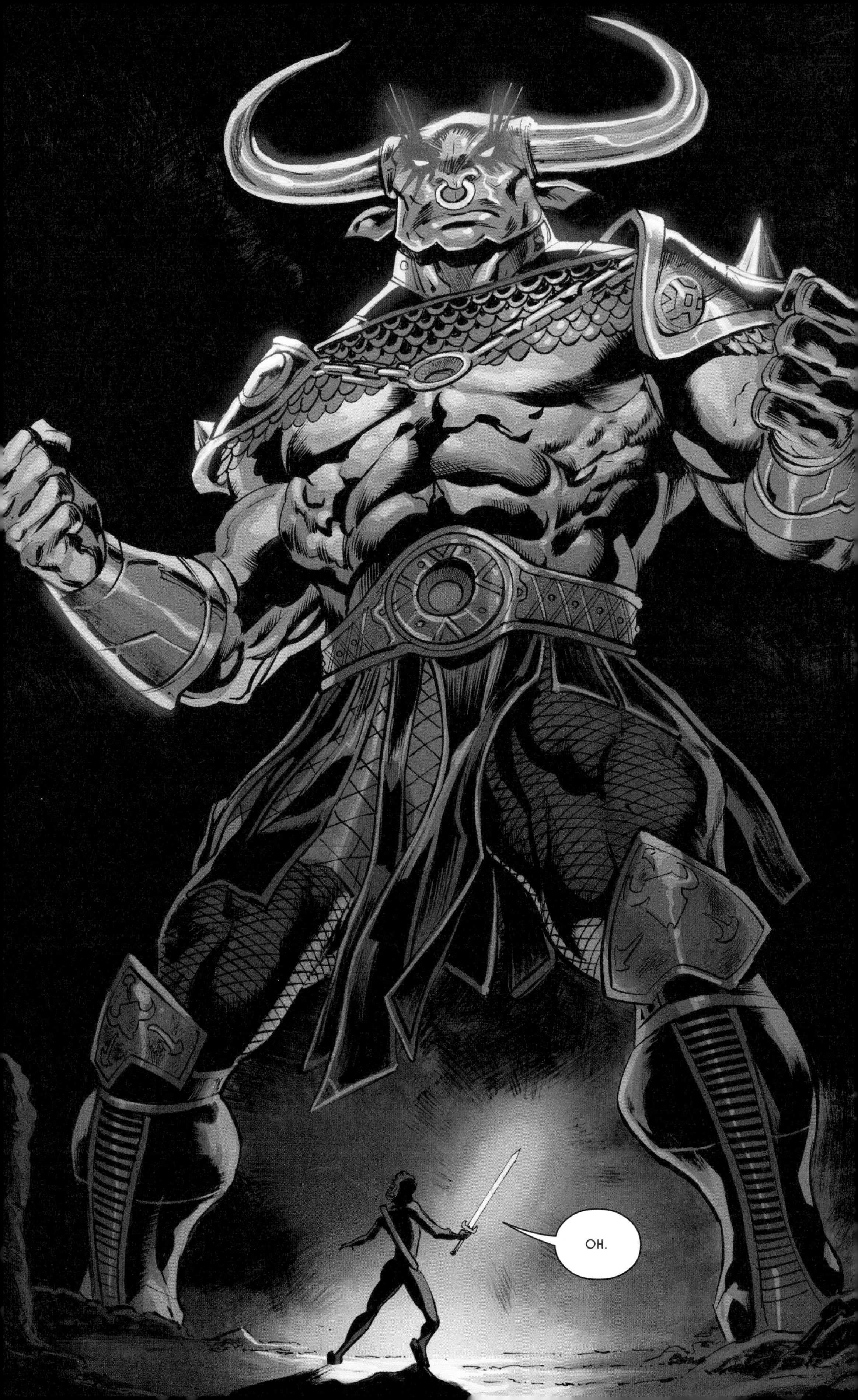
OH.

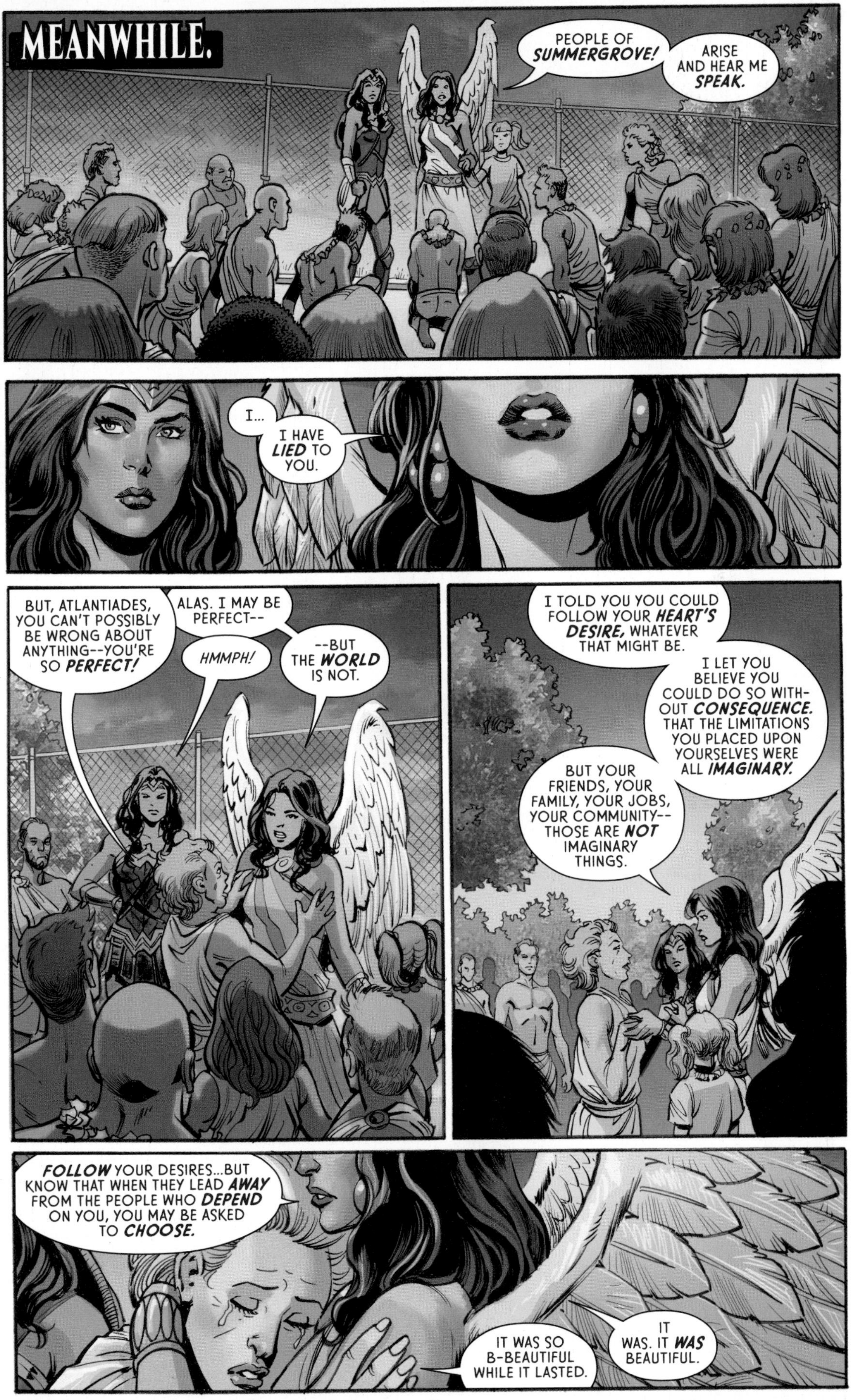
MEANWHILE.
PEOPLE OF SUMMERGROVE!
ARISE AND HEAR ME SPEAK.
I...
I HAVE LIED TO YOU.
BUT, ATLANTIADES, YOU CAN'T POSSIBLY BE WRONG ABOUT ANYTHING--YOU'RE SO PERFECT!
ALAS. I MAY BE PERFECT--
HMMPH!
--BUT THE WORLD IS NOT.
I TOLD YOU YOU COULD FOLLOW YOUR HEART'S DESIRE, WHATEVER THAT MIGHT BE.
I LET YOU BELIEVE YOU COULD DO SO WITHOUT CONSEQUENCE. THAT THE LIMITATIONS YOU PLACED UPON YOURSELVES WERE ALL IMAGINARY.
BUT YOUR FRIENDS, YOUR FAMILY, YOUR JOBS, YOUR COMMUNITY--THOSE ARE NOT IMAGINARY THINGS.
FOLLOW YOUR DESIRES...BUT KNOW THAT WHEN THEY LEAD AWAY FROM THE PEOPLE WHO DEPEND ON YOU, YOU MAY BE ASKED TO CHOOSE.
IT WAS SO B-BEAUTIFUL WHILE IT LASTED.
IT WAS. IT WAS BEAUTIFUL.

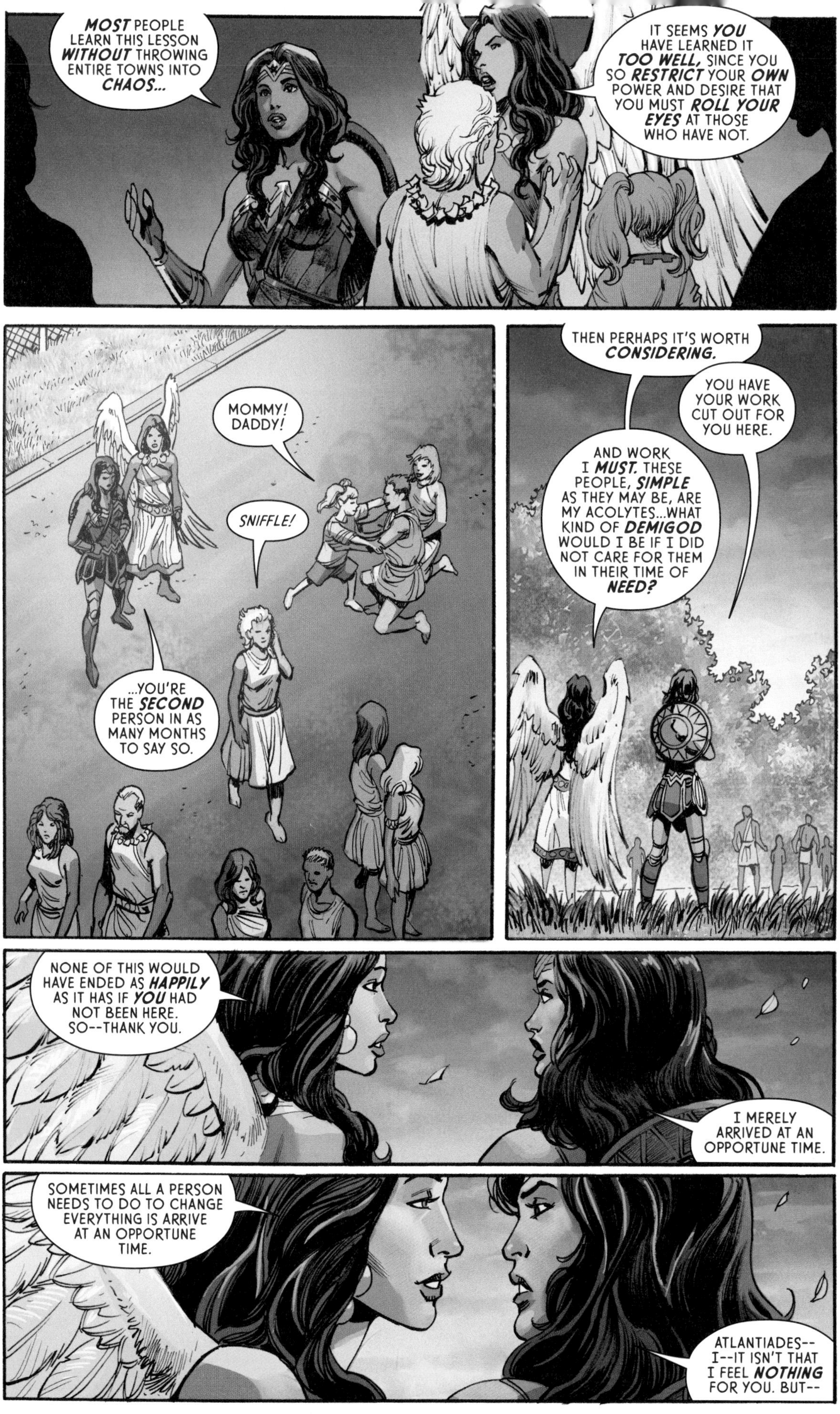
MOST PEOPLE LEARN THIS LESSON WITHOUT THROWING ENTIRE TOWNS INTO CHAOS...
IT SEEMS YOU HAVE LEARNED IT TOO WELL, SINCE YOU SO RESTRICT YOUR OWN POWER AND DESIRE THAT YOU MUST ROLL YOUR EYES AT THOSE WHO HAVE NOT.
MOMMY! DADDY!
SNIFFLE!
...YOU'RE THE SECOND PERSON IN AS MANY MONTHS TO SAY SO.
THEN PERHAPS IT'S WORTH CONSIDERING.
YOU HAVE YOUR WORK CUT OUT FOR YOU HERE.
AND WORK I MUST. THESE PEOPLE, SIMPLE AS THEY MAY BE, ARE MY ACOLYTES...WHAT KIND OF DEMIGOD WOULD I BE IF I DID NOT CARE FOR THEM IN THEIR TIME OF NEED?
NONE OF THIS WOULD HAVE ENDED AS HAPPILY AS IT HAS IF YOU HAD NOT BEEN HERE. SO--THANK YOU.
I MERELY ARRIVED AT AN OPPORTUNE TIME.
SOMETIMES ALL A PERSON NEEDS TO DO TO CHANGE EVERYTHING IS ARRIVE AT AN OPPORTUNE TIME.
ATLANTIADES-- I--IT ISN'T THAT I FEEL NOTHING FOR YOU. BUT--

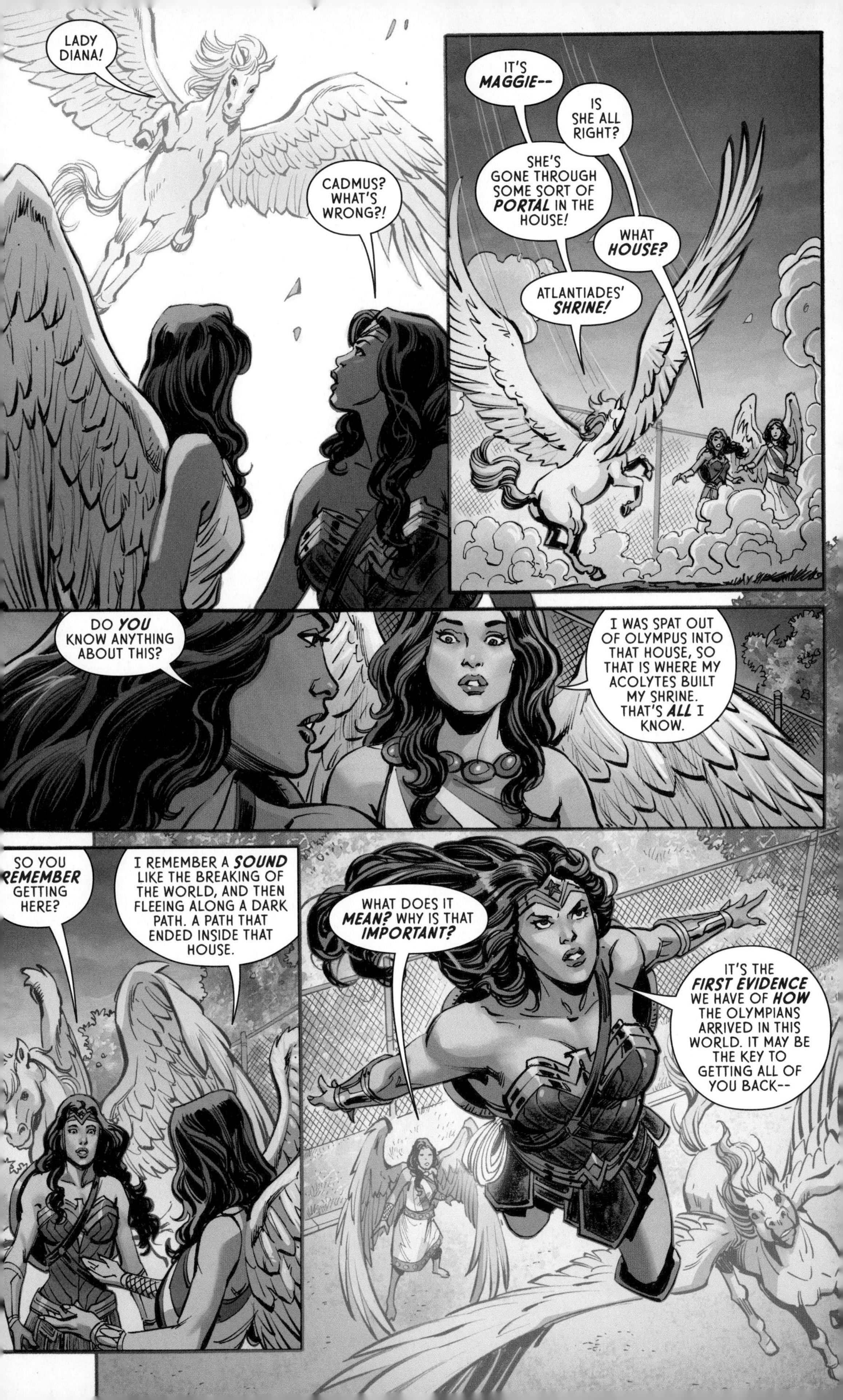
LADY DIANA!
CADMUS? WHAT'S WRONG?!
IT'S ***MAGGIE***--
IS SHE ALL RIGHT?
SHE'S GONE THROUGH SOME SORT OF ***PORTAL*** IN THE HOUSE!
WHAT ***HOUSE?***
ATLANTIADES' ***SHRINE!***
DO ***YOU*** KNOW ANYTHING ABOUT THIS?
I WAS SPAT OUT OF OLYMPUS INTO THAT HOUSE, SO THAT IS WHERE MY ACOLYTES BUILT MY SHRINE. THAT'S ***ALL*** I KNOW.
SO YOU ***REMEMBER*** GETTING HERE?
I REMEMBER A ***SOUND*** LIKE THE BREAKING OF THE WORLD, AND THEN FLEEING ALONG A DARK PATH. A PATH THAT ENDED INSIDE THAT HOUSE.
WHAT DOES IT ***MEAN?*** WHY IS THAT ***IMPORTANT?***
IT'S THE ***FIRST EVIDENCE*** WE HAVE OF ***HOW*** THE OLYMPIANS ARRIVED IN THIS WORLD. IT MAY BE THE KEY TO GETTING ALL OF YOU BACK--

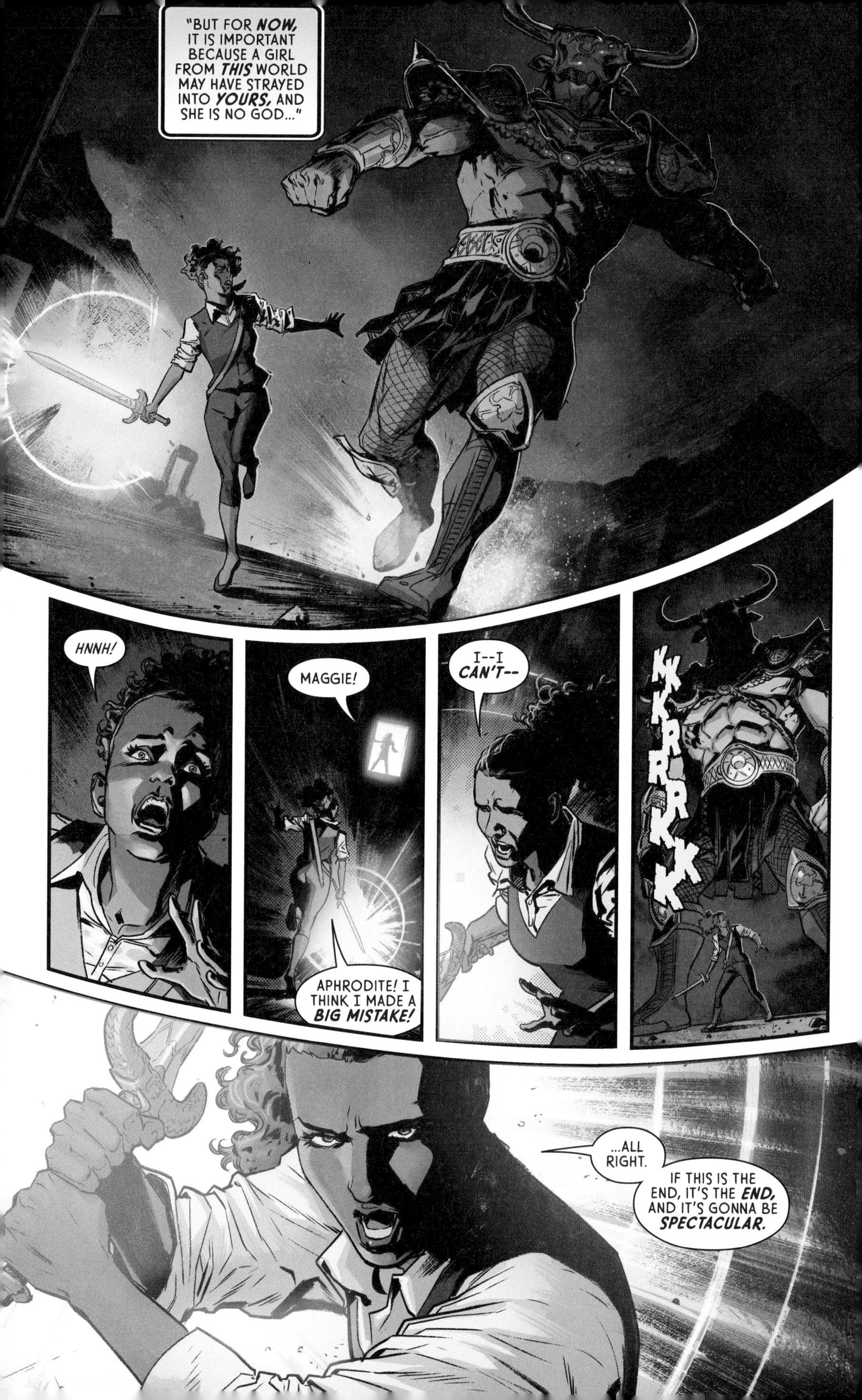

"BUT FOR NOW, IT IS IMPORTANT BECAUSE A GIRL FROM THIS WORLD MAY HAVE STRAYED INTO YOURS, AND SHE IS NO GOD..."
HNNH!
MAGGIE!
APHRODITE! I THINK I MADE A BIG MISTAKE!
I--I CAN'T--
KKKRRRRKKK
...ALL RIGHT.
IF THIS IS THE END, IT'S THE END, AND IT'S GONNA BE SPECTACULAR.

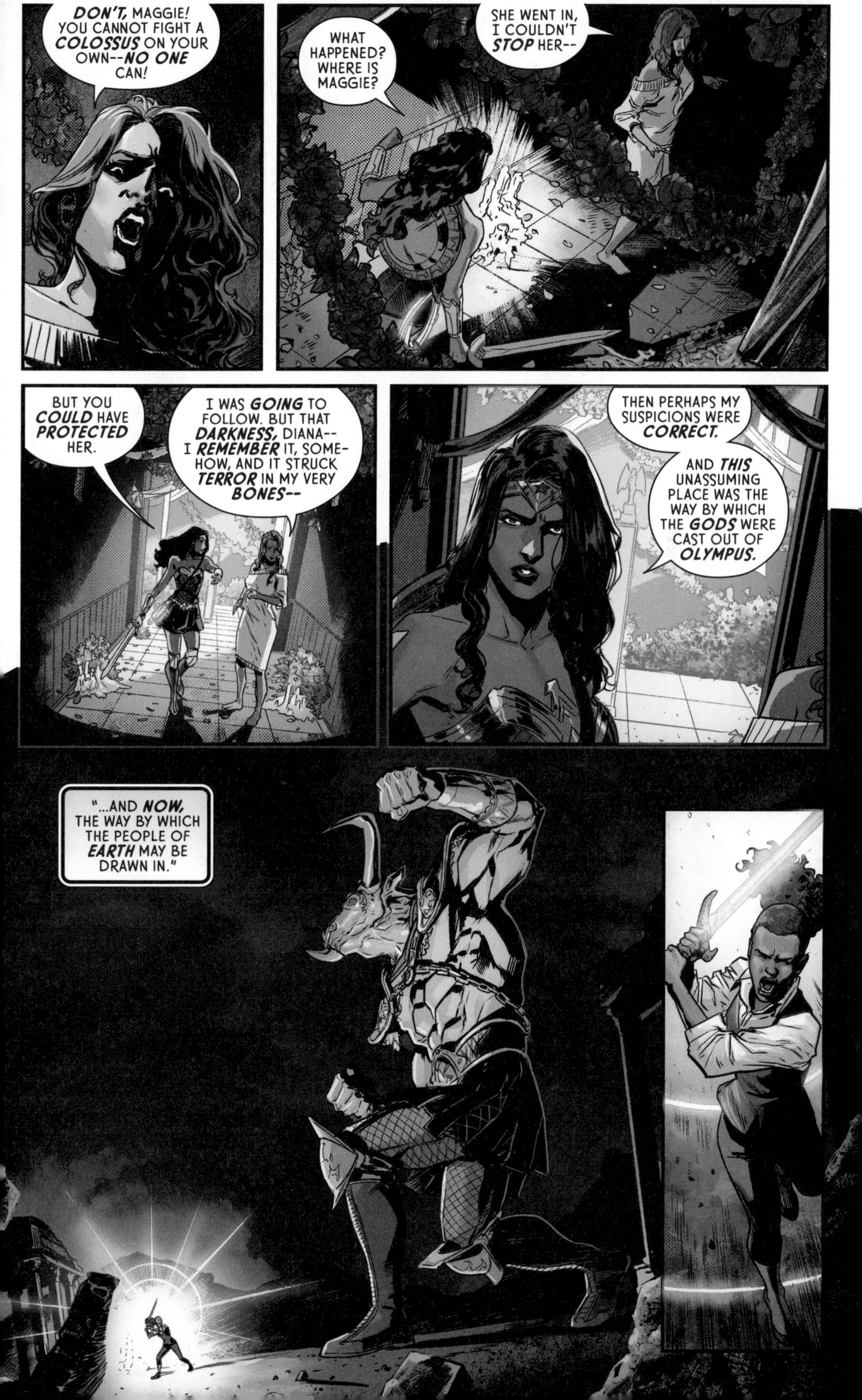

DON'T, MAGGIE! YOU CANNOT FIGHT A COLOSSUS ON YOUR OWN--NO ONE CAN!
WHAT HAPPENED? WHERE IS MAGGIE?
SHE WENT IN, I COULDN'T STOP HER--
BUT YOU COULD HAVE PROTECTED HER.
I WAS GOING TO FOLLOW. BUT THAT DARKNESS, DIANA-- I REMEMBER IT, SOMEHOW, AND IT STRUCK TERROR IN MY VERY BONES--
THEN PERHAPS MY SUSPICIONS WERE CORRECT.
AND THIS UNASSUMING PLACE WAS THE WAY BY WHICH THE GODS WERE CAST OUT OF OLYMPUS.
"...AND NOW, THE WAY BY WHICH THE PEOPLE OF EARTH MAY BE DRAWN IN."

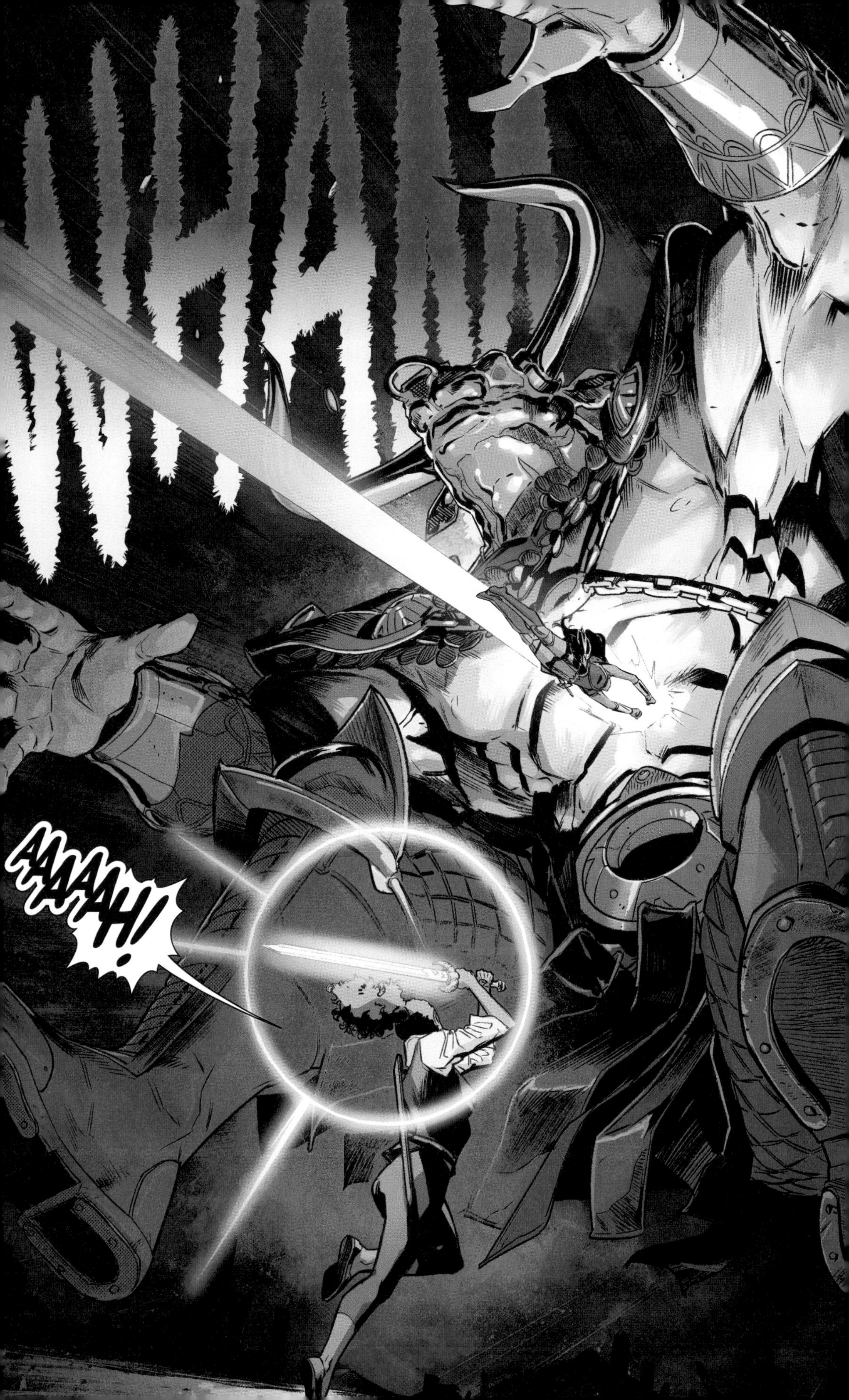
AAAAAAH!

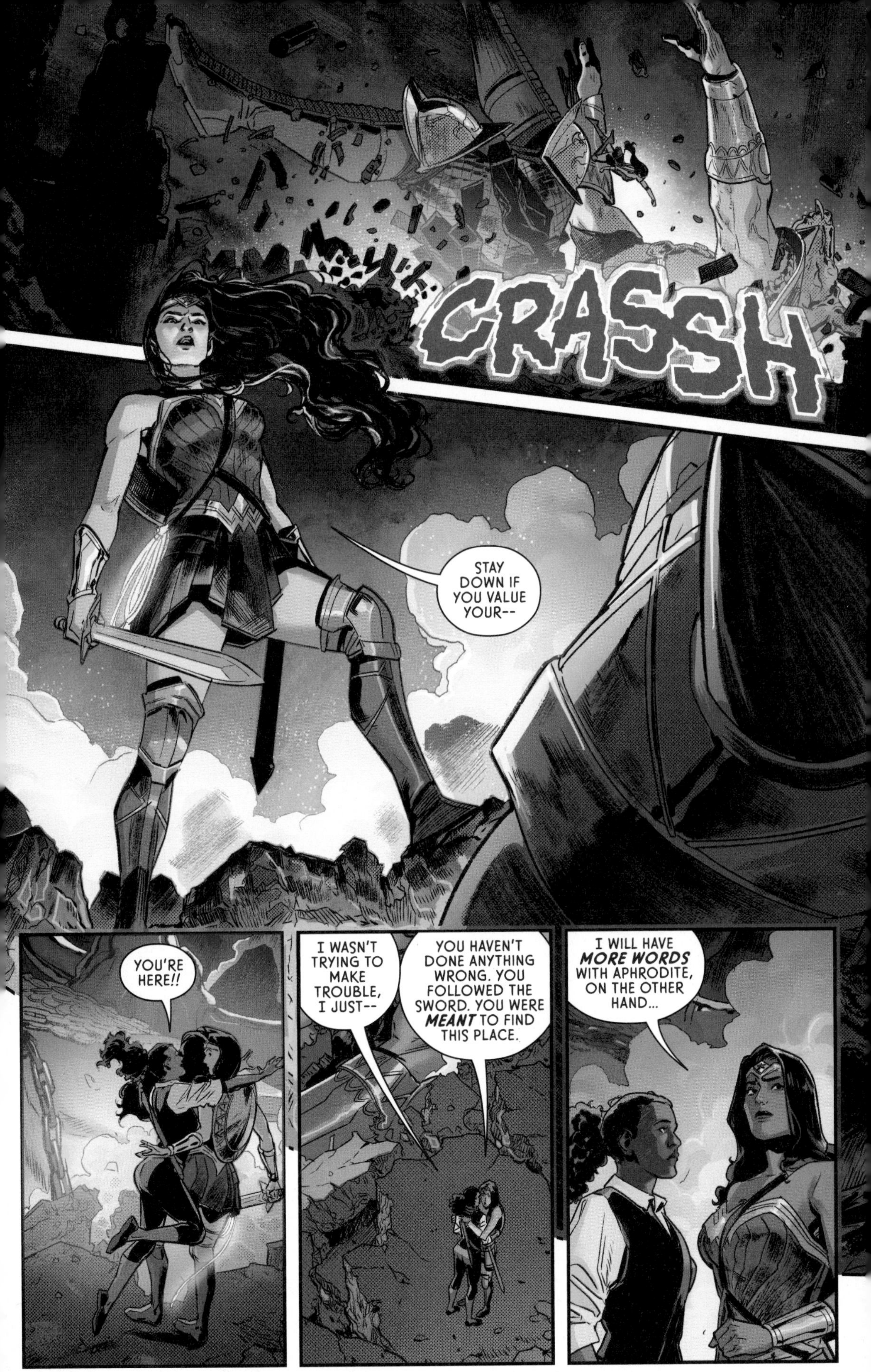
CRASSH
STAY DOWN IF YOU VALUE YOUR--
YOU'RE HERE!!
I WASN'T TRYING TO MAKE TROUBLE, I JUST--
YOU HAVEN'T DONE ANYTHING WRONG. YOU FOLLOWED THE SWORD. YOU WERE MEANT TO FIND THIS PLACE.
I WILL HAVE MORE WORDS WITH APHRODITE, ON THE OTHER HAND...

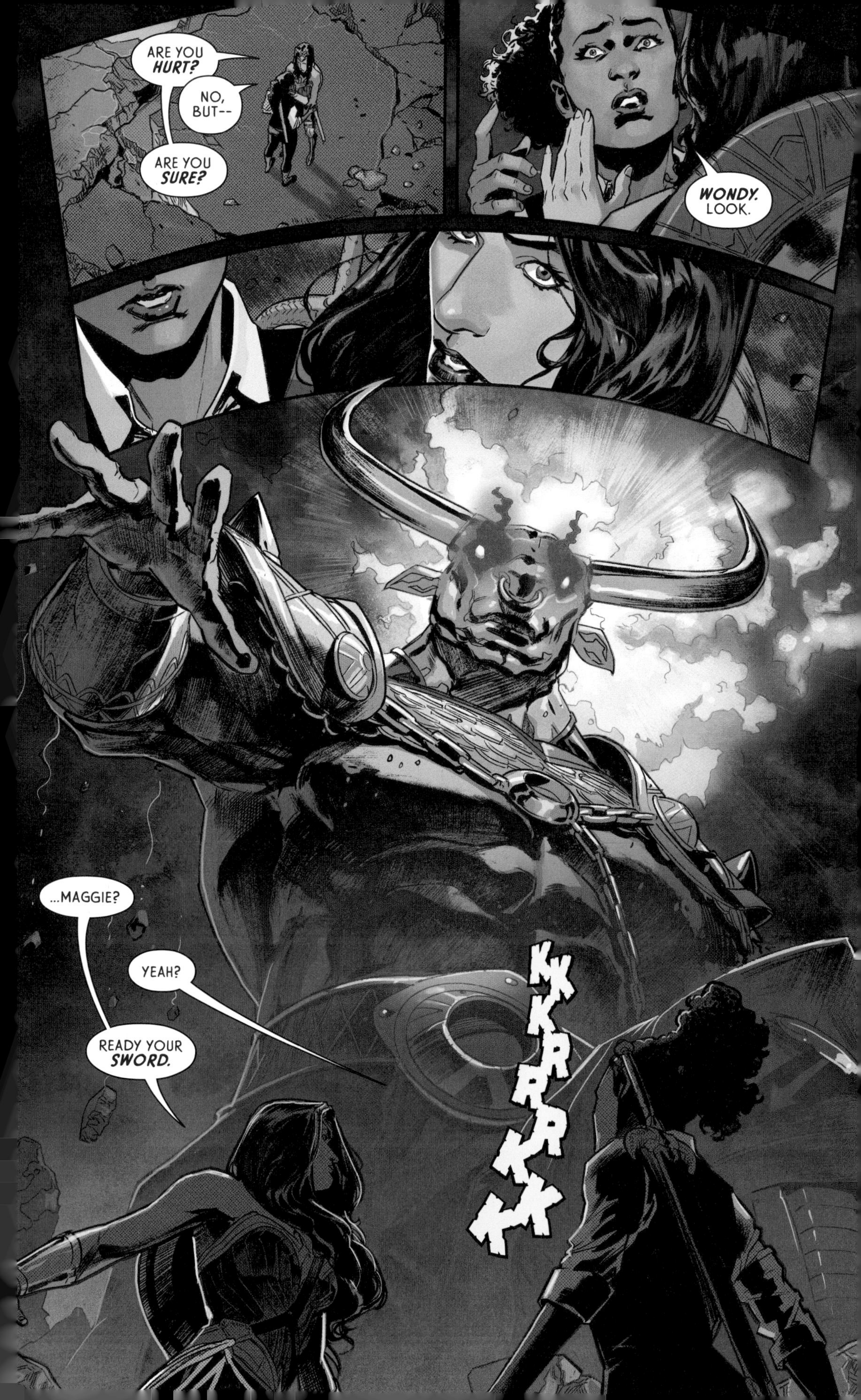

ARE YOU HURT?
NO, BUT--
ARE YOU SURE?
WONDY. LOOK.
...MAGGIE?
YEAH?
READY YOUR SWORD.
KKRRRKKK

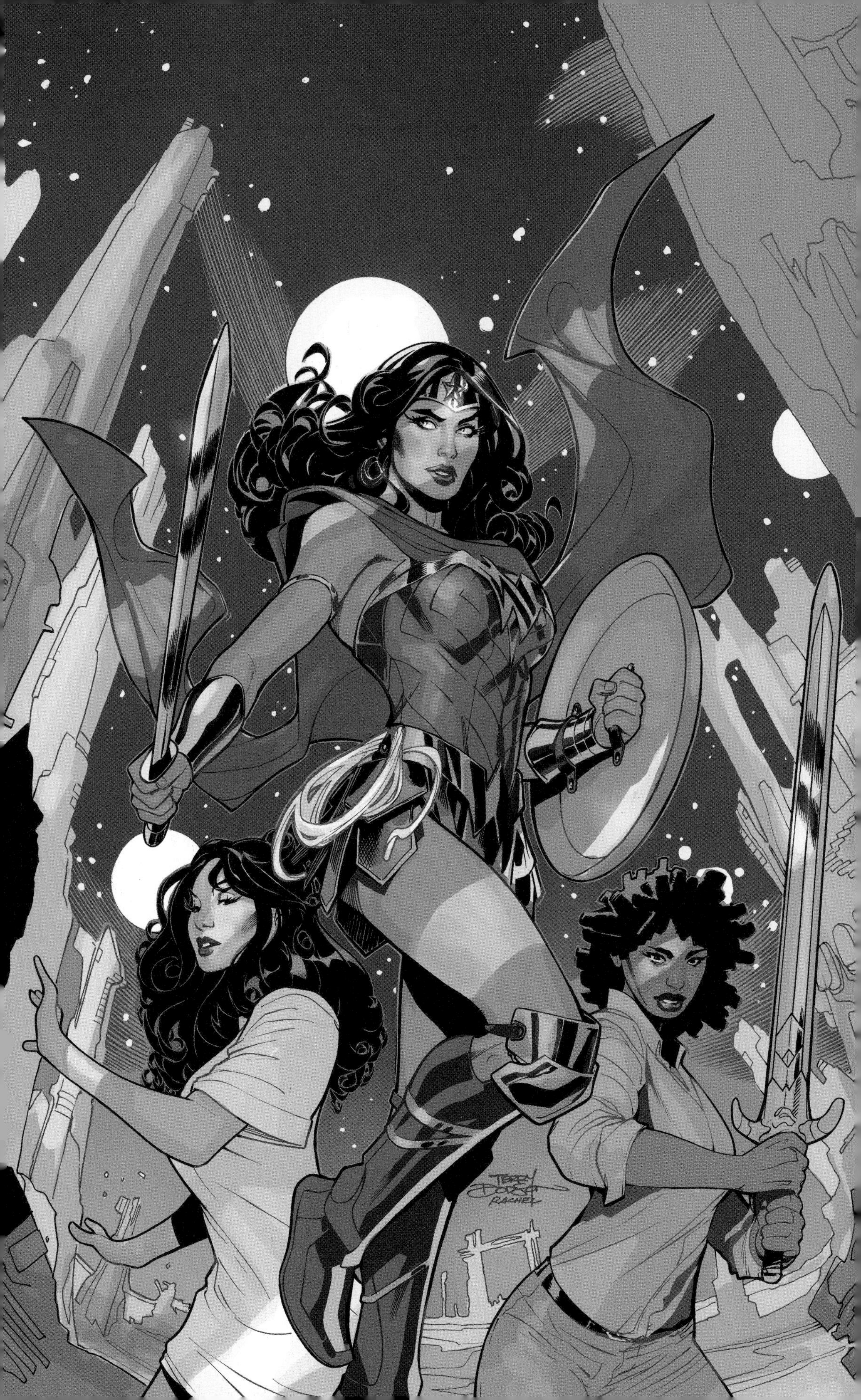

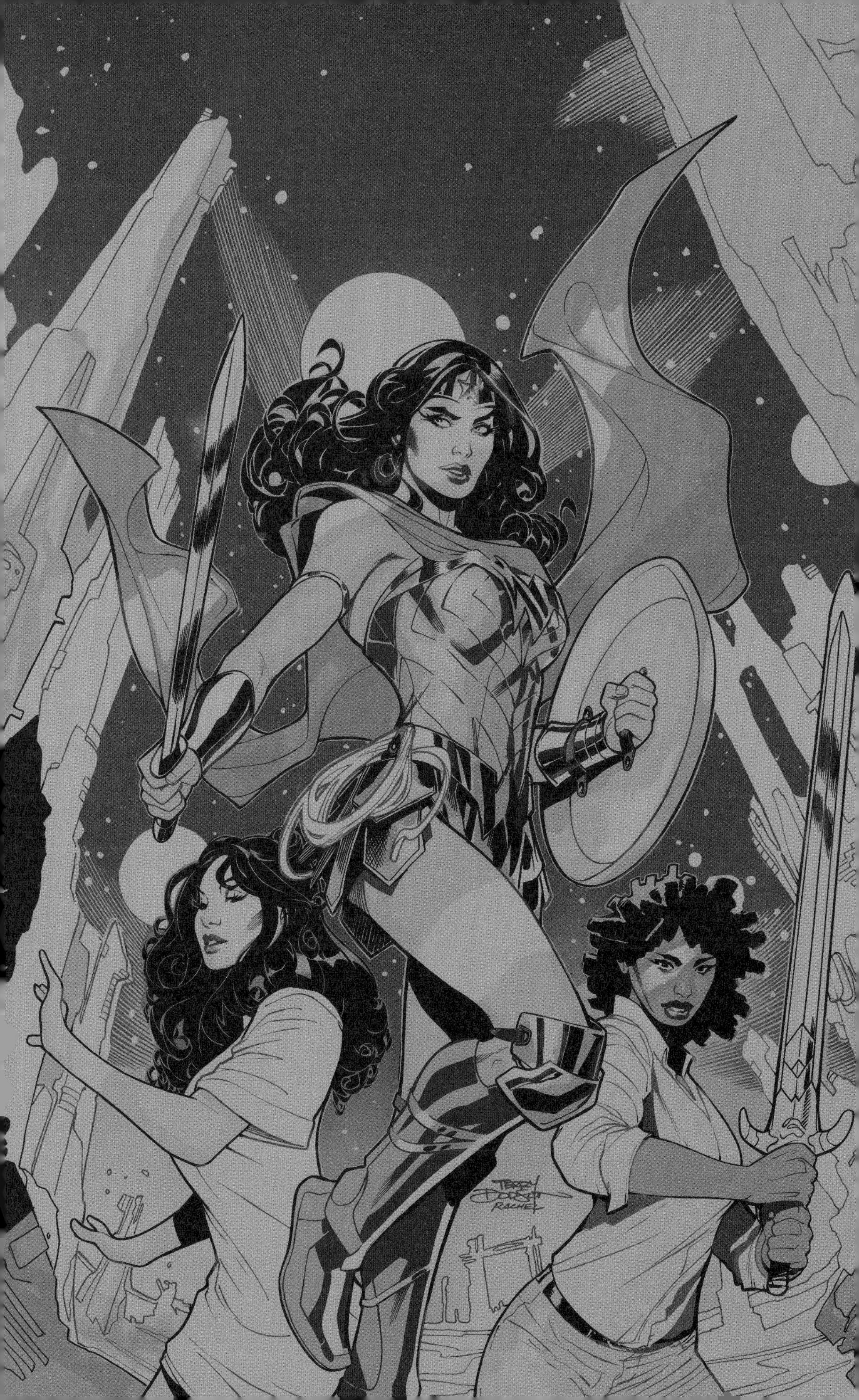
TERRY DODSON RACHEL

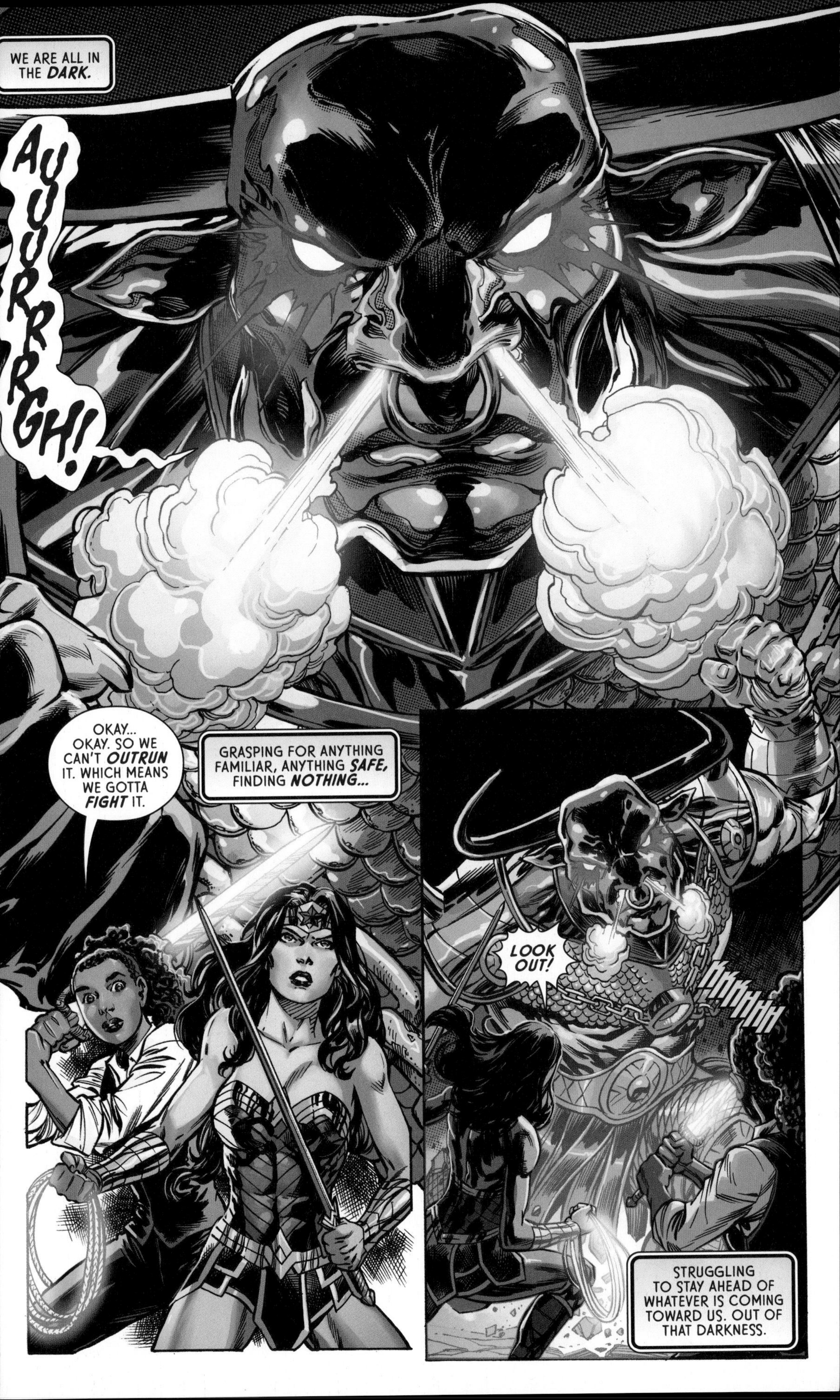
WE ARE ALL IN THE DARK.
AYUURRRGH!
OKAY... OKAY. SO WE CAN'T OUTRUN IT. WHICH MEANS WE GOTTA FIGHT IT.
GRASPING FOR ANYTHING FAMILIAR, ANYTHING SAFE, FINDING NOTHING...
LOOK OUT!
STRUGGLING TO STAY AHEAD OF WHATEVER IS COMING TOWARD US. OUT OF THAT DARKNESS.

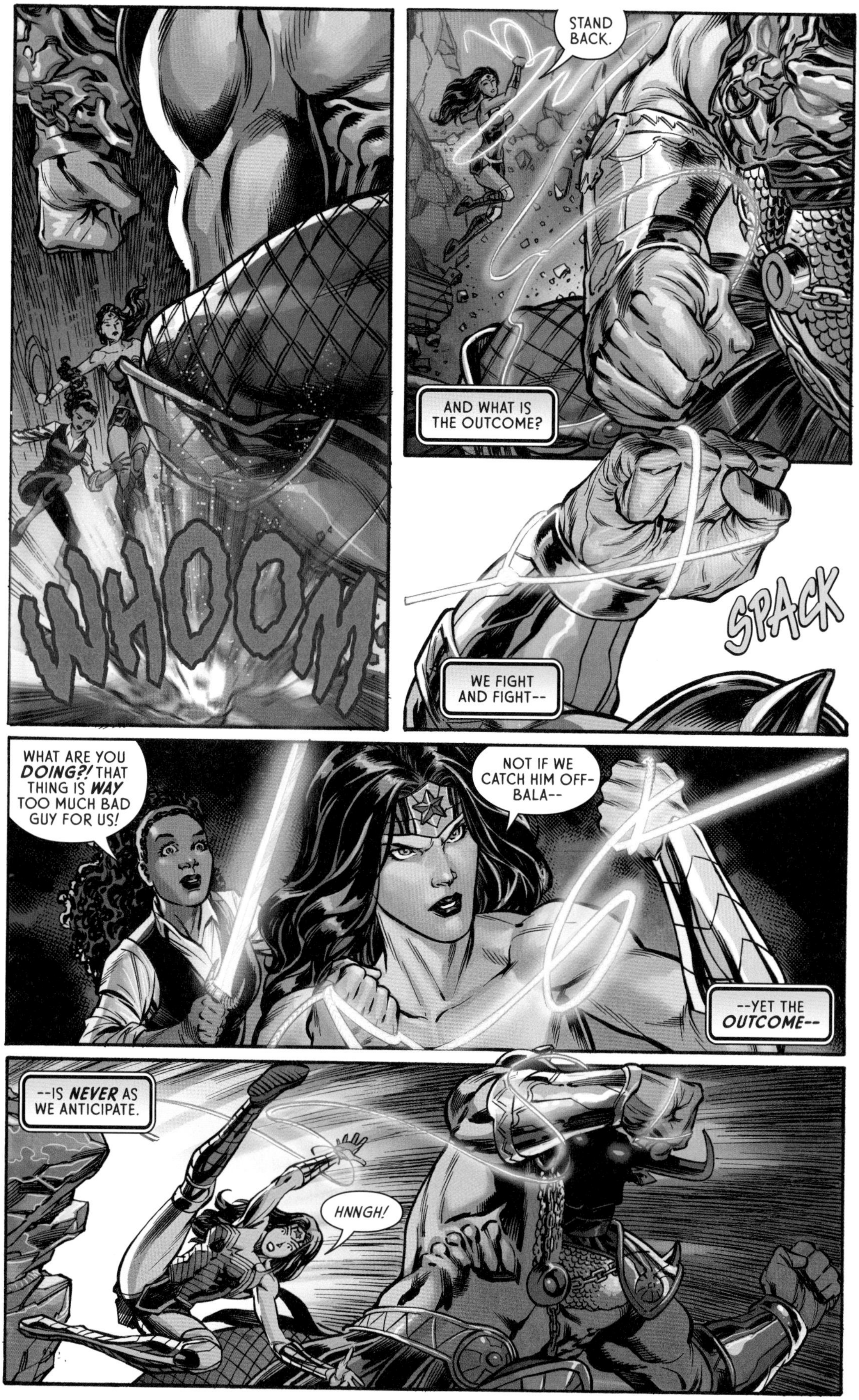
WHOOM
STAND BACK.
AND WHAT IS THE OUTCOME?
SPACK
WE FIGHT AND FIGHT--
WHAT ARE YOU *DOING?!* THAT THING IS *WAY* TOO MUCH BAD GUY FOR US!
NOT IF WE CATCH HIM OFF-BALA--
--YET THE *OUTCOME*--
--IS *NEVER* AS WE ANTICIPATE.
HNNGH!

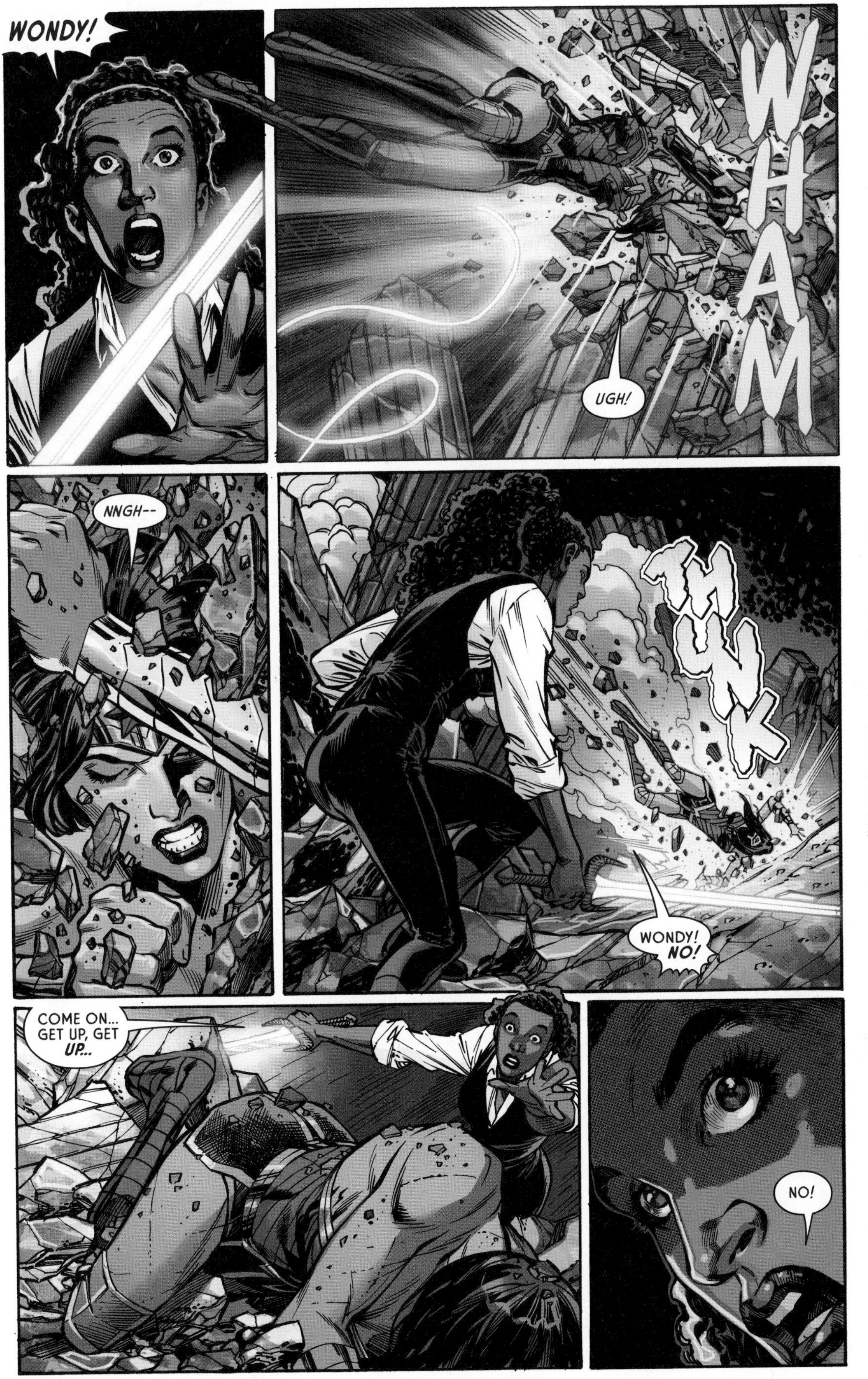
WONDY!
WHAM
UGH!
NNGH--
THUNK
WONDY! NO!
COME ON... GET UP, GET UP...
NO!

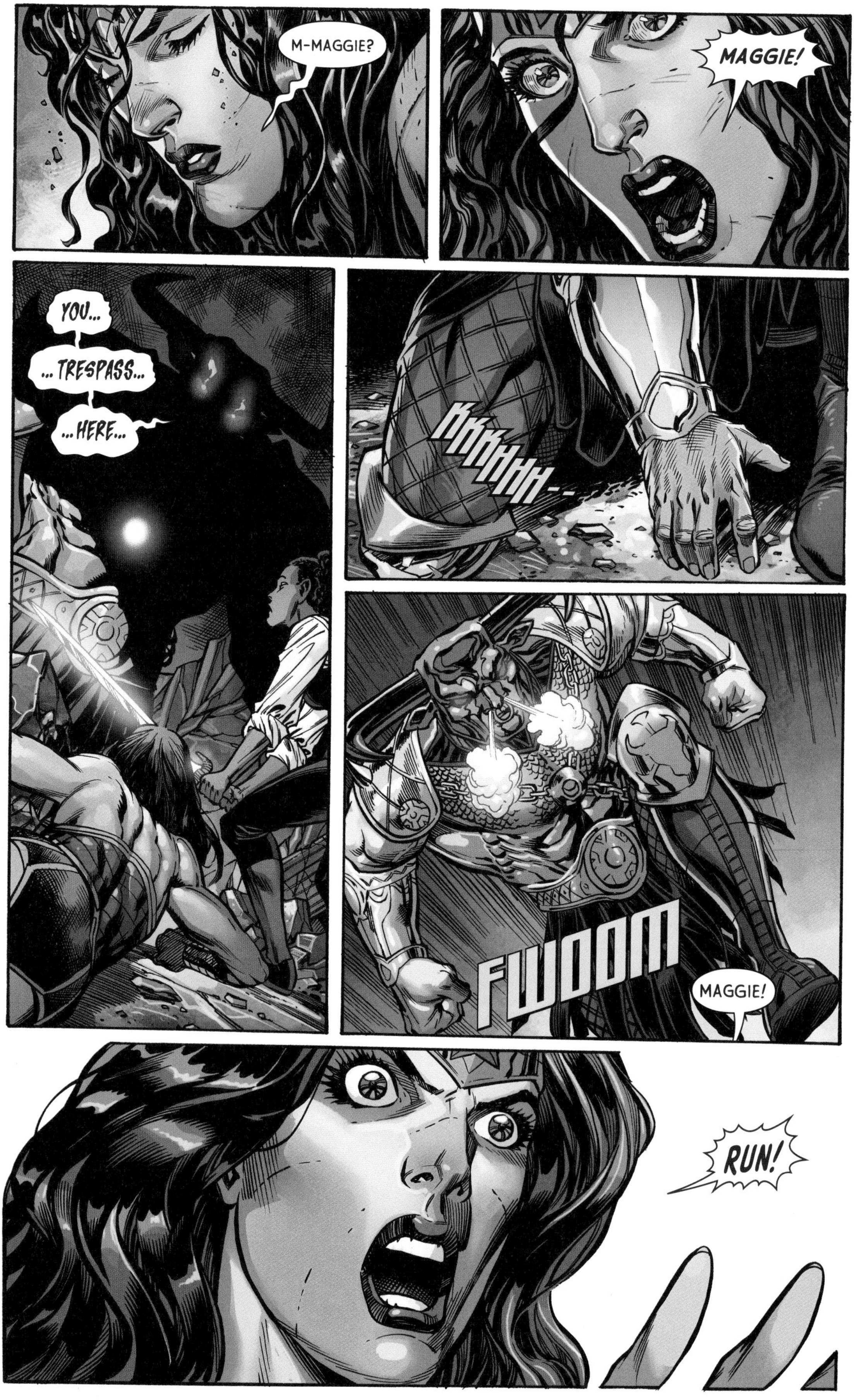
M-MAGGIE?
MAGGIE!
YOU...
...TRESPASS...
...HERE...
KKKHHH--
FWOOM
MAGGIE!
RUN!

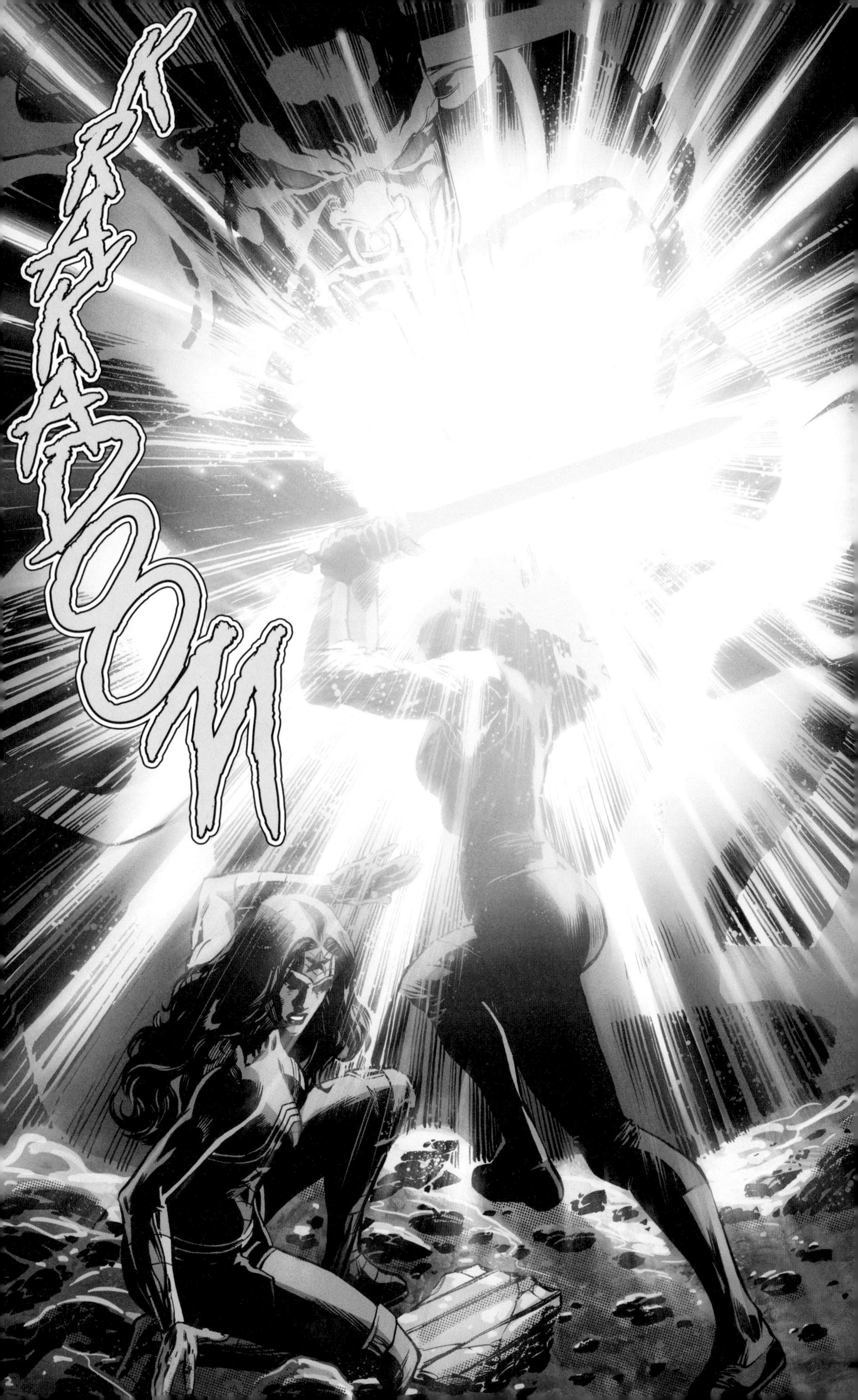
KRAKADOOM

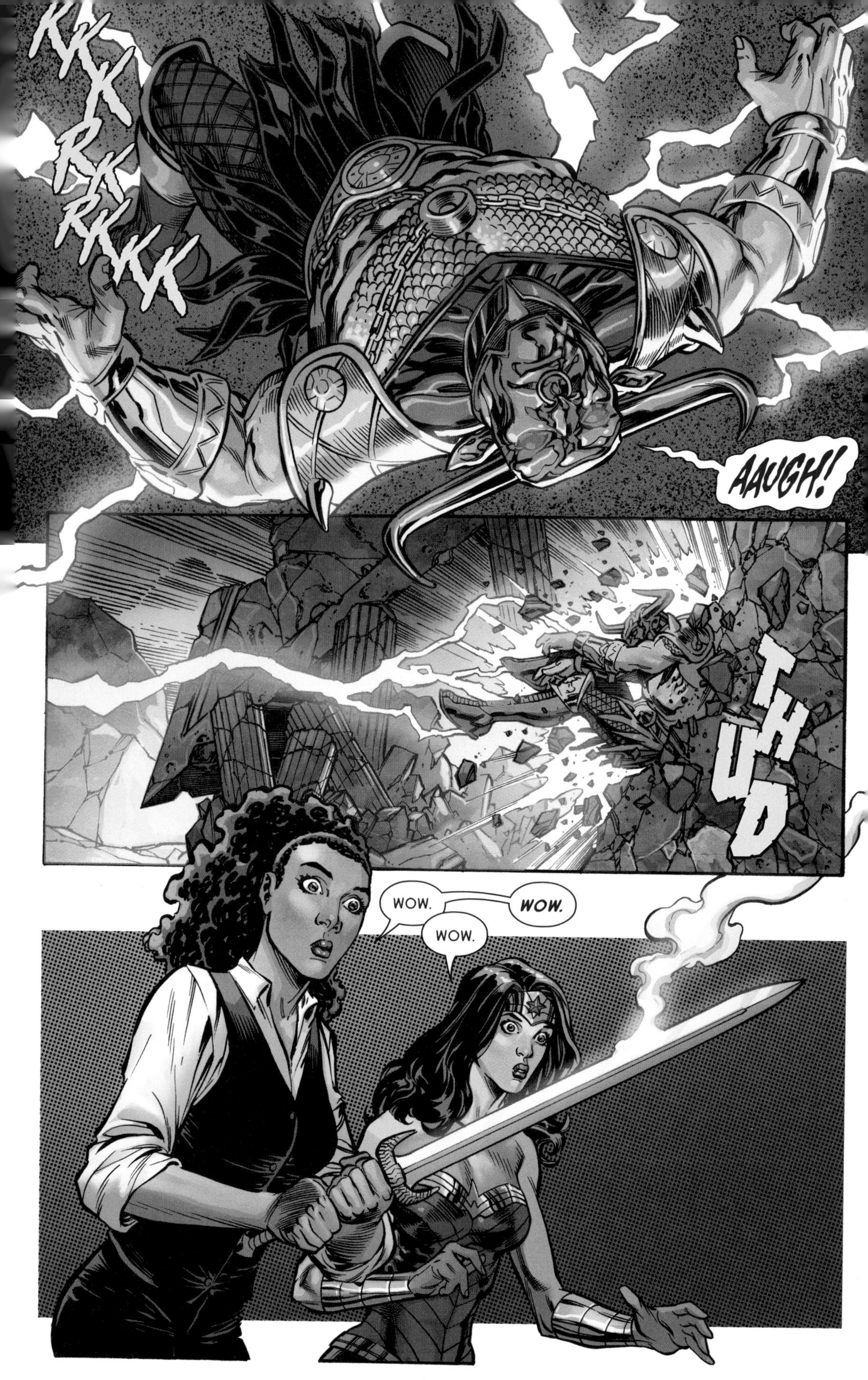
KKKRRKKK
AAUGH!
THUD
WOW.
WOW.
WOW.

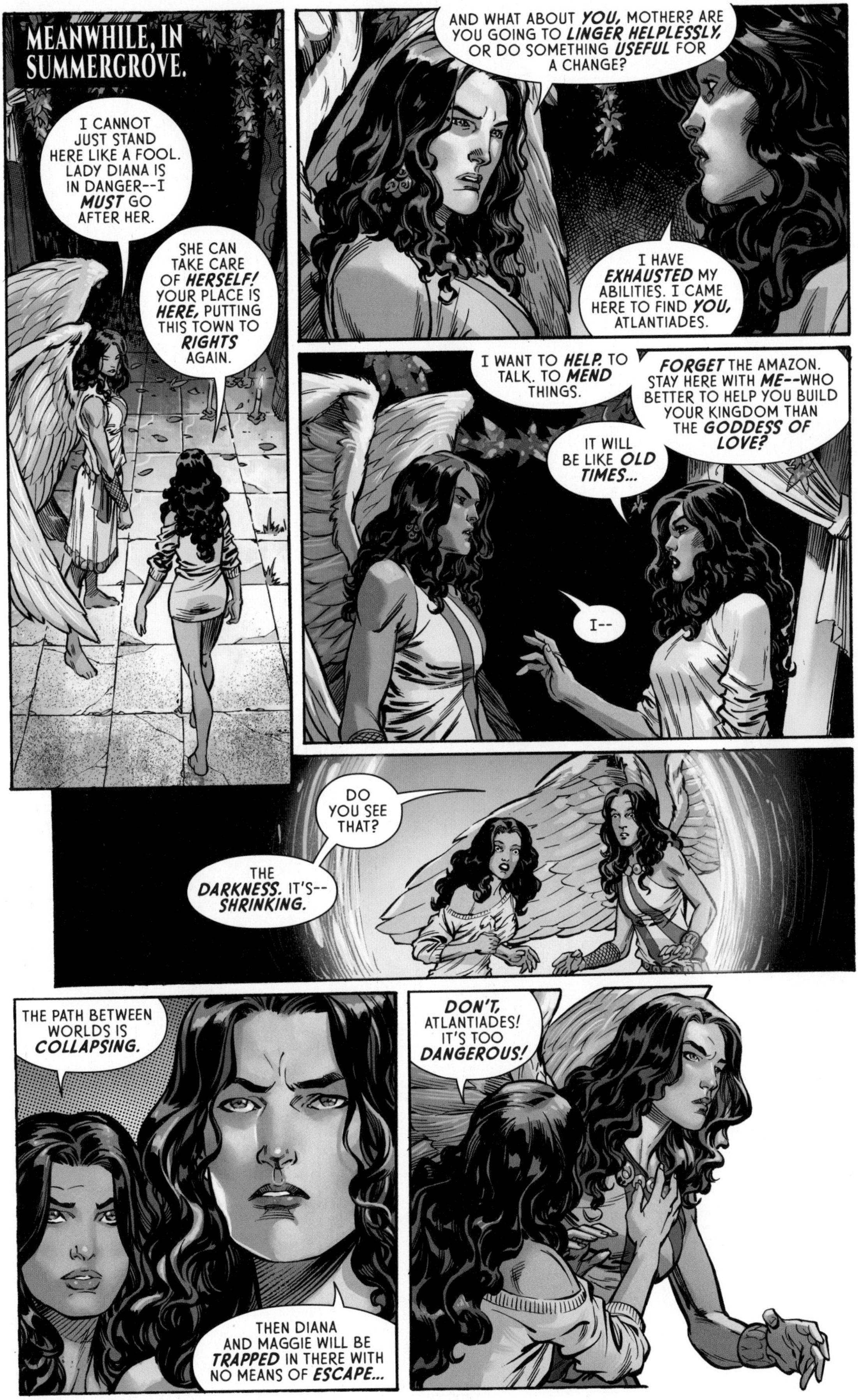
MEANWHILE, IN SUMMERGROVE.
I CANNOT JUST STAND HERE LIKE A FOOL. LADY DIANA IS IN DANGER--I MUST GO AFTER HER.
SHE CAN TAKE CARE OF HERSELF! YOUR PLACE IS HERE, PUTTING THIS TOWN TO RIGHTS AGAIN.
AND WHAT ABOUT YOU, MOTHER? ARE YOU GOING TO LINGER HELPLESSLY, OR DO SOMETHING USEFUL FOR A CHANGE?
I HAVE EXHAUSTED MY ABILITIES. I CAME HERE TO FIND YOU, ATLANTIADES.
I WANT TO HELP. TO TALK. TO MEND THINGS.
FORGET THE AMAZON. STAY HERE WITH ME--WHO BETTER TO HELP YOU BUILD YOUR KINGDOM THAN THE GODDESS OF LOVE?
IT WILL BE LIKE OLD TIMES...
I--
DO YOU SEE THAT?
THE DARKNESS. IT'S--SHRINKING.
THE PATH BETWEEN WORLDS IS COLLAPSING.
THEN DIANA AND MAGGIE WILL BE TRAPPED IN THERE WITH NO MEANS OF ESCAPE...
DON'T, ATLANTIADES! IT'S TOO DANGEROUS!

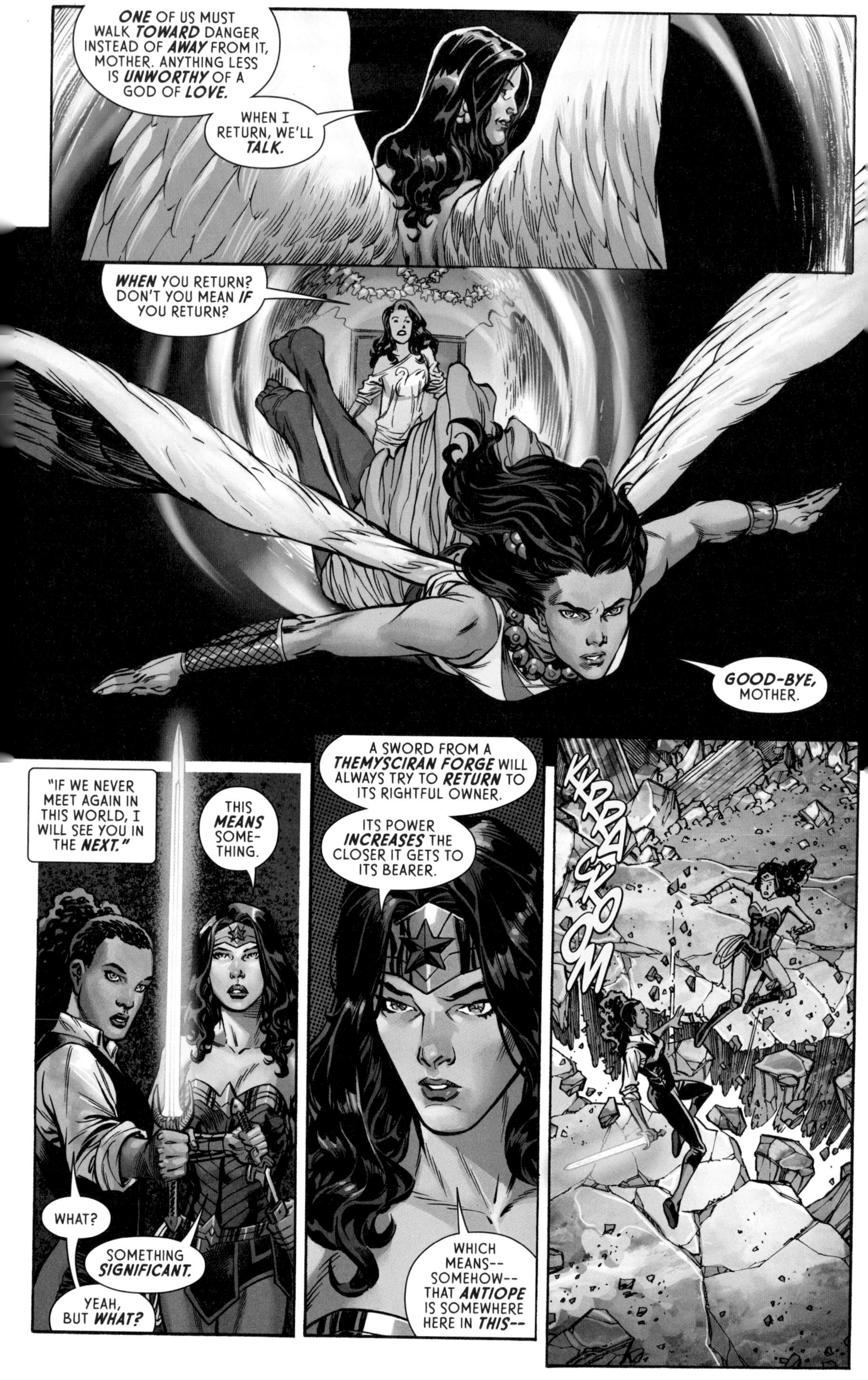
ONE OF US MUST WALK TOWARD DANGER INSTEAD OF AWAY FROM IT, MOTHER. ANYTHING LESS IS UNWORTHY OF A GOD OF LOVE.
WHEN I RETURN, WE'LL TALK.
WHEN YOU RETURN? DON'T YOU MEAN IF YOU RETURN?
GOOD-BYE, MOTHER.
"IF WE NEVER MEET AGAIN IN THIS WORLD, I WILL SEE YOU IN THE NEXT."
THIS MEANS SOME-THING.
WHAT?
SOMETHING SIGNIFICANT.
YEAH, BUT WHAT?
A SWORD FROM A THEMYSCIRAN FORGE WILL ALWAYS TRY TO RETURN TO ITS RIGHTFUL OWNER.
ITS POWER INCREASES THE CLOSER IT GETS TO ITS BEARER.
WHICH MEANS-- SOMEHOW-- THAT ANTIOPE IS SOMEWHERE HERE IN THIS--
KKRRAKOOM

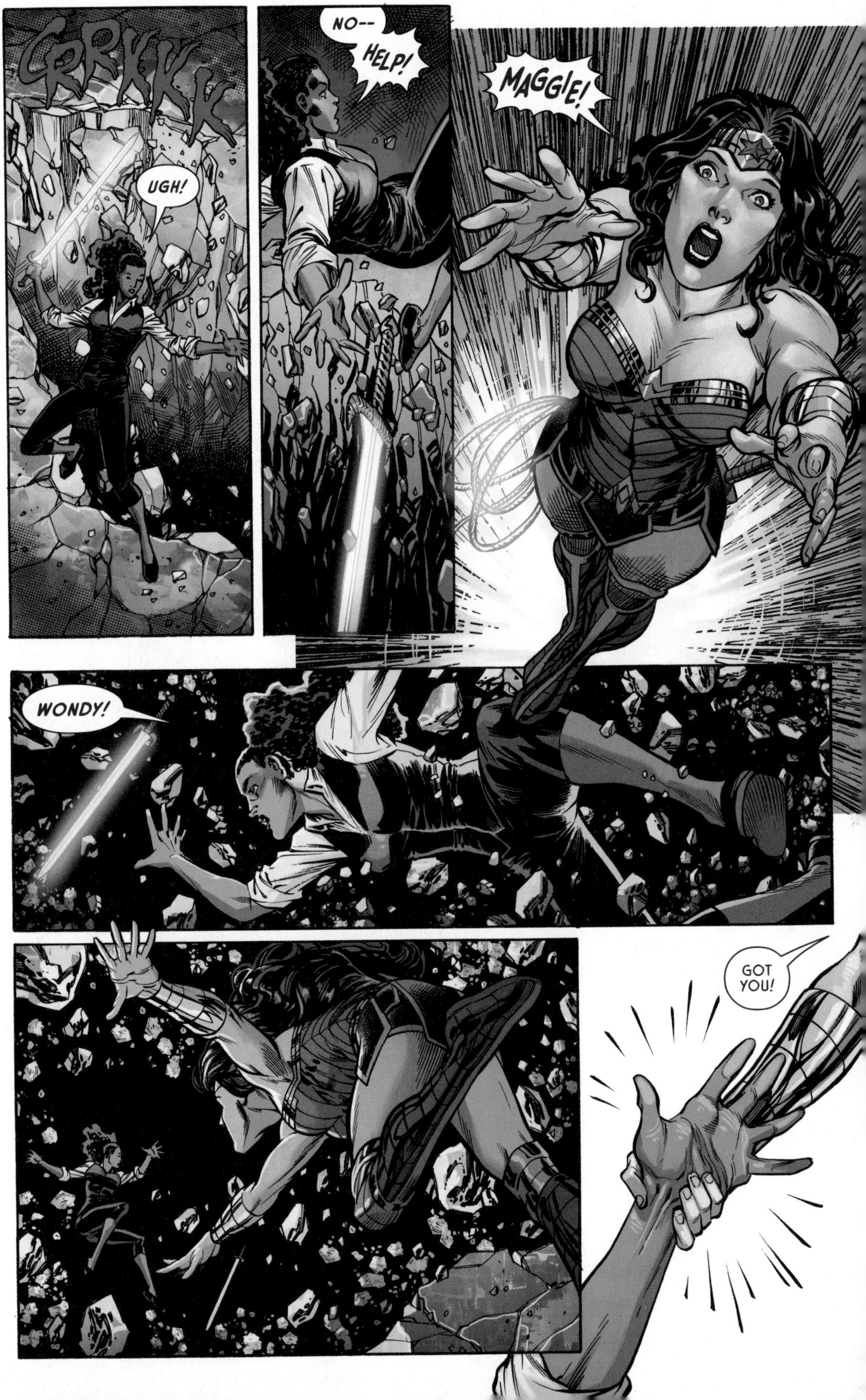
CRRKKK
UGH!
NO--
HELP!
MAGGIE!
WONDY!
GOT YOU!

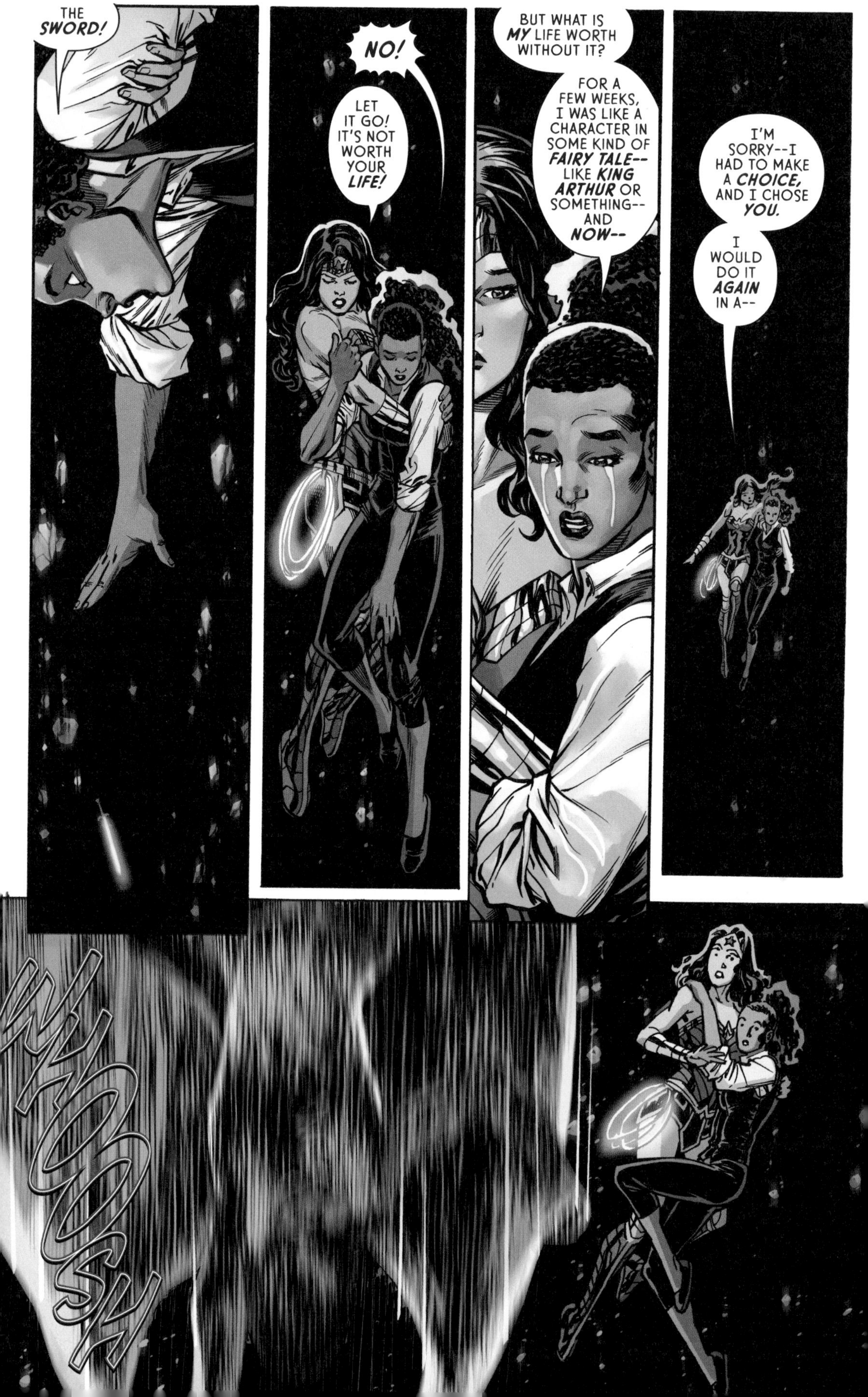
THE SWORD!
NO!
LET IT GO! IT'S NOT WORTH YOUR LIFE!
BUT WHAT IS MY LIFE WORTH WITHOUT IT?
FOR A FEW WEEKS, I WAS LIKE A CHARACTER IN SOME KIND OF FAIRY TALE-- LIKE KING ARTHUR OR SOMETHING-- AND NOW--
I'M SORRY--I HAD TO MAKE A CHOICE, AND I CHOSE YOU.
I WOULD DO IT AGAIN IN A--
WHOOOOSH

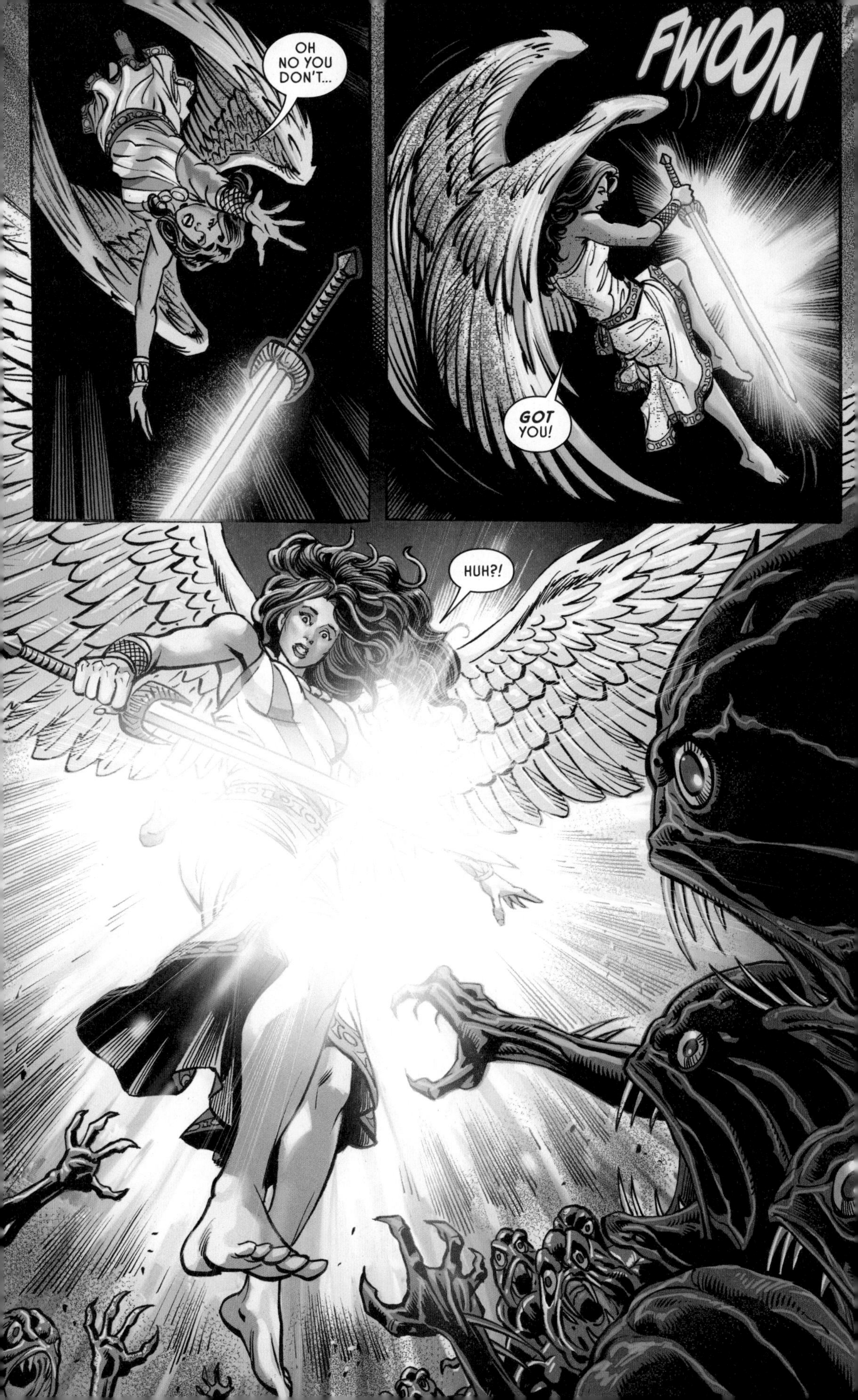
OH NO YOU DON'T...
FWOOM
GOT YOU!
HUH?!

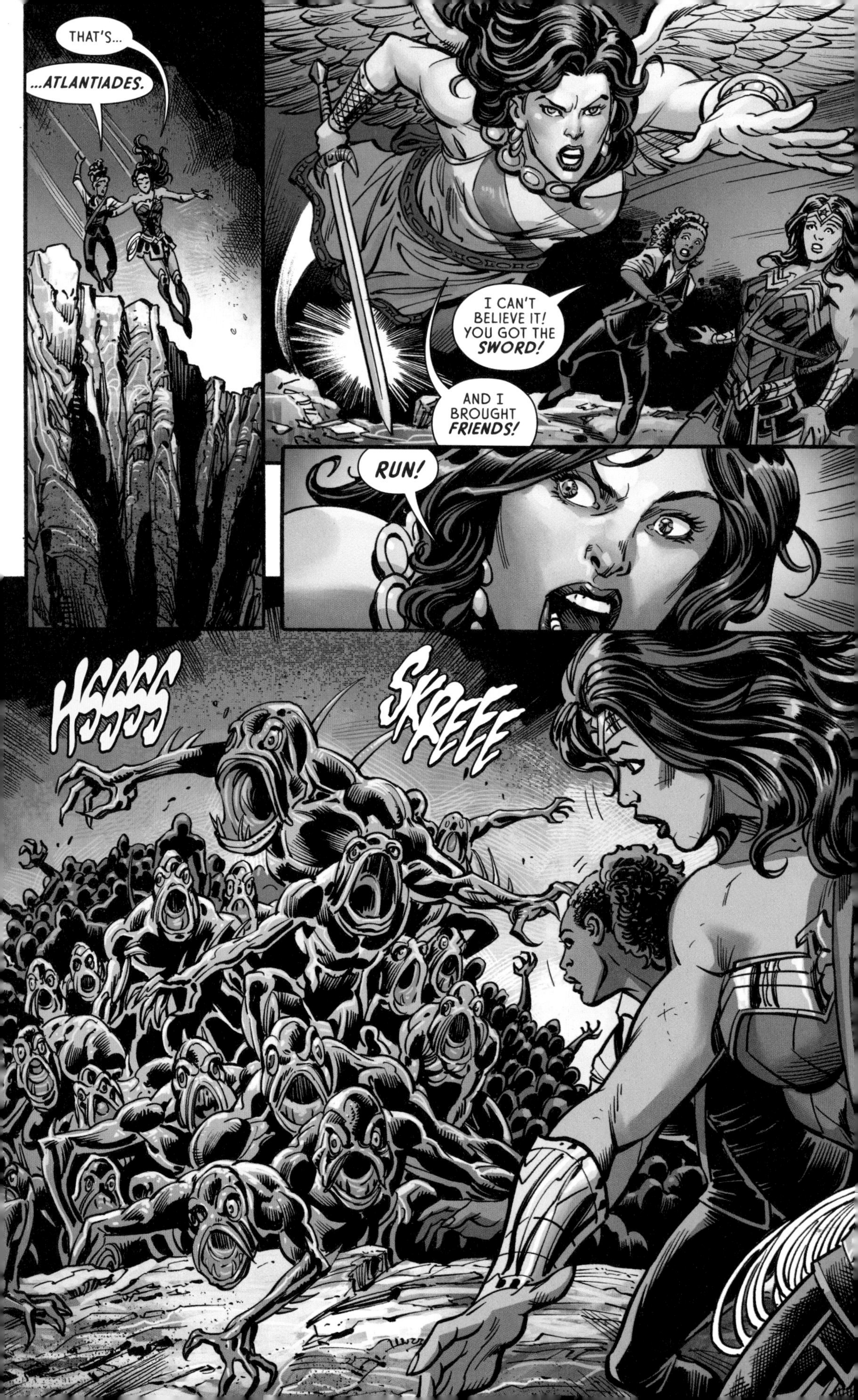
THAT'S...
...ATLANTIADES.
I CAN'T BELIEVE IT! YOU GOT THE SWORD!
AND I BROUGHT FRIENDS!
RUN!
HSSSS
SKREEE

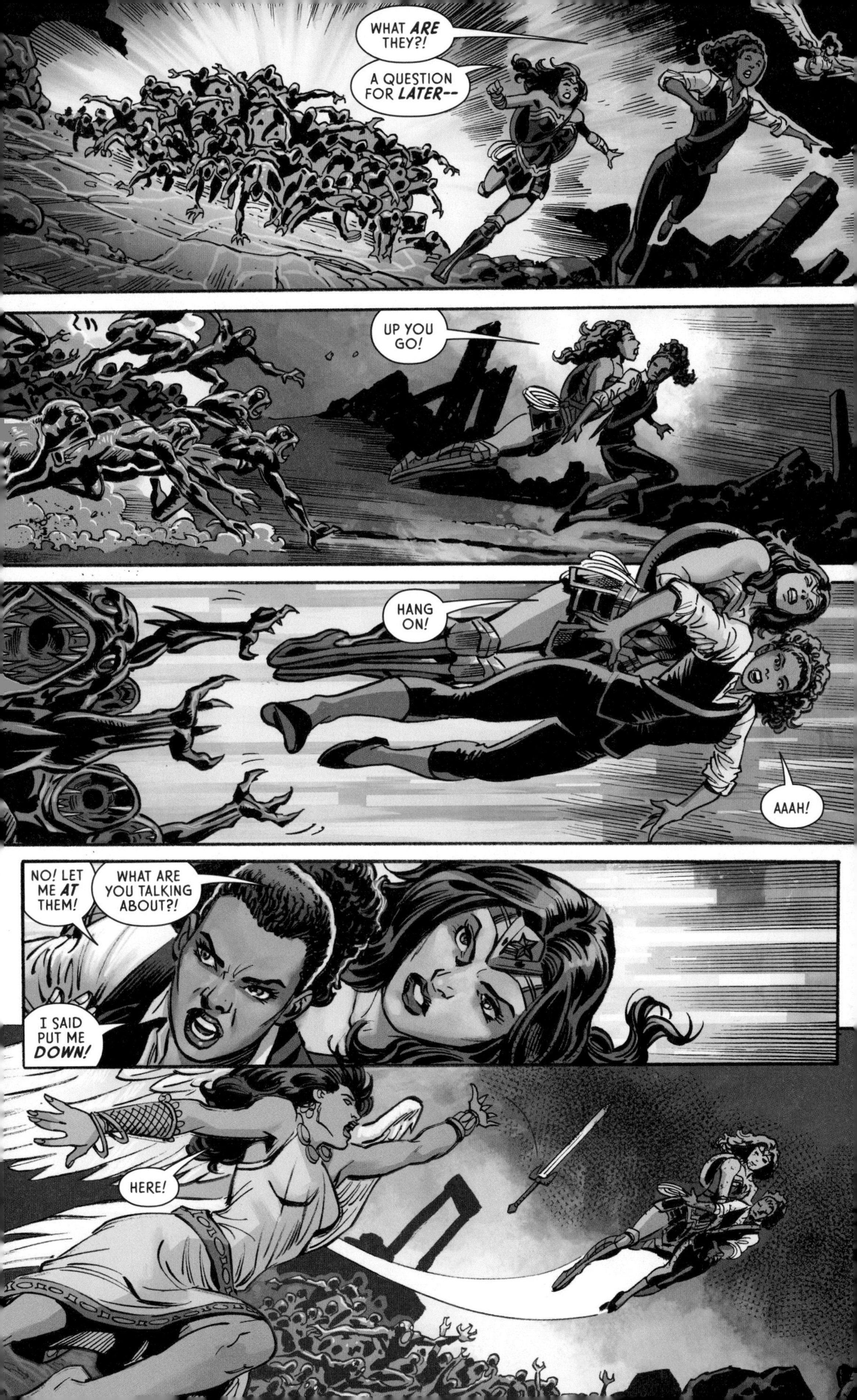

WHAT ARE THEY?!
A QUESTION FOR LATER--
UP YOU GO!
HANG ON!
AAAH!
NO! LET ME AT THEM!
WHAT ARE YOU TALKING ABOUT?!
I SAID PUT ME DOWN!
HERE!

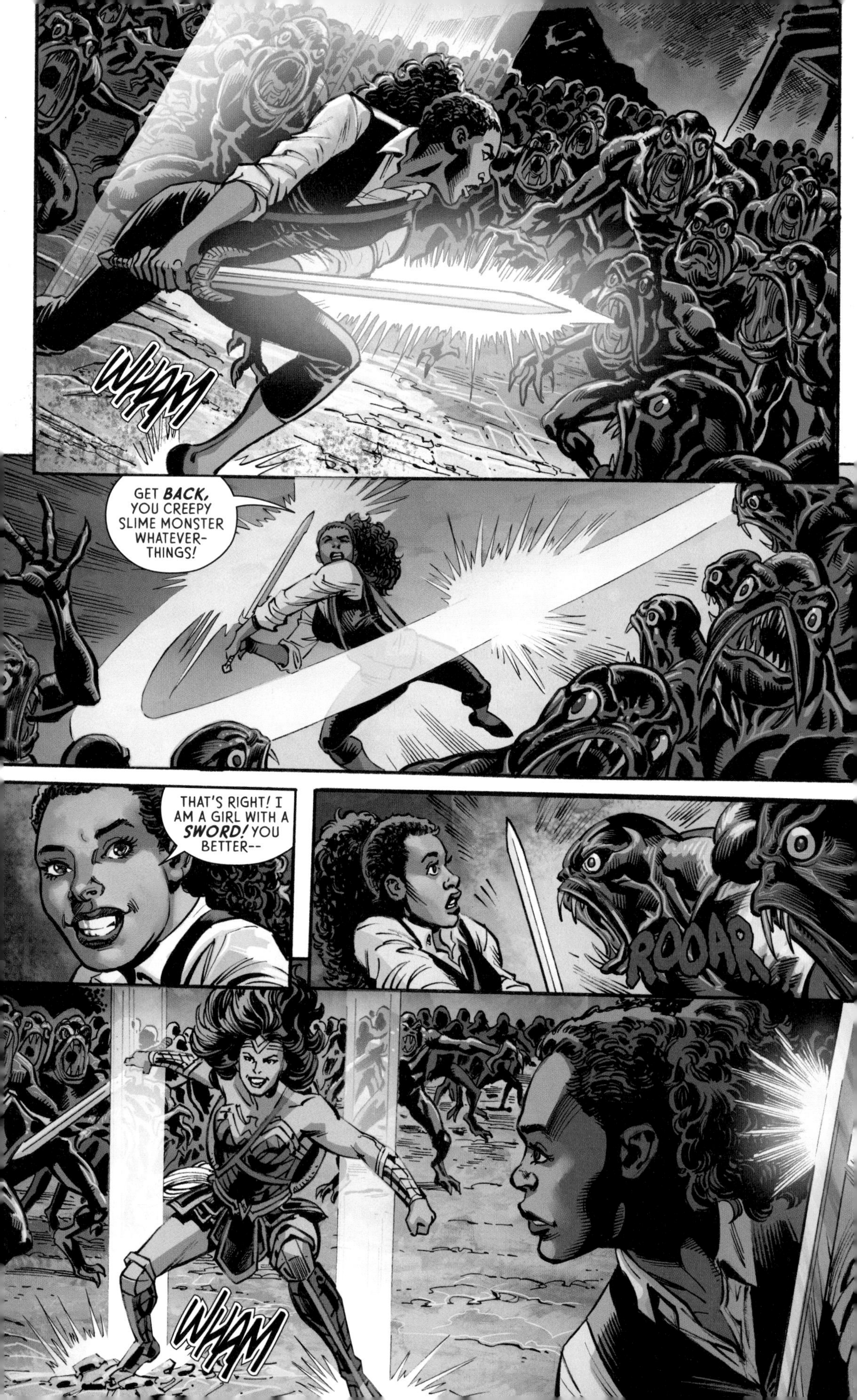

WHAM
GET BACK, YOU CREEPY SLIME MONSTER WHATEVER-THINGS!
THAT'S RIGHT! I AM A GIRL WITH A SWORD! YOU BETTER--
ROOAR
WHAM

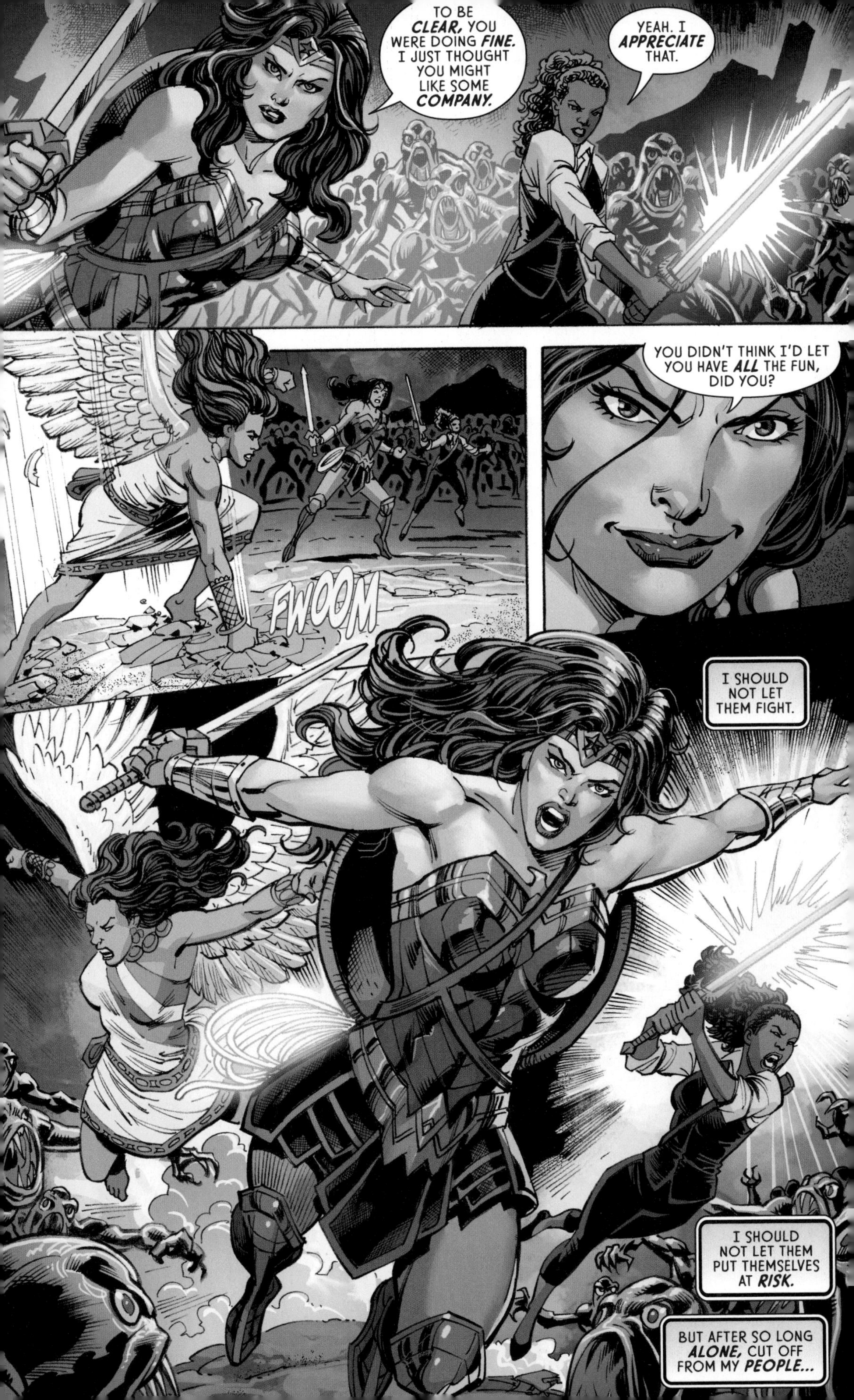
TO BE CLEAR, YOU WERE DOING FINE. I JUST THOUGHT YOU MIGHT LIKE SOME COMPANY.
YEAH. I APPRECIATE THAT.
FWOOM
YOU DIDN'T THINK I'D LET YOU HAVE ALL THE FUN, DID YOU?
I SHOULD NOT LET THEM FIGHT.
I SHOULD NOT LET THEM PUT THEMSELVES AT RISK.
BUT AFTER SO LONG ALONE, CUT OFF FROM MY PEOPLE...

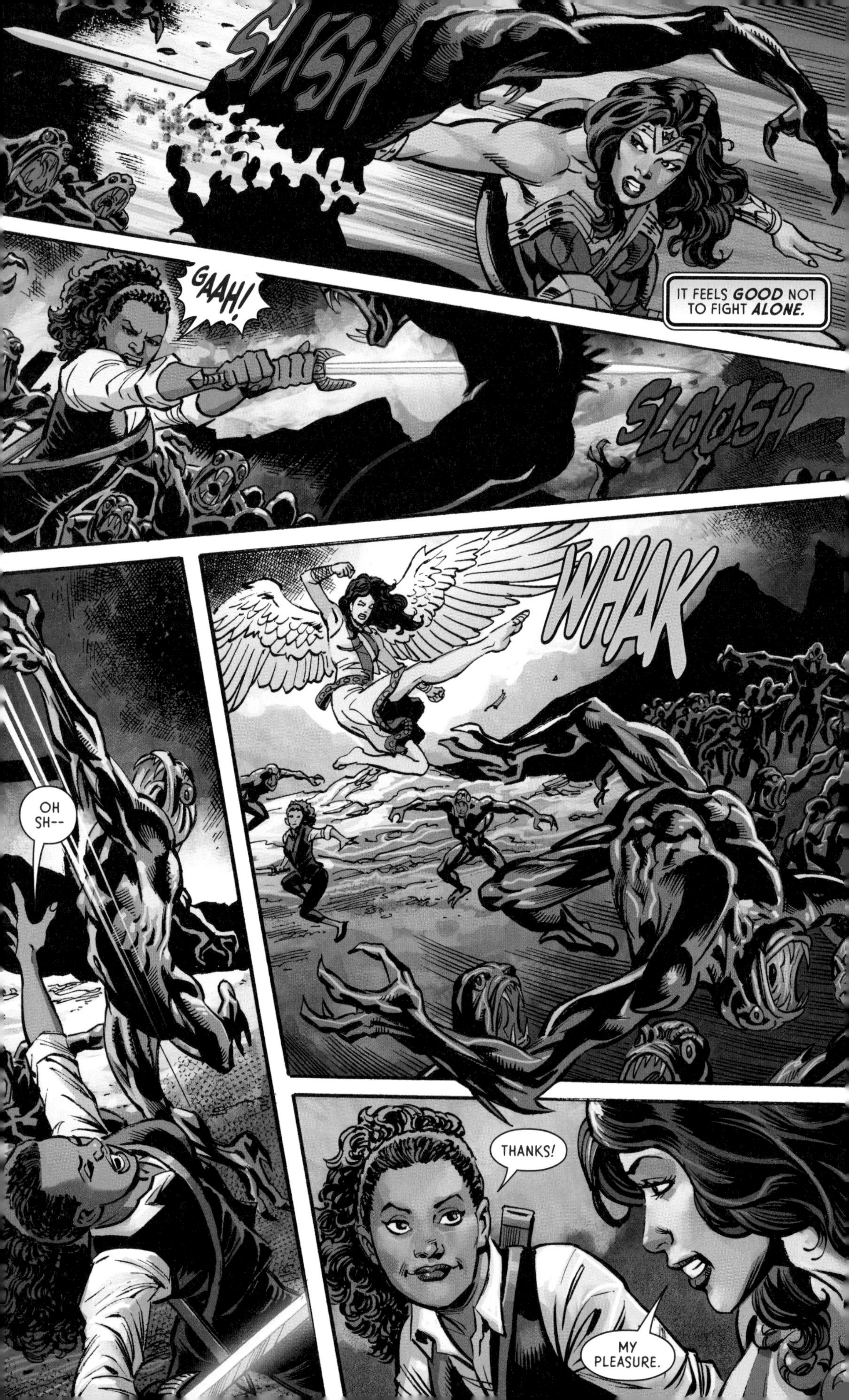
SLISH
IT FEELS GOOD NOT TO FIGHT ALONE.
GAAH!
SLOOSH
WHAK
OH SH--
THANKS!
MY PLEASURE.

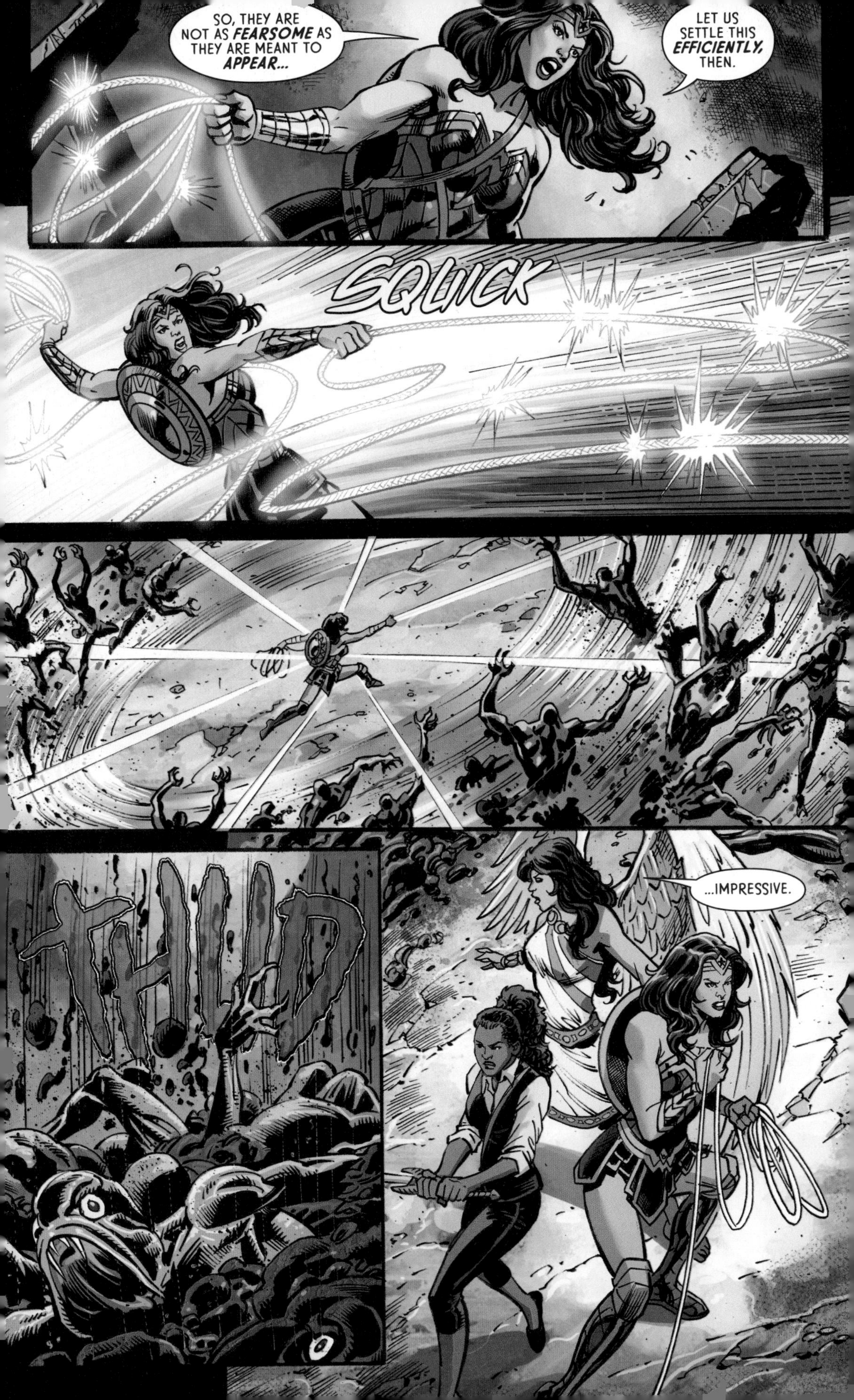
SO, THEY ARE NOT AS FEARSOME AS THEY ARE MEANT TO APPEAR...
LET US SETTLE THIS EFFICIENTLY, THEN.
SQUICK
THUD
...IMPRESSIVE.

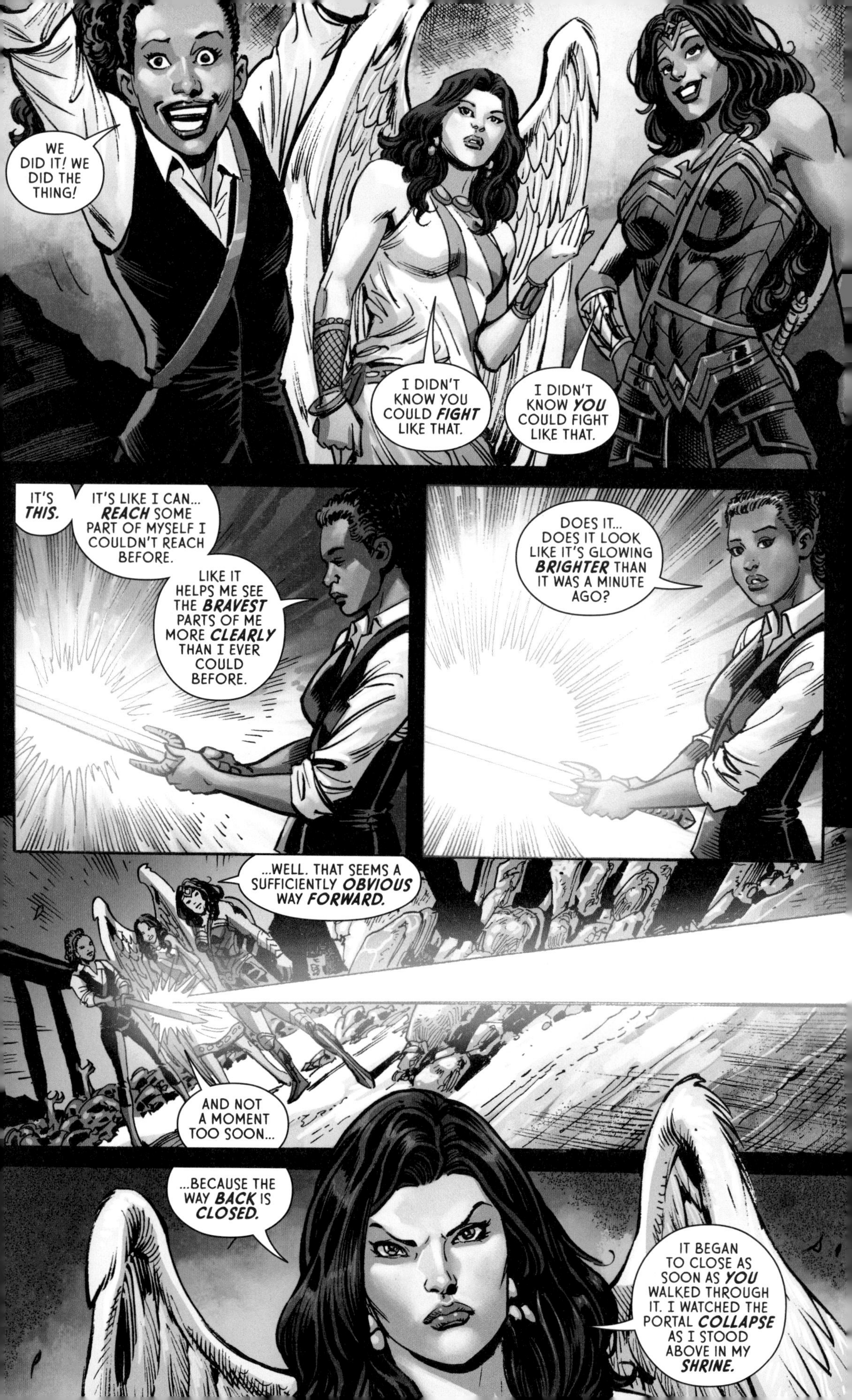
WE DID IT! WE DID THE THING!
I DIDN'T KNOW YOU COULD FIGHT LIKE THAT.
I DIDN'T KNOW YOU COULD FIGHT LIKE THAT.
IT'S THIS.
IT'S LIKE I CAN... REACH SOME PART OF MYSELF I COULDN'T REACH BEFORE.
LIKE IT HELPS ME SEE THE BRAVEST PARTS OF ME MORE CLEARLY THAN I EVER COULD BEFORE.
DOES IT... DOES IT LOOK LIKE IT'S GLOWING BRIGHTER THAN IT WAS A MINUTE AGO?
...WELL. THAT SEEMS A SUFFICIENTLY OBVIOUS WAY FORWARD.
AND NOT A MOMENT TOO SOON...
...BECAUSE THE WAY BACK IS CLOSED.
IT BEGAN TO CLOSE AS SOON AS YOU WALKED THROUGH IT. I WATCHED THE PORTAL COLLAPSE AS I STOOD ABOVE IN MY SHRINE.

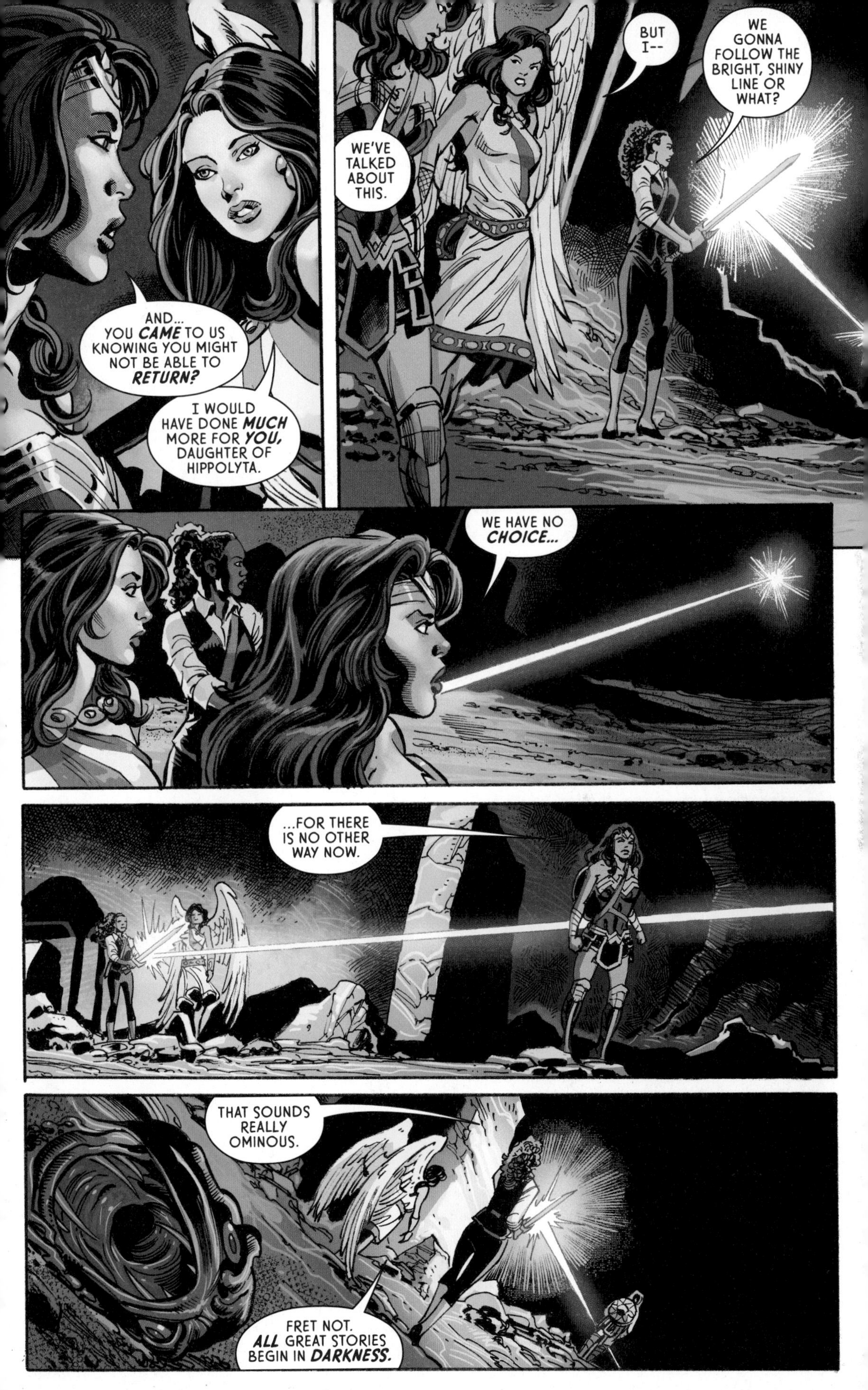
AND... YOU CAME TO US KNOWING YOU MIGHT NOT BE ABLE TO RETURN?
I WOULD HAVE DONE MUCH MORE FOR YOU, DAUGHTER OF HIPPOLYTA.
WE'VE TALKED ABOUT THIS.
BUT I--
WE GONNA FOLLOW THE BRIGHT, SHINY LINE OR WHAT?
WE HAVE NO CHOICE...
...FOR THERE IS NO OTHER WAY NOW.
THAT SOUNDS REALLY OMINOUS.
FRET NOT. ALL GREAT STORIES BEGIN IN DARKNESS.

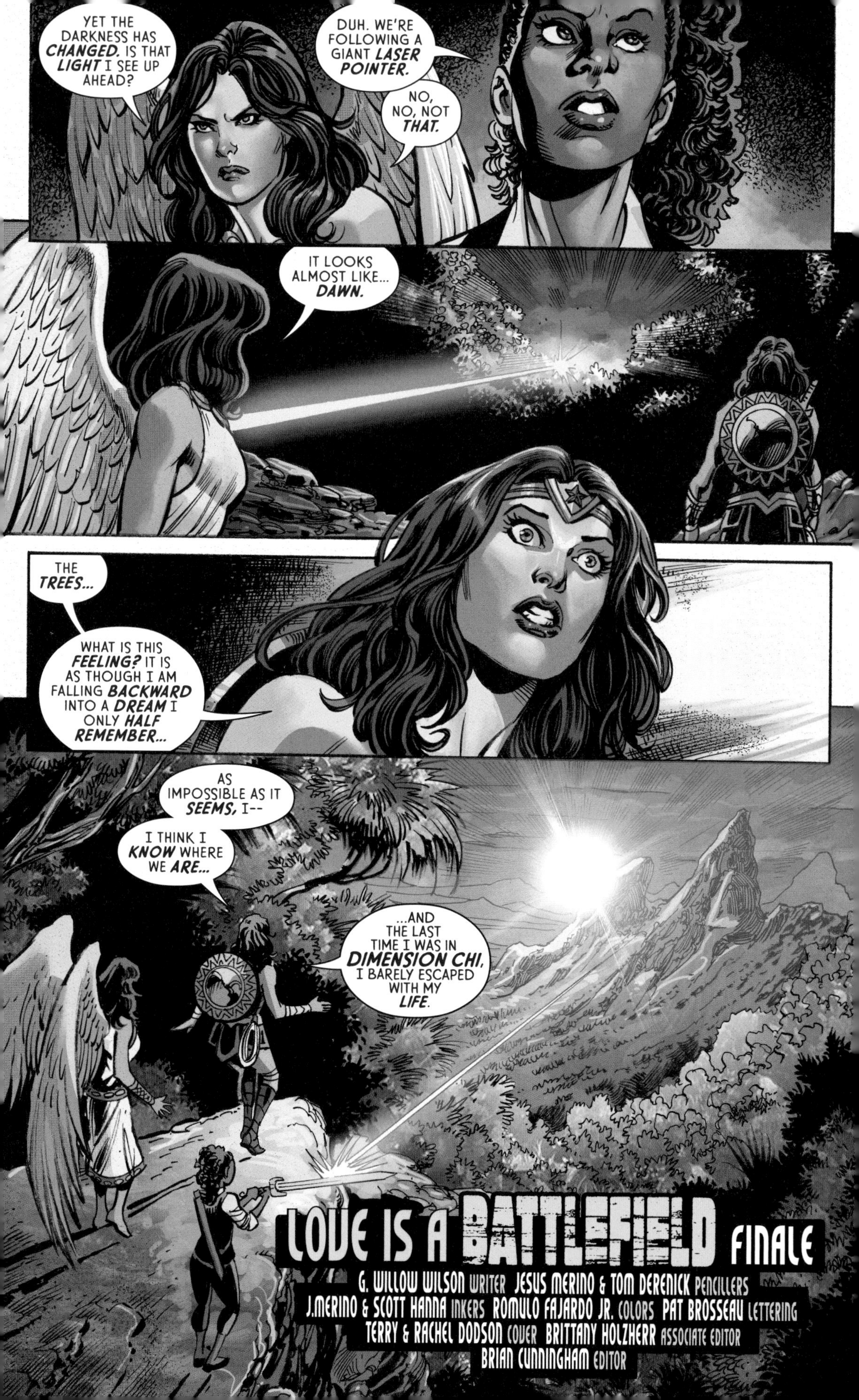
YET THE DARKNESS HAS CHANGED. IS THAT LIGHT I SEE UP AHEAD?
DUH. WE'RE FOLLOWING A GIANT LASER POINTER.
NO, NO, NOT THAT.
IT LOOKS ALMOST LIKE... DAWN.
THE TREES...
WHAT IS THIS FEELING? IT IS AS THOUGH I AM FALLING BACKWARD INTO A DREAM I ONLY HALF REMEMBER...
AS IMPOSSIBLE AS IT SEEMS, I--
I THINK I KNOW WHERE WE ARE...
...AND THE LAST TIME I WAS IN DIMENSION CHI, I BARELY ESCAPED WITH MY LIFE.
LOVE IS A BATTLEFIELD FINALE
G. WILLOW WILSON WRITER JESUS MERINO & TOM DERENICK PENCILLERS
J.MERINO & SCOTT HANNA INKERS ROMULO FAJARDO JR. COLORS PAT BROSSEAU LETTERING
TERRY & RACHEL DODSON COVER BRITTANY HOLZHERR ASSOCIATE EDITOR
BRIAN CUNNINGHAM EDITOR

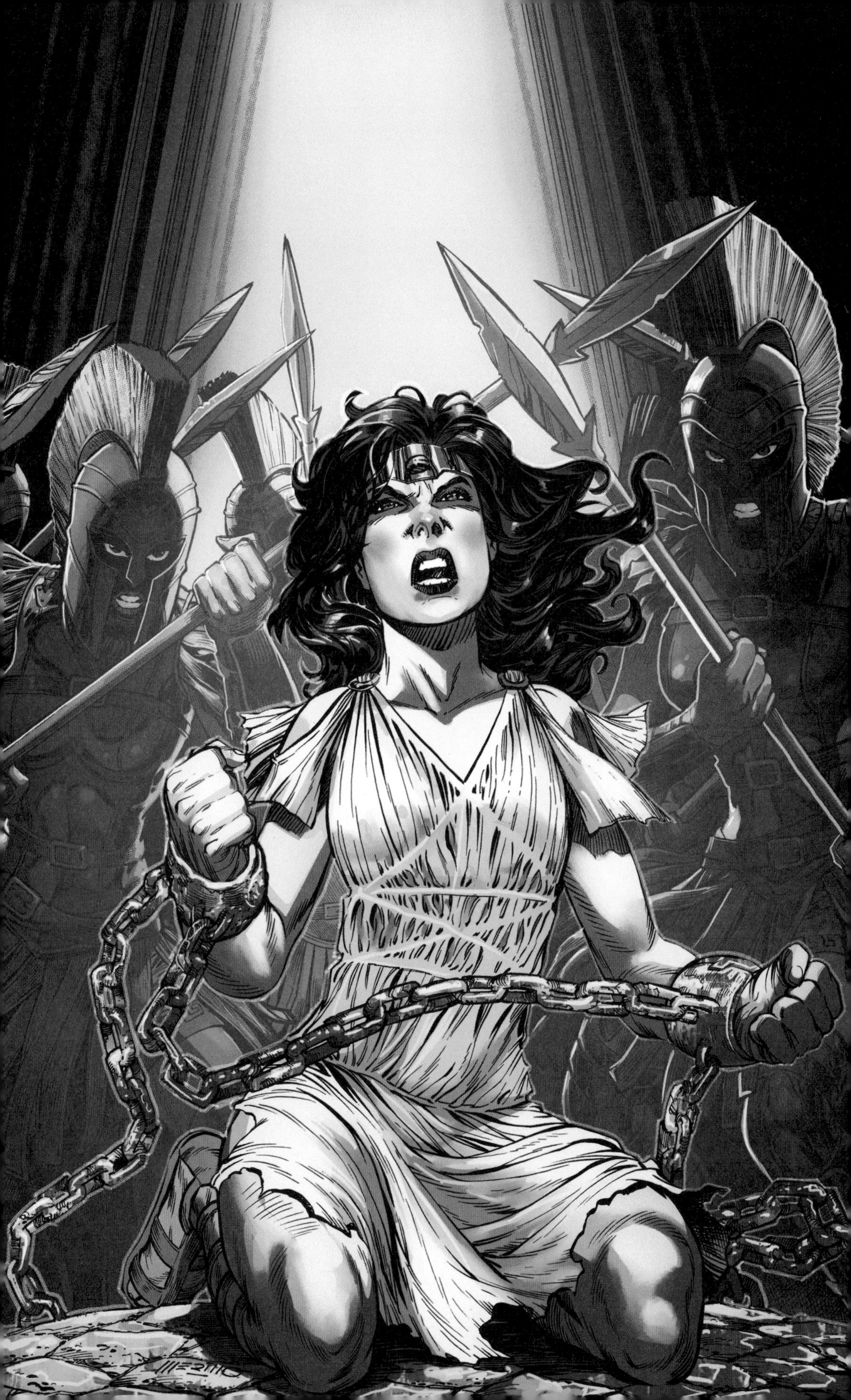

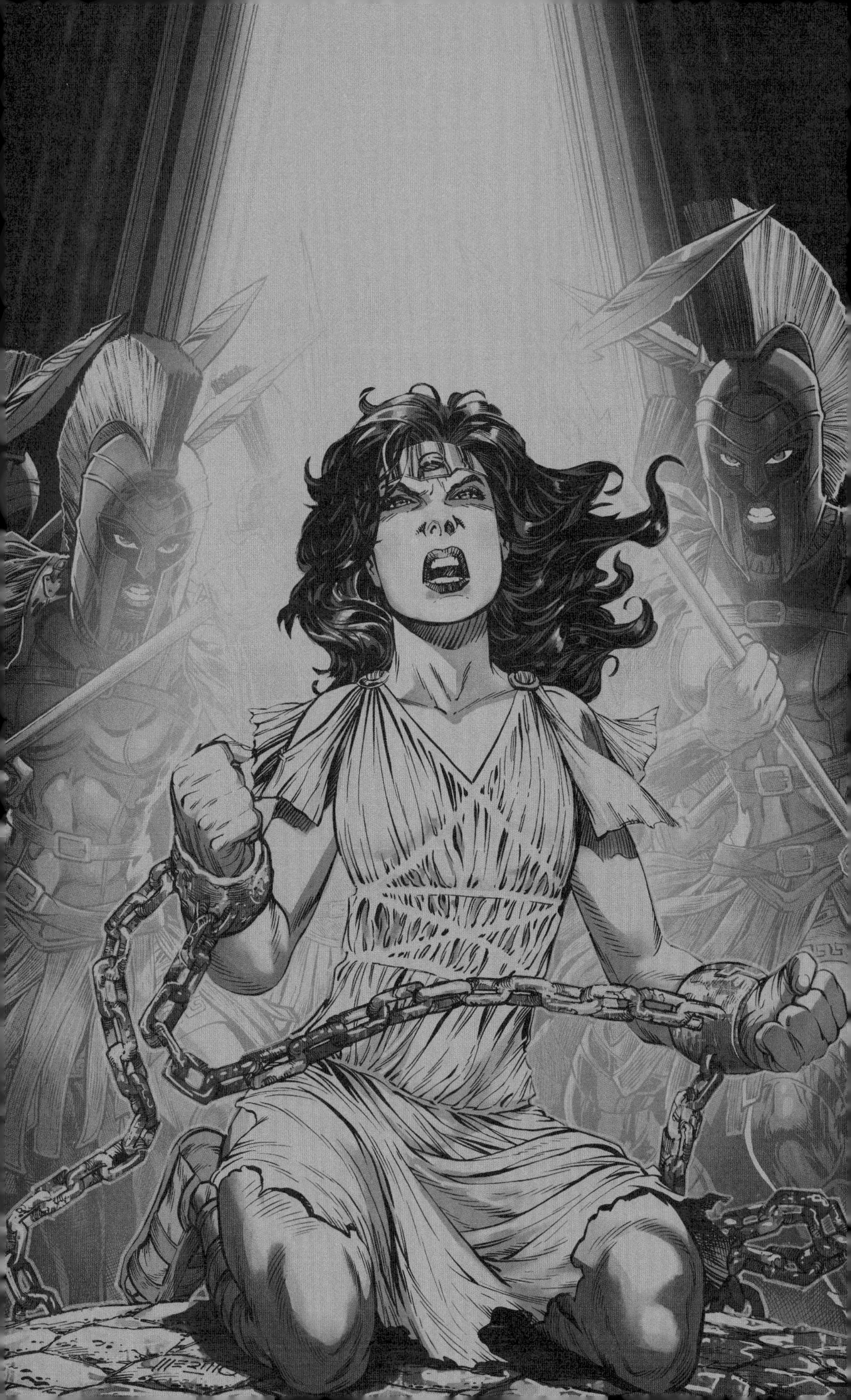

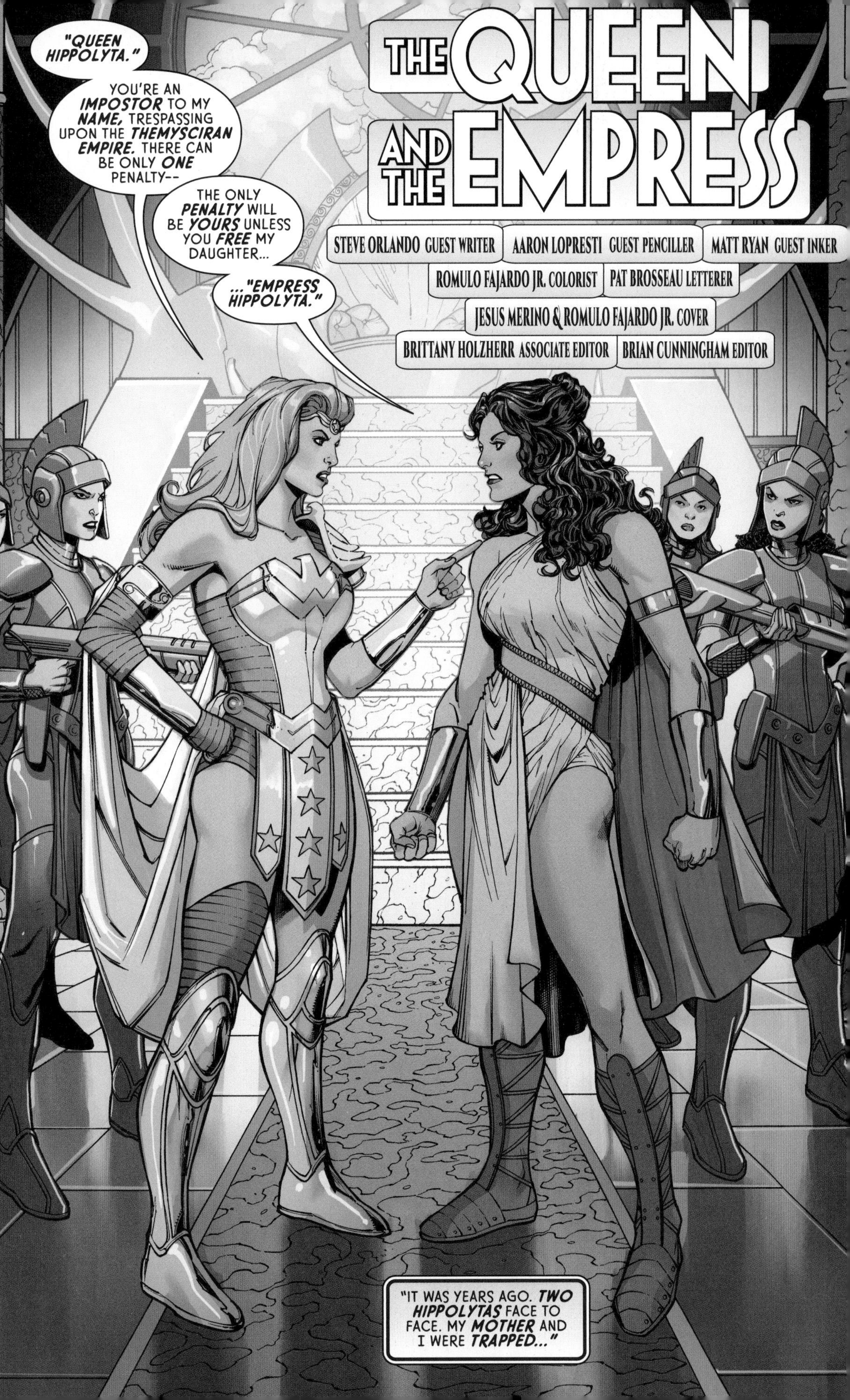
"QUEEN HIPPOLYTA."
YOU'RE AN IMPOSTOR TO MY NAME, TRESPASSING UPON THE THEMYSCIRAN EMPIRE. THERE CAN BE ONLY ONE PENALTY--
THE QUEEN AND THE EMPRESS
STEVE ORLANDO GUEST WRITER
AARON LOPRESTI GUEST PENCILLER
MATT RYAN GUEST INKER
ROMULO FAJARDO JR. COLORIST
PAT BROSSEAU LETTERER
JESUS MERINO & ROMULO FAJARDO JR. COVER
BRITTANY HOLZHERR ASSOCIATE EDITOR
BRIAN CUNNINGHAM EDITOR
THE ONLY PENALTY WILL BE YOURS UNLESS YOU FREE MY DAUGHTER...
..."EMPRESS HIPPOLYTA."
"IT WAS YEARS AGO. TWO HIPPOLYTAS FACE TO FACE. MY MOTHER AND I WERE TRAPPED..."

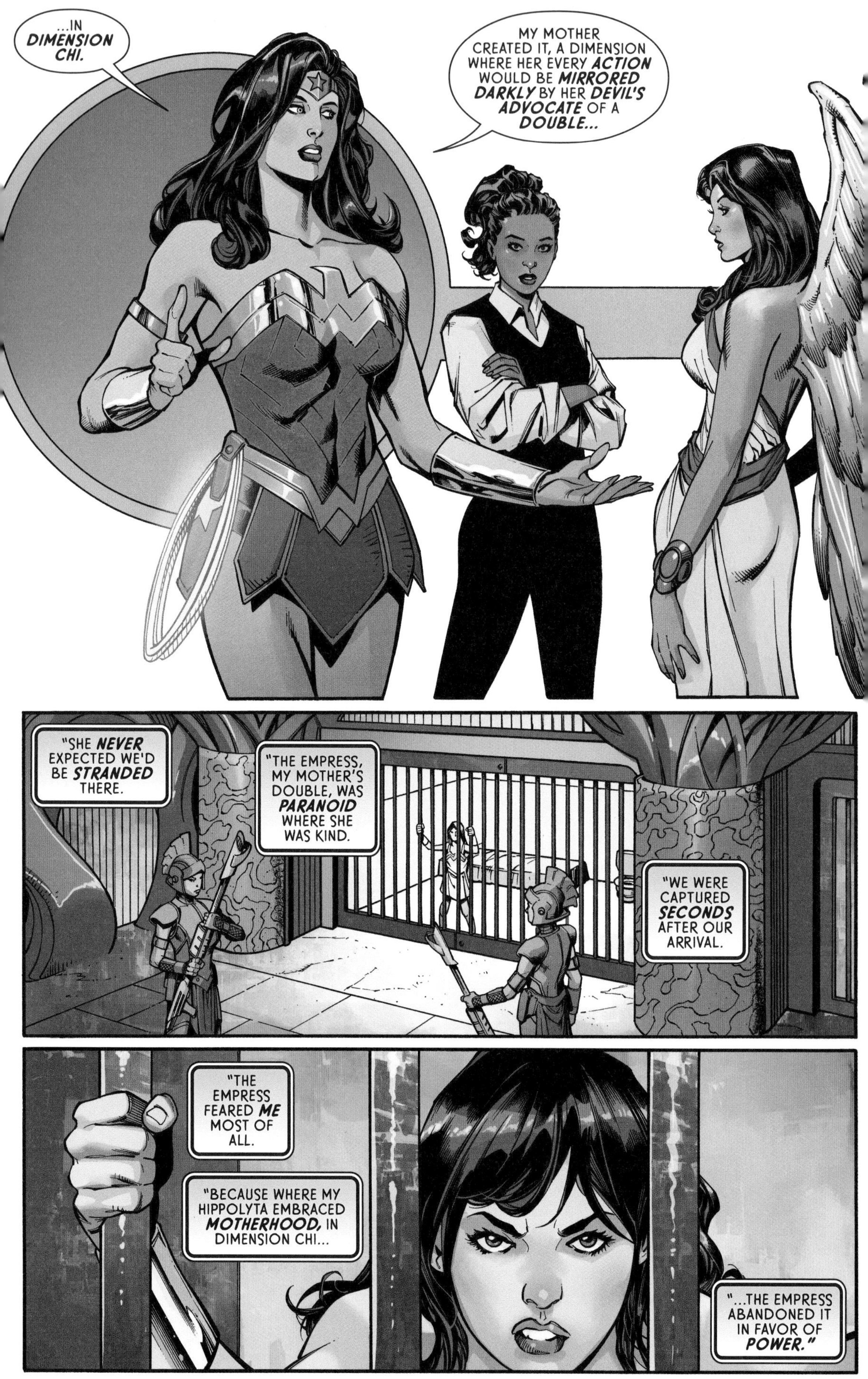
...IN DIMENSION CHI.
MY MOTHER CREATED IT, A DIMENSION WHERE HER EVERY ACTION WOULD BE MIRRORED DARKLY BY HER DEVIL'S ADVOCATE OF A DOUBLE...
"SHE NEVER EXPECTED WE'D BE STRANDED THERE.
"THE EMPRESS, MY MOTHER'S DOUBLE, WAS PARANOID WHERE SHE WAS KIND.
"WE WERE CAPTURED SECONDS AFTER OUR ARRIVAL.
"THE EMPRESS FEARED ME MOST OF ALL.
"BECAUSE WHERE MY HIPPOLYTA EMBRACED MOTHERHOOD, IN DIMENSION CHI...
"...THE EMPRESS ABANDONED IT IN FAVOR OF POWER."

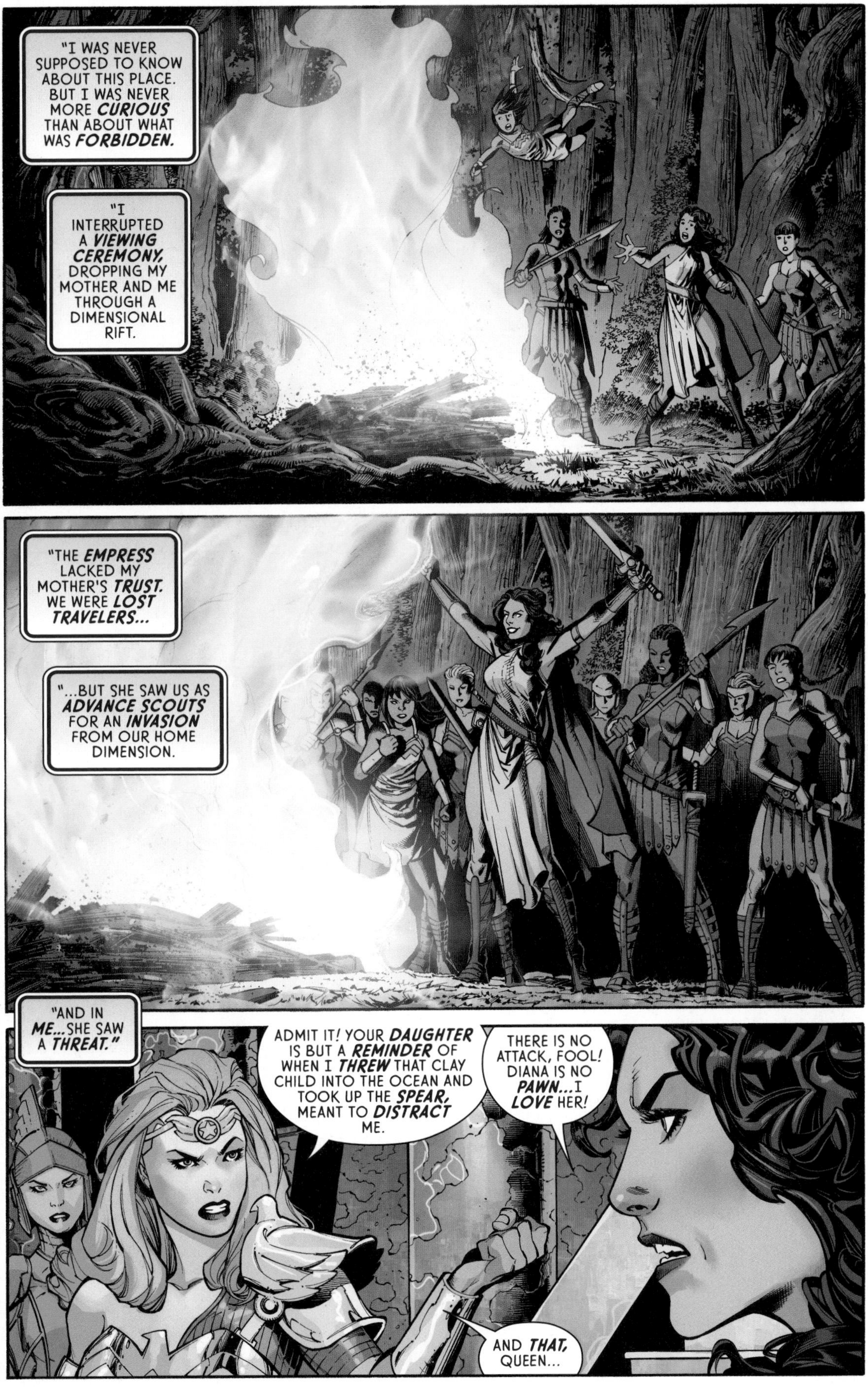
"I WAS NEVER SUPPOSED TO KNOW ABOUT THIS PLACE. BUT I WAS NEVER MORE CURIOUS THAN ABOUT WHAT WAS FORBIDDEN.
"I INTERRUPTED A VIEWING CEREMONY, DROPPING MY MOTHER AND ME THROUGH A DIMENSIONAL RIFT.
"THE EMPRESS LACKED MY MOTHER'S TRUST. WE WERE LOST TRAVELERS...
"...BUT SHE SAW US AS ADVANCE SCOUTS FOR AN INVASION FROM OUR HOME DIMENSION.
"AND IN ME...SHE SAW A THREAT."
ADMIT IT! YOUR DAUGHTER IS BUT A REMINDER OF WHEN I THREW THAT CLAY CHILD INTO THE OCEAN AND TOOK UP THE SPEAR, MEANT TO DISTRACT ME.
THERE IS NO ATTACK, FOOL! DIANA IS NO PAWN...I LOVE HER!
AND THAT, QUEEN...

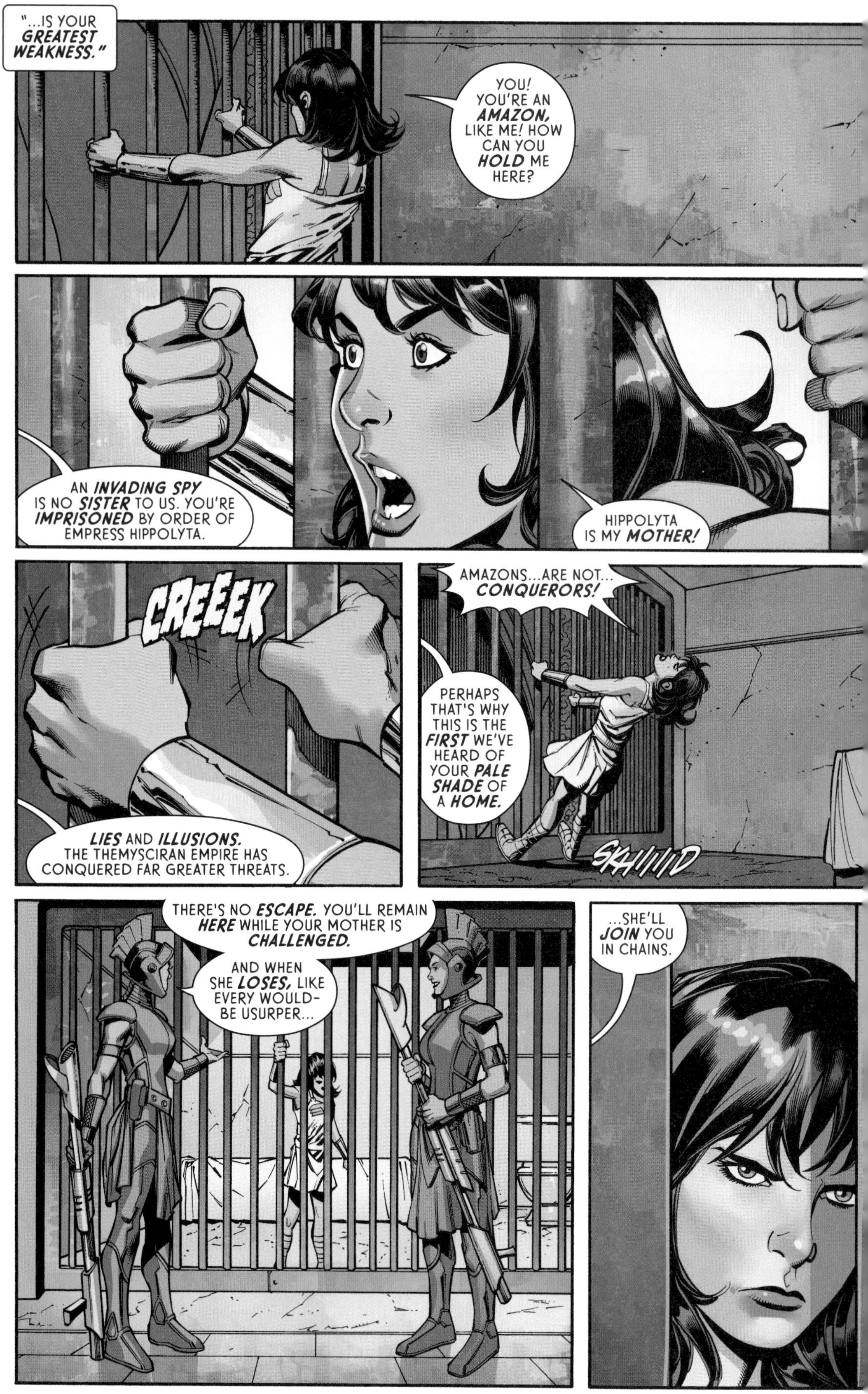
"...IS YOUR GREATEST WEAKNESS."
YOU! YOU'RE AN AMAZON, LIKE ME! HOW CAN YOU HOLD ME HERE?
AN INVADING SPY IS NO SISTER TO US. YOU'RE IMPRISONED BY ORDER OF EMPRESS HIPPOLYTA.
HIPPOLYTA IS MY MOTHER!
CREEEK
LIES AND ILLUSIONS. THE THEMYSCIRAN EMPIRE HAS CONQUERED FAR GREATER THREATS.
AMAZONS...ARE NOT... CONQUERORS!
PERHAPS THAT'S WHY THIS IS THE FIRST WE'VE HEARD OF YOUR PALE SHADE OF A HOME.
SKIIIID
THERE'S NO ESCAPE. YOU'LL REMAIN HERE WHILE YOUR MOTHER IS CHALLENGED.
AND WHEN SHE LOSES, LIKE EVERY WOULD-BE USURPER...
...SHE'LL JOIN YOU IN CHAINS.

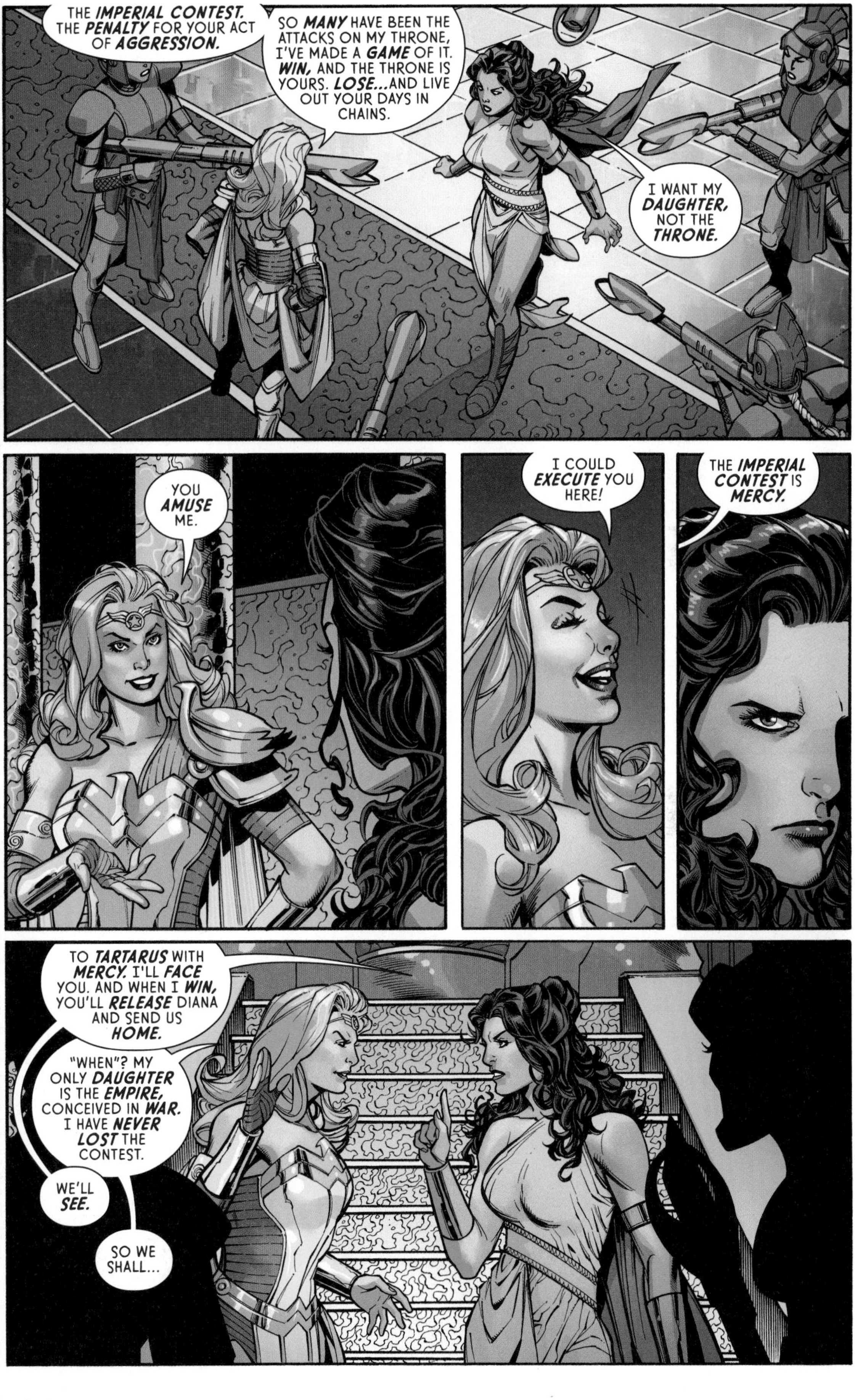
THE IMPERIAL CONTEST. THE PENALTY FOR YOUR ACT OF AGGRESSION.
SO MANY HAVE BEEN THE ATTACKS ON MY THRONE, I'VE MADE A GAME OF IT. WIN, AND THE THRONE IS YOURS. LOSE...AND LIVE OUT YOUR DAYS IN CHAINS.
I WANT MY DAUGHTER, NOT THE THRONE.
YOU AMUSE ME.
I COULD EXECUTE YOU HERE!
THE IMPERIAL CONTEST IS MERCY.
TO TARTARUS WITH MERCY. I'LL FACE YOU. AND WHEN I WIN, YOU'LL RELEASE DIANA AND SEND US HOME.
"WHEN"? MY ONLY DAUGHTER IS THE EMPIRE, CONCEIVED IN WAR. I HAVE NEVER LOST THE CONTEST.
WE'LL SEE.
SO WE SHALL...

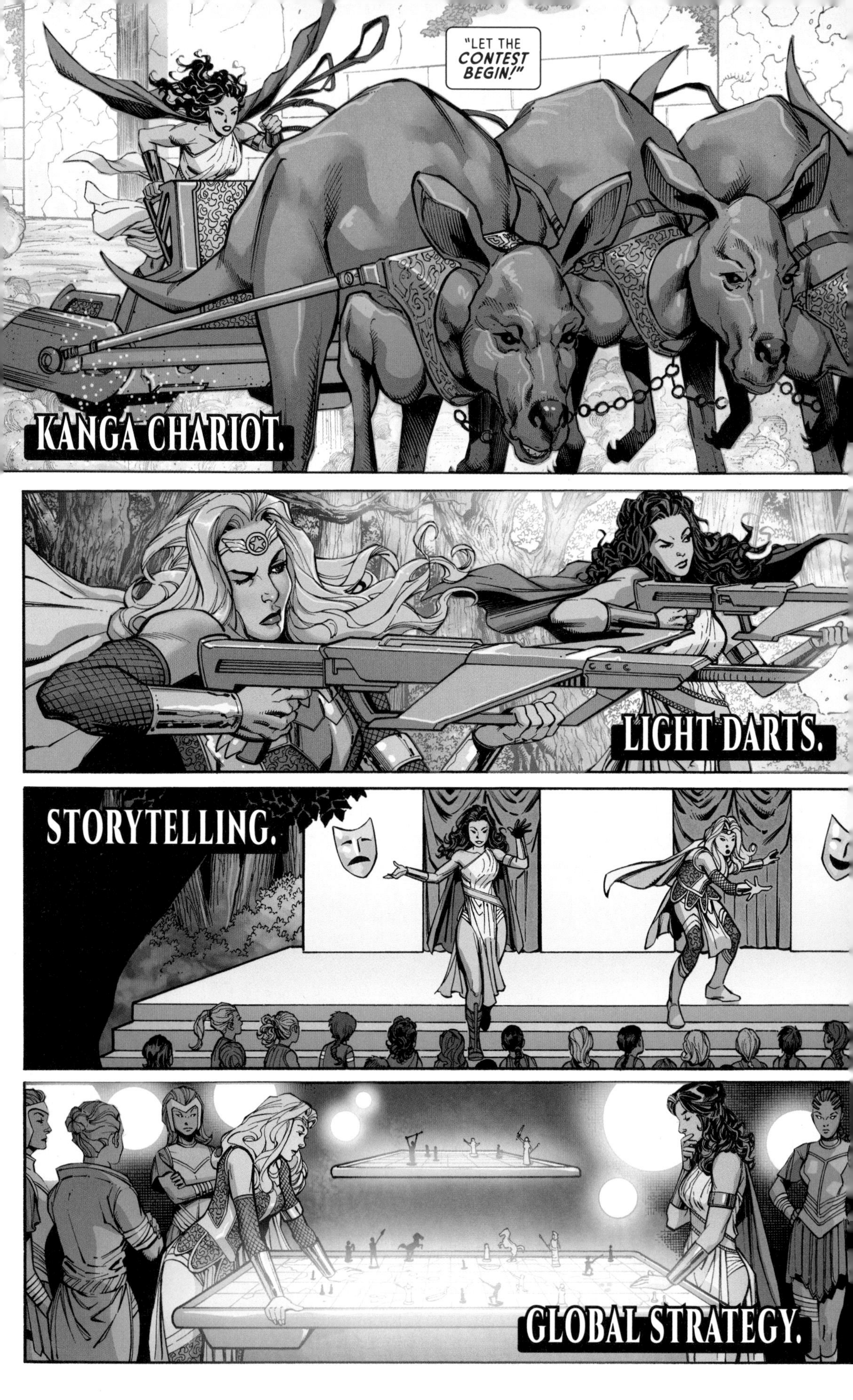
"LET THE CONTEST BEGIN!"
KANGA CHARIOT.
LIGHT DARTS.
STORYTELLING.
GLOBAL STRATEGY.

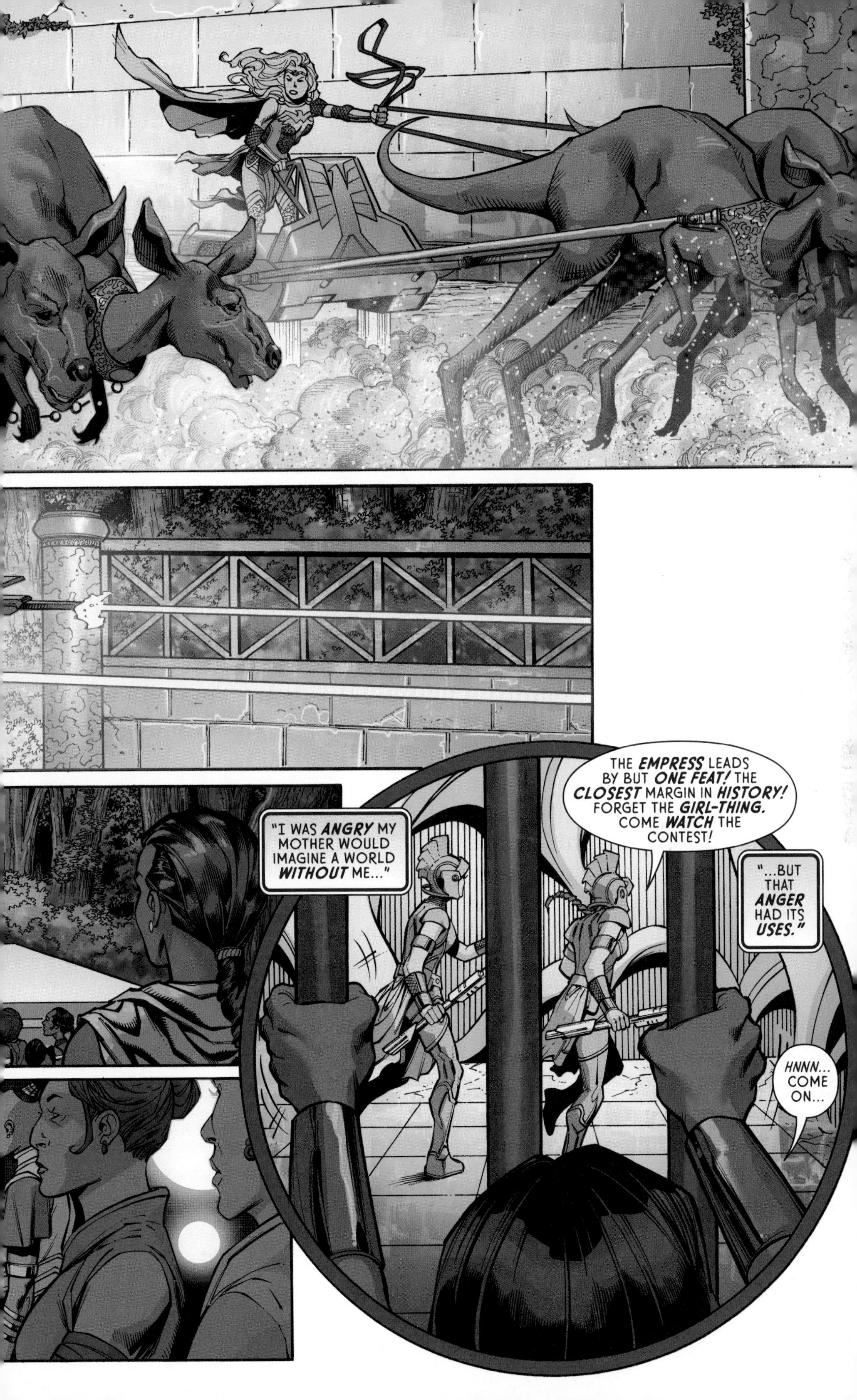
"I WAS ANGRY MY MOTHER WOULD IMAGINE A WORLD WITHOUT ME..."
THE EMPRESS LEADS BY BUT ONE FEAT! THE CLOSEST MARGIN IN HISTORY! FORGET THE GIRL-THING. COME WATCH THE CONTEST!
"...BUT THAT ANGER HAD ITS USES."
HNNN... COME ON...

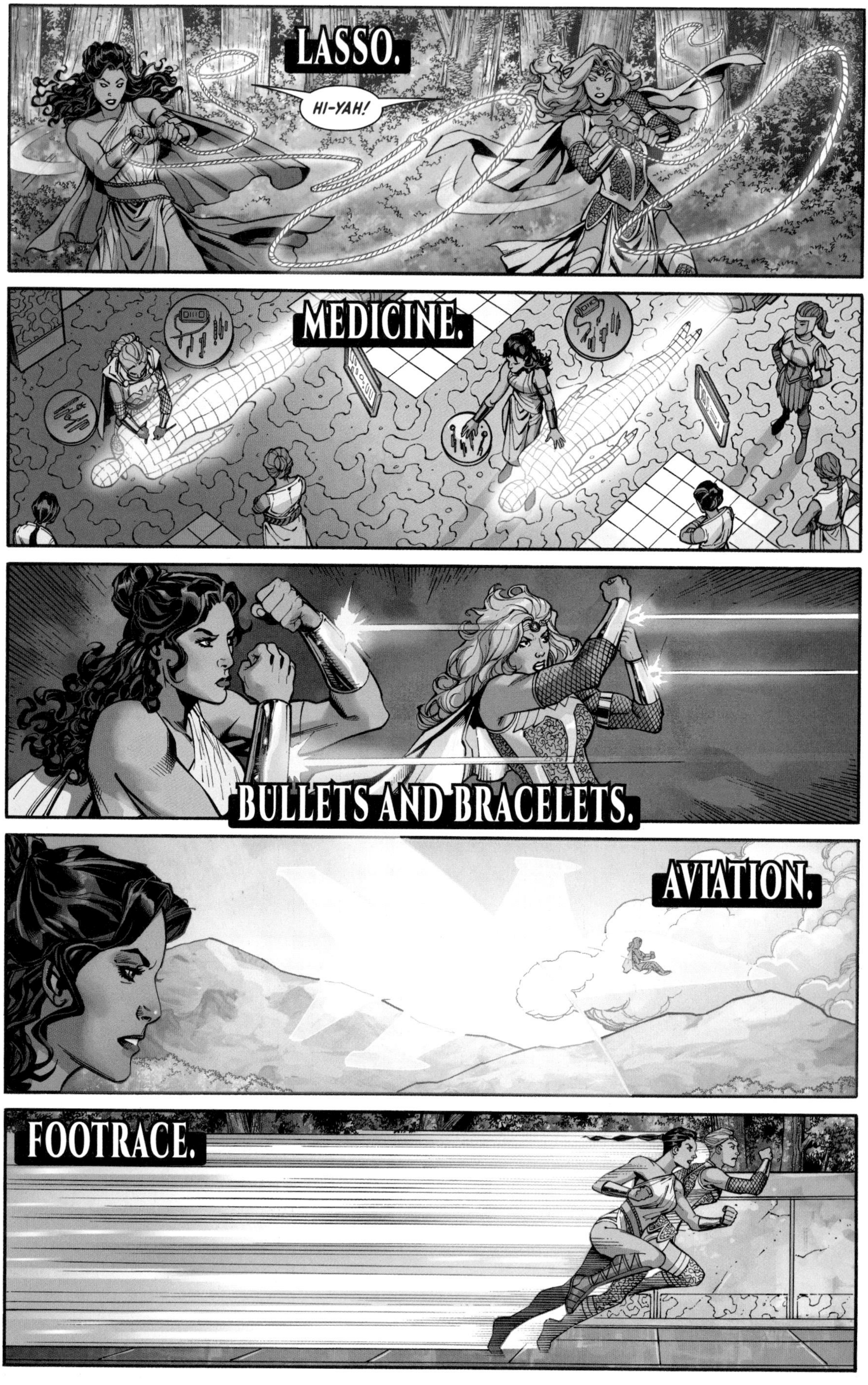
LASSO.
HI-YAH!
MEDICINE.
BULLETS AND BRACELETS.
AVIATION.
FOOTRACE.

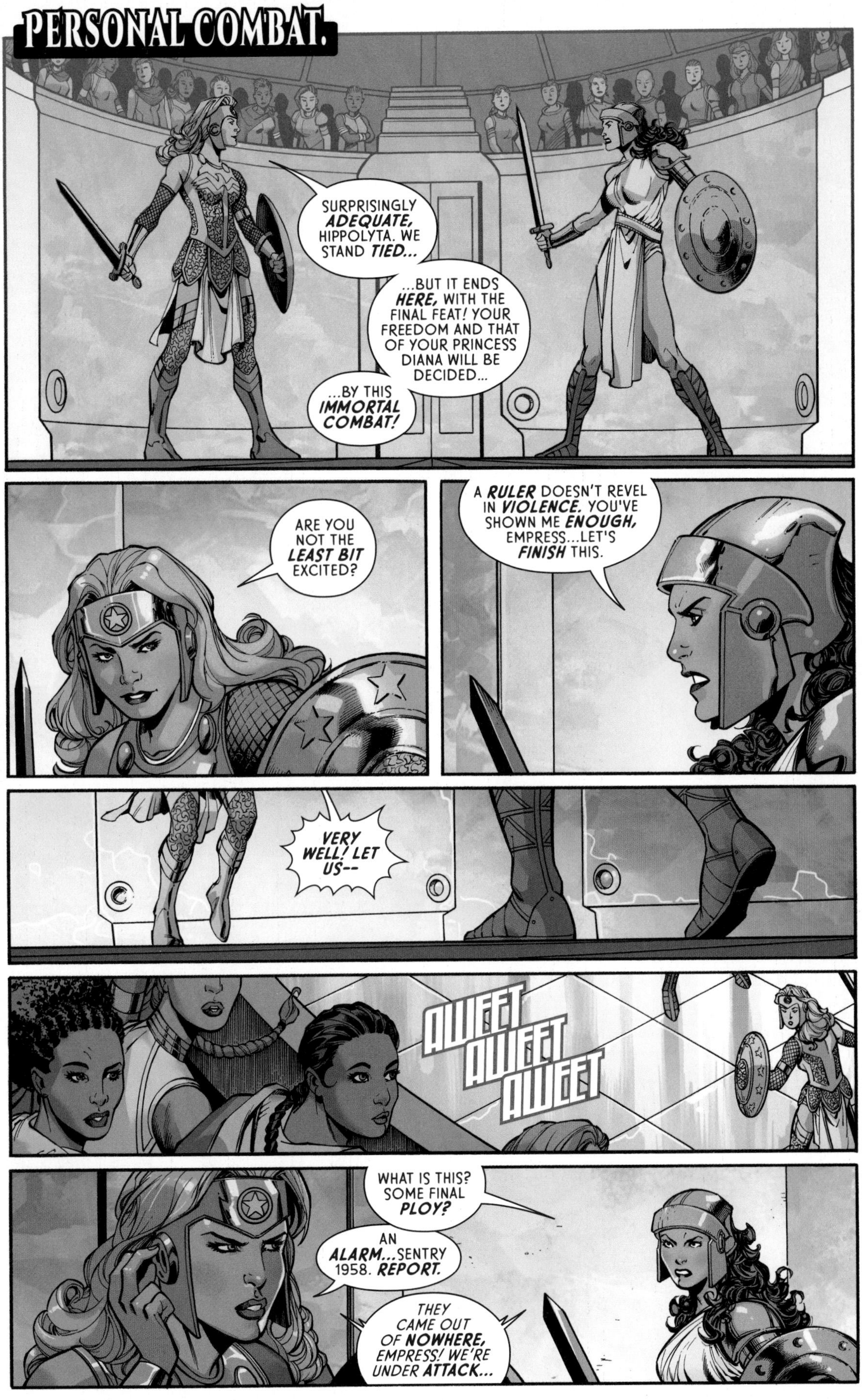
PERSONAL COMBAT.
SURPRISINGLY ADEQUATE, HIPPOLYTA. WE STAND TIED...
...BUT IT ENDS HERE, WITH THE FINAL FEAT! YOUR FREEDOM AND THAT OF YOUR PRINCESS DIANA WILL BE DECIDED...
...BY THIS IMMORTAL COMBAT!
ARE YOU NOT THE LEAST BIT EXCITED?
A RULER DOESN'T REVEL IN VIOLENCE. YOU'VE SHOWN ME ENOUGH, EMPRESS...LET'S FINISH THIS.
VERY WELL! LET US--
AWEET AWEET AWEET
WHAT IS THIS? SOME FINAL PLOY?
AN ALARM...SENTRY 1958. REPORT.
THEY CAME OUT OF NOWHERE, EMPRESS! WE'RE UNDER ATTACK...

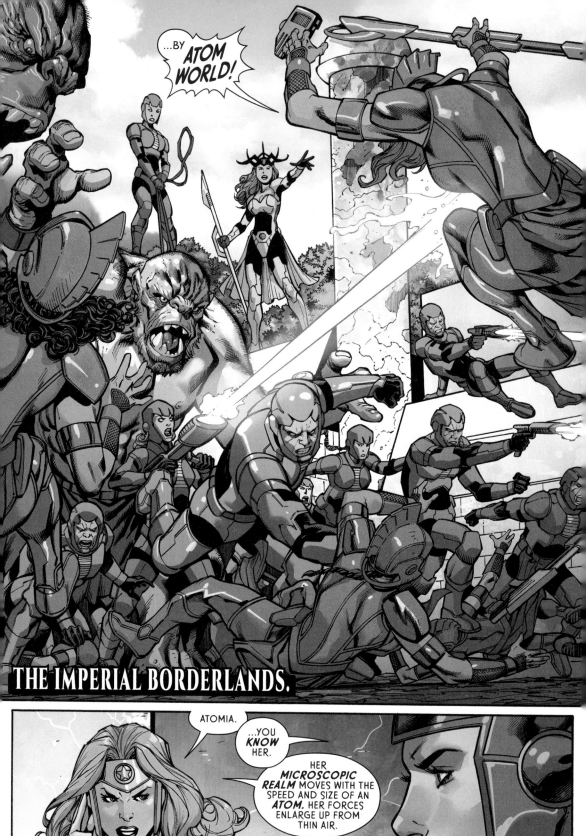

...BY **ATOM WORLD!**

THE IMPERIAL BORDERLANDS.

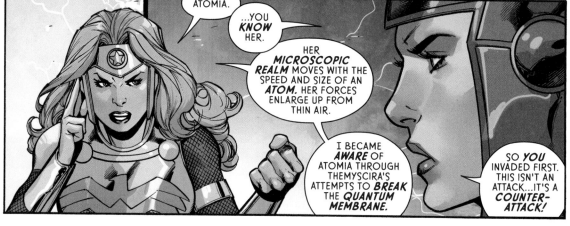

ATOMIA.

...YOU **KNOW** HER.

HER **MICROSCOPIC REALM** MOVES WITH THE SPEED AND SIZE OF AN **ATOM.** HER FORCES ENLARGE UP FROM THIN AIR.

I BECAME **AWARE** OF ATOMIA THROUGH THEMYSCIRA'S ATTEMPTS TO **BREAK** THE **QUANTUM MEMBRANE.**

SO **YOU** INVADED FIRST. THIS ISN'T AN ATTACK...IT'S A **COUNTER-ATTACK!**

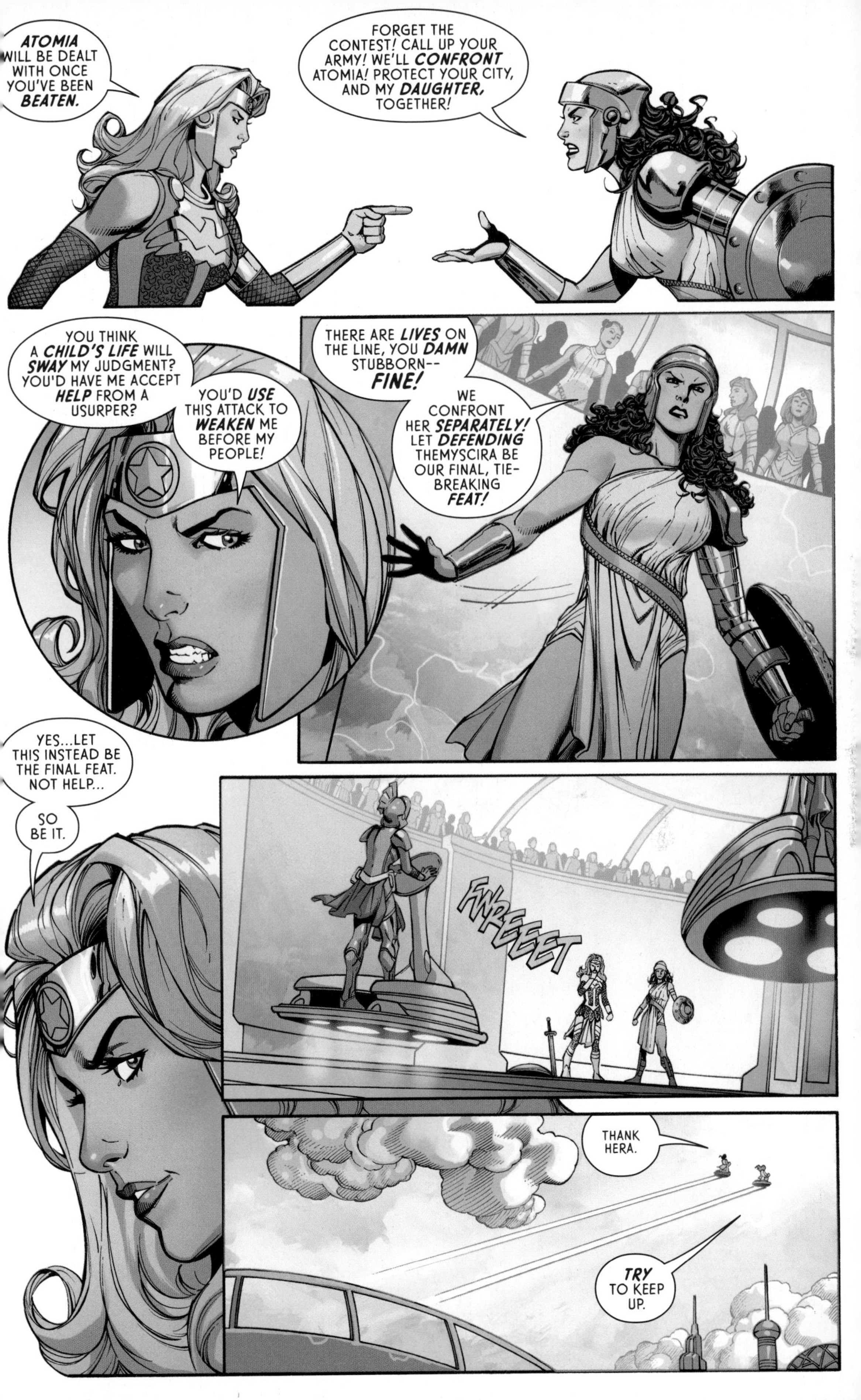
ATOMIA WILL BE DEALT WITH ONCE YOU'VE BEEN BEATEN.
FORGET THE CONTEST! CALL UP YOUR ARMY! WE'LL CONFRONT ATOMIA! PROTECT YOUR CITY, AND MY DAUGHTER, TOGETHER!
YOU THINK A CHILD'S LIFE WILL SWAY MY JUDGMENT? YOU'D HAVE ME ACCEPT HELP FROM A USURPER?
YOU'D USE THIS ATTACK TO WEAKEN ME BEFORE MY PEOPLE!
THERE ARE LIVES ON THE LINE, YOU DAMN STUBBORN-- FINE!
WE CONFRONT HER SEPARATELY! LET DEFENDING THEMYSCIRA BE OUR FINAL, TIE-BREAKING FEAT!
YES...LET THIS INSTEAD BE THE FINAL FEAT. NOT HELP...
SO BE IT.
FWREEEET
THANK HERA.
TRY TO KEEP UP.

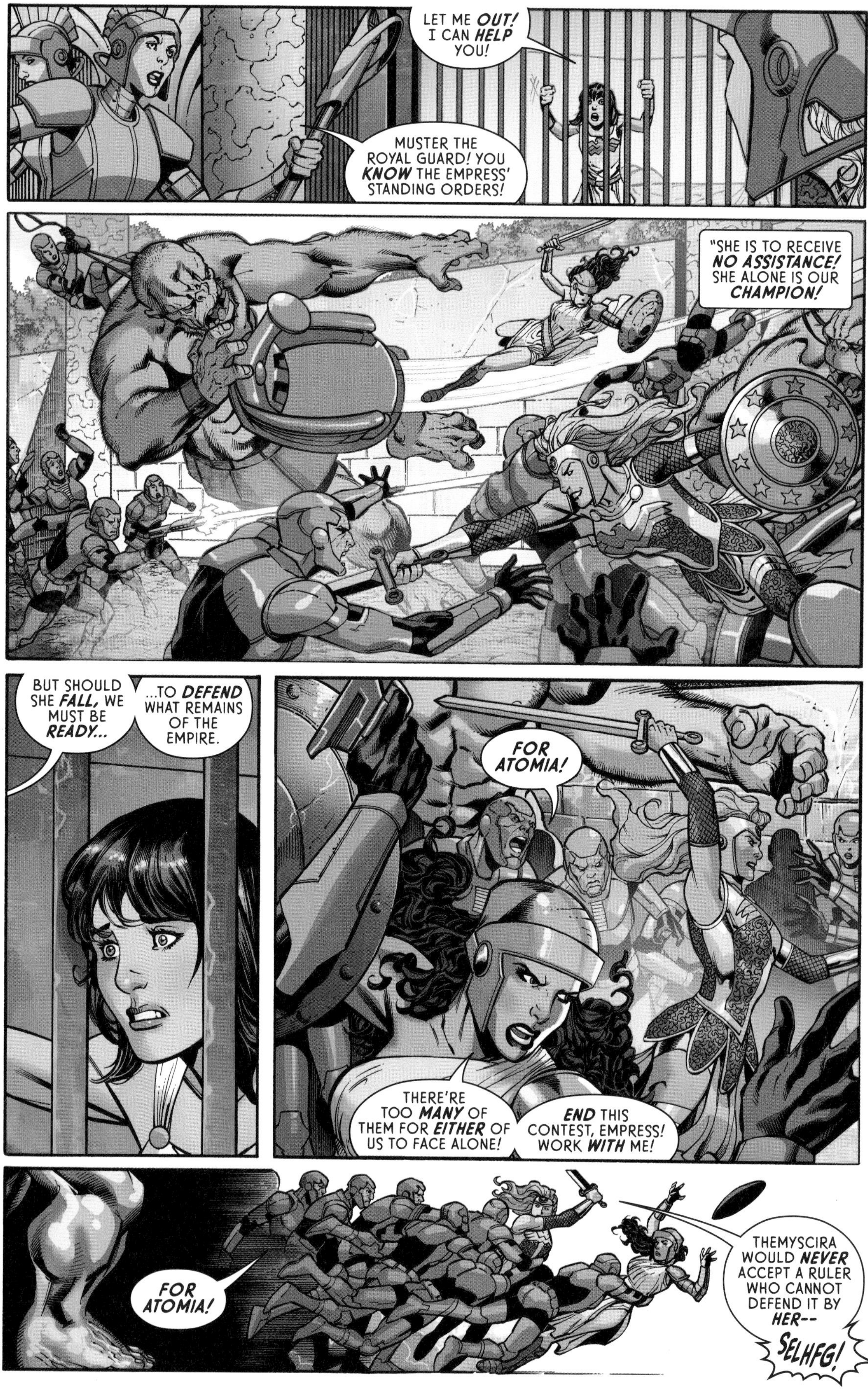
LET ME OUT! I CAN HELP YOU!
MUSTER THE ROYAL GUARD! YOU KNOW THE EMPRESS' STANDING ORDERS!
"SHE IS TO RECEIVE NO ASSISTANCE! SHE ALONE IS OUR CHAMPION!
BUT SHOULD SHE FALL, WE MUST BE READY...
...TO DEFEND WHAT REMAINS OF THE EMPIRE.
FOR ATOMIA!
THERE'RE TOO MANY OF THEM FOR EITHER OF US TO FACE ALONE!
END THIS CONTEST, EMPRESS! WORK WITH ME!
FOR ATOMIA!
THEMYSCIRA WOULD NEVER ACCEPT A RULER WHO CANNOT DEFEND IT BY HER--
SELHFG!

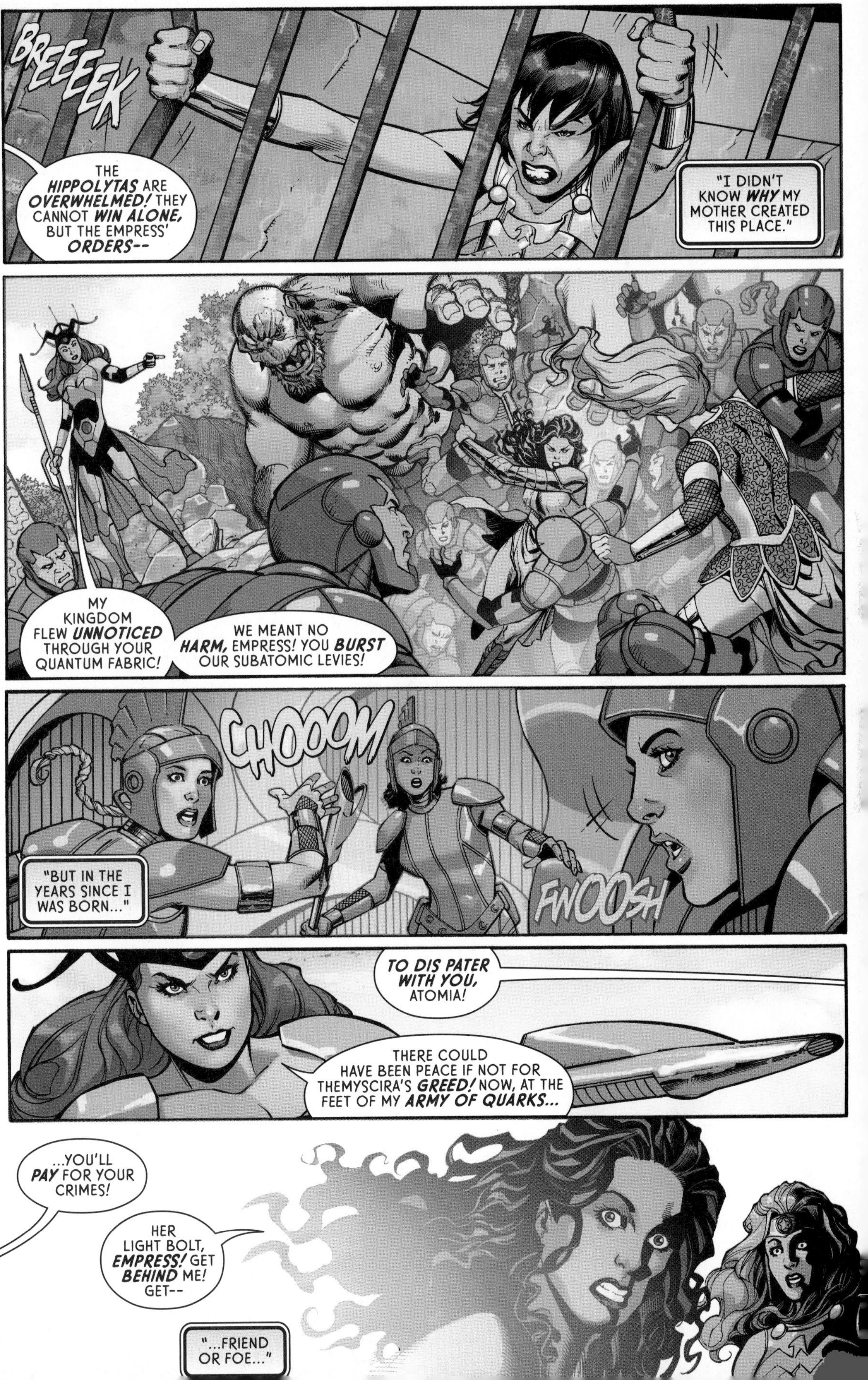
BREEEEK
THE HIPPOLYTAS ARE OVERWHELMED! THEY CANNOT WIN ALONE, BUT THE EMPRESS' ORDERS--
"I DIDN'T KNOW WHY MY MOTHER CREATED THIS PLACE."
MY KINGDOM FLEW UNNOTICED THROUGH YOUR QUANTUM FABRIC!
WE MEANT NO HARM, EMPRESS! YOU BURST OUR SUBATOMIC LEVIES!
CHOOOM
"BUT IN THE YEARS SINCE I WAS BORN..."
FWOOSH
TO DIS PATER WITH YOU, ATOMIA!
THERE COULD HAVE BEEN PEACE IF NOT FOR THEMYSCIRA'S GREED! NOW, AT THE FEET OF MY ARMY OF QUARKS...
...YOU'LL PAY FOR YOUR CRIMES!
HER LIGHT BOLT, EMPRESS! GET BEHIND ME! GET--
"...FRIEND OR FOE..."

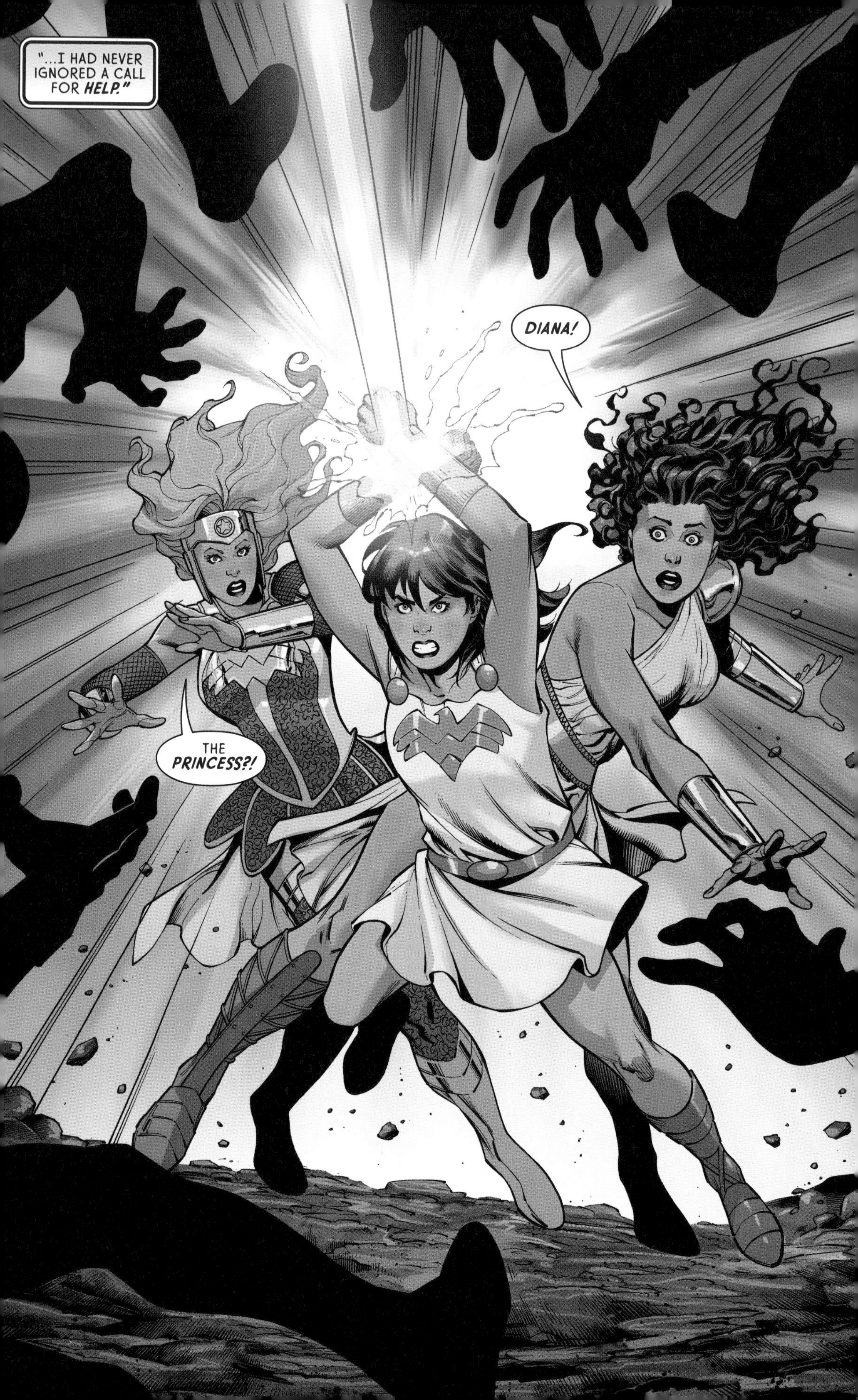
"...I HAD NEVER IGNORED A CALL FOR HELP."
DIANA!
THE PRINCESS?!

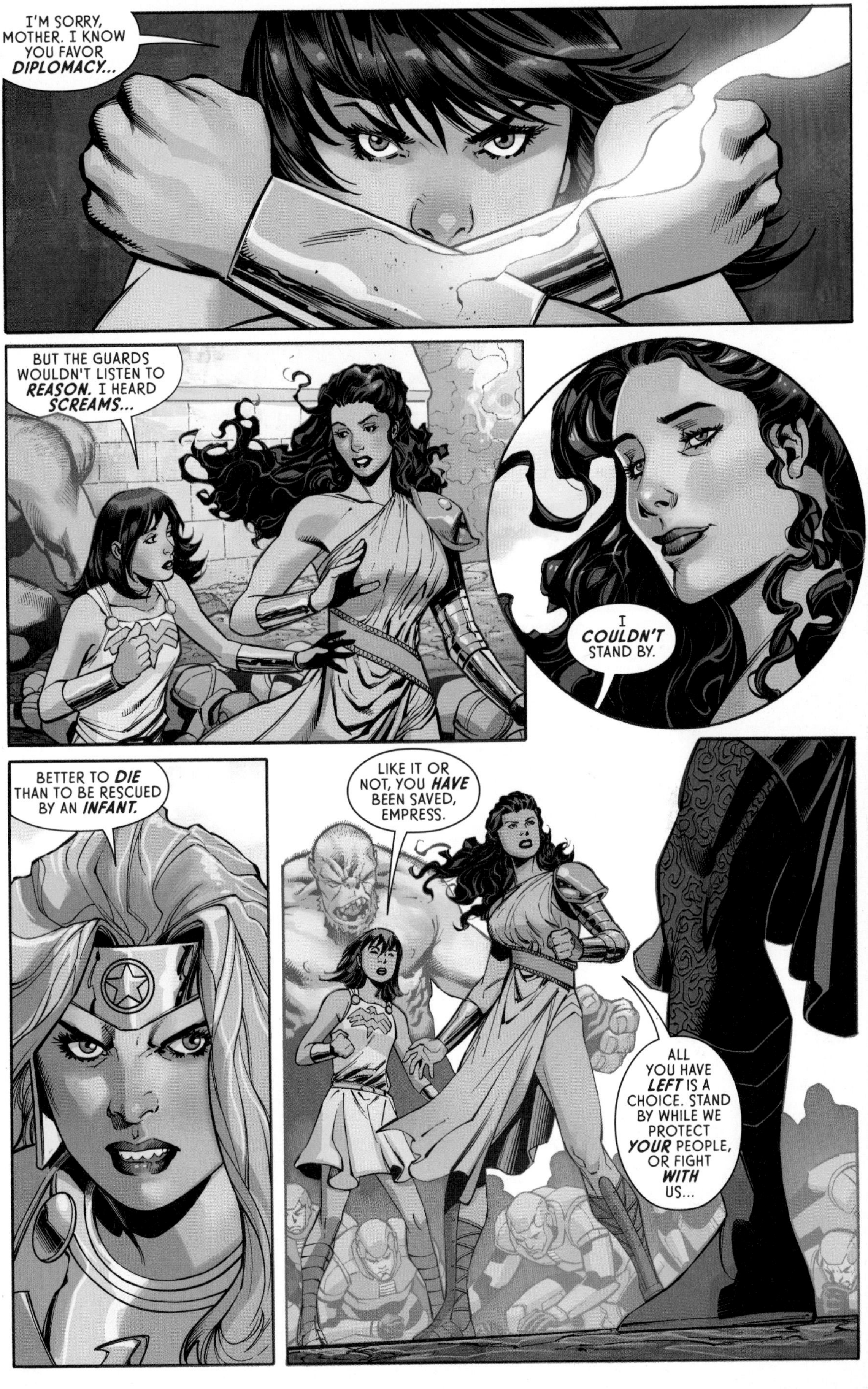
I'M SORRY, MOTHER. I KNOW YOU FAVOR DIPLOMACY...
BUT THE GUARDS WOULDN'T LISTEN TO REASON. I HEARD SCREAMS...
I COULDN'T STAND BY.
BETTER TO DIE THAN TO BE RESCUED BY AN INFANT.
LIKE IT OR NOT, YOU HAVE BEEN SAVED, EMPRESS.
ALL YOU HAVE LEFT IS A CHOICE. STAND BY WHILE WE PROTECT YOUR PEOPLE, OR FIGHT WITH US...

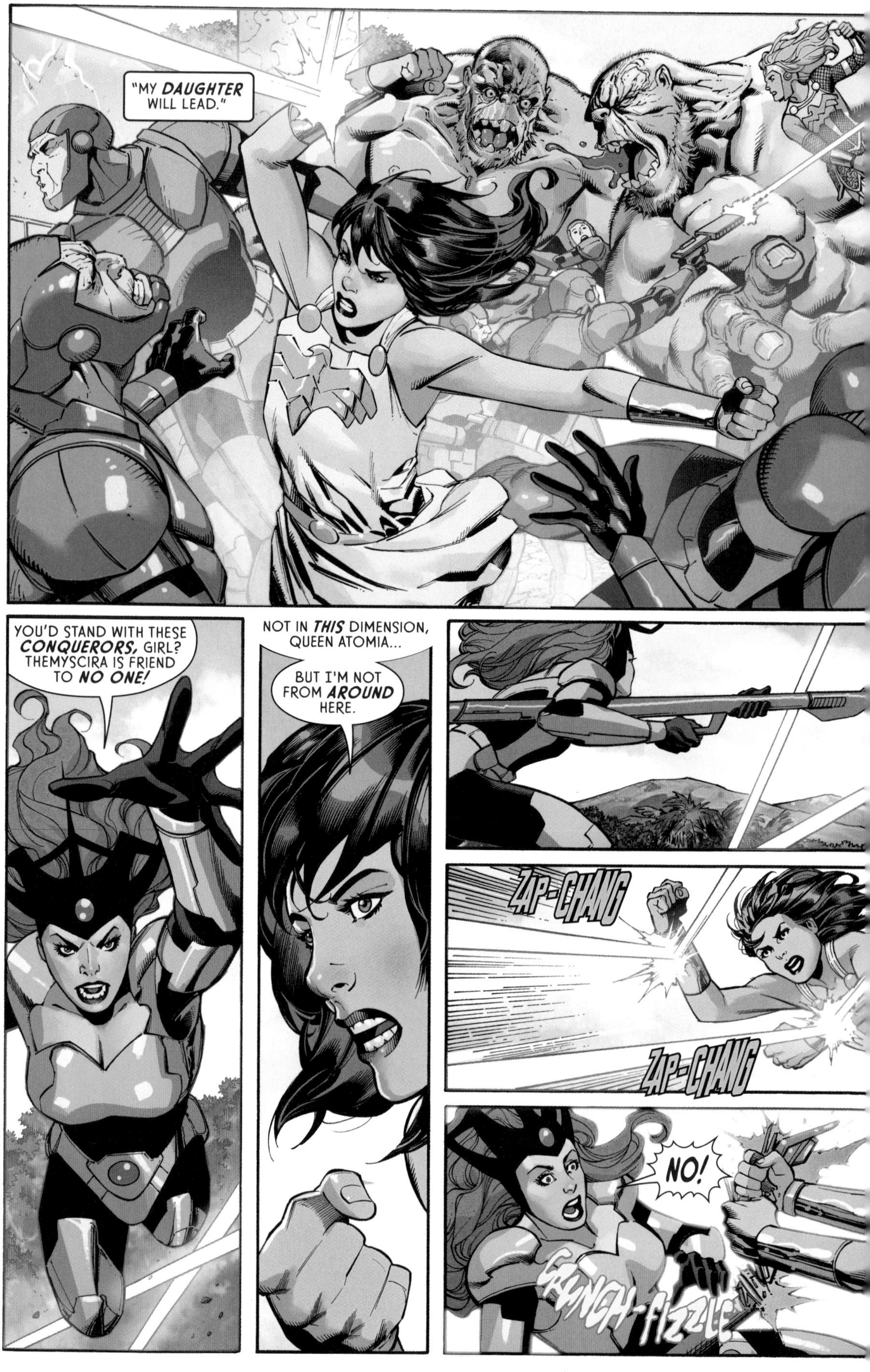
"MY DAUGHTER WILL LEAD."
YOU'D STAND WITH THESE CONQUERORS, GIRL? THEMYSCIRA IS FRIEND TO NO ONE!
NOT IN THIS DIMENSION, QUEEN ATOMIA...
BUT I'M NOT FROM AROUND HERE.
ZAP-CHANG
ZAP-CHANG
NO!
CRUNCH-FIZZLE

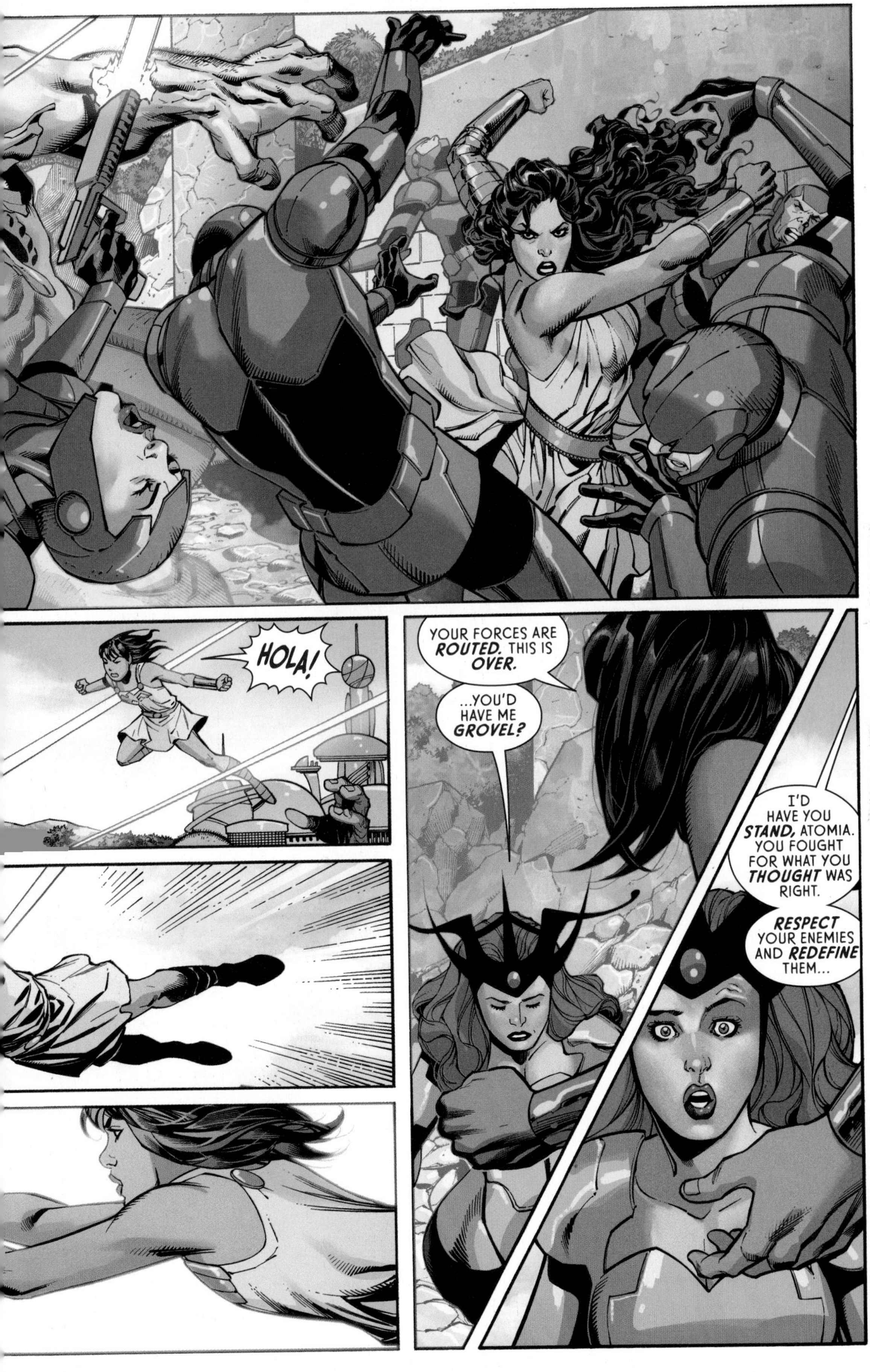

HOLA!
YOUR FORCES ARE ROUTED. THIS IS OVER.
...YOU'D HAVE ME GROVEL?
I'D HAVE YOU STAND, ATOMIA. YOU FOUGHT FOR WHAT YOU THOUGHT WAS RIGHT.
RESPECT YOUR ENEMIES AND REDEFINE THEM...

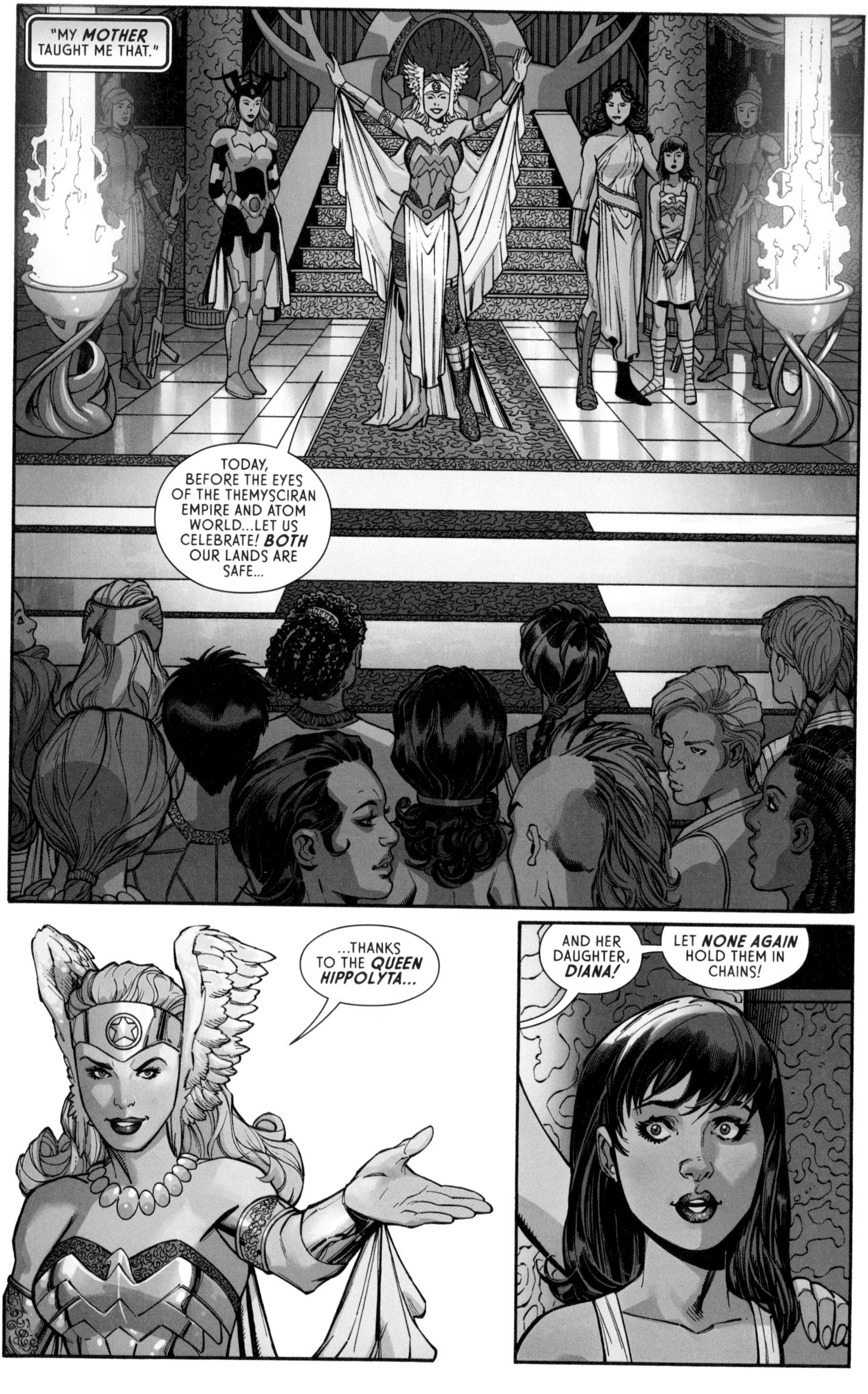
"MY MOTHER TAUGHT ME THAT."
TODAY, BEFORE THE EYES OF THE THEMYSCIRAN EMPIRE AND ATOM WORLD...LET US CELEBRATE! BOTH OUR LANDS ARE SAFE...
...THANKS TO THE QUEEN HIPPOLYTA...
AND HER DAUGHTER, DIANA!
LET NONE AGAIN HOLD THEM IN CHAINS!

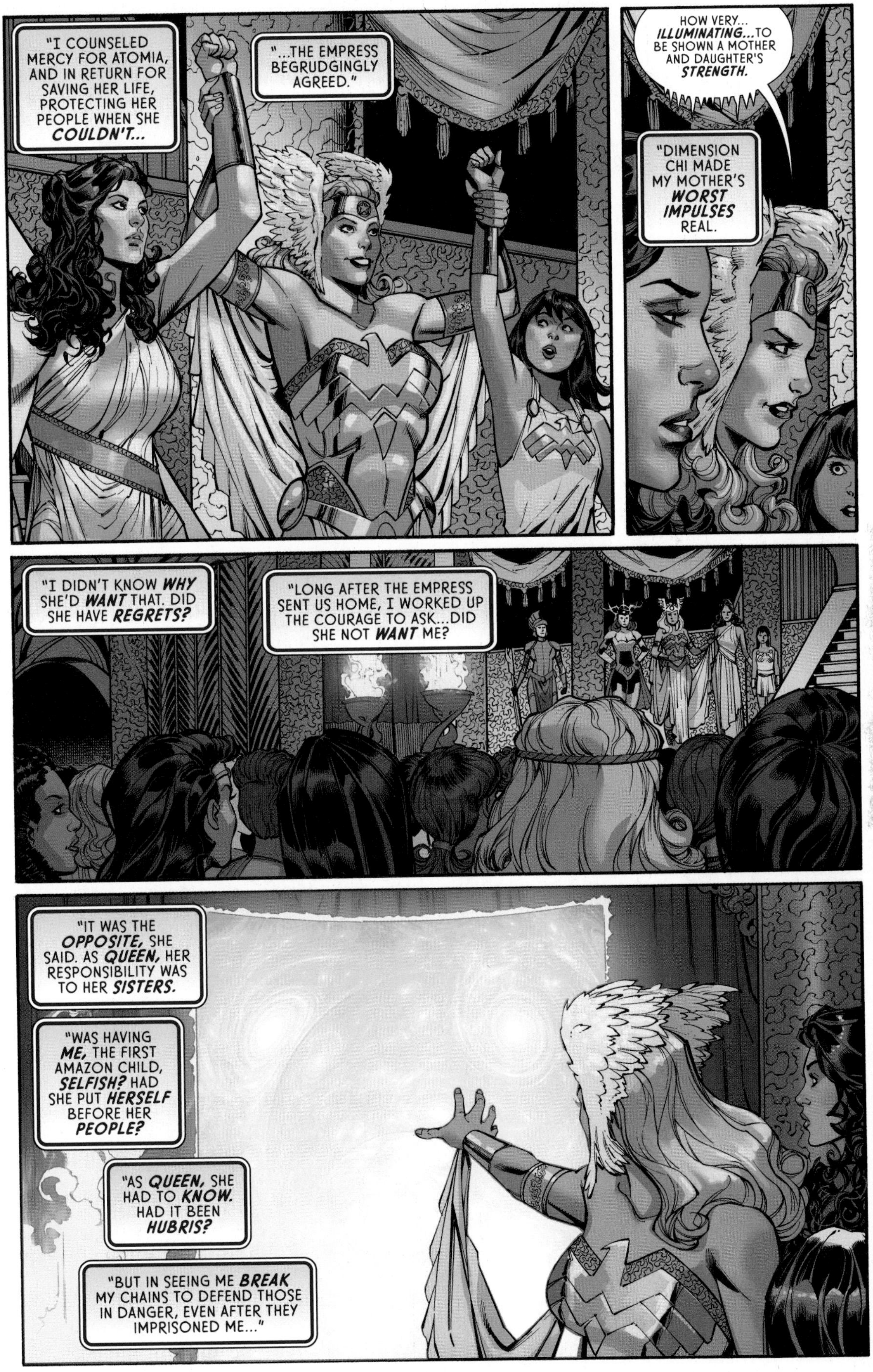
"I COUNSELED MERCY FOR ATOMIA, AND IN RETURN FOR SAVING HER LIFE, PROTECTING HER PEOPLE WHEN SHE COULDN'T...
"...THE EMPRESS BEGRUDGINGLY AGREED."
HOW VERY... ILLUMINATING...TO BE SHOWN A MOTHER AND DAUGHTER'S STRENGTH.
"DIMENSION CHI MADE MY MOTHER'S WORST IMPULSES REAL.
"I DIDN'T KNOW WHY SHE'D WANT THAT. DID SHE HAVE REGRETS?
"LONG AFTER THE EMPRESS SENT US HOME, I WORKED UP THE COURAGE TO ASK...DID SHE NOT WANT ME?
"IT WAS THE OPPOSITE, SHE SAID. AS QUEEN, HER RESPONSIBILITY WAS TO HER SISTERS.
"WAS HAVING ME, THE FIRST AMAZON CHILD, SELFISH? HAD SHE PUT HERSELF BEFORE HER PEOPLE?
"AS QUEEN, SHE HAD TO KNOW. HAD IT BEEN HUBRIS?
"BUT IN SEEING ME BREAK MY CHAINS TO DEFEND THOSE IN DANGER, EVEN AFTER THEY IMPRISONED ME..."

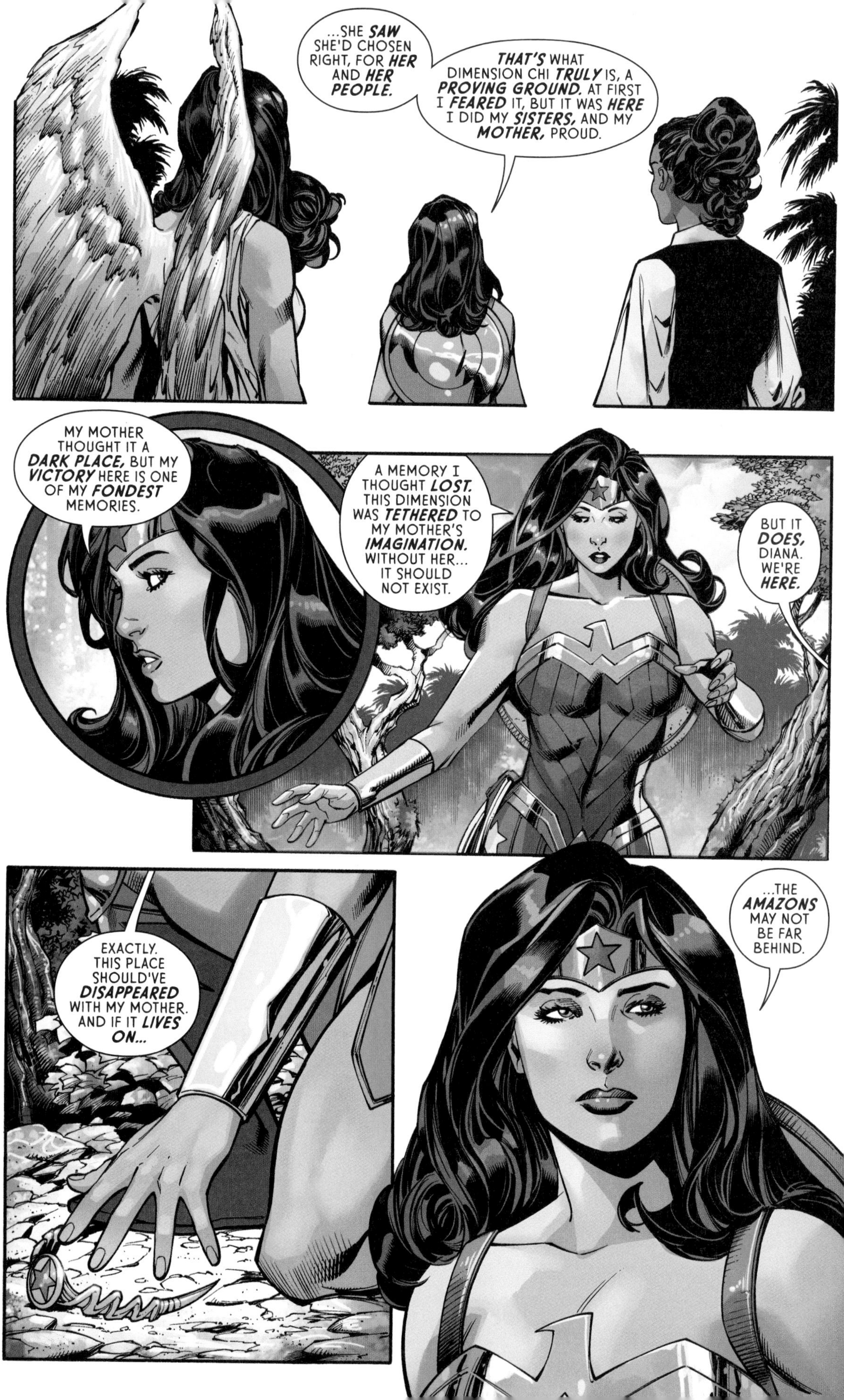
...SHE SAW SHE'D CHOSEN RIGHT, FOR HER AND HER PEOPLE.
THAT'S WHAT DIMENSION CHI TRULY IS, A PROVING GROUND. AT FIRST I FEARED IT, BUT IT WAS HERE I DID MY SISTERS, AND MY MOTHER, PROUD.
MY MOTHER THOUGHT IT A DARK PLACE, BUT MY VICTORY HERE IS ONE OF MY FONDEST MEMORIES.
A MEMORY I THOUGHT LOST. THIS DIMENSION WAS TETHERED TO MY MOTHER'S IMAGINATION. WITHOUT HER... IT SHOULD NOT EXIST.
BUT IT DOES, DIANA. WE'RE HERE.
EXACTLY. THIS PLACE SHOULD'VE DISAPPEARED WITH MY MOTHER. AND IF IT LIVES ON...
...THE AMAZONS MAY NOT BE FAR BEHIND.

VARIANT COVER GALLERY

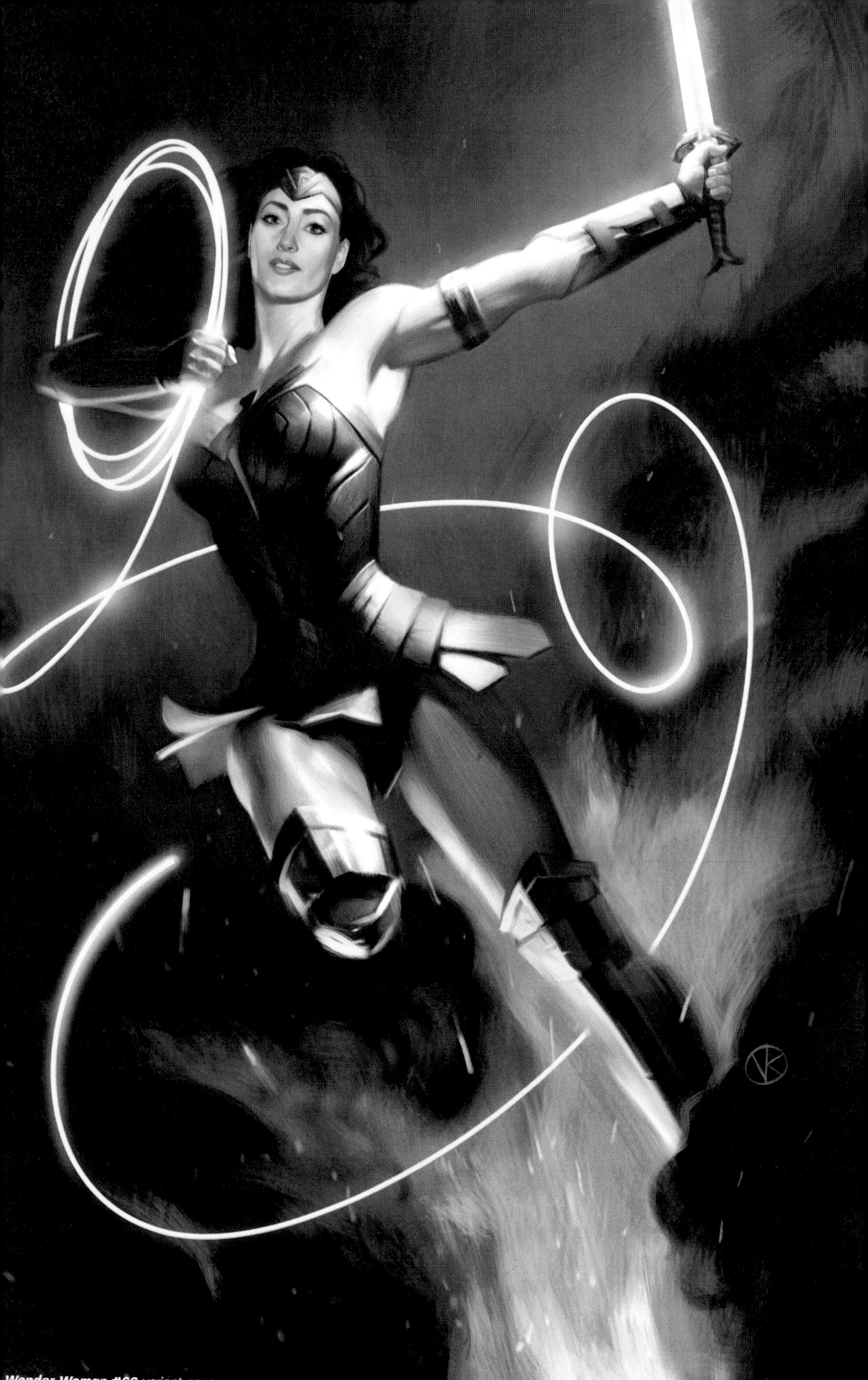

***Wonder Woman* #66** variant cover
by **VIKTOR KALVACHEV**

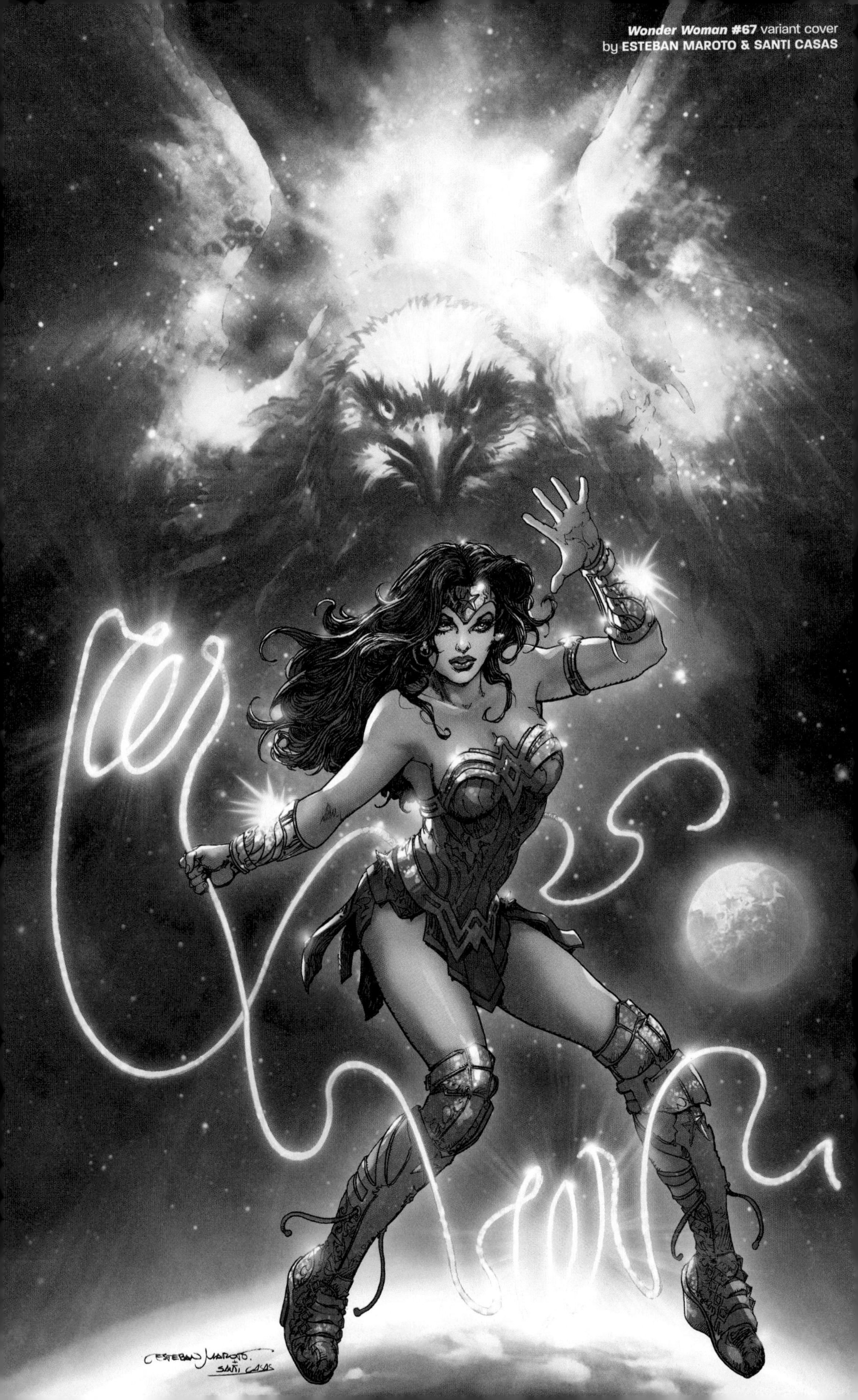
ESTEBAN MAROTO
SANTI CASAS

Wonder Woman **#67** variant cover
by **ESTEBAN MAROTO & SANTI CASAS**

***Wonder Woman* #68** variant cover
by **KAARE ANDREWS**

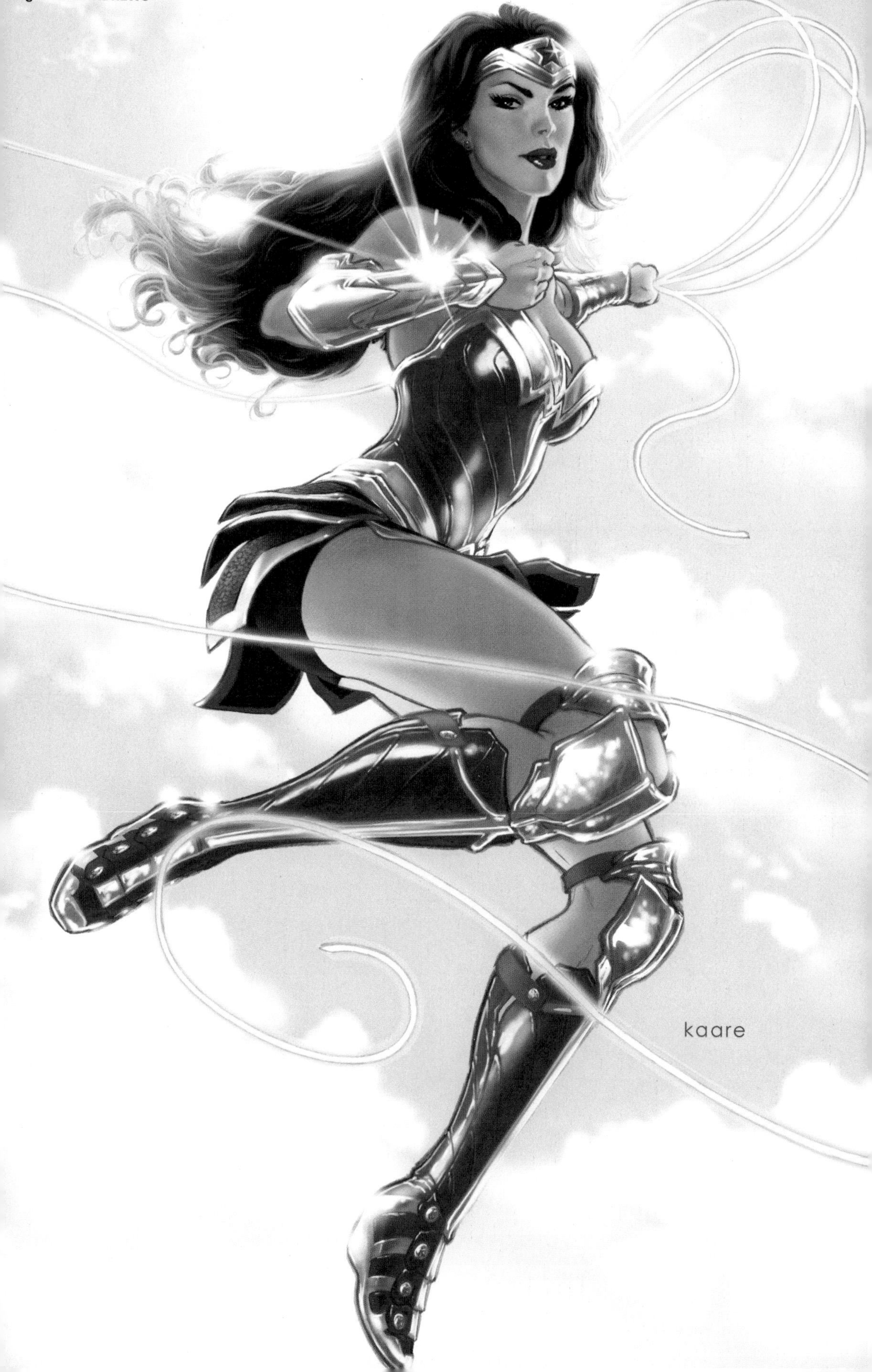
kaare

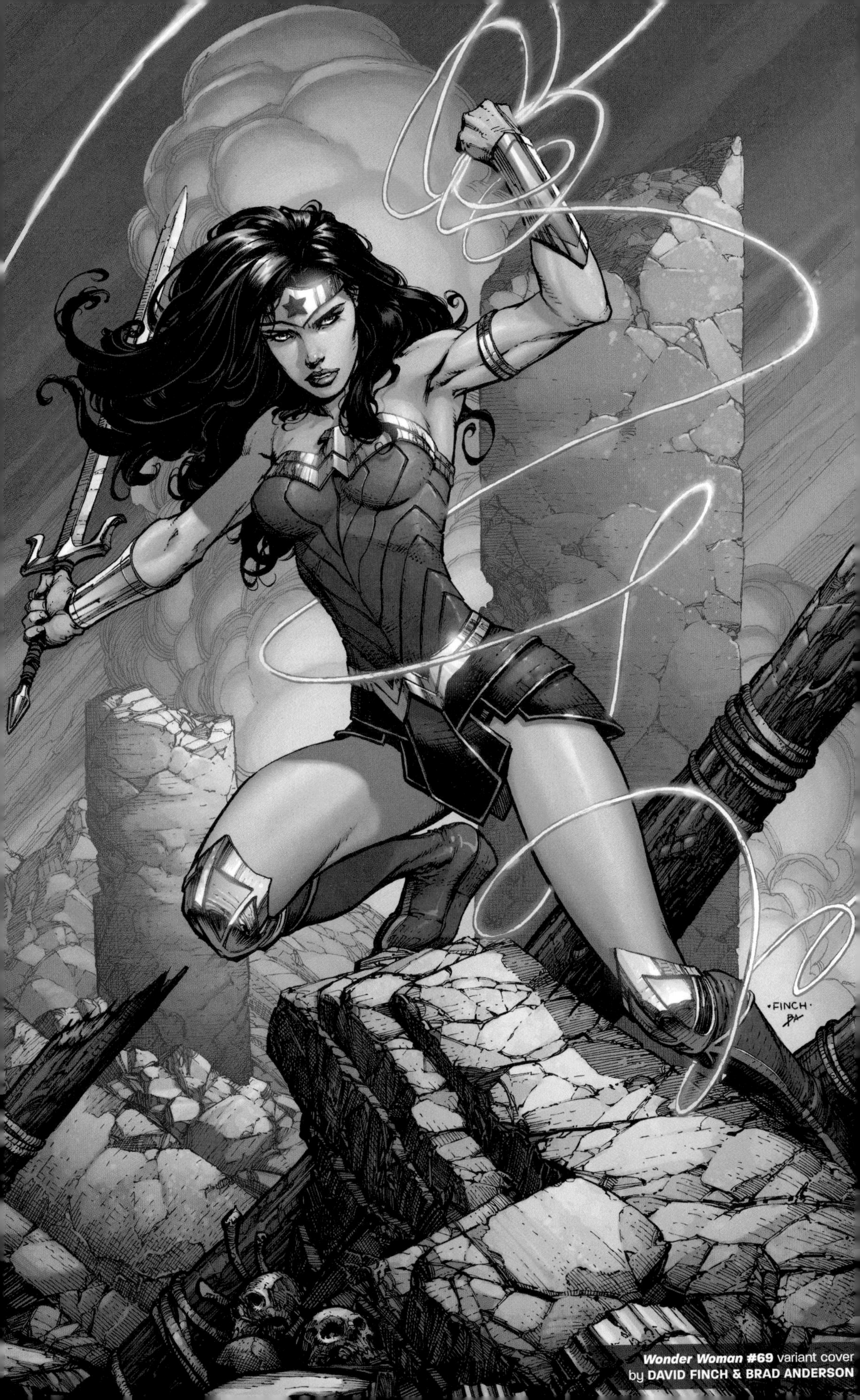
FINCH

***Wonder Woman* #69** variant cover
by **DAVID FINCH & BRAD ANDERSON**

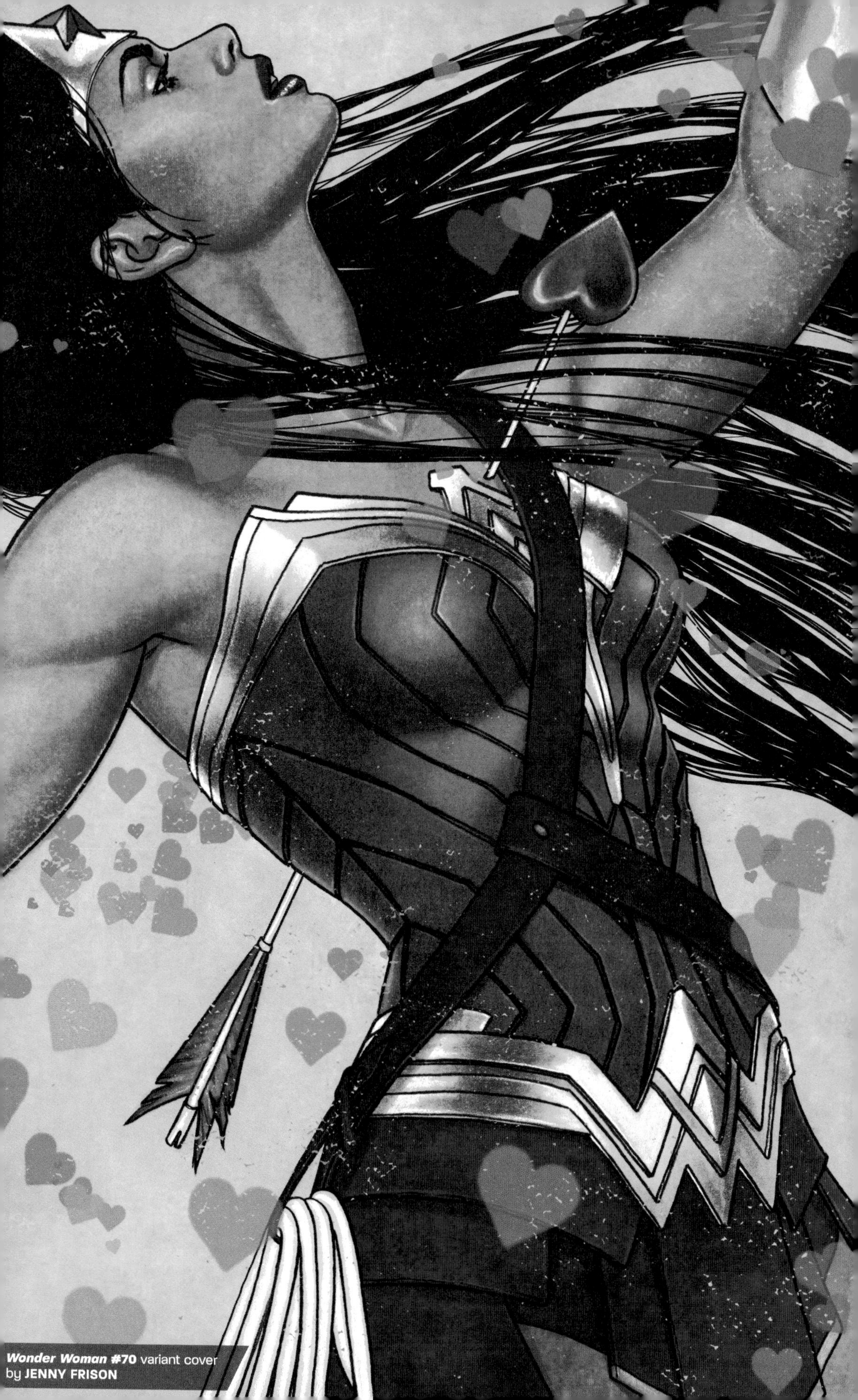

***Wonder Woman* #70** variant cover
by **JENNY FRISON**

***Wonder Woman* #71** variant cover
by **JENNY FRISON**

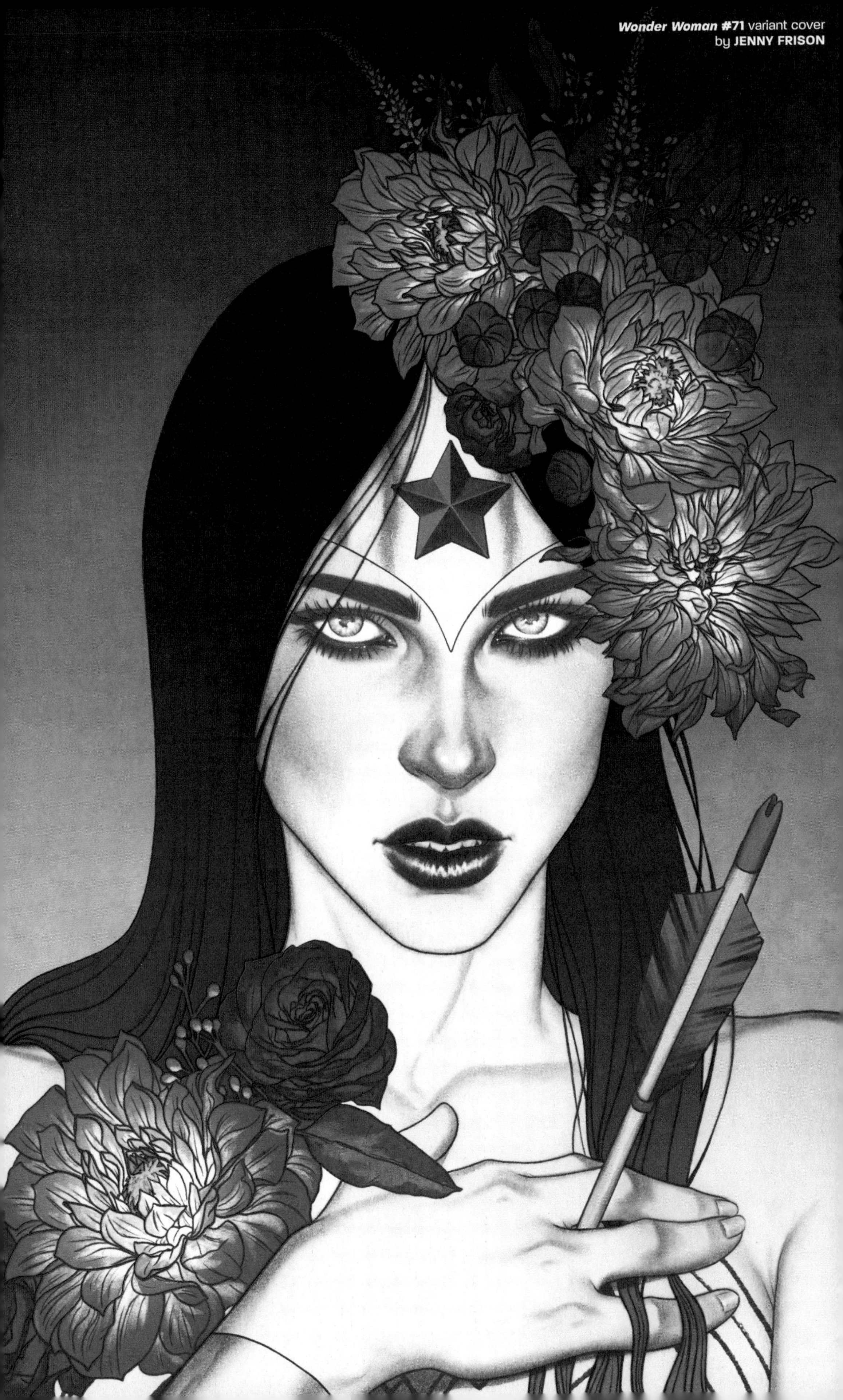

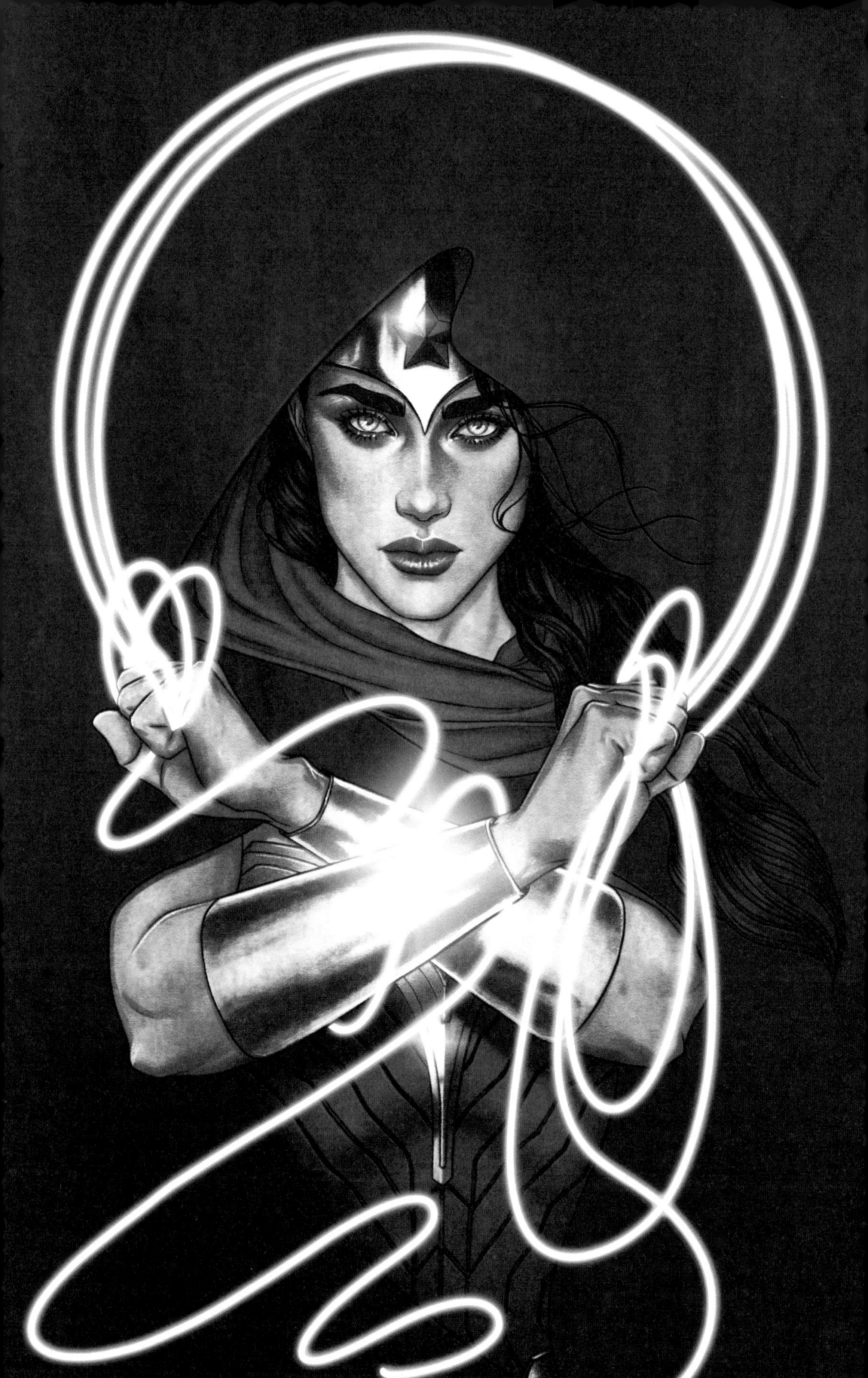

***Wonder Woman* #72** variant cover
by **JENNY FRISON**

Wonder Woman **#73** variant cover
by **JENNY FRISON**

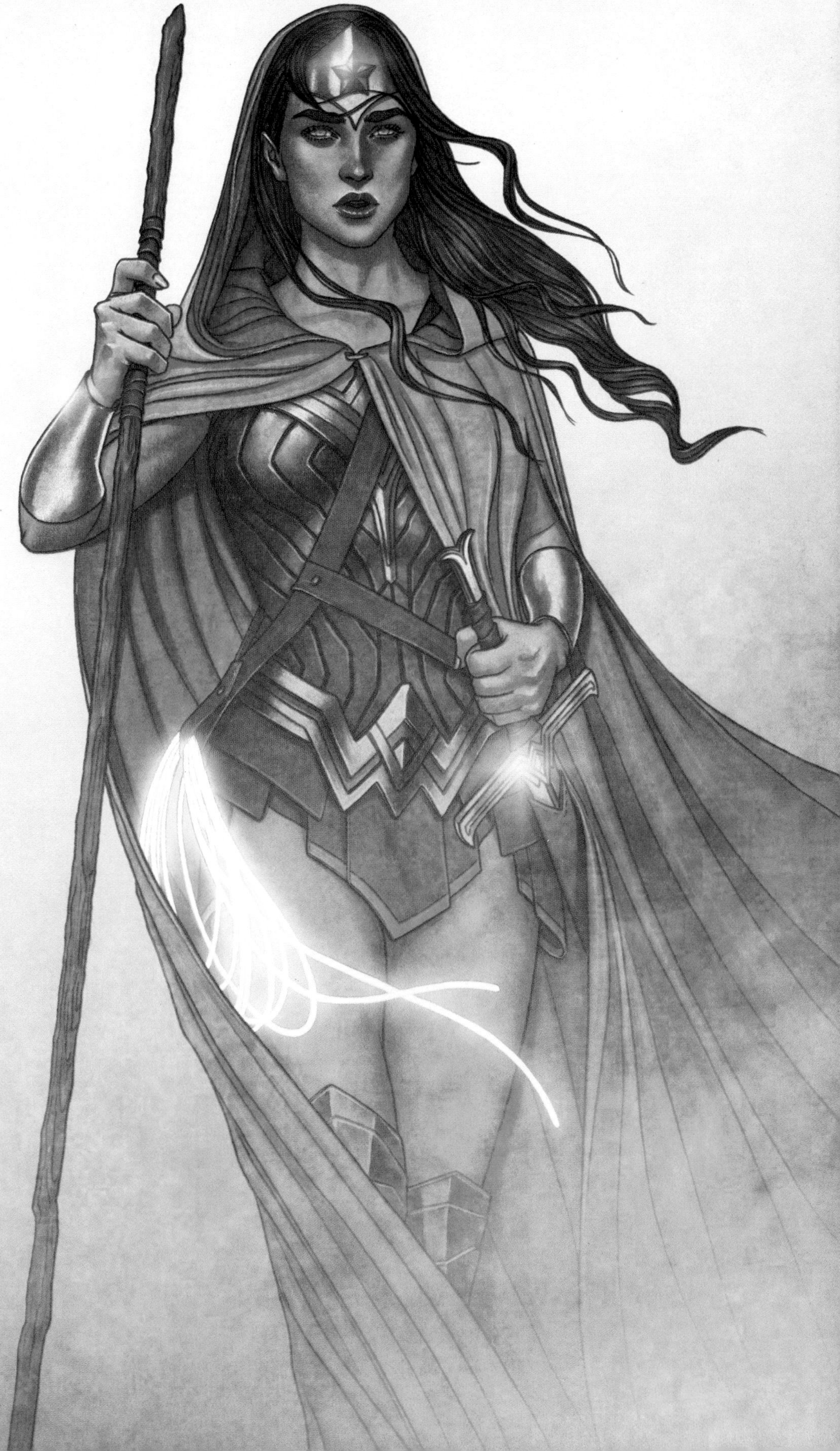

"Clear storytelling at its best. It's an intriguing concept and easy to grasp."
– THE NEW YORK TIMES

"Azzarello is rebuilding the mythology of Wonder Woman."
– CRAVE ONLINE

WONDER WOMAN
VOL. 1: BLOOD
BRIAN AZZARELLO
with CLIFF CHIANG

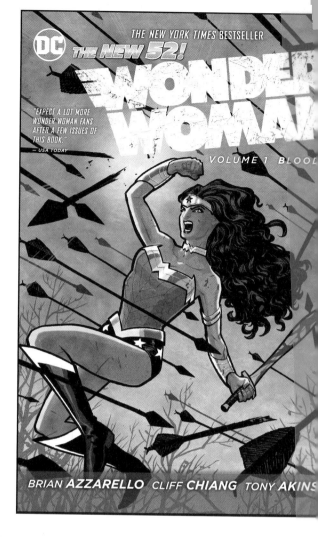

VOLUME 1 BLOO...

BRIAN **AZZARELLO** CLIFF **CHIANG** TONY **AKINS**

**WONDER WOMAN
VOL. 2: GUTS**

**WONDER WOMAN
VOL. 3: IRON**

READ THE ENTIRE EP...

Get more DC graphic novels wherever comics and books are sold!

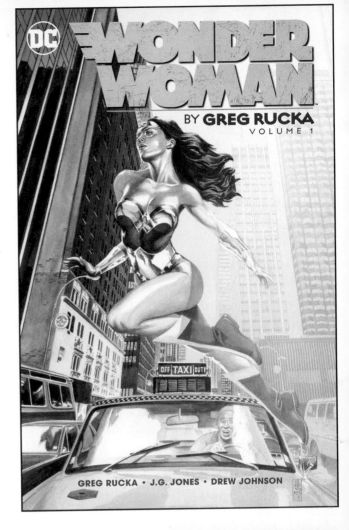

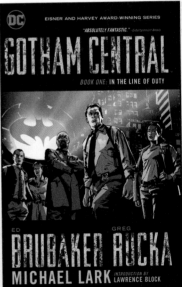

"A triumphant blend of Golden Age concepts with modern themes."
–PUBLISHERS WEEKLY

"Earth One graphic novels—a series that allows for fresh takes on classic characters, untethered as it is from past and current continuity."
–WASHINGTON POST

WONDER WOMAN
EARTH ONE
VOL. 1
GRANT MORRISON and YANICK PAQUETTE

WONDER WOMAN
EARTH ONE
VOLUME ONE
GRANT MORRISON
YANICK PAQUETTE
NATHAN FAIRBAIRN
DC
PAQUETTE NF 14

GREEN LANTERN
EARTH ONE
VOLUME ONE
GABRIEL HARDMAN
CORINNA BECHKO
JORDAN BOYD
DC

GREEN LANTERN EARTH ONE VOL. 1

TEEN TITANS
EARTH ONE
VOLUME ONE
JEFF LEMIRE
TERRY DODSON
RACHEL DODSON
CAM SMITH
BRAD ANDERSON
DC
THE NEXT CHAPTER IN THE
#1 NEW YORK TIMES BEST-SELLING EARTH ONE SERIES

TEEN TITANS EARTH ONE VOL. 1

COMPLETE YOU
EARTH ONE COLLECTIO

BATMAN EARTH ONE VOL
BATMAN EARTH ONE VOL.
BATMAN EARTH ONE VOL.
SUPERMAN EARTH ONE VOL
SUPERMAN EARTH ONE VOL.
SUPERMAN EARTH ONE VOL.
TEEN TITANS EARTH ONE VOL.

Get more DC graphic novels wherever comics and books are sold!

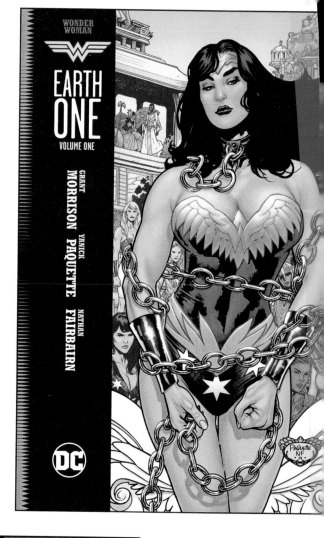

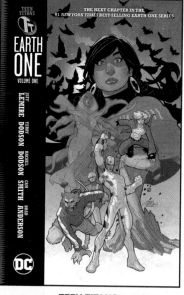